Woman's Cause

Woman's Cause

The Jewish Woman's Movement
in England and the
United States,
1881–1933

LINDA GORDON KUZMACK

OHIO STATE UNIVERSITY PRESS

Columbus

Library of Congress Cataloging-in-Publication Data
Kuzmack, Linda Gordon.
  Woman's cause : the Jewish woman's movement in England and the United
States, 1881–1933 / Linda Gordon Kuzmack.
    p. cm.
  Includes bibliographical references.
  ISBN 0-8142-0515-1 (alk. paper)
  ISBN 0-8142-0529-1 (pbk.: alk. paper)
  1. Women, Jewish—England—History.   2. Women, Jewish—United States—
History.   3. Feminism—England—History.   4. Feminism—United States—
History.   5. Women in Judaism—England—History.   6. Women in Judaism—
United States—History.   I. Title.
HQ1172.K89   1990
305.42′089′924042—dc20   89-72158
                                                                  CIP

∞ The paper in this book meets the guidelines for permanence and durability
of the Committee on Production Guidelines for Book Longevity of the Council on Library Resources.

                        Printed in the U.S.A.

              9 8 7 6 5 4 3 2 1

For Arnold, Mark, and Eric

Contents

Illustrations

Acknowledgments

IT IS a pleasure to thank everyone who helped make this book possible. Howard M. Sachar, my dissertation adviser, encouraged me to undertake a comparative study and guided me skillfully through the complex process. Jonathan D. Sarna and Ellen M. Umansky shared their extensive knowledge of Judaism and feminism from the earliest stages of research to the final publication of *Woman's Cause*. This work could never have been written without them.

Several scholars contributed research sources, illuminated problems and new insights, and read all or portions of the dissertation and the book, including Paula Hyman, Hasia Diener, Sue Levi Elwell, Marion Kaplan, Gary Loeb, and Gerald Sorin. Robert W. Kenny and Leo Ribuffo provided thoughtful commentary. Barbara Kanner fostered my involvement in feminist scholarship. Rabbi Eugene J. Lipman and the late Leila Rosen Young listened to my ideas and gave me friendship and support.

The Memorial Foundation for Jewish Culture subsidized much of my research in several cities. Thanks to a grant from the American Jewish Archives, I discovered material at the AJA that provided my first significant documentation on Jewish women in England, as well as invaluable information on American Jewish women. Faculty and staff at the Archives and the Hebrew Union College-Jewish Institute of Religion were particularly helpful and gracious in advising me, particularly the distinguished Jacob R. Marcus, Jonathan D. Sarna, Michael E. Meyer, Abraham Peck, Fannie Zelcer, and the Archives' staff.

It was extraordinarily difficult to obtain substantial documentation from England, because papers, letters, and diaries are scattered across the country in several archives, libraries, Jewish organizations, and private hands. Without the contribution of people who believed in my work and were willing to ferret through shelves, boxes, and attics to help me, I could never have amassed the evidence I needed to prove the existence of Jewish feminism in England. I am profoundly grateful to the help I received from Beth Zion Lask Abrahams, R. D. Barnett, Chaim Bermant, Edward Bristow, Richard W. Davis, Hannah Feldman, William J. Fishman, Ruth Winston-Fox, the late David

Franklin, Phyllis J. Gerson, Lily Glass, Dr. I. Sidney Gold, Trude Levi, Jane E. Levy, Mrs. L. L. Loewe, V. D. Lipman, Hyam Manoby, Gwen Montagu, Alan Montefiore, Joseph Munk, Aubrey Newman, Claire Rayner, Rabbi Jacqueline Tabick, John J. Tepfer, Bernard Wasserstein, and staff members of the Jewish Historical Society of England and the New West End Synagogue. Shirley Winterbotham undertook research for me in England with dedication and skill.

Many thanks to Charlotte Dihoff, my editor, for her encouragement and patience, and to Sally Serafim, my copyeditor, for her meticulous reading of this manuscript.

Both my parents died before the publication of *Woman's Cause.* Because they knew I was working on this book and encouraged me throughout, its publication has an extra special meaning for me and my family. Above all, my deepest gratitude goes to my husband Arnold, and my sons Mark and Eric, for their love and patience.

Abbreviations

AFL	American Federation of Labor
AJ	*American Jewess*
AJA	American Jewish Archives
AJH	*American Jewish History*
AJHS	American Jewish Historical Society
CCAR	Central Conference of American Rabbis
CJW	Council of Jewish Women Papers
EEF	East End Federation
EJ	*Encyclopedia Judaica*
FS	*Feminist Studies*
FWZ	Federation of Women Zionists
HIAS	Hebrew Immigrant Aid Society
HUC-JIR	Hebrew Union College-Jewish Institute of Religion
ICW	International Council of Women
ILGWU	International Ladies Garment Workers' Union
JAPGW	Jewish Association for the Protection of Girls and Women
JC	*Jewish Chronicle*
JFO	Jewish Feminist Organization (Germany)
JG	*Jewish Guardian*
JJS	*Jewish Journal of Sociology*
JLWS	Jewish League for Woman Suffrage
JQR	*Jewish Quarterly Review*
LL	London Library
LNA	Ladies National Association
LTS	Leeds Tailoresses' Society
ML	Mocatta Library (London)
NYPL	New York Public Library
NAW	*Notable American Women*
NAWSA	National American Woman Suffrage Association
NCJW	National Council of Jewish Women
NCW	National Council of Women
NFTS	National Federation of Temple Sisterhoods
NFWW	National Federation of Women Workers
NUSEC	National Union of Societies for Equal Citizenship
NUWSS	National Union of Women's Suffrage Societies

NUWW	National Union of Women Workers
NWP	National Women's Party
PAJHS	*Proceedings of the American Jewish Historical Society*
UAHC	Union of American Hebrew Congregations
WCJW	World Council of Jewish Women
WCTU	Women's Christian Temperance Union
WIZO	Women's International Zionist Organization
UJW	Union of Jewish Women
WPPL	Women's Protective and Provident League
WSP	Woman Suffrage Party
WSPU	Women's Social and Political Union
WTUL	Women's Trade Union League
WUPJ	World Union for Progressive Judaism
WV	*Woman Voter*
YWHA	Young Women's Hebrew Association

Introduction

"WE HAVE created a bond of sisterhood," exulted Rosa Sonneschein, publisher of *The American Jewess*, Jewish women's first independent newspaper, in 1895. Urging Jewish women to follow the journal into the "universal sisterhood" of the secular woman's movement, the *American Jewess* campaigned for national, Jewish communal and religious suffrage "in the pulpit and the pew."

Across the Atlantic, England's Jewish League for Woman Suffrage, the world's only Jewish woman's suffrage organization, "held their banner high" in 1912 marching for their "holy cause and therefore Jewish cause." Militant Jewish suffragists smashed windows and disrupted worship services "for denying freedom to women." In the United States, aristocrat Maud Nathan became the most prominent among thousands of Jewish women who acclaimed the suffrage campaign's "opening of prison doors," and immigrant Rose Schneiderman envisioned the ballot as a "tool in the hands of working women."

Woman's Cause suggests that Jewish feminists participated in national English and American feminist movements during the late nineteenth and early twentieth centuries to a greater degree than is commonly recognized; simultaneously, they created a feminist movement that was distinctively Jewish. Interacting with both their non-Jewish peers and the Jewish community, Jewish women, like their Christian counterparts,[1] participated in the social service, equal rights, and socialist feminism[2] described by Olive Banks and other scholars.

Secular and Jewish feminist movements stimulated each other. Jewish women played a role in nearly every major national feminist venture at the turn of the century, including campaigns for social reform, feminist trade unionism, suffrage, and welfare feminism. At the same time, membership in national women's organizations encouraged Jewish women to create a similar network of Jewish groups. Jewish women's participation in the International Council of Women from 1904 onward triggered formation of an informal ICW Jewish women's caucus in the same year. The caucus' work on behalf of Jewish women's concerns culminated in the founding of the World Council of Jewish Women in 1923.

1

For many female Jewish activists, American and English alike, feminism became a vehicle for social acceptance in their respective countries, emancipation in national and communal life, and acquisition of limited practical power in national, religious, and communal affairs.

Woman's Cause compares and contrasts Jewish feminism in England and the United States between 1881, when East European Jewish immigration flooded both countries, and 1933, when Hitler's rise to power changed the Jewish world. This method illuminates the similarities and differences between Jewish feminists, and the nature of their participation in national and international feminism. This approach owes a debt to comparative studies of secular feminism by Olive Banks, Richard Evans, William O'Neill, and Ross Paulson.[3]

Jewish feminism paralleled its secular counterpart in several ways, reflecting many of the same attitudes toward class structure, pace, and degree of feminist militancy.

The woman's movement developed as nineteenth-century women, separated into the private sphere of domesticity while their menfolk performed in public life, forged a close-knit "sisterhood" with female relatives and friends. Women's supportive relationship provided an emotional bonding enabling them to emerge into public life and create a network of organizations devoted to social and religious causes. These groups, suggests Mary P. Ryan, generated a politically oriented "woman's movement" demanding social reform and woman's equality.[4] Barbara Welter defines this process as the "cult of true womanhood," and Nancy F. Cott sees it as "domestic feminism."[5] Gerda Lerner suggests that feminism began when women recognized the separate interests of women as a group and rejected their subordinate place in history.[6]

Jewish women participated in secular feminism and adapted its several aspects to a Jewish context. Olive Banks, William O'Neill,[7] and others define nineteenth-century "social feminists" as those who participated primarily in social reform woman's organizations as an expression of their belief in women's rights. Banks suggests these groups were "feminist" even when they focused exclusively on social reform because they "tried to *change* the position of women, or the ideas about women."[8] Paula Hyman suggests that female Jewish clubwomen and social service volunteers were "feminist in a larger sense" because they "enhanced the self-worth of women and worked on their behalf."[9]

Militant or "radical" feminists, note Eleanor Flexner and Aileen Kraditor, campaigned primarily or exclusively for political rights and suffrage.[10] Jewish suffragists marched, threw stones, were imprisoned or force-fed for demanding the national franchise, and were often ostracized by the Jewish community for demanding equality in Jewish religious and communal life. Radical socialist Jewish feminists organized women's trade unions, led strikes, and agitated for protectionist legislation for women. Whether moderate or radical, female Jewish activists often validated their contemporary feminist tactics with arguments culled from Jewish tradition and secular feminist theory.

Who were these *Jewish* feminists? Sharing the class attitudes of their non-Jewish peers, the majority were acculturated upper- or middle-class Anglo-Jewish women of German-Jewish or Sephardic descent. Eastern European immigrant women played a more active role among feminists in America than in England, protesting against the trade-union movement that denied them equal wages. Jewish feminists undertook three types of activity:

1. They modified or rejected traditional Judaism by moving from the home into the public sphere and by demanding a more equal role in Jewish religious and communal life;
2. The majority joined secular as well as Jewish women's organizations;
3. They founded a Jewish woman's movement by creating politically oriented Jewish women's groups affiliated with the secular woman's movement.

Jewish women's organizations deliberately identified themselves with the secular "woman's movement" by affiliating with national and international secular woman's organizations and by employing secular feminist terminology such as "sisters" and "sisterhood."

Nevertheless, Jewish women's overriding allegiance to the Jewish community has made it difficult for scholars such as Deborah Grand Golumb to define as feminist even the organizers of the 1893 Congress of Jewish Women, because she claims they "identified themselves first as Jews and only second as females."[11]

Jewish women felt they had no other choice. By the late nineteenth century, America and the woman's movement were influenced by Christian religious doctrine and secular racist propaganda, both of which identified Jews as members of an alien race. To avoid this charge, Jewish feminists, like other Jews, eagerly defined themselves as members of a religious group rather than as a separate nation or people, and avoided controversies over race and sex that increased their vulnerability as Jews.

Women who sought to live as feminists and as Jews weighed their desire for emancipation against traditional Judaism's attitudes toward women and the Jewish community's struggle for social acceptance by the majority culture. Christian-centered attitudes within secular feminism played roles as well. Early leaders of the feminist movement, almost entirely Christian until the turn of the twentieth century, initially regarded Jews with caution, suspicion, or dislike, depending upon their degree of class, religious, and social bias.

Sephardic or German-Jewish women's social status and commitment to social reform forged their entree into national feminism. Yet, Jewish women remained distinct within the larger feminist movement, partly because of the drive for Jewish acculturation and fears of anti-Semitism.[12]

However, Jewish women were also preoccupied with their struggle against their second-class status in their own religious and communal life. Traditional Judaism's attitudes toward sex-role differences profoundly affected all aspects of Jewish women's lives. Three millennia of tradition glorified Jewish women in the roles of wife and mother because they were vital to the Jewish family, which was perceived as the key to Jewish survival. Jewish women were expected to go outside the home primarily to perform acts of private charity: feeding the poor or tending the sick.[13] Deborah the Judge and other independent biblical heroines who had saved the Jewish people were often viewed with ambivalence by rabbinic commentators because of their visibly public acts. This attitude was not exclusively Jewish; Joan Kelly argues that all recorded societies have designated women as "the other," either as a hereditary inferior order or as a minority group. Certainly, biblical teachings reflected the attitude of surrounding cultures in the ancient Near East.[14]

Traditional Judaism viewed women as the hidden "other" in many ways. Rabbinic Jewish law mandated that women were not required to attend regular synagogue services because they were not obligated to perform time-bound religious tasks, which included daily and Sabbath worship, due to their household tasks. Because they were not obligated, women were not considered full participants in communal prayer. In the synagogue, women were permitted to attend services, but they were confined behind a screen or upstairs in the synagogue gallery. They were not counted in the quorum of ten (*minyan*) required for communal prayer.[15] With some variations in time and place, tradition usually dictated that women could not recite the blessings over the Torah, read from the Torah scroll, or study sacred texts. Jewish women were also excluded from religious and communal decision-making.[16]

During the Talmudic and medieval periods, a few women did write religious prayers or teach religious law and custom, but usually from behind a screen. This practice was continued into the nineteenth century by a handful of learned East European women, a few of whom were dubbed "rabbi" by their peers because of their scholarship. In Poland, for instance, Hannah of Ludmir functioned as a Hasidic *rebbe* of a small sect. Ostracized by the Orthodox Jews of Ludmir, she and her group fled to Jerusalem to escape communal wrath. However, with the exception of Hannah, women rarely even attempted to act as communal religious leaders.[17]

Yet, despite the restrictions in religious law that emphasized their family role, Jewish women have always worked. Historically, state-imposed restrictions on the occupations of Jewish men severely limited their wages. In addition, some men devoted their lives to studying sacred texts, deeming such study more holy, and therefore more important, than earning a living. Therefore, women's income remained essential to the survival of most Jewish families. Jewish women's employment did not violate the traditions related to their role as homemakers, since until the age of industrialization their work could be performed at home.[18] Nineteenth-century Jewish women's need to work outside the home proved a crucial element in the emergence of the Jewish woman's movement.

Jewish women attempted to strike a balance between their desire for emancipation and reverence for Jewish tradition, their hope for acculturation and fear of anti-Semitism. The combination fomented a tension that Jewish feminists attempted to resolve as they sought to join the woman's movement.

Every study has its limitations. *Woman's Cause* will focus on women whose feminist activities directly affected the Jewish community. This encourages a greater understanding of the correlation between distinctly Jewish feminism and secular feminism. My research examines Jewish feminists who worked primarily within Jewish organizations and those who concentrated their activities on secular feminist groups, but became role models for Jewish women working within the Jewish community because of their outstanding reputations.

As a result of this emphasis upon the Jewish community, there will be no discussion of radicals such as Emma Goldman who separated themselves from Jewish life. Except for a brief mention, there will be no examination of the woman's Zionist movement; to do so requires a thorough examination of its role within the Zionist movement as a whole. Radicalism of nonaffiliated Jews and women's participation in Zionism deserve further research. Joan Dash's penetrating biography, *Summoned to Jerusalem: The Life of Henrietta Szold*, is an excellent study of the founder of Hadassah and American woman's involvement in Zionism.

To avoid frequently changing terminology, this book will follow the American preference for "woman's movement" rather than the English "women's movement," and use the American term "suffragists" rather than the English "suffragettes."

A comparative study must necessarily be less detailed than one would wish. It is hoped that this book will encourage further research on the role of Jewish women and on the connections between feminist issues yesterday and today.

1

Prologue—Idealized Ladies

ENGLAND

I was this day united in the holy bonds of matrimony to Moses Montefiore. . . . Oh! may I continually be thankful to God for his great goodness towards me and my family; suffer me not, Good Heavens, to be ungrateful for Thy bounty, but if misfortune or disappointments are to befall me may I bear them with resignation!
—*Judith Montefiore*, Diary, *June 10, 1812*

JUDITH COHEN Montefiore, wife of the renowned Jewish philanthropist and diplomat Moses Montefiore, has become the almost stereotypical ideal of nineteenth-century Anglo-Jewish womanhood. In a country and era in which class and wealth determined status and opportunity, her social prominence, legendary devotion to her husband, personal modesty, and "good works" established her as a living legend.[1] Montefiore and her counterparts in the United States became the ultimate role models for successive generations of Jewish women who sought to emerge from the home and take their places in communal and national public life.

THE JEWS IN ENGLAND

Jewish emancipation in England, unlike Continental Europe, progressed gradually after the readmission of Jews to England in 1655. Parliament never laid down conditions for Jewish citizenship, as did the Paris Sanhedrin for French Jewry or the Prussian Diet for German Jewry. As Howard Sachar has noted, Jews were more fully accepted in England than in any other European country, with the possible exception of Italy.[2]

Nevertheless, the linkage between England's Established Anglican church and the State, as well as the relatively rigid social hierarchy centered around a royal court, produced a limited social exclusion, economic restrictions, and legal and political discrimination against Jews. As we shall see, these limitations were felt more keenly on England's small island than in the larger United States, pressuring Anglo-Jewry into an intense drive for social acceptance and political enfranchisement.

By the eighteenth century, Ashkenazic Jews from Germany and Poland had immigrated to England. They took full advantage of the new opportunities, quickly becoming more powerful than their more acculturated Sephardic co-religionists from Holland. Some Ashkenazim became wealthy businessmen, although most Jews were employed in middle- and lower-class occupations.[3] Eagerly integrating themselves into the larger society, by the mid–nineteenth century upper- and middle-class Jews perceived themselves and sought to be viewed by native Britons as members of a Dissenting church who were full English citizens in all aspects of daily life.[4]

By the nineteenth century, England's toleration had promoted the social integration of the paladins of Sephardic and Ashkenazic Jewish society, the Montefiores, Rothschilds, Goldsmids, and Cohens. Termed the "Cousinhood" by author Chaim Bermant, these families had become the ruling elite of Anglo-Jewish society. Like their non-Jewish counterparts, their financial success allowed them to buy the landed estates that represented power and patronage. The Cousinhood was not merely a cluster of relatives, but almost an organic unit.[5] Following Victorian custom, the cousins intermarried among themselves to strengthen family-dominated businesses as well as their position in English society.

Religiously observant and communally responsible, the Cousinhood guarded the Jewish community against persistent social hostility and led the successful fight for Jewish political emancipation during the same era as Roman Catholics received their own emancipation. In 1858, Lionel Rothschild was admitted to the House of Commons, and the process was completed in 1871, when Nathan Rothschild was created a Baron and admitted to the House of Lords. During the same year, Jews and Nonconformists were permitted to receive degrees at Oxford and Cambridge universities.[6] Riding a wave of English liberalism, Anglo-Jewry garnered social acceptance as English citizens while maintaining Jewish distinctiveness at home and Jewish kinship abroad.

JUDITH COHEN MONTEFIORE

Judith Cohen Montefiore, daughter of one of Anglo-Jewry's leading families, dedicated her life to her husband, Moses Montefiore. She presided with culture, brilliance, and grace over the elegant dinners and parties essential to Moses Montefiore's career, and her devoted "Monte" insisted that she was the cause of his diplomatic and business success.[7] The glittering receptions conducted by Montefiore and her Anglo-Jewish peers had their Continental counterparts, including the *salons* ruled over by German-Jewish hostesses such as Rachel Levy Varnhagen.[8]

Committed to God, family, and duty, Lady Montefiore attended synagogue services whenever "her health and the weather permitted." By the nineteenth century, the synagogue had become the center of Jewish public life in England as well as the United States, combining worship, charitable and burial services, and social functions. Anglo-Jewry remained almost entirely Orthodox; indeed, Moses Montefiore opposed a modest attempt at reform at the West End Synagogue. Historically, some Jewish women had always attended services, although few attended regularly. Tradition told women their family duties did not require regular worship, confined them to a separate section and forbade them to take part in synagogue management. Christian women, spurred by the nineteenth-century Evangelical revival sweeping England and America, which urged a return to God and morality, had begun attending worship services in increasing numbers, and Jewish women were beginning to emulate their example.

Although Lady Montefiore's public worship was similar to the church-going practices of her Gentile peers, her male family and friends tried to keep her at home, claiming Jewish tradition decreed that it was "not considered essential" for a woman to attend synagogue. "Surely," she disagreed tartly, "at a place of devotion the mind ought to testify due respect and gratitude towards the Almighty."[9] Given her social distinction, Lady Montefiore's visibility during synagogue worship established a powerful incentive for other Jewish women to follow her example.

She preferred to remain quietly at home, yet Lady Montefiore traveled around the world with Montefiore on his numerous expeditions on behalf of world Jewry, often at the risk of her own health.[10] She capped her public role by publishing the first guidelines for Anglo-Jewish women's social conduct, *A Jewish Manual*, by "A Lady," in 1846.

WOMEN'S SEPARATE SPHERES

Montefiore's public devotion to God, family, and social obligations symbolized the expansion of women's role in nineteenth-century England and the United States. The industrial revolution had separated work and home for the majority of citizens. A doctrine of separate spheres relegated public life to men, and the home to women. Wives, essentially their husbands' property, were expected to maintain the home as their husbands' refuge from the outside world. Medical and legal theories reinforced women's segregation, claiming that women were more emotional than men and were naturally dependent upon fathers or husbands. Law and custom determined women's legal dependence and social subordination to their husbands. Wives were expected to be innocent, pure, gentle, and self-sacrificing helpmeets.[11]

Judith Lady Montefiore exemplified the new cult of domesticity, which glorified women's roles as wives, mothers, and mistresses of households.[12] Although not in itself feminist, the cult of domesticity contained the preconditions for feminism by assigning a separate vocation of domesticity to "womanhood" that gave women a consciousness of their separate identity. Nancy Cott contends that without this self-perception, no group of women would ever have created the issue of "women's rights."[13] Implicitly, Montefiore expanded the concept of Jewish womanhood to include an increasingly public role alongside one's husband. Her near-veneration in the Jewish community and English society established a precedent, encouraging upper- and middle-class Anglo-Jewish women to become more active in English as well as Jewish life.

LOUISE LADY ROTHSCHILD

Louise Lady Rothschild,[14] the niece of Judith Lady Montefiore, founded the first serious volunteer philanthropic organization of Anglo-Jewish women. As the wife of Baron Anthony de Rothschild, a scion of Anglo-Jewry's preeminent banking family, she held an unrivaled social position in Anglo-Jewish life. Cultivated, well-educated, and surfeited with luxury, Rothschild dismissed her social obligations as a "grand bore."[15] Imbued with a powerful sense of moral obligation, she focused her life around religion and service to others. Even at sixteen, the future Louise Rothschild was animated by the same devotion to "religious spirit" which inspired Queen Victoria at the same age to declare: "I will be good."[16] Rothschild's sense of duty dominated her entire married life:

> My present duties are to give an example of virtue and piety; to influence, if possible, the conduct of those around me; to make my husband as happy as lies in my power, fulfilling his desires and in all things giving way to his wishes. . . .[17]

Louise Lady Rothschild. Courtesy, National Portrait Gallery,
London

Lady Rothschild's philanthropy extended far beyond the socially
acceptable mode of dropping off baskets of food for sick families in
the villages surrounding her estate. She became famous for her philanthropic works, ranging from nursing sick villagers to founding vil-
lage schools to participating in the management of the Jews' Free
School.[18] It was one of several charitable schools established by the
Anglo-Jewish community to educate and Anglicize the poor. Communal leaders hoped it would educate Jewish students both secularly

and religiously, and combat Protestant missionary societies' attempts to convert Jewish children in missionary-run free schools for Jewish students.[19]

English and American Jewish communities had established a network of charitable organizations to both assist and acculturate the Jewish poor. In England, Jewish communal affairs were governed by two institutions. The Board of Deputies of British Jews acted as the legal representative of the Jewish community, and the Board of Guardians managed community-wide charitable institutions. Although the Boards exerted no legal authority over Anglo-Jewry, they demonstrated considerable leadership at a time when Continental Jewish communities legally taxed and controlled their members.[20] Most charity work in England was organized on denominational lines. Because Jews felt themselves to be a "small minority," Jewish communal workers usually joined only Jewish philanthropic organizations, adopting the form of England's church-affiliated philanthropies.[21]

Jewish women had volunteered in Anglo-Jewish charitable schools since 1662. By 1812, several women taught at Jews' Hospital, one of several free schools for working-class children sponsored by the Jewish community. Amelia Solomon and Rachel Hart created a program to train the school's girls in moral welfare, so that they might become "fit members of society." The anonymous Jewish woman author of *The Jewish Preceptress* (1818) admonished Free School pupils to reject idleness as the "perverter of moral virtue" and "creator of all the poverty and criminality that besmirched the reputation of the Jewish community."[22]

Louise Lady Rothschild launched Jewish women into organized philanthropy when she founded the first independent Jewish women's philanthropic associations in 1840, the Jewish Ladies' Benevolent Loan Society and the Ladies' Visiting Society. Like other nineteenth-century Anglo-Jewish philanthropies, Rothschild's societies combined traditional Jewish concepts with westernized organizational methods consciously based upon Octavia Hill's Charity Organization Society.[23] The Society waged a crusade against impulsive charity, believing that it fostered inefficient administration and encouraged the poor to lie in order to receive funds. Instead, volunteers were trained to encourage their clients to become independent through thrift and self-help.[24]

The societies became the "first link in the chain" to unite London's upper-class West End with the working-class East End. A bastion of Rothschild women composed the executive councils of Lady

Rothschild's benevolent societies, supported by their husbands' financial assistance and "warm approval." Rothschild female cousins reinforced each other in this new venture as they had throughout their lives. Typical of the female friendship of the nineteenth century described by Carroll Smith-Rosenberg, the ties between the Rothschild cousins provided an underlying structure on which clustered groups of female relatives and friends.[25]

Like their Christian counterparts, the societies' volunteers, or "friendly visitors," examined the home conditions of Jewish families seeking assistance, gave personal advice, and attempted to determine the most effective and efficient manner of philanthropic help. The Jewish poor were admonished to cultivate thrift, self-sufficiency, and a reverence for the upper classes, so they might be considered worthy English citizens.[26] Working-class Jewish women were often bitterly resentful: "We do not want to be talked to or taught, we do not drink, and we know how to bring up our children religiously and soberly."[27]

Always concerned for her "less favoured sisters," Louise Lady Rothschild initiated and financed programs for immigrant girls after thousands of East European Jews flooded England from 1881 onwards. In 1885, Rothschild created the first Jewish working girls' club, the West Central Friday Night Club. Led by noted social worker Emily Harris, West Central developed an extensive program serving a variety of social, educational, and recreational purposes.[28]

West Central aroused a furor. Opponents charged that it contributed to the deterioration of the family by taking girls away from their families during their leisure hours. Supporters argued that the club drew girls from the "temptations of the cheap music halls & tawdry entertainments" and "offered tranquil and peaceful change, and their own society." Despite the clamor, West Central established a communally acceptable precedent for socializing immigrant and working girls. As we shall see, Lily Montagu assumed leadership of the club in 1893, expanding West Central from a relatively small group into Anglo-Jewry's premier girls' club and settlement house.[29]

Lady Rothschild's leadership endowed women's philanthropic organizations with an unrivaled social cachet, establishing a precedent that enabled upper- and middle-class Anglo-Jewish women to create a plethora of charitable groups. These emulated the Christian women's benevolent societies that had been created in the wake of the Evangelical revivalism sweeping England and the United States. Drawing upon the cult of domesticity's elevation of women's moral role, evangelists called for women as well as men to inspire, uplift, and improve whole communities and social institutions[30] through personal chastity, honesty, and concern for others expressed through good works.

The Evangelical revival insisted that the nation's moral health depended upon a strong family life, which inculcated Christian values and taught children to be good citizens. Girls were raised to believe that they had a particular religious obligation to help family and society, particularly its weak and unprotected citizens, through public as well as private philanthropy.[31] As women became active in charitable societies, many came to believe that a woman's vocation as moral protector of the family might also take her outside the home to take care of others. Women's involvement in Evangelical activities was facilitated by the trend toward smaller families among upper- and middle-class women, due to later marriages and newly obtainable birth control information, as well as a flood of labor-saving inventions that gave women more leisure time for charitable work.[32]

Beginning with the Evangelical revival, the cult of separate spheres ultimately engendered among women a common identity, solidarity, and new social power. In turn, these generated a separate network of relationships among women that fostered the creation of politically active women's organizations concerned with religious and political reform. These organizations became the catalysts enabling women to obtain limited political achievements in national life.[33]

Women's benevolent societies began this process by forming the basis for the emergence of women in public life through philanthropic service. These societies gave women a consciousness of their identities as women and an outlet for their unused energies, developed a sense of group identity, and trained women in organizational skills.[34] Jewish women emulated this pattern by creating their own parallel organizations.

Following Louise Rothschild's example, Jewish women adapted Evangelical women's associations onto a Jewish framework, creating their own women's organizations that focused upon their own concerns. They drew upon Jewish women's historical involvement in communal charity, integrating Jewish concepts and traditions into the forms developed by secular women's organizations. The success of Jewish women's benevolent societies laid the groundwork for the emergence of England's first politically oriented Jewish feminist movement.

THE EMERGENCE OF ANGLO-JEWISH EQUAL RIGHTS FEMINISM

Equal rights feminism emerged separately from Evangelicalism. The Enlightenment doctrines of reason, natural law, and equality had formed the theoretical basis of Mary Wollstonecraft's path-breaking treatise, A Vindication of the Rights of Woman (1792). Influenced by Wollstonecraft, England's feminist "bluestockings" in the 1830s and 1840s argued for correction of inequities facing women in marriage, education, and unemployment. Radical thinkers sought political reform and girls' education as tools for achieving women's rights.[35]

In 1856, a coterie of women created the Langham Place group to defend Carolyn Norton in her landmark legal battle to obtain a divorce. After Norton's victory, the Langham Place women successfully campaigned for the passage of the 1857 Married Woman's Property Bill and the Divorce Bill, which provided England's first limited protections for married women. However, it was not until 1893 that married women were declared legally independent persons and gained the right to control their own property and personal earnings.[36]

Aware that few opportunities for education and employment were open to single women, many of whom barely survived on family charity or below-subsistence wages, the Langham Place group embarked upon a major campaign for higher education for women. Led by Emily Davies, Langham Place feminists contended that education would provide the key to women's economic independence as well as social and political equality.[37] This campaign drew Louisa Lady Goldsmid into the Langham Place circle in the mid-1860s.

Goldsmid may well have been influenced by two trends that expanded women's scope: nascent Reform Judaism, and the contemporary wave of women authors. Like their Gentile counterparts, Jewish women writers were concerned with morality, domestic themes, and the proper role of women, as well as with the problems of anti-Semitism,[38] missionaries, assimilation, and intermarriage.[39]

Grace Aguilar (1816–47), an unmarried Jewish woman author and teacher, was the most prominent Jewish poet of her day as well as a popular and prolific novelist, essayist, translator, short-story writer, and author of one of the first histories of the Jews in England. In Women in Israel, which extolled biblical women, she attempted to "convince every woman of Israel of her immortal destiny, her solemn responsibility, and her elevated position."

Over a hundred Anglo-Jewish women responded with a collective letter of appreciation to Aguilar: "You have taught us to know and appreciate our dignity. . . . You have vindicated our social and spiritual equality. . . ."[40] Acclaimed as a "genius," Aguilar critically influenced a generation of Jewish women, from Anglo-Jewish essayist Charlotte Montefiore to American Rebecca Gratz, pioneer founder of the Jewish Sunday School movement.[41]

In addition to Aguilar's proto-feminism, Louisa Lady Goldsmid was undoubtedly influenced by the reformist lifestyle of her husband's family. Her father-in-law, Isaac Goldsmid, and her husband, Francis Goldsmid, were leaders of the movement for Jewish political emancipation and founders of the West London Synagogue, England's first Reform congregation.

Mid-nineteenth-century Reform Judaism primarily sought to eliminate what they perceived as embarrassing, outmoded "Orientalisms" in ritual and to create a decorous atmosphere imitative of the Anglican church.[42] The Goldsmids were leaders of a small group of upper-class Jews who founded the West London Synagogue for this purpose in 1840. Because of the innate conservatism of Anglo-Jewry, West London's cautious changes bore little relation to German Reform Judaism; and, although it initially caused a furor because it violated communal discipline, its influence quickly became more social than religious. By the turn of the century, the congregation had ceased to be an energizing liberal force.[43] Nevertheless, West London's founders were considered radical reformers, and Lady Goldsmid's involvement in the woman's movement fit the family pattern.

At the urging of her old friend Emily Davies, Lady Goldsmid joined Davies's campaign to establish a women's college at Cambridge University to train England's surplus of unmarried gentlewomen for employment. Davies's proposal aroused a storm of controversy, since most academic and medical authorities insisted that women's supposed delicacy, modesty, and inability to match men's intellectual abilities prohibited them from the usual program of study.[44]

Aware of this opposition, Goldsmid urged Davies to proceed with caution and initially hesitated to help her long-time friend. Goldsmid, commented Davies, "could not make up her mind to take any part at present. She thought we had better wait till the ferment about the franchise is over."[45] Nevertheless, Goldsmid finally made up her mind to publicly support her friend. She convinced Davies, however, that the education campaign could be won only if it broke away from the suffrage movement. Davies agreed. "I think with Lady Goldsmid that 'We had better quietly withdraw and stick to our "middle-class" (i.e., education).'"[46]

Throwing herself into the education campaign, Goldsmid became a member of the first Executive Committee of Emily Davies's College for Women (later Girton College), serving from 1872 until her death in 1909. After her husband's death, she founded a scholarship in his memory and made other gifts to the college. Goldsmid's involvement ensured that Jewish women were admitted to Girton.[47]

At Davies's request, Goldsmid also joined the Langham Place suffrage committee, which had been organized in London to support John Stuart Mill's proposed suffragist amendment to the 1867 Reform Bill. When the bill failed, the committee disbanded and the battle for suffrage declined for the next two decades. During that period, Goldsmid and others focused on the successful campaign to secure the 1870 Married Women's Property Act.[48]

By supporting Girton College, Lady Goldsmid opened up new professional opportunities for Jewish as well as non-Jewish women. In the Jewish and secular world alike, a college education ensured respectable social status and financial independence. Upper- and middle-class Jewish parents, like their Gentile peers, now sought these newly trained governesses and teachers to educate their daughters.[49] In the Jewish community, the growing numbers of female Jewish teachers of secular subjects encouraged the Jewish community to employ women as teachers in religious schools and as charitable workers in community service organizations. As we shall see, Lady Goldsmid later extended her dedication to women's education and employment to working-class women as well. The process of education, professionalization, and employment fostered by Lady Goldsmid would become the basis for Jewish women's widespread involvement in public life.

UNITED STATES

AMERICA'S JEWS

The nineteenth-century American Jewish community was created by two successive waves of Jewish immigrants who came to America seeking the American promise of toleration, opportunity, and escape from the religious restrictions of European Jewish *kahals*. The first to arrive were Sephardic and Ashkenazic Jews who had escaped the Spanish rulers of seventeenth-century Brazil, the West Indies, and Holland (1655–1815). By the eighteenth century they were joined by the second wave of German Jews who came in two groups. The first were primarily traditional and unlearned Ashkenazi German Jews (1815–30) who fled anti-Semitic restrictions imposed during the conservative reaction in Germany that followed the Napoleonic Wars. By the late 1840s, they were joined by German-Jewish intellectuals who had been caught up in the unsuccessful 1848 revolution. The rapidly increasing numbers of German Jews soon dominated American Jewish life.

Like their English co-religionists, the vast majority of early American Jews rushed to take advantage of their new emancipation by seeking acceptance in all aspects of American life. This was easier in the New World than in England, because American society promoted separation of church and state, an officially classless society, and values that emphasized personal initiative and independence.

American Jews fought relatively few battles state by state for political emancipation, and waged some struggles against barriers erected by an established church or an upper-class social aristocracy. Immigrants' infatuation with America stemmed from Americans' belief that "equal hats" made people equal.[50] Members of America's burgeoning middle class, Jews were encouraged to pursue the economic success that facilitated their social mobility. The nation's relative lack of anti-Semitism further accelerated Jewry's progress. Even though most Americans considered their country a Christian nation, the Constitution and Bill of Rights engendered a religious tolerance and pluralism[51] which ensured that social anti-Semitism rarely took legal form.

Nevertheless, Jews were surrounded by the ambivalence of their Christian neighbors. Nineteenth-century America was increasingly uneasy in a period of growing industrialization and a constant influx of European immigrants who came to be seen as corrupters of the cities and therefore as enemies of the traditional "good society." Needing stability, Americans turned to the traditional values inherent in small-town life. In this atmosphere, even the most sympathetic Christians might admire the Hebrew Bible as Christian Scripture but condemn Jewry's rejection of Christ. Therefore, comments Naomi Cohen, despite the unparalleled American legal tolerance, the effect of emancipation, in America as well as England, was to make many Jewish citizens more self-conscious than at any previous era in Jewish history.[52]

Still, the unprecedented tolerance in America encouraged Jews to create a particularly American Jewish identity, which fused Jewish tradition with American notions of social and political opportunity. After the influx of East European immigrants began in 1881, German Jews became the aristocracy of American Jewry. They led the way toward Jewish acculturation as Americans and away from ethnic and religious identification as Jews. Reveling in the buoyant conviction that, in America, "nothing is impossible,"[53] most Jewish immigrants had migrated to urban areas, where occupational opportunities provided social mobility and it was easier to create new religious forms. As the familiar network of tradition and collective memory began gradually to pull apart, American Jews substituted a new group of religious and philanthropic institutions which synthesized Jewish and American values.[54]

American life hastened the process of acculturation. Maintaining traditional values of marriage and children for women[55] did not prevent Jewish women's involvement in public activity. The majority of Jewish men worked on Saturday, because civil law decreed their businesses must be closed on Sunday. Husbands abandoned their traditional task of religious instruction of their children and curtailed their attendance at Sabbath services. Faced with these changes, rabbis, like Christian ministers, discovered that filling their synagogues depended upon the increasing numbers of Jewish women who came to worship. "The young Jewess attends service at the sanctuary, and the young Jew attends service at the counting house," bemoaned the *Jewish Messenger.*[56]

WOMEN IN AMERICA

Jewish women benefited from America's version of the Evangelical revival, known as the "Second Great Awakening" (1790–1835). It generated a cult of domesticity that varied only slightly from its counterpart in England. Rooted in the American Revolution's emphasis on personal liberty, the cult hastened the process of Jewish acculturation, and infused the anti-slavery and woman's movements. "Remember the Ladies," cautioned Abigail Adams to her husband, "Remember all men would be tyrants if they could."[57] As we shall see, the emphasis upon personal liberty in the United States engendered a more vigorous and widespread feminist movement there than in England. In contrast, England's tolerance of eccentricity and militancy encouraged a more radical suffragist movement than in the United States.

REBECCA GRATZ

Philadelphia aristocrat Rebecca Gratz (1781–1869) reshaped American Jewish religious education by founding the first Jewish Sunday School in the United States in 1838. She served as the Hebrew Sunday School's first superintendent and its president for more than twenty-five years. Gratz shattered Jewish tradition by hiring women teachers to instruct students in Hebrew Sunday School classrooms where boys and girls studied together. In the process, she opened up new opportunities in teaching for women and new educational opportunities for children. An elegant and popular figure, Gratz, according to legend, served as Sir Walter Scott's model for Rebecca in his novel *Ivanhoe.*[58]

Gratz became the ideal for thousands of middle-class American Jewish women who emerged from the home into public life.

The doctrine of separate spheres laid the basis for the "feminizing" of certain vocations in America and England by linking women's nurturing functions with philanthropy and teaching. Unmarried women, once relegated to the fringes of society, received new approval by devoting themselves to serving others through these "women's vocations."[59] As population figures rose, America and England experienced a significant increase in the numbers of single women. Depending upon their class and financial situation, respectable unmarried women devoted themselves to philanthropic vocations or to employment as teachers or authors, careers that permitted personal flexibility. Given these new options, women increasingly chose not to marry because they viewed marriage as restricting their personal liberty. Many turned to the woman's movement to seek redress of legal, economic, and social inequalities.[60]

Like certain other women of her day, Gratz believed that "there appears no condition in human life more afflictive and destructive to happiness and morals than an ill-advised marriage." She did "not know why married life affords so few examples [of happiness], it must surely be their own faults who choose their destiny when it is otherwise."[61] Gratz's determination to remain single and pursue a career was profoundly influenced by several unmarried women authors, especially Jewish writer Grace Aguilar and American poet Penina Moise (1797–1880).[62] America's first Jewish lyric poet, Moise became famous for her synagogue hymns. A versatile author, she also penned epigrams satirizing the social stigma attached to unmarried women:[63]

> And am I no longer betrothed, dear mother?
> Oh Cupid! suppose I should ne'er get another?[64]

Searching for a meaning for her own life, Gratz formulated her plans for the first Jewish Sunday School movement at a time when rabbis were searching for an alternative to the traditional day school (cheder) for boys. The majority of Jewish children attended American public schools while Jewish religious education suffered from assimilation and a lack of trained teachers. In 1838, Gratz founded the Hebrew Sunday School Society and opened the first Jewish Sunday School to serve Philadelphia's Jewish community, particularly its working-class children.

Gratz was encouraged and guided by Isaac Leeser, rabbi of Philadelphia's Mikve Israel congregation and one of the most influential scholar-rabbis of nineteenth-century America. Leeser sought to inte-

Rebecca Gratz. Courtesy, American Jewish Historical
Society

grate Jewish values with the demands of America's secular culture
and lifestyle.[65] His newspaper, the *Occident*, simultaneously glorified
Jewish women's role as wives and mothers and reinforced their traditional role in the synagogue, while praising Jewish women's benevolent societies and their participation in a wide range of philanthropic
activities.[66] He supported Gratz's Sunday School although it had no
Jewish precedents. Gratz's role models were the Evangelical Christian
Sunday School movement and the Society of Friends, which had permitted women to function as missionaries and teachers since colonial
days.[67]

Gratz hired women as religious education teachers, a sphere previously reserved for men, and permitted women to teach both boys
and girls, which was unprecedented in Jewish religious custom. Classroom texts equating Judaism and motherhood further reinforced an
attitude of respect toward women educators.[68] The Sunday School

rapidly inspired followers, beginning in 1838 with Charleston's first Sunday School, which was an extension of Congregation Bet Elohim. The two schools gradually became models for similar schools across the country. By 1881, Gratz's Sunday School was venerated by the Jewish community as a women's institution that served as a model for teaching Jewish immigrants.

Rebecca Gratz's work in the Sunday School movement as well as her efforts in women's philanthropic organizations earned her an international reputation as an exemplar of Jewish womanhood. Immortalized by renowned authors and artists and fawned over by Philadelphia society, Gratz was eagerly imitated by Jewish women who ventured into volunteer service and professional careers.[69] Her stature gained respectability for the growing numbers of Jewish women who remained single in order to preserve their independence. Gratz set the standard for Jewish women who wished to move into public life while remaining committed to the Jewish community.

THE "WOMAN QUESTION"

> Carry out the republican principal of universal suffrage, or strike it from your banners, and substitute "Freedom and Power to one half of society, and Submission and Slavery" to the other.
> —Ernestine Rose, "On Legal Discrimination," 1851

Ernestine Rose, the first nationally known Jewish suffragist in the United States, rejected Rebecca Gratz's model of service in favor of international radical feminism.[70] Raised in an ultra-orthodox Jewish community in Poland, she rebelled against her father's choice of a husband and fled to England, where she became a disciple of utopian reformer Robert Owen. Westernized, secularized, and radicalized, she married William E. Rose in 1836 and accompanied him to the United States.[71]

Despite her Polish-Jewish origins, Rose's path to feminism was strikingly similar to that of her Christian peers. Like Susan B. Anthony, Elizabeth Cady Stanton, and many others, she was profoundly influenced by European pacifist and feminist philosophy and infuriated by the second-class treatment of female abolitionists and temperance activists.[72] Rose traveled the United States on behalf of abolition, temperance, and women's rights, often speaking on platforms with Anthony and Stanton. She presented the first petition for a Married Woman's Property Law to the New York State Legislature in 1836. Rose delivered a stirring address at the first women's rights convention in Seneca Falls, New York, in 1848, and spoke at succeeding national women's rights conventions throughout her life.[73] Although she returned to England with her husband in 1869, she remained active in international feminist affairs.

Rose was the only nationally prominent Jewish feminist in pre–Civil War America. The fledgling status of the Jewish community hampered Jewish women, even more than men, who might wish to champion unpopular causes. There were only 15,000 Jews in America in the 1830s, when Rose and her husband voyaged to America. After 1848, thousands of Central European Jews emigrated to the United States in the wake of the failure of Europe's liberal revolutions. By 1860, near the end of Rose's career in the United States, the number of Jews totaled nearly 150,000.[74] Nevertheless, although Jews were slowly gaining a foothold in the upwardly mobile American middle class, they still confronted social exclusion, economic restrictions, and occasional legal discrimination in certain states.

Given this situation, Jewish women, like their fathers, brothers, and husbands, refrained from supporting controversial causes. Moreover, feminism and many other radical causes were often promoted by Christian evangelicals whose attitudes toward Jews and attempts at their conversion fostered deep suspicion in the Jewish community.[75] As we shall see in chapter 2, the nineteenth-century feminist movement was riddled with Christian anti-Judaism and political anti-Semitism, which significantly inhibited Jewish membership.

Moreover, Jewish women were considered outsiders both as women and as Jews by most elements of American society. Even American feminists might accept Jews in theory but reject them in fact. Lydia Maria Child, for example, attacked prejudice against Jews and "colored people," but condemned Jews as having "humbugged the world. . . ."[76] Under these circumstances, a Jewish feminist would have to be willing to risk being doubly vilified as a feminist and a Jew. Moreover, during Rose's lifetime Jewish women were still heavily circumscribed by restrictions emanating from Judaism's ideals of female modesty, duty, and service to family and community.

In rejecting her father's traditionalism, Ernestine Rose also appears to have dissociated herself from the American Jewish community. She never publicly identified herself as a Jew while speaking on feminist issues, and committed herself to secularized international feminism, setting a precedent for a later group of Jewish feminists. As a result, she did not become a role model for the majority of Jewish women of her generation who identified themselves as Jews. Nevertheless, she could never escape her Jewish heritage. Rabbi Isaac M. Wise's newspaper supplement for Reform Jewish women, *Deborah*, frequently reported her speeches and identified her as a "Jewess," giving her a nationwide prominence in the Reform Jewish community that may well have influenced the movement's early concern with "the Woman Question" and its halting steps toward religious emancipation for women.[77]

REFORM JUDAISM

Reform Judaism profoundly influenced the emergence of a Jewish women's movement in both England and the United States, but at different times in each country. Originating in 1820s Germany, Reform Judaism was inspired philosophically by the Enlightenment and politically by Jewry's emancipation from the ghetto. Seeking to combine modernity with Jewish values, early reformers rejected Jewish law in favor of prophetic ethics. They claimed to be German citizens adhering to the Jewish religion, rather than members of a biblically mandated Jewish people or nation.[78] Developing new approaches to ritual and Jewish life, they sought to elevate the status of women in Judaism. In 1837, Reform Rabbi Abraham Geiger issued the first known call for the religious emancipation of Jewish women:

> Let there be from now on no distinction between duties for men and women, unless flowing from the natural laws governing the sexes; no assumption of the spiritual minority of woman . . . no institution of the public service . . . which shuts the doors of the temple in the face of woman; no degradation of woman in the form of the marriage service, and no applying the fetters which may destroy woman's happiness.[79]

German Reformers declared that girls would be educated equally with boys and would be eligible for confirmation. Jewish women could be admitted to the *minyan*, the legal quorum of ten required for a religious service. Reformers also abolished the man's traditional morning benediction thanking God for "not having made me a woman." Several edicts on marriage and divorce further helped to reinforce the conviction that "It is our sacred duty to declare . . . the complete religious equality of woman with man."[80]

Reform was transported to both England and the United States, but it became a major force in American Jewish life, while remaining a relatively minor movement that did not become more than marginally influential in England until the early twentieth century. Even then, as we shall see, the majority of progressive worshipers turned more toward the new movement of Liberal Judaism than toward classical Reform.

After 1848, Reform Jews from Germany settled across America, from the Atlantic to the Pacific. German Reformers founded syn-agogues and religious schools combining German Reform teachings and emphasis upon decorum with the independence of America's Protestant congregationalist churches.[81] Describing themselves as American citizens of the Jewish religion, Reformers simplified their ritual, preached in English or German rather than Hebrew, and used an English-Hebrew prayerbook.[82] America's frontier spirit and inde-pendent congregationalism encouraged the growth of the new move-ment.

Nevertheless, Reform desperately needed adequate financial sup-port and active congregants to shore up its fledgling synagogues. Faced with the exigencies of building a new movement plus the demands of American life, which forced men to work on the Jewish Sabbath, rab-bis acknowledged the presence of the women filling their pews. Rabbi Isaac M. Wise, who popularized an Americanized Reform Judaism, introduced mixed choirs, mixed seating, and confirmation to his con-gregations, beginning in 1846.[83] Equal participation in worship, ar-gued Wise, should be a religious obligation for every woman.[84] Wise even argued that women should have the right to vote in the syn-agogue and hold seats in their own right.[85] Inspired by Wise, the practice of having family pews soon spread to Reform congregations across the country,[86] but women seatholders did not get the right to vote until the end of the century.

Asserting Jewish women's right to fulfill religious obligations equally with men, increasing numbers of Reform rabbis introduced mixed consecration ceremonies for boys and girls. Confirmation re-placed the *bar mitzvah* ceremony in some synagogues in order to include women in a ritual acknowledging their coming of age in re-ligious life.[87] Rabbi David Einhorn encouraged an 1869 conference of Reform rabbis to approve significant changes in religious laws affect-ing women, including the equalization of the position of women in marriage and divorce.[88]

Wise's newspaper supplement *Deborah* and Einhorn's newspaper *Sinai* encouraged Jewish women to become active in Reform Juda-ism's social, religious, educational, and philanthropic activities.[89] Re-form women responded in significant numbers.[90] Jewish women distributed food and clothing, nursed the sick and wounded, estab-lished nursery schools, and provided emergency shelters and employ-ment. Indeed, Reform Jewish women insisted upon their right to work in the community, "for the good of the community."[91] They not only cited Jewish teachings as validity for their charitable activities but, like their Christian counterparts, justified their work as a proper extension of women's moral obligations in the home.[92]

As one result of the drive for emancipation, the Reform movement improved girls' religious education, drawing girls into the Sunday School format pioneered by Rebecca Gratz in 1838, instituting new schools for the higher religious education of both girls and boys, and attempting unsuccessfully to establish a Jewish women's college.[93]

Religious changes affecting Reform women indirectly influenced increasing numbers of traditional Jewish women as well. In New York, a synagogue in uptown Harlem permitted some departures from traditional religious practice. Mixed seating was allowed during services, ostensibly because there was no gallery for the women. In 1876, the congregation's newly formed ladies' auxiliary took exclusive control of educational activities. Women of the congregation served on the school committee and acted as an unpaid staff for the school, although their husbands controlled the purse strings.[94]

Heatedly debating "the Woman Question" generated by the early American suffrage movement, Reform communities tended to support the secular drive for women's emancipation. Reform rabbis argued that the woman's movement's values were compatible with Reform's stress on prophetic ethics and reflected the future trend of women's role in the majority culture; Jewish women's involvement in the American women's movement would strengthen the burgeoning Reform movement by encouraging their participation in religious life.[95]

While mid-nineteenth-century Reform Jewish women were active in charitable organizations and Reform temples, Minna Cohen Kleeberg (1841–78) was one of a handful who became visible as passionate supporters of religious and political suffrage. A poet and principal of a Sunday School she founded with her husband, she scathingly attacked Jewish men's daily prayer thanking God they were not born as women, commenting pungently, "Thank God I was not created a man!"[96]

A combination of *realpolitik* and religious-ethical convictions determined Reform rabbis' advocacy of religious equality for women. Wise and his colleagues appear to have decided that the values implicit in the American woman's movement were compatible with Reform's stress on prophetic ethics. They estimated that Jewish involvement in the woman's movement would encourage Jewish women's participation in religious life and so strengthen Reform Judaism.[97] They judged correctly. As we shall see, the emancipation of women significantly influenced the growth of the Reform movement as well as the development of politically conscious Jewish women's organizations after 1881.

CONCLUSION

Judith Lady Montefiore, Louise Lady Rothschild, and Rebecca Gratz embodied Jewish values and acculturated dreams to their many followers. They epi.omized westernized Jewry's ultimate goal: combining Jewish values and identity with social acceptance in the larger world. Socialization with Christian women encouraged these women to clothe their philanthropic and educational activity with secular forms and Jewish substance. Acclaimed in the national as well as the Jewish world, they became role models for generations of Jewish women who wished to emerge from the home into public life.

These idealized Jewish ladies of mid-nineteenth century America and England struggled to redefine the meaning of Jewish womanhood in the modern, religiously tolerant, secular world to which Jewry had only recently gained access. Jews grappled daily with the problem of how to maintain Jewishness while asserting citizenship. Similarly, Jewish wives and mothers expanded their role in the home, the center of Jewish life, to include limited philanthropic and religious activities. Rothschild and Gratz promoted a mushrooming network of female benevolent societies and charitable schools, creating a new touchstone of self-identity for Jewish women who adapted the cult of separate spheres to their own needs. As single Jewish women, Gratz and Aguilar encouraged the perception that their charitable work was a new form of devotion to family and community. In doing so, they laid the groundwork for a new generation of single Jewish women to enter the public sphere.

Yet, despite many similarities, concepts of Jewish womanhood developed somewhat differently in England and the United States. Living in the goldfish bowl of a small island, perpetually on the lookout for social anti-Semitism, English Jews rigorously adhered to England's class-dominated customs, identified themselves as English citizens of a Dissenting English church, and maintained conventional social, religious, and communal forms. This situation caused even the most progressive Jews to be cautious in their reforms. For Anglo-Jewish women, surrounded by the combined strictures of Victorian England and traditional Judaism, each step toward independent organizations, higher education, or suffrage for women became a radical and threatening venture.

In this atmosphere, Louise Lady Rothschild remained socially and religiously orthodox, pioneering girls' clubs to assist her "less fortunate sisters," but unprepared to join the fledgling English woman's movement. Nevertheless, as we shall see, Lady Rothschild's social status and family connections engendered a personal security that encouraged her not only to create girls' clubs, but also to educate her daughters to assume an even more public role on behalf of women. Rothschild's legacy established the preconditions for a network of Anglo-Jewish women's organizations that later triggered creation of a Jewish woman's movement in England.

In the United States, Rebecca Gratz and, later, the Reform movement were spurred to independent action by the young country's devotion to progress, the opportunities available to the Jewish middle classes, an emphasis upon personal independence, and rejection of a central authority by synagogues and Jewish community groups. Reform Judaism gained a major hold upon Jewish life in the United States approximately forty years before its weaker counterpart would do so in England.

These conditions shaped the first hesitant appearance of radical Jewish feminism. Only one isolated Jewish woman in each country supported suffrage before 1881. Louise Lady Goldsmid, a committed member of the Anglo-Jewish community, focused her primary efforts upon education and employment for women. As we shall see, she was also instrumental in convincing liberal Anglo-Jewish men and women to support the women's trade union movement. The American Ernestine Rose, on the other hand, maintained no perceptible ties to the Jewish community, devoting her allegiance to suffrage and the international feminist movement. Her approach reflected the more flexible position of Jewry, the relative permeability of class barriers, and the slightly more open social behavior permitted women in mid-nineteenth-century America.

Montefiore, Rothschild,[98] Goldsmid, Gratz, and Rose, each in her divergent way, set the stage for the development of new concepts of ideal Jewish womanhood. Each became a role model for a new generation of Jewish women groping for new ways to assert their independence and emancipation.

2

"Bond of Sisterhood"

UNITED STATES

THE IMMIGRANTS

In 1881, East European immigrants began to flood the United States and England, fleeing the Russian pogroms and policies of starvation that followed the assassination of Czar Alexander II. Their arrival established German Jews as a functional aristocracy. Their earlier presence and their Americanized or Anglicized cultural, religious, and political attitudes clearly distinguished them from the newcomers. Reinforcing this conception of a Jewish elite by participation in the cultural and philanthropic events of upper-class America, German Jews ensured their gradual social acceptance within the larger society.[1]

So long as the newcomers had remained in Russia, the German Jewish community had been overcome with sympathy. Once they emigrated, however, German Jews became more ambivalent. German Jewish businessmen had achieved the middle-class citizen's dream of personal success.[2] They feared that their hard-won social status would be jeopardized by the large numbers of "alien" Jews who were markedly different in dress, speech, and living patterns[3] and who were accused by anti-Semites of undermining traditional American values as well as America's economic and social order.[4]

Despite these concerns, German Jewish leaders empathized with their co-religionists' plight, and quickly expanded Jewish philanthropic services to meet the emergency. Since the number of male volunteers was utterly inadequate to handle the task, communal leaders appealed to women to help fill the gap. Their eager response shaped the first phase of the Jewish woman's movement in England and the United States.

JEWISH WOMEN'S RESPONSE

In the wake of mass immigration, American Jewish women expanded the scope of their existing benevolent societies, created new charitable organizations,[5] and sought membership in all-male philanthropic organizations throughout the 1880s. B'nai B'rith was American Jewry's oldest and largest fraternal and service organization. Its lodges did not permit ladies' auxiliaries until 1897, and the first chapter of B'nai B'rith Women was not formed until 1909.[6] Jewish women also sought to join the Young Men's Hebrew Association (YMHA), which offered social, cultural, educational, recreational, and philanthropic programs for middle- and working-class Jews. The New York "Y" created the first women's auxiliary in 1888, and by 1894 there were similar auxiliaries in nine other cities.[7]

Jewish newspapers recorded Jewish women's increasing activism within the multitude of Jewish educational and social agencies functioning in each city. New York, the center of immigrant life, became the focal point for women's participation in a range of charitable services, including the Hebrew Free School Association, the Montefiore Hospital, and the United Hebrew Charities.[8]

Reform Jewish women had created local Temple Sisterhoods to assist their synagogues by the 1890s, often intertwining their religious and philanthropic obligations. *Grande dame* Hannah Einstein, already the first woman board member at United Hebrew Charities, became president of Temple Emanu-El's Sisterhood in 1897 and president of the New York Federation of Sisterhoods in 1899.[9]

Jewish women were welcomed as charitable volunteers, teachers, or even school board members because the Jewish community put a high priority on Americanizing and educating immigrants. However, like their Christian counterparts,[10] Jewish women still held little real influence in the Jewish or secular arenas. To deal with issues of paramount concern to themselves, Jewish women adapted the national model of women's clubs which was rapidly spreading throughout the United States.

JEWISH MEMBERSHIP IN WOMEN'S CLUBS

Nineteenth-century middle-class women's network of personal relationships had generated a host of organizations devoted to self-improvement for members and service to less fortunate working and immigrant women.[11]

The women's club movement began when journalist Jane Croly created Sorosis as a Boston cultural organization in 1868. Following her example, middle-class women across the country founded dozens of popular clubs which combined literary study and social service. These clubs became a source of intellectual stimulation, social service, and feminine sisterhood for their members.[12]

Club membership made a statement about women's changing status. A "club" rather than a "society" was a radical departure for women's groups, since they were patterned after men's clubs with their public interests. Club members' devotion to "sisterhood" and the social reform emphasis of the General Federation of Women's Clubs, founded in 1899, formed a cornerstone of social feminism.[13]

Jewish women sought to join American women's clubs to improve their social status and cultural education as well as to participate in clubs' charitable endeavors. Club membership soon became a hallmark of German-Jewish women's acceptance into American life and the primary stepping-stone into American organizational and political life. Deborah Grand Golumb suggests that Jewish women were easily accepted into women's clubs because they shared the progressive concerns of their Christian counterparts. Women's clubs shared racial and economic biases, rather than the religious exclusivity of men's clubs, so they were content to admit middle- and upper-class Jewish women. Clubs served as Jewish women's stepping stones from benevolent societies to city, state, and national organizations.[14]

The first women's club with a Jewish membership was founded in 1846 as Immanuel Lodge of the United Order of True Sisters, a fraternal organization for German-Jewish women. The lodge was a secret society whose structure was modeled after B'nai B'rith; it was organized by members of Temple Emanu-El of New York City. Its purpose was to help its members "to become familiar with current arts and affairs and to foster solidarity among the women of the Temple."[15] The Lodge expanded into a national organization in 1851. A significant departure for Jewish women's groups, the new United Order of True Sisters provided a meeting place, forum, and social service center for its members.[16]

THE 1893 CONGRESS OF JEWISH WOMEN

> It is almost impossible to gauge the great influence of the 1893 Women's Congresses! The cause of women's suffrage . . . actually became fashionable!
> —Hannah Greenbaum Solomon, Fabric of My Life, p. 109

In 1891, leaders of the General Federation of Women's Clubs invited Chicago matron Hannah Greenbaum Solomon to organize a Jewish Women's Congress as part of the Women's Congress at the 1893 Chicago World's Columbian Exposition (World's Fair).[17] Solomon and her sister were the first Jewish members of the Chicago Women's Club in 1877. Commenting on the clubwomen's enthusiastic welcome to their Jewish colleagues, Solomon later noted the "privilege and pleasure" she had enjoyed in working with her "Christian sisters."[18]

Clubwork became Solomon's stepping-stone into feminist social reform, buttressed by the moral stanchion of Reform Rabbi Emil G. Hirsch of Chicago's Temple Sinai, where Solomon and her family were members. Hirsch firmly supported the emancipation of Jewish women, urging them to join the "army" battling for social reform and demand their right to equality, education, and entry into the professions and public charitable work.[19]

To organize the Jewish Women's Congress, Solomon gathered a committee of upper-class German-Jewish women, many of whom were members of the Chicago Women's Club and Reform Jews. Locating and organizing women for a national congress proved so difficult that the Jewish Women's Congress' working committee concluded that Jewish women needed a national organization publicly identified with the woman's movement. This organization must create a network of Jewish women who could reinforce each other while beginning to forge political influence for women within the Jewish community.[20]

To galvanize support, the working committee sought a cadre of nationally recognized speakers who would command the respect of secular as well as Jewish women's groups and attract an audience of Jewish women from across the United States. The committee was successful on both counts. Four distinguished Jewish women were invited to deliver papers at the general Women's Congress and the World Parliament of Religions on topics including women's education, social emancipation and suffrage, and immigration.[21] Their appearance at major, non-Jewish World's Fair events underscored German-Jewish women's increasing acceptance into the wider American society and their public commitment to women's emancipation.

The Jewish Women's Congress itself generated tremendous excitement:

> September 5, 1893. Women elbowed, trod on each other's toes and did everything else they could do without violating the proprieties to gain the privilege of standing edgewise in a hall heavy with the fragrance of roses. They filled all the seats some time before the opening of the Jewish Women's Congress. By 10 o'clock the aisles were all filled, ten minutes later there was an impossible jam at the doors that reached far down the corridor. Few men were present. They were thrust into the

background into the remotest corners. They had no place on the program and seemed to look upon themselves as interlopers. But the ladies did not consider them so: they did not consider them at all: they had something better to think about.[22]

Ray Frank, America's first Jewish woman preacher, electrified the Congress with her opening prayer and speech for women's emancipation, demanding that "Jewish women must break the shackles that bind them."[23] A host of speakers urged the women to forge ties of Jewish sisterhood to expand women's role in home, synagogue, and community. Learned papers were delivered by outstanding Jewish women on clubwork, social service, religion, the professions, arts, and business. Rebekah Kohut, author and editor of the Jewish women's journal *Helpful Hints*, had remained home at the plea of her rabbi-scholar husband, Alexander. Her absence lent an especial poignancy to her paper, read by another, which connected women's "messianic mission" to their duties for home, Judaism, and the Jewish community.[24]

FOUNDING THE NCJW

Conference co-organizer Sadie American, an outspoken feminist, called for creation of a national Jewish women's organization with four central aims: (1) to study Judaism; (2) to provide Sabbath schools for the poor; (3) to undertake philanthropic work; (4) to act as a forum for the exchange of ideas among all Jewish women.[25] These four objectives formed the core of the resolution creating the National Council of Jewish Women (NCJW). Hannah G. Solomon was elected its first president and Sadie American its corresponding secretary.

The new NCJW's first task was to initiate an ambitious program of Jewish study. Council members formed study circles to improve their own Jewish knowledge of Judaism and created Sabbath Schools to educate Jewish working-class children.[26] The women's study of religious texts led them into two different arenas. They concluded that as a " 'religious body,' it behooves us to do philanthropic work."[27] Traditional values reinforced NCJW's charitable work, and validated their progress into the arena of social reform. As we shall see, studying Jewish literature and ritual also led the NCJW to seek greater participation in ritual and voting rights for women in the synagogue. The combined goals identified them as feminists who learned to wage political campaigns to ensure emancipation for their members and to improve the lives of less fortunate women and children.[28]

Jewish Women's Congress speakers identified themselves with the equal rights and social service goals of America's woman's movement, adapted to fit the needs of Jewish women. As we shall see, that message infused the NCJW, shaped its policies, and inspired its social reform and legislative efforts, causing it to become America's first independent, politically conscious Jewish women's organization.

RELIGION AND FEMINISM: RAY FRANK

> From time immemorial the Jewish woman has remained in the background. . . . She has gathered strength and courage to come forward . . . to battle for herself if necessary.

In 1890, Ray Frank delivered the sermon at the Kol Nidre evening service ushering in the Day of Atonement, Judaism's most sacred holiday, for the Jewish community of Spokane, Washington. Frank was the first woman in Jewish history to deliver a Kol Nidre sermon, and her appearance launched her on a national career as a religious leader.[29] Worshipers jammed synagogues from coast to coast to hear the diminutive woman lionized by the Jewish press as the "Maiden in the Temple" and a "later-day Deborah."[30]

The first Jewish woman in America to attempt spiritual leadership, Frank symbolized Jewish women's desire for increased equality in religious life. Believing that as a woman she had a special mission to help revitalize Judaism, she was propelled toward feminism by her commitment to Judaism. Her visibility in Reform synagogue pulpits opened the way for women's greater participation in Reform Jewish life, and inspired an organized demand for religious equality by the Jewish Women's Congress, the NCJW, and, as we shall see, Rosa Sonneschein's *American Jewess.*

A California teacher and journalist who volunteered to teach religious school, Ray Frank's (1864/5–1948) classroom lectures attracted so many adults that the rabbi asked her to deliver synagogue sermons. She had no Jewish role models, since Reform Judaism had not progressed beyond mixed seating and mixed choirs, and traditional Judaism did not even count women in the quorum needed for worship. As a result, she looked toward female Christian ministers.

By the late nineteenth century, the woman's movement and the examples of certain Utopian movements encouraged a few Christian women to seek careers as ministers. The majority of American Christians opposed women's right to preach, citing church doctrines that insisted women remain "silent in the churches."[31] Religious feminists argued that the Church Fathers had taught that women and men were *equally* welcome in Christianity, and that their call to preach came from the Holy Spirit.[32] In response, a limited number of churches

Ray Frank Litman. Courtesy, American Jewish Historical Society

permitted women to preach and occasionally to act as ministers. The Quakers, Universalists, Unitarians, and Congregationalists resolved this issue earlier than most Methodists, Presbyterians, Lutherans, or Episcopalians. Radical sects such as Seventh Day Adventists, Christian Scientists, and Shakers had female founders or leaders.[33]

Despite the lack of Jewish role models, Ray Frank's concern about the spiritual neglect in America's Jewish communities drove her to travel across the country urging Jews to return to Judaism. In 1893, wishing to improve her own Jewish education, Frank took a few courses in Jewish ethics and philosophy at Hebrew Union College, the rabbinical seminary for Reform Judaism.[34] She studied at the College for a few months and then left; it is unclear whether she left of her own volition or because seminary authorities convinced her that women should not attempt rabbinic studies. Although she never graduated and never claimed to be a rabbi, she received several requests to function as a congregational rabbi.[35] She rejected these offers, but remained highly ambivalent about the rabbinate for women:

> It has been said that I am ambitious to be ordained a Rabbi. . . . I . . . do not aspire to the office of Rabbi, I could never be one; that is thoroughly masculine. But I do aspire to that work which the rabbis seldom care to do. . . . I never wish to be a salaried preacher because one who is paid by others must to a very great extent say what will please the ones who pay him.[36]

Defending women's emancipation while remaining uncertain regarding its ultimate goals, Frank relegated the rabbinate to a "masculine" status while treating it with ostensible contempt. Her speech to the Jewish Women's Congress demanded new vistas for women in religious life. Asserting that women are "the stronger spiritually," she insisted that "We are capable of fulfilling the office [of rabbi]."[37] Nevertheless, she promoted a traditional concept of motherhood: "Sisters, our work in and for the synagogue lies in bringing to the Temple the Samuels to fulfill the Law."

Torn between opportunity and tradition, Frank admired feminists such as Charlotte Perkins Stetson but doubted she could go as far.[38] Although she supported women's emancipation, she opposed the suffrage campaign.[39] Later, women's participation in World War I convinced Frank to reverse her position, and she helped found the League of Women Voters in Champaign-Urbana.[40]

Unsure of how to achieve emancipation for women,[41] and unclear in her objectives, Frank intertwined Judaism, women's equality, and women's duty as homemakers in her lectures across the United States. Despite her intellectual confusion, the *American Jewess*, the country's first independent newspaper for Jewish women, acclaimed her as an "arch-angel" in the same category as the "genius" Susan B. Anthony.[42]

In 1899, Ray Frank reached a crucial turning point. Citing the need to repair her health, she left the United States for an extended sojourn in Europe. There she met economist Simon Litman, married him in 1901, and returned with him to the University of Illinois. As a childless faculty wife, she devoted herself to the local League of Women Voters and gave a few speeches on women and Judaism, but she never resumed her preaching career. In 1915, she founded a study circle from among a small Jewish campus group called Menorah; it became a precursor of the B'nai B'rith Hillel Foundation's campus religious studies programs.[43]

Simon Litman's memoir of his wife sheds only faint light on Frank's reasons for abruptly severing her career. During his visits with her in Europe, she seemed like "one who has been recovering from a breakdown from what I could not tell." On the surface, Frank was a smiling, fun-loving, eloquent, solicitous, and questioning woman. However, she usually wore a "solemn, almost tragic expression" and appeared "weary and disillusioned." Often "withdrawn into herself," she remained "absorbed in deep thoughts to the extent of not knowing what was going on around her."[44] Litman's description, the ambivalence in Frank's own speeches, and her refusal to resume her career after her marriage suggest that her breakdown was probably caused by a tension between her preacher's role and traditional American and Jewish condemnation of women religious leaders.[45]

Ray Frank solved her internal conflict by abandoning her attempts at religious leadership, unlike England's Lily Montagu, who, as we shall see, functioned successfully as a rabbi-without-title. However, there are interesting parallels between the two preachers. Frank and Montagu both sought to prove that raising women's religious status was a valid extension of their roles as moral guardians of home and society. Rejecting the Orthodoxy of their parents, both women turned instead toward progressive Judaism as a vehicle for their own careers and as the key to revitalizing the Jewish faith.[46] Their newly gained religious mantle sanctified religious emancipation as well as social activism for a new generation of Jewish women.

Frank's inability to maintain her career may be due to several causes. She lacked American role models, although she did correspond frequently with Lily Montagu and other Anglo-Jewish feminists such as author Nina Davis and activist Nettie Adler.[47] Adulation from prominent American admirers such as essayist Ambrose Bierce[48] evidently did not provide enough emotional support. Unlike Lily Montagu, she did not have a tight-knit family and class structure to support her. Even her advocates among Reform members of the National Council of Jewish Women were ambivalent about the extent of religious emancipation for Jewish women. Without strong familial or organizational support, Frank was emotionally unable or unwilling to continue her religious leadership.

Nevertheless, Ray Frank's impact extended beyond her brief career. Before she began to preach, Reform women's influence in the synagogue was limited to mixed seating, mixed choirs, and often a ma-

jority presence during worship. Frank's status as a preacher
encouraged Jewish women to demand more equal participation in synagogue ritual and laid the basis for a successful campaign for religious
education and synagogue voting privileges for women.

THE WOMAN MOVEMENT

Jewish women seeking to join the American feminist movement faced
the Christian anti-Judaism and social anti-Semitism of the era. At
the 1885 National Woman Suffrage Association convention, Elizabeth
Cady Stanton proposed a resolution denouncing Christianity's position on women. Her co-workers persuaded her to substitute "Judaism" for "Christianity" in order not to offend good Christians. They
were apparently not concerned about the few early Jewish feminists
such as Nina Morais Cohen, an NCJW leader from Minneapolis, active suffragist, and delegate to the 1888 International Conference of
Women. Stanton's resolution read in part:

> Whereas, the dogmas incorporated in the religious creeds derived from
> Judaism, teaching that woman was an afterthought in creation, her sex
> a misfortune, marriage a condition of subordination, and maternity a
> curse, are contrary to the law of God as revealed in nature and the pre-
> cepts of Christ; and
> Whereas, These dogmas are an insidious poison, sapping the vitality of
> our civilization, blighting woman and palsying humanity; therefore,
> Resolved, That we denounce these dogmas. . . . we call upon the Chris-
> tian ministry's leaders of thought, to teach and enforce the fundamental
> idea of creation. . . . in true religion there is neither male nor female,
> neither bond nor free, but all are one [in Christ Jesus].[49]

Originally written by Clara Bentwick Colby, this statement was
intended to delineate the religious underpinnings of society's anti-
suffrage posture. At the same time, its message combined Christian
anti-Jewish attitudes toward the Old Testament with the new racial
anti-Semitism that was permeating contemporary Europe and America. The measure was voted down because NWSA members wanted
to avoid grappling with the question of the effect of religion upon
their role as women. The debate never considered the question of
Jewish feminists' sensibilities.

Widely circulated and debated, Stanton's statement provided an
acceptable rationale for continuing anti-Jewish sentiment within the
woman's movement. Anna Howard Shaw was the second president of
the National American Women's Suffrage Association and a friend
and suffrage colleague of Nina Morais Cohen. In 1888, Shaw delivered
a sermon at the International Council of Women that attempted to

prove Christianity's support of women's equality. To make her point, she, like other ministers of her day, contrasted a supposedly pure Christianity with a distorted picture of Judaism, presenting St. Paul's vision of a Jew who was "bound by the prejudice of past generations" and "educated in the school of an effete philosophy."[50] The anti-Jewish hostility of Stanton, Colby, and their circle, as well as the ambivalence of Shaw and others who were friendly to German-Jewish suffragists, help explain Jewish women's reluctance to become involved in the suffrage movement.

By 1890, the newly named National American Woman Suffrage Association still faced persistent attempts to inject antireligious elements into the NAWSA platform. However, attitudes toward Jews were becoming less hostile, even though feminist groups remained Christian-centered. In 1895, the Women's Christian Temperance Union (WCTU) proposed to admit Catholic as well as Jewish women as members. However, they refused to eliminate the word "Christian" in their name. The *American Jewess* recommended that if the WCTU really wished to involve Jews, it should substitute "Humanity" for "Christianity."[51] The suggestion was never adopted.

In 1895, Elizabeth Cady Stanton published the first volume of her *Woman's Bible*, an analysis by different commentators of the first five books of the Bible (Genesis through Deuteronomy). While the vicious anti-Semitism of the 1885 resolution is absent, the *Woman's Bible* frequently blamed the Hebrew Bible for the subservient position of women in the world. One commentary, for example, insisted that the second creation story was "manipulated by some Jew in an endeavor to give 'heavenly authority' for requiring a woman to obey the man she married." Stanton herself claimed that the Hebrew Bible was responsible for dooming humanity because it cast Eve, allegedly the first woman, as the one responsible for bringing "sin and death into the world."

In 1896, NAWSA voted to reject Stanton's *Bible*:

> This association is non-sectarian, being composed of persons of all shades of religious opinion, and has no official connection with the so-called "Woman's Bible" or any theological publication.[52]

Several reasons lay behind this refusal to alienate church members or Jews. The "Social gospel" encouraged women to expand their roles as moral guardians in the church as well as in society. Second-generation suffragists were no longer willing to antagonize potential members who belonged to Christian churches. At the same time, many of the younger suffragists wished to accept Jewish members.

Some recognized that the suffrage campaign needed a wider political base, concluding that NAWSA could not afford to lose potential members,[53] including upper- and middle-class German-Jewish women who had become relatively socially acceptable in American society. Still others sincerely believed in the social reformers' vision of creating an ideal city through cooperation of all peoples and religions.

Nevertheless, suffragists feared that admitting German Jews might open the door to East Europeans. Along with the rest of the country, NAWSA's members feared the impact of votes cast by male immigrants who followed the voting instructions of conservative political and business interests. If East European women obtained the franchise, it was believed that they would follow their husbands' voting pattern.

Carrie Chapman Catt, NAWSA's third president, who campaigned with upper-class German-Jewish women, argued that the immigrants were a "great danger" and that giving the vote to immigrant males would threaten the state.[54] This attitude on the part of Catt and other NAWSA leaders alienated immigrants as well as established Jewish women's groups, who never believed suffragists' claims that their anti-foreign, anti-immigrant stand was not intrinsically anti-Jewish. Yet, as we shall see, not all German-Jewish suffragists supported granting the franchise to East European newcomers.

NAWSA's rejection of the *Woman's Bible* did not end some members' conscious anti-Semitism or eliminate the movement's Christian orientation. However, the continued subtle exclusion of Jewish women from inner circles of the suffragist leadership was qualitatively different from the anti-Jewish feeling of the early nineteenth century. The 1896 resolution signaled a progressive decline in anti-Jewish feeling among second-generation suffragists that made it possible for growing numbers of Jewish women to join the movement.

ROSA SONNESCHEIN AND THE AMERICAN JEWESS

> We have created a bond of sisterhood . . . [for national and] religious suffrage . . . [in] the pulpit and the pew.
> —The American Jewess, *July 1895, April 1898*

In 1895, Rosa Sonneschein founded the *American Jewess* as a feminist platform advocating women's social, political, communal, and religious emancipation. Inviting Jewish women to "follow us to the goals of universal sisterhood," the newspaper dedicated itself to campaign for national, communal, and religious suffrage.

What the Jewish women of America want, and a result they may justly exert their energies to attain is equal rights in the Synagogue.[55]

Sonneschein's monthly journal simultaneously became an advocate for Jewish concerns and a defender of all socially or politically disenfranchised groups, including East European immigrants, the working classes, Blacks, and Catholics.[56] The *American Jewess* published social, religious, and literary articles in a format that included beautiful pictures, woodcuts, and engravings. Its financial support came from private contributions and extensive advertising. A member of a flourishing Jewish press, the *American Jewess* attracted 29,000 readers; its influence, however, extended far beyond its immediate German-Jewish readership.[57]

Born in Hungary, Rosa Sonneschein had suffered in an arranged marriage to brilliant, radical, and erratic German Reform rabbi Solomon Hirsch Sonneschein, with whom she had three children. Rosa accused her husband of adultery and drunkenness, while he accused her of frigidity. Even though women could, with difficulty, legally seek divorce after 1888, Rosa Sonneschein permitted her husband to divorce her so as not to "ruin" his career.[58] Lacking alimony, she supported herself as a journalist.

Seeking sympathetic understanding from equally independent female minds, Sonneschein gravitated toward the woman's movement, as had other divorced women in similar situations.[59] Its network of supportive relationships appears to have met her needs and dramatically changed her life. Addressing the Press Congress at the 1893 World's Fair, Sonneschein called for a new woman's literary magazine that would "connect with a cord of mutual interest the sisters dwelling throughout . . . the country."[60]

Sonneschein claimed that her newspaper's battle against the "injustice that is done to women the world over" helped to decrease anti-Semitism within the feminist movement. As proof of her success, she contended that the *American Jewess* was the only Jewish publication "largely read by non-Jews," especially non-Jewish women activists.

We have created a bond of sisterhood, doing our share to weaken existing prejudices against the Jewess by bringing to public notice the Jewess of to-day.[61]

Rapidly becoming a standard-bearer of the feminist movement within the Jewish community, the *American Jewess* campaigned for the abolition of still-pervasive legal restrictions on women, the admission of women onto school boards, and women's participation in social reform. "Woman's rights" agitation, asserted the journal, demanded higher education and employment training for women to help them discover the "independence and self-reliance" to earn a living.[62] "It is a stern fact that woman must support herself, whether she likes it or not. . . ." argued the *American Jewess*. The journal campaigned for Jewish women's right to become professional nurses, physicians, and lawyers and urged better pay and working conditions for women teachers, businesswomen, factory workers, and union organizers. Sonneschein's newspaper bitterly reproached middle-class women who, sheltered by their husbands' comfortable income, attacked the concept of working women, without acknowledging that the latter could not survive without employment.[63]

Since many working women remained single, the *American Jewess* insisted that women should be able to choose whether or not to marry without fear of ridicule. "Many a woman considers it criminal to encourage love she cannot return, and the charge is laid at her door of never having a single proposal." A man "chooses a wife or not, as he pleases. Why should not a woman be granted an equal privilege?"[64]

American Jewess columnist Sarah Drukker brilliantly spearheaded the journal's crusade for national woman suffrage. "The injustice that is done to women the world over," she declaimed, "is due to man's monopoly of political rights." "Suffrage," insisted Drukker, "is the crowning glory of progress."

> It is never considered unwomanly to help men into power, it is never considered unwomanly for a mother to canvas for her son, to get him into office, but it is considered unwomanly for a woman to ask for liberty for herself.[65]

The *American Jewess* supported and often vied with the fledgling National Council of Jewish Women for leadership of the campaign for Jewish religious suffrage. The journal went beyond the NCJW's official position, however, in asserting unqualified support for national suffrage and demanding that Jewish women receive the right to religious leadership, including the rabbinate.

Sonneschein editorialized that Jewish women were "fully as capable to fill the pulpit as the pew" and glorified preacher Ray Frank as the epitome of the female rabbi. Praising Frank as an "arch-genius" whose "platform is the world," Sonneschein proudly reported a Chicago synagogue's offer to Frank in 1896 to become their rabbi, which Frank carefully refused.[66]

Mounting a campaign for religious and political suffrage, Sonneschein convinced leading Reform rabbis such as Emil G. Hirsch, mentor to Hannah G. Solomon and the NCJW, to publish supportive articles in the *American Jewess*.[67] Reform rabbis had officially declared their theoretical support for religious suffrage a few years earlier in a resolution approved by the Central Conference of American Rabbis.[68] However, no synagogue had yet put this resolution to the test.

Jewish women would win their battle for religious suffrage because they were united in "sisterhood," Sonneschein's editorials prophesied in the new language of the women's movement. Scathingly denouncing anti-suffragist rabbis,[69] she insisted that congregations must change with the times. When Chicago's Temple Isaiah granted religious suffrage to women, she boasted that the victory properly was due to efforts by the *American Jewess*:

> We are . . . very much pleased to note that the suggestion of its editor, that our women be admitted to equal membership, has borne fruit. The New Congregation of Chicago [Temple Isaiah] . . . has been the first Jewish congregation to adopt the idea. A resolution was unanimously carried which admits both married and single women to full membership.[70]

Although the NCJW was also campaigning for religious equality and the right to vote in the synagogue, Sonneschein insisted that the *American Jewess* was primarily responsible for the victory in every Reform temple which gave the vote to women:[71]

> In all humility we wish to say that this important fact was accomplished through the influence of "The American Jewess," and through the direct efforts of its editor. . . . [the proof is that] not only did we receive a letter of thanks from the talented Rabbi of Temple Isaiah, but the London "Jewish Chronicle" . . . commented favorably on this congregational innovation.[72]

To encourage further progress, the *American Jewess* praised every step taken by rabbis and synagogues that promoted equality, from election of women to synagogues' Sabbath School Boards to women's greater participation in worship. Firmly believing that equality for Jewish women could be secured only through women's communal visibility and effective organization, the *American Jewess* paid especial tribute to female leaders of synagogue Sunday Schools and Jewish women's organizations such as the National Council for Jewish Women.[73]

Despite its extensive support of feminism and the NCJW, in 1899 the *American Jewess* published a series of editorials attacking the NCJW for holding a public event on the Sabbath. Perhaps in reprisal, several Council members withdrew their financial contributions from the paper, causing a financial crisis. The *American Jewess* closed later the same year, unable to expand its reading audience beyond a small group of dedicated Jewish women.[74]

The *American Jewess* and the NCJW significantly influenced the development of Jewish feminism. The journal chronicled the growing numbers of traditional as well as Reform Jewish women who became active in Jewish synagogue and communal life. Under the glare of publicity, Reform temples increasingly granted suffrage to their women. The new political leverage of the *American Jewess* and the NCJW encouraged Reform Jewish women to deliver sermons, become members of Sunday School and synagogue boards, and acquire a modest influence in the Reform movement at large and in wider Jewish communal life.[75]

Moreover, the *American Jewess* appears to have somewhat contributed to modifying the Christian bias of feminist organizations and making secular feminism an option for greater numbers of Jewish women who wished to move beyond Jewish issues and champion women's emancipation on the national scene. Differences in approach between Christian and Jewish feminists, however, held significant implications for the future. Aware of Jewish vulnerability and persistent social anti-Semitism, Jewish women who retained their Jewish cultural or religious connections always considered the well-being of the Jewish community simultaneously with feminist concerns. Jewish tradition also affected their approach to feminism. Among Jewish women, feminism was not usually anti-male, nor did it constitute a rejection of men. Instead, Jewish feminists attempted to convince men to accept women as their equals in all religious, cultural, social, and political arenas.

Sharing this attitude toward feminism, the NCJW and the *American Jewess*, despite their differences, formed a fragile alliance to seek religious and communal equality. However tentative their cooperation, they succeeded in affecting a larger group of synagogues and Jewish communities than did Anglo-Jewish feminists in England during this period. As we shall see, the NCJW would use these efforts as the basis for future ventures that would establish it as the preeminent Jewish women's organization in the United States until World War II.

ENGLAND

By 1881, when the Prince of Wales attended the synagogue marriage of his friend Leopold de Rothschild to Mlle. Marie Perugia, British Jewry's social acceptance appeared complete. Part of the Prince of

Wales's intimate social circle, the elite of the "Cousinhood" held high positions in the British government, frequented England's great houses, and flourished in the business and professional world. Approximately 60,000 Jews lived comfortably in England, with major settlements in London and the great northern industrial cities and smaller clusters scattered throughout provincial towns.[76]

In the same year, tens of thousands of East European Jews began emigrating to England. They settled primarily in London's East End and in the northern industrial cities. Between 1881 and 1909, the number of aliens in England rose from 135,000 to 287,000. The vast majority consisted of East European Jews.[77]

Fearful of their arrival, native Anglo-Jews anticipated an anti-Semitic reaction. They already felt more exposed to anti-Semitism than did their American co-religionists. Selective social exclusion, occasional anti-Semitic harangues in journals and newspapers such as the *Evening News* and incidents in Parliament[78] reminded them of the limits of English tolerance. The sheer number of immigrants, their distinctive clothing and customs, and their prevalence in the "sweated" clothing trades justified Anglo-Jews' fears, for the newcomers did arouse a new wave of anti-Semitism.

English workers protested Jewish labor and business competition, and social reformers blamed "sly" Jewish immigrants for brutal conditions in garment industry sweatshops.[79] A clamor arose for anti-alien legislation, which the Jewish community equated with anti-Semitism. "Practically the whole agitation against the Russian and Polish immigrant is the result of antipathy towards Jews," asserted the *Jewish Chronicle*.[80]

In this atmosphere, the native Anglo-Jewish community fruitlessly attempted to persuade the newcomers to return home. Soon convinced that the immigrants would remain, Jewish communal leaders decided to Anglicize, educate, and provide job training for the immigrants. Anglo-Jewish leaders acknowledged that they acted out of a mixture of motives: a genuine concern for fellow Jews was combined with a desire to provide "self-protection" against anti-Semitic slurs.[81]

JEWISH WOMEN'S "JUST CAUSE"

Given the pressure to acculturate the immigrants as rapidly as possible, the Jewish community dramatically expanded its social services. Anglo-Jewish women threw themselves into the "just cause." Like their Christian counterparts, Jewish women were buttressed, spiritually and financially, by a strong religious commitment, new leisure time, and male patronage and support as they ventured beyond benevolent societies into social service. Anglo-Jewish women claimed that they were particularly effective as volunteers because women were "much more attentive to religious and social observances than men."[82]

While many Anglo-Jewish women still preferred to contribute privately to charities, significant numbers joined volunteer organizations. Some raised money for immigrant services by holding "Penny Dinners." Others financed the Jewish Convalescent Home for Infants or donated money to Louise Lady Rothschild's Jewish Ladies Benevolent Loan Society.[83] Female Jewish charity recipients were evidently scrupulously honest; 99 percent of the clients of Lady Rothschild's benevolent society repaid their loans.[84]

At the same time, Jewish women changed the direction of their benevolent societies and created new, independent social service institutions. Like male-run Anglo-Jewish communal organizations, the Jewish women's philanthropic organizations were modeled after England's Charity Organization Society, founded by Octavia Hill. The women's organizations helped immigrants with "housekeeping and other domestic arrangements" and increased benefits to Jewish widows; they also multiplied their clothing collections by over 1,000 items per year, but still could not meet the demand.[85]

By 1884, the women had become so indispensable that the Board of Guardians created the Ladies' Conjoint Visiting Committee, the first breach in the community's exclusively male leadership. Rapidly increasing its scope and influence, the Conjoint provided advice and financial assistance throughout the East End. Simultaneously, the *Jewish Chronicle*'s "letters to the editor" pages were flooded with social service recommendations by prominent Jewish women, which were ignored by male-run communal boards but implemented by Jewish women's organizations such as those founded and directed by Mrs. Alice Model.[86]

Mrs. Model founded the Sick Room Helps Society in 1895 as an at-home maternity nursing service for Jewish working women. Beginning with 27 maternity cases, by 1901 the Society cared for 837 patients. The Sick Room Helps Society also founded a "Provident," or Women's Sick Benefit Society, a self-help cooperative savings organization administered by East End residents that boasted a thousand members by 1902. In 1911, Mrs. Model created a cooperative Self-Help Society for Jewish working girls, which provided health care, emergency funds, and burial services for its members. By encouraging working-class clients to vote and contribute to organiza-

tional management, she encouraged independence and fostered interaction between Jewish gentlewomen and working-class immigrant
women.[87]

REFORM JUDAISM

As in the United States, the growing impact of Anglo-Jewish women
upon volunteer philanthropy and their entry into teaching and selected other professions triggered a search for equality in religious life
by the late 1880s.[88] They could not have chosen a better time, for
Jewish men were leaving the synagogue in droves, bored by long, in-
comprehensible services in Hebrew, dry sermons, and the need to
work on the Sabbath. The loss of congregants, combined with the
impact of Darwinism, the rise of secularism, and modern Biblical
criticism, generated a debate over modernizing worship that filled
Jewish newspapers and journals through the turn of the twentieth
century.[89]

While men were leaving the synagogue, growing numbers of Anglo-Jewish women, like their Christian counterparts, thronged to worship services and performed much of the charitable work of the
synagogue. Since fewer men were visible, Jewish women's activities
began to significantly influence religious life. To help revitalize Jewish
worship, for example, Jewish women recommended specific changes
in synagogue ritual, including greater participation by women.[90]

Up to this time, the small Reform Jewish movement in England
had only superficially modified a few ritual forms and remained very
traditional in substance. Faced with the loss of many of their male
congregants, and asserting that women's participation in ritual "strengthened" the synagogue, Reform ministers (rabbis) responded to wom-
en's demand for involvement in ritual, despite vociferous objections
from the Chief Rabbi.[91]

Several Jewish ministers and choirmasters suggested that women
be permitted to sing in a synagogue choir while remaining in their
customary seats. The presence of women in Christian church choirs
provided an acceptable precedent for Jews, declared the *Jewish Chronicle*. Filling the *Chronicle*'s pages for months, the issue had an impact
far beyond the immediate controversy. As noted earlier, mixed choirs
defined the difference between Reform and Orthodox Judaism in England, and lay the groundwork for a series of steps improving women's
role in religious affairs. Although England's Chief Rabbi, Hermann
Adler, avoided deciding the issue, several synagogue choirs welcomed
women, stating that they had greatly strengthened synagogue life.[92]

Mixed choirs paved the way for further steps. In 1888, the radical reformer Rev. F. D. Fay initiated a confirmation ceremony for girls, arguing that confirmation studies prepared girls to be knowledgeable Jewish mothers. However, confirmation did not become a regular event until 1896, when a number of girls committed themselves to the program.

Rev. Fay and other Jewish ministers also instituted religious education and confirmation ceremonies for girls in Reform synagogues. Confirmations for girls increased in popularity over the next forty years, providing a new generation of Jewish women with a grounding in Judaism. Rev. Fay even called for permitting women to be counted in the *minyan*, the quorum necessary for worship. His proposal met with a thunderous silence from other ministers, despite approval from the *Jewish Chronicle*.[93]

As newly Jewishly educated women filled the synagogues, they demanded changes to meet their needs. In 1893, Manchester's Jewish women organized special Sabbath services for women, conducted by sympathetic Jewish ministers. Lively and energetic, without the "listlessness" so common at regular synagogues, these services continued for several years. At the same time, Jewish women attended nontraditional services conducted by Reform ministers in West London Synagogue and in outlying Hampstead.[94] In 1896, the first group of women to attend a congregational meeting demanded votes for women seatholders in West London and several other synagogues. As we shall see, progressive Jewish women eventually achieved religious suffrage as the result of a tumultuous turn-of-the-century campaign, inspired in great part by the new Liberal Jewish movement founded by Lily Montagu.

By the end of the nineteenth century, Jewish women gained new confidence and new political skills as they won the right for women to sing in the choir, and for girls to be confirmed and receive equal religious education with boys. Jewishly educated Reform Jewish women's synagogue participation and the influence of these women in modernizing worship gave them their first taste of religious status; this, in turn, helped to validate their increasing participation in philanthropic volunteerism on behalf of East European immigrants.

1902 CONFERENCE OF JEWISH WOMEN

> The Great Hall commenced to fill with delegates and members, all looking and feeling very serious, and naturally impressed with the importance of the work in hand . . . there was no confusion, only a pleasant and subdued excitement.

In 1902, a group of Anglo-Jewish women's organization leaders opened the first Conference of Jewish Women. Conference president Julia

Cohen (Mrs. Nathaniel), whose husband's family virtually ran the Board of Guardians, presided over a committee of prominent Anglo-Jewish gentlewomen. Mrs. Millicent Garrett Fawcett, leader of the National Union of Women's Suffrage Societies (NUWSS), was an honored guest, establishing the Conference's connection with the English women's movement.[95]

Conference proceedings showcased women's leadership abilities and created England's first national umbrella organization for Jewish women's groups. Male communal leaders, originally resistant, eventually touted the event as a "great triumph . . . a red-letter day in the history of the community."[96] Indeed, the conference determined the social service agenda for Jewish women until World War I.

Mrs. Cohen's opening speech revealed the tension between activism and conservatism, not only among Anglo-Jewish women, but among secular English feminists as well. She urged women to become social service volunteers at the same time that she stressed the "line of demarcation" between men's public spheres and women's domestic role. Conferees should focus on public activities deemed suitable for women: "friendly visiting" in homes and schools, sanitation, and nursing.

The class gulf yawned wide as speakers condemned the "thoughtless pity" for immigrants that ran "rife" in the Jewish community. Agreeing with Octavia Hill, they advocated new scientific nursing and social work methods rather than simply handing out money or clothing.[97] Regarding religious participation, speakers suggested a program of religious education for girls equal to that for boys.[98]

THE UNION OF JEWISH WOMEN

The conference's final session founded the first Union of Jewish Women in Great Britain on June 1, 1902. In class-conscious Britain, the Union's unimpeachably aristocratic officers guaranteed the respect of male communal leaders and English women's groups alike: Julia Cohen and a bastion of Rothschild women served as president and vice-presidents, and a cadre of prominent Anglo-Jewish women comprised the Executive Council. The Countess Dowager of Desart, a leader of the International Council of Women (ICW), joined the Executive Committee, presaging an alliance between the UJW and the international women's movement.[99]

Defining the Union in terms of the women's movement, the Union's official report declared it to be an "all-embracing sisterhood," forming a "bond between Jewish women of all degrees and all shades of opinion, religious, social and intellectual."[100] However, although it theoretically welcomed Jewish women "of all degrees," until World War I its members were primarily upper-class women who came in contact with working-class women when providing food, clothing, or medical care. The UJW's aim was "to promote the social, moral and spiritual welfare of Jewish women, and to induce practical co-operation between Jewish women workers throughout the country."[101]

Unlike America's NCJW, which focused on immigrant concerns, the UJW concentrated on helping the "better educated Jewess."[102] The Union saw itself as a "Guild of Service" within the Englishwomen's social service tradition. Its professional social staff trained upper- and middle-class Anglo-Jewish women as volunteers for a range of educational and philanthropic organizations. Avoiding conflict with philanthropies benefited by the Jewish Board of Guardians, it served as a link between charitable institutions and women who needed help.

Drawing upon the advice of the Council of Jewish Women in the United States, the UJW organized a system of volunteers trained to help "gentlewomen" seeking employment and to assist Jewish charitable institutions.[103] The Union's small loan fund supported a limited amount of job training and personal assistance to "necessitous ladies, allowing them to tide over a difficult period." By the end of its first year, the *Jewish Chronicle* hailed the Union as being more effective than its male-run counterparts:

> While the male writers and thinkers of the community have been
> scribbling "co-operation," and chattering "co-operation," their sisters
> have quietly girdled the Kingdom with an effective organization of mu-
> tual help.

The *Chronicle* cited this effectiveness as further justification for the emancipation of Jewish women: "The work of the Union amply justifies the more responsible position which English Jewesses now occupy in the communal work and counsels; and we strongly recommend it."[104]

By the end of the Union's first few years, its education and job training programs had helped to increase middle-class Jewish women's financial security and social mobility. The UJW's large-scale enrollment of volunteers and vocational education for "gentlewomen" also substantially increased opportunities for female Jewish volunteers, nurses, social workers, and teachers in the Jewish community. These accomplishments laid the groundwork for later UJW campaigns to provide professional opportunities for women and obtain equal rights for women in the synagogue. Still, the UJW continued to limit its work to "gentlewomen" until World War I.

CONCLUSION

Jewish women's clubs and social service organizations fostered the emergence of a distinctive Jewish woman's movement aligned with secular feminism that, allowing for some variation, followed similar patterns in England and the United States.

The massive influx of East European immigrants proved to be a watershed for newcomers and native Sephardic and German-Jewish women alike. The Jewish community's desperate need for social service volunteers to meet the emergency, reinforced by the precedent of Christian women's organizations, launched modern Jewish feminism. The National Council of Jewish Women and the Union of Jewish Women deliberately styled their self-improvement studies and social service tasks after the manner of national women's groups, and publicly framed their mandate in relation to the secular woman's movement. These and other independent Jewish women's organizations forged a separate group consciousness and sense of their distinctive identity as Jewish women by strengthening members' self-esteem, Judaic knowledge, political philosophy, and desire for equality. As Rosa Sonneschein, the NCJW, and the UJW all demonstrated, maintaining their Jewish convictions caused Jewish feminists to create organizations to fit their distinctive needs and goals while asserting their "sisterhood" with their Christian peers.

Reform Judaism reinforced the process by giving Jewish women's organizations the theological arguments for public service through its insistence upon prophetic justice and compassion. All organization members justified their action in this manner, however, whether they were Reform, Conservative, or Orthodox. Women's growing activism in the synagogue strengthened their influence in religious life and their claims for equality in synagogue and community.

Membership in Jewish women's clubs and greater participation in religious life established a religious sanction for Jewish women's communal activism; this was the first step toward acquiring limited influence on communal social service. Nevertheless, Jewish women's intensive participation in communal charitable work did not provide the communal power their contributions appeared to justify.

Still, despite many similarities, there were clear differences in Jewish women's evolution toward feminism in England and the United States. Anglo-Jewish society in England, restricted by the class system and fearful of rising anti-Semitism, remained conservative, and tolerated fewer innovations than did the Jewish community in the United States. In contrast, America's vast landscape, economic and social mobility, and separation of church and state permitted Jews to engage in unconventional activities while ignoring occasional social anti-Semitism and anti-Jewish harangues.

As a result, Anglo-Jewish feminism progressed somewhat differently from its American counterpart. On the one hand, England's first Conference of Jewish Women took place nearly a decade after the Congress of Jewish Women convened in America. The Union of Jewish Women focused on "necessitous ladies," while the National Council of Women undertook charitable work with Jewish working-class immigrants. As already noted, Reform Judaism became significant in Britain approximately forty years after it spread throughout the United States. Anglo-Jewish women campaigned for places in the choir and confirmation for girls while Ray Frank preached across the United States and American Jewish women demanded votes in the synagogue. To some degree, Jewish feminism in America was more vigorous than its English counterpart. On the other hand, as we shall see in chapter 3, Jewish women in England pioneered the Jewish community's international anti–white slavery effort nearly twenty-three years before American Jewish women joined the campaign. In areas such as anti–white slavery or suffrage, we shall discover that Jewish women in England pursued unpopular ventures either earlier or with greater militancy.

By the end of the nineteenth century, Jewish women's increasing contributions to American Jewish religious and communal life, June Sochen notes, began to gradually erode traditional Jewish attitudes towards women and to reshape the Jewish community.[105] Her comments apply equally well to Jewish women's accomplishments in England.

At the same time, upper- and middle-class Jewish women in both countries were beginning to join secular feminist organizations in considerable numbers. Because Jewish women's influence in the Jewish community remained minimal, they increasingly turned toward the woman's movement to correct this imbalance, asserting their sisterhood with their non-Jewish peers. Jewish women's determination to identify themselves in terms of their Jewishness as well as their womanhood, however, colored their relationship with secular, but Christian-oriented, feminism. Nevertheless, by the early twentieth century, Jewish women's organizations in England and the United States, having progressed beyond social service into politically oriented social reform, were poised to share joint endeavors.

3

A "Holy War"

ENGLAND

THE ROTHSCHILDS, PURITY, AND PROSTITUTION

> *Our own people disown us, their Law forbids them to receive us*
> *again, and we will not enter a Christian Home, we have no wish to*
> *join your Church, for, however bad we may be, we will not give up*
> *our own Faith.*
> —*A prostitute to Constance Rothschild Battersea's*
> *missionary friend, in Cohen,* Rothschild, *p. 204*

IN THE spring of 1885, Constance Rothschild Battersea learned from
a missionary about the desperate plight of London's Jewish prostitutes. Only Christian missions[1] would give them food and lodging,
and no Jew, prostitutes believed, would help them. Horrified, Battersea
founded the Jewish Ladies Society for Preventive and Rescue Work,
later renamed the Jewish Association for the Protection of Girls and
Women (JAPGW). Her action launched Anglo-Jewish women into organized English feminism and established the roots of an Anglo-Jewish woman's movement seventeen years before the founding of the
Union of Jewish Women.

The daughter of Baron Anthony and Louise de Rothschild, Constance inherited her mother's strong sense of duty to the poor, independent spirit, and social entrée to the topmost echelons of English
society. As young girls, Constance and her sister Anne were surfeited
with luxury, taught by their mother to educate and care for the less
fortunate, and surrounded by their parents' distinguished guests,
most of whom were Christian. As adults, both sisters married Christians and assumed a social life revolving around the Royal Court.[2]

Ambivalent about Judaism, Constance felt that Jewish tradition
regarded her, as a woman, as useless and excluded her from the important aspects of religious life. Yet, although she rejected her parents'

53

Constance Battersea. Courtesy, National Portrait Gallery,
London

Orthodox synagogue, Constance never converted and remained deeply
attached to Jews as a people.[3] Her determination to protect the rights
of women, and Jewish women in particular, appears to stem in part
from her complex attitude toward her Jewishness.

After her marriage to Cyril Flower, later Lord Battersea, Constance
combined a lavish social life with charitable activities and speeches
for temperance. In 1881, fellow temperance worker Fanny Morgan, a
suffragist, introduced Lady Battersea to the woman's movement. Battersea financed Morgan's political career, including her successful
campaign to be elected mayor of Brecon.[4] Increasingly involved in
women's issues, in 1885 Battersea created the JAPGW. In the early
1890s she became active in prison reform for women and the National
Union of Women Workers, later known as the National Council of
Women. Elected president of the NUWW in 1901, she was hailed by

the Jewish press as a symbol of social acceptance for the Jewish community as a whole.[5] "Never shall I forget how women of different or opposed creeds and churches joined in giving me their unanimous support," commented Battersea. In 1902, she persuaded the newly founded Union of Jewish Women to formally ally itself with the National Union of Women Workers and the International Council of Women.[6] In 1899, she began her involvement with the ICW.

Battersea's life work, however, was triggered by her 1885 encounter with a Christian missionary seeking help for Jewish prostitutes whom the Jewish community claimed did not exist, yet condemned "as too vile even to be saved from the gutter."[7] Judaism traditionally idealized its women as models of sexual purity who lived by a strict code of religious morality. No Jewish community in the world publicly acknowledged Jewish prostitution, and the majority of Jews did not believe that Jewish streetwalkers existed. Lady Battersea, claimed her missionary friend, was "the only person in this huge City of London" who might help the outcasts.[8] Confronted with this dilemma, Battersea "set out" to tackle "rescue work" by founding the Jewish Association for the Protection of Girls and Women.

ANTI-SEMITISM AND THE "GREAT SOCIAL EVIL"

Battersea founded the JAPGW in the wake of a nationwide anti-prostitution campaign and the furor aroused by journalist W. T. Stead's 1885 exposés of child prostitution and white slavery. William Sanger's 1858 *History of Prostitution* had charged that most prostitutes were recent immigrants.[9] Stead's articles fanned the prejudice by accusing immigrant East European Jews of being the source of the traffic and the corruptors of innocent English girls and women.[10] The charges infuriated a British public already engaged in "social gospel" crusades for moral reform and sexual purity.

Stead's "Maiden Tribute of Babylon" series spawned new social reform organizations as well as official studies, commissions, and legislation designed to halt the "great social evil." The reformers found ready support from English workers who already blamed Jewish immigrants for rising unemployment, overcrowding, and unsanitary living conditions. Fueling this resentment, Stead's articles unleashed a wave of anti-Semitic newspaper stories, titillating fiction, and reports on white slavery filled with ostensibly Jewish names. The publicity popularized ancient canards that Jews were Christ-killers who ritually murdered Christian children to obtain their blood for the baking of unleavened Passover bread.[11]

Inflamed by these stories, roving mobs in London's East End, home of the city's immigrant Jews, verbally heckled or physically assaulted Jews in the streets or in their homes. When the "Jack the Ripper" murders broke in 1888, three years after Stead's articles, Jews in London's working-class Whitechapel district were accused of the murders by East End residents, newspapers, and even police officials, although no evidence ever existed to implicate any Jew. Bands of vigilantes roamed the East End, forcing Jews to lock themselves in their homes for safekeeping.[12]

Even social reformers who conceded Jews' personal morality accused East European Jews of causing communal immorality. The economist Beatrice Potter, later the wife and colleague of Sidney Webb, conducted a survey of East London for Charles Booth in 1889. She concluded that Jews were highly moral, and confirmed that the few Jewish petty criminals confined themselves to non-violent crimes such as betting on cards, dice, and horses.[13] Nevertheless, Potter accused Jewish immigrant employers of undefined "unsavory" Jewish practices, which she alleged caused the garment industry's "sweating" system that chained thousands of immigrants to home-based "sweatshops" at below-subsistence wages for twelve to fourteen hours a day.[14]

Inflammatory publicity, the Booth study, social reform crusades, angry mobs, and the Jack the Ripper murders fueled a successful drive for the 1906 Aliens Act, which limited the immigration of foreigners into Britain.

WHITE SLAVERY

While the furor grew over the sweating system, evidence was mounting concerning Jewish prostitution in England. Judaism's glorification of wives and mothers and its strict condemnation of sexual immorality had convinced most Jews that Jewish prostitution did not exist. Nevertheless, a handful of Jewish prostitutes had always plied their trade in any country, including England, although they remained relatively few and unacknowledged throughout history.

In post-1881 Eastern Europe, however, official policies of pogroms, starvation, and repression forced growing numbers of Jews to make a living as procurers and prostitutes. Traffickers, many of whom were Jewish, tricked or forced East European Jewish girls and women to become prostitutes in brothels in several countries, including England and the United States.[15] A flamboyant International Brotherhood of Jewish traffickers operated from Buenos Aires and elsewhere in South America and around the world. Picking up girls in Russia or Poland, traffickers would ship them to England and Western Europe, America, Greece, Egypt, and elsewhere.

Bertha Pappenheim, president of Germany's Jewish Feminist Organization,[16] blamed Jewish prostitution on the terrible poverty and anti-Semitism suffered by East European Jews, as well as Judaism's notions of the "inferiority of the female sex." Marion Kaplan describes Pappenheim's searing condemnation of a traditional Judaism that permitted East European Jewish young women to remain unskilled, ignorant, and relegated to an inferior social and religious status.[17] Such women were easy targets for *stille chuppah*, a secret marriage.

As the JAPGW discovered, traffickers commonly deceived their victims with false promises of marriage and decent living conditions. The "wedding," however, was a *stille chuppah* or secret marriage. According to Jewish law, a rabbi is not required at a religious wedding; any two adult males can witness the ceremony. Young women would be told they were participating in a legal religious ceremony, but would not realize that the ceremony was invalid in civil law because it was not performed by an agent of the state (rabbi) and was not registered by the state. While a few of the young women who were "married" by *stille chuppah* were prostitutes, the majority were tricked into the vice that followed. Since a young woman and her parents would be totally disgraced if she slept with a man not her husband, a false "husband" could easily force his "wife" into prostitution by threatening to heap scandal upon her family if she protested.[18]

If a false "husband" deserted his "wife," the situation was worse, because a traditional Jewish woman needed a *get*, a religious certificate of divorce, in order to remarry, but only the husband could issue the *get*. Without this document, no traditionally observant man would marry an *agunah*, a wife whose husband had disappeared. Without the option of remarriage, threatened by procurers with scandal and starvation, *agunot* could be easily forced into prostitution. Moreover, an *agunah* could not even be legally helped in England. Because a woman's "marriage" had not been registered according to English law, she had no claim on her "husband." East European Orthodox rabbis were reluctant to help stop this practice by expelling from the community men who conducted such weddings or by modifying Jewish law to ease the problem of *agunot*, despite efforts by Bertha Pappenheim, the JAPGW, and other Jewish feminists. Pappenheim estimated that by 1929 over 20,000 *agunot* in Europe had been tricked by traffickers' rosy promises.[19]

Despite the seriousness of their vice, traffickers represented only a fractional minority of any Jewish community. Yet, in England, Western Europe, and the United States, the traffickers' Jewishness combined with the sexual nature of their crime attracted attention out of all proportion to their numbers. Growing publicity about Jewish prostitution and white slave traffic in England embarrassed Jewish community leaders, who tried to pretend Jewish streetwalkers did not exist. Anyone who publicly contacted these disowned women risked being shunned by the entire Anglo-Jewish community. In founding the JAPGW, Battersea was fully aware of the danger to her reputation, but remained committed to her task because, she commented, "We were women alone, working for women."[20]

THE JAPGW

Despite communal hostility, fear, and indifference, Constance Rothschild Battersea founded the Jewish Association for the Protection of Girls and Women in 1885, rallying her family and friends to join the JAPGW's Executive Council. The mixture of anti-Semitism, Jewish traffickers, and Jewish victims demanded creation of a distinctively Jewish organization. Sensitive to social reformers already in the field, the JAPGW worked closely with feminist and inter-denominational anti–white slavery organizations such as William Coote's National Vigilance Association.[21]

The JAPGW, Battersea insisted, was part of a larger campaign for the moral reform of all English society, as a "continuation of work initiated by Mrs. Josephine Butler and carried on by Mr. [W. T.] Stead, for suppression of the White Slave Traffic."[22] In the tradition of Butler's Ladies National Association (LNA), Battersea's JAPGW had difficulty with the concept of willing prostitutes, and insisted that all streetwalkers were innocent victims of male dominance or seduction, or of kidnapping, sexual imprisonment, or starvation.[23]

Like Butler's LNA, the JAPGW was composed of an interlocking network of nationally prominent middle- and upper-class women closely connected to women's temperance, educational, and suffrage campaigns. Some would also become members of the Liberal Jewish movement, which was founded by Lily Montagu in 1902. JAPGW members absorbed the lessons of sexual politics taught by the LNA. Forty years before creation of the JAPGW, Butler and LNA members were considered dangerous radicals and were physically harassed because they visited brothels and engaged in public debate over sexual issues.[24] In founding the JAPGW, Constance Lady Battersea could not be certain that her status as a Rothschild would protect her against similar attacks, given the Jewish community's dread of publicity concerning Jewish prostitution.

Nevertheless, the LNA had also proved that pure wives and mothers could wage political campaigns in areas that affected their homes and families. Butler's success established a precedent that enabled Battersea to validate the JAPGW's existence to a few male Jewish communal and religious leaders such as the Rev. Simeon Singer and Liberal theologian Claude Montefiore.

RESCUE AND PREVENTION HOMES

Following the pattern of Christian rescue groups, the Battersea and JAPGW leadership opened several homes to rescue girls from dangerous situations, provide moral education, and train them for honest employment. The JAPGW sent "friendly visitors" to these institutions, as well as to homes and jobs where girls were placed. The friendly visitor's task was "to keep a watchful eye" on JAPGW girls and provide advice and assistance as needed.[25] Volunteers repeatedly noted, however, that some girls were "beyond help," frequently returning to delinquency despite regular visits.[26]

Charcroft House, the first Jewish rescue home, was opened in 1885 as a shelter for immigrant girls rescued from the docks by JAPGW agents. Gentlewomen volunteers lectured the girls in moral behavior and trained them in domestic tasks for future occupations as servants. One young woman placed as a maid wrote

> Just a line to thank you very much for your kindness. . . . I have plenty to do all day but I am finished at five every night and dress for dinner. I must tell you that I have a comfortable little room to myself and I rather like it.[27]

Battersea quickly learned that there would be few permanent successes in dealing with Jewish prostitutes, most of whom could be influenced for a short time because they were emotional, "with true feeling." However, she warned Charcroft volunteers, they had to be prepared for failures and "heart-breaking disappointments."[28] While several alumnae of the Home were successfully placed in domestic service, most had poor job records. Two "feeble-minded" girls remained at the Home for the rest of their lives, since no other facility would accept them. Several others returned to prostitution and ended up in prison, where they were visited by Charcroft staff.[29]

Sara Pyke House was a residential home for "friendless" girls, designed to teach religion, morality, and a trade. It was the first stop for all unprotected Jewish immigrant girls and a few Christian girls

as well who landed in London. Sara Pyke House became more than
a rescue home; it became a place to which

> all in difficulty come. They come for advice, they come to beg; fathers
> and mothers come to ask that difficult daughters may be kept under
> wise control. . . . one man wrote to ask if we could recommend to him
> a good school, and another asked for references of the girl to whom he
> was about to propose. An elderly woman asked to be allowed to leave
> her valuables in charge of "the ladies" while she went into the hospital
> for an operation.[30]

In 1908, 82 out of 617 girls cared for by the JAPGW stayed in Sara
Pyke House for some period of time. Some of these girls were eventually placed in domestic service, others were eventually sent to
friends of families, and still others were returned to their native countries. A few remained as permanent lodgers after they obtained jobs.[31]
Agents from the house rescued sixteen-year-old, fatherless "Kitty"
from her mother, a hawker whose home was "frequented by most
undesirable elements." The girl herself was being "persuaded" by her
mother "to find her living on the streets." Three months of Sara Pyke
House's training enabled her to find a good job.[32]

The House eventually expanded into a permanent residence for
"respectable and industrious working girls," and those "whose home
surroundings may be unsatisfactory." Desperate to show their new
stability, the JAPGW noted that the girls paid a bit from their earnings
toward room and board and flaunted, as a sign of status, the pathetic
"flourishing feathers of their hats and the impossible shades and
shapes of their garments."[33]

The Industrial Training School was founded by the JAPGW at the
turn of the century as the only Jewish home in England for delinquent
girls. It provided Jewish religious education as well as vocational training for former prostitutes, enabling them to find legitimate work in
domestic service and trades.[34] From 1906 to 1911, the School admitted sixty-two girls between fourteen and twenty years of age. Nine-
teen left the school for a job or were returned to their parents. Not
all were juvenile delinquents; some were simply neglected children
rescued by the School's volunteers.[35]

Laundry work, household chores, study, and prayers formed the
bulk of a school day. From six in the morning to eight thirty in the
evening, residents' lives were filled with hard work, fresh air, a carefully controlled lifestyle, and a sparse but "nutritious" diet. A "lady
doctor" regularly monitored the girls' health, and a local synagogue
allotted eight free seats to school inmates.[36]

The Domestic Training Home prepared young women for domestic service, while accepting a few governesses as boarders. By 1911, thirty-seven girls were admitted to the Home, thirty girls were on the waiting list, and fifteen were employed. The Home also became a model training center for Jewish women wishing to become matrons, or managers, of other homes. Its Jewish environment attracted impecunious middle-class women who sought one of the few respectable employment opportunities that permitted women to wield authority.[37]

The JAPGW's rescue homes continued their operations into the late 1920s, despite the 1911 National Insurance Act, which forbade government assistance to organizations that helped prostitutes. Private contributions made up the difference.[38]

Rescue homes not only provided an alternative for Jewish immigrant girls. For the first time, Anglo-Jewish women gained some understanding of the problems of immigrant girls and women. Simultaneously, the "gentlewomen" received invaluable training in social service, organizational management, and communal and national politics. Discovering that they could manage these homes raised Jewish women's self-esteem and concepts of themselves as women. They also began to explore the political reforms necessary to complete the task at hand.

RESCUE WORK

Rescue work formed a major portion of JAPGW activities. Between 1904 and 1910, the Association conducted 198 investigations regarding suspicious people or houses and dealt with 23 convicted cases of international trafficking and 39 cases of suspected trafficking. Association agents claimed to have prevented 29 women from being abducted into white slavery. Forty-four missing girls were reported as having "gone away with men of bad character." Two hundred twenty-two girls became prostitutes. These totals represented only the cases that could be discovered.[39]

By 1912, the international ramifications were so massive that the JAPGW split its tasks in half. Constance Battersea and her ladies' committees handled the rescue, job training, and residential homes for women and girls. A special Gentleman's Committee assigned male agents to meet immigrant girls at the dock, and directed the international rescue work along the lines of William Coote's National Vigilance Association. After World War I, when Englishwomen had won the vote and were striking out in new directions, Battersea and other women joined male JAPGW leaders in the leadership of international rescue operations.

IMPLICATIONS

Perhaps only a Rothschild, protected by inviolable class status and a secure position in the upper reaches of English as well as Jewish society, could undertake an anti–white slavery crusade without also destroying her position in Jewish and English society. Constance Rothschild Battersea took a great risk in 1885. The Jewish community's refusal to admit the very existence of Jewish prostitution, combined with traditional Judaism's reluctance to permit women a place in public life, presaged intense resistance to any Jewish woman who attempted a Jewish crusade similar to that of Josephine Butler's in the 1840s. The flood of Jewish immigration, which aroused anti-Jewish hostility intensified by unemployment, overcrowding, and sexual scandal, appeared to threaten the hard-won social stability of native, acculturated Anglo-Jewry. As a result, the Jewish community publicly ignored prostitution and white slavery as late as 1908 when the *Jewish Chronicle* upbraided community leaders for the "burning social scandal" and urged support for the JAPGW.

Battersea also had to overcome English feminists' resistance to accepting Jewish women. Battersea's superior class status, her membership in the Royal circle, and her friendship with Lady Aberdeen and Countess Desart of the International Council of Women provided social entrée into the National Union of Women Workers and the class-conscious woman's movement. As a delegate to several ICW Congresses from 1904 onwards, where she represented both the JAPGW and the NUWW, Battersea indicated her concern with feminist issues that extended beyond strictly Jewish interests. Her prominence in the NUWW and the ICW signaled the first crack in the monolithic Christian façade of English and international feminism.

Constance Rothschild Battersea's JAPGW identified itself with woman's movement goals. It became the first Jewish organization to publicize the exploitation of prostitutes and rescue women forced into white slavery. In the process, Edward Bristow concludes, it became the first Jewish organization to bring sensitive issues of concern to women to the popular consciousness.[40] Battersea became a link between English and Jewish feminism, as she convinced numbers of upper- and middle-class Anglo-Jewish women to join English feminist groups and encouraged them to create Jewish women's organizations that allied themselves with the woman's movement.

THE UNITED STATES

[The fight against the white slave traffic] is a world movement for
humanity, and for humanity's sake, and for the moral betterment
of the world, we, who have handed down the ten Commandments,
should lend our strength to this movement.
                    —Proceedings of the Triennial Conventions of the
                         National Council of Jewish Women, 1908

In 1908, Sadie American, president of the New York Section of the
National Council of Jewish Women (NCJW) from 1902 to 1908, called
upon the NCJW to wage a "holy war" against white slavery in the
United States. Assuming leadership of what had become a volatile
and embarrassing situation, the NCJW forced Jewish community
leaders to grapple with a problem they, like their English co-religionists, would have preferred to ignore.

The NCJW's anti–white slavery campaign launched Jewish women
beyond study groups and genteel charity into political social reform
activities focusing upon girls and women. In the process, the NCJW
cemented its alliance with the woman's movement, which had begun
with its creation at the Chicago World's Fair in 1893.

SOCIAL PURITY AND THE "SOCIAL GOSPEL"

By the 1890s, America's Christian clergy had begun to preach a "social gospel" that commanded churches to undertake a mission to
eradicate poverty and corruption in the nation's cities. Against the
background of migration to the cities by native Americans as well as
foreigners, and a significant rise in poverty, crime, and vice, social
reformers termed prostitution the nation's "great social evil" and
instituted a new wave of repressive moral reform measures against
prostitutes.

American feminists had been concerned about the welfare of prostitutes since the Evangelical revival of the 1830s. By the 1880s, a new
coalition of religionists, temperance workers, and suffragists protested against laws mandating new restrictions against streetwalkers.
Emulating England's Josephine Butler, they waged a national campaign for new social purity legislation that recognized men's responsibility for the "downfall" of women, urged chastity for both sexes,
and urged greater sympathy toward prostitutes. Like other feminist
activists, these female reformers claimed that their ostensible moral
superiority to men justified protecting the morality of society.[41]

Sadie American. Courtesy, American Jewish Historical
Society

ANTI-SEMITISM

The nationwide concern for protecting young women was intensified
by rumors which claimed that widespread immigration to the cities
by poor whites, Blacks, and foreigners—particularly East European
Jews—was exposing America to the risk of a drastic increase in prostitution, venereal disease, and crime, and a loss of traditional values.
Even middle-class Jews in Washington, D.C., were not immune to the
racial bias around them. NCJW members were horrified that immigrant families owned grocery stores in alleys "populated exclusively
by the lowest class of Negroes."[42]

Social Darwinist and racist ideas imported from Europe inflamed
nativists who claimed that "alien hordes" were bringing vice to
America's cities and poisoning the national racial stock.[43] Like author
Edward Bellamy in his utopian novel, *Looking Backward*, a vocal
middle-class minority of populists and reformers insisted that the

solution to corruption was racial unity among native white Americans and a return to basic American values.[44]

Fears of pollution often centered on the thousands of East European Jewish immigrants who flooded America after 1881. Charges that newly arrived Jews were corrupting America's cities stemmed from European theories about an international Jewish conspiracy and dire warnings about Jewish power. These theories had been circulated by European missionaries since the 1840s, and they were published anew in 1878 with F. W. Mathias's translation of Osman Bey's *The Conquest of the World by the Jews*. American authors and churchmen such as L. C. Newman and Samuel H. Kellog trumpeted the theories from their books and pulpits.[45] Although religious attacks differed from the secular, they reinforced the popular image of a Jewish menace. Even so, articles in the Jewish press and the indifference of leading Jewish rabbis indicate that these charges gained far less credence in America than in Europe.

European racial theories did gain some respectability, however, even among some Jewish thinkers who argued whether or not there was a Jewish *race*, and whether that term should be defined in an anthropological, social, cultural, or religious manner. However, these same theories quickly became weapons against Jews, ranging from innocent notions that all Jews were "dark" to accusations that Jews were destroying "racial purity" and generating a "mongrelization of the races." Faced with a rising fear of racial "corruption" by immigrants, American conservatives and progressives alike gradually shifted toward greater suspicion and rejection of Jews. Goldwin Smith portrayed Jews as unpatriotic parasites. Mixing sympathy with suspicion, sociologists Jacob Riis and Edward A. Ross asserted that Jews manipulated money without working for it and destroyed ethical standards in business and the professions. The press railed against "obnoxious" Jewish traits.[46]

Whipped up by theorists and journalists, crowds demonstrated against Jewish merchants, and Theodore Bingham, police commissioner of New York City, claimed falsely in 1908 that half the city's criminals were Jewish. At the same time, clubs, resorts, and colleges began to restrict the entrance of middle-class Jews. Nevertheless, anti-Semitism in the United States was relatively less violent, less racist, and less central to those who promoted it than its European counterpart.[47]

Similar to the pattern in England, the anti-Semitic furor over Jewish immigrants fueled a mixture of anti–white slavery literature, studies, and investigations that accused Jews of being primarily responsible for the international traffic in women. Filled with the names of Jewish traffickers, books and articles charged that a network of international Jewish organizations with ties to commercial vice conspired to control the global economy. Nativist and anti-Semitic literature aroused the public image of lustful, bearded foreigners preparing to sacrifice helpless young women.

Newspapers warned Americans to beware of the "Polish pollution . . . which is already corrupting the manhood and youth of every large city in the nation." G. K. Turner's articles on immigrant vice in New York exposed the connection between white slavery and Tammany Hall politicians, some of whom were Jewish, and also accused Jews of responsibility for the majority of America's white slave traffic. The NCJW's Sadie American feared that the "whole" 1911 International Anti–White Slavery Conference "would be turned into detestation and denunciation of the Jews because of the Jewish traffickers."[48]

JEWISH PROSTITUTION

Out of the welter of distortion and fact, credible evidence began to emerge indicating that some Jews were involved in prostitution and white slavery, although the congressional Dillingham Commission proved that no single monopoly, Jewish or non-Jewish, controlled the traffic.[49] Social worker Frances Kellor's investigation revealed a national network of employment agencies that recruited prostitutes. A group of Jewish communal leaders known as the Committee of Fifteen published a report in 1902 documenting an extensive network of Jewish vice in New York.[50] The Committee confirmed that the same International Brotherhood documented by the JAPGW in London operated regularly out of Buenos Aires.

A small subculture of Jewish criminals was primarily engaged in non-violent crime. Most were pickpockets, thieves, or even horse-poisoners. Stiff Rivka, a rare example of a female Jewish professional thief, would sit in the front row of a synagogue's women's gallery so she could identify women wearing jewelry. After services, Rivka would jostle her victim and steal her brooch. Still, the majority of offenses for which Lower East Side Jews were charged by police and the courts were primarily petty violations of corporation ordinances. Due to ignorance of the law, Jews would play handball on the sidewalk or dispose of garbage improperly.[51]

Yet, Jewish prostitution flourished within Jewish areas of major cities. In 1911, thirty out of sixty-six crime-ridden hotels that were obliged to put up a cash bond in order to obtain their licenses were

Jewish. Eighty of the 181 most notorious hotels closed or fought by the Committee of Fourteen, another anti-prostitution group, between 1907 and 1911 were either Jewish- or German-owned.[52] Rosie Hertz was one of the most colorful women involved in "the trade." One of the first Jewish madams in New York, Rosie ran a brothel on East First Street that became "as much a fixture on the Lower East Side as the Brooklyn Bridge." Known to area residents as "Mother Hertz," Rosie wore an apron and a wig, like any pious Jewess, and spoke frequently of God. However, she was one of the most notorious "breeders" of prostitutes in the city.[53]

In some sections of the country, a few Jewish prostitutes achieved considerable fame for their skills. A red-headed Jewish whore was all the rage in turn-of-the-century San Francisco. The famous madam Nell Kimbrell commented that "a redheaded Jew girl was supposed to be just pure fire and smoke." Jewish prostitutes flourished in Rocky Mountain mining camps, western bordellos, the Canal Zone, and Alaska.[54]

Studies showed that immigrant girls and factory workers were particularly vulnerable to being seduced, tricked, or forced into prostitution. As the demand for industrial workers transformed the nature of women's work, immigrant Jewish girls found employment away from home in factories, where they were exposed to the secular world.[55] Acculturation was more rapid in America than in England, where most girls employed in the garment trades worked at home or in sheltered workshops in which it took longer to become modernized. Therefore, in greater numbers than their counterparts in England, first generation East European Jewish girls in America rejected the demure dress and amusements allowed by tradition. Some girls sought the prostitutes' "feathered hats and freedom" in order to escape their brutal poverty, tedious factory work, and severe alienation from their families caused by immigration, as documented by social worker Alice Mencken's study of 300 Jewish female delinquents in 1924.[56]

Mamie Pinzer (1885–?) came from a broken and disturbed immigrant Jewish family, and her bitterest memories were of a mother who turned her over to the authorities for living with a man. After she left prison, Pinzer survived as a morphine-addicted prostitute in Philadelphia. She refused to accept domestic or factory work: ". . . I just cannot be moral enough to see where drudgery is better than a life of lazy vice." With the help of aristocrat Fanny Quincy Howe, however, Mamie attended secretarial school and learned to survive in a "respectable" business. Her major accomplishment was opening her

apartment as a "half-way" house for prostitutes. Decades ahead of
her time, she acted as a "peer counselor" to those who suffered from
the same lack of love she had experienced in childhood.[57]

The majority of Jewish prostitutes plied their trade among primarily Jewish clientele, although most Jews never even knew of their
existence. While a few contemporary estimates claimed that there
were between 10,000 and 30,000 Jewish prostitutes at the turn of the
twentieth century, actual documentation yields fewer numbers. The
Rockefeller Grand Jury collected only 6,000 names in 1910. In a study
of Manhattan's night court, the Yiddish newspaper *Warheit* showed
that only 27 percent of the convicted prostitutes were Jewish. One of
the most dependable studies, based on a sample of 647 prostitutes
released from Bedford Hills Reformatory up to 1910, showed that the
Jewish proportion of these prostitutes was about 19 percent, the same
as the Jewish proportion of the city. Police records show that approximately 17 percent of all prostitutes arrested in Manhattan from 1913
to 1930 were Jewish, less than the Jewish proportion of the population.[58]

JEWISH COMMUNAL REACTION

As evidence mounted about Jewish prostitution, communal leaders
intensified Americanization projects in philanthropic programs in order to improve East European immigrants' chances to be considered
"worthy" American citizens. At the same time, Jewish leaders financed campaigns against prostitution in New York and Chicago.
Communal worker David Blaustein, one-time director of the Educational Alliance, undertook the effort in conjunction with leading rabbis and communal leaders. Under Blaustein's direction, Jewish immigrants organized against Jewish prostitution and threw procurers
out of their neighborhoods. Yet, as Edward Bristow notes, such protest
was difficult to sustain and could not be decisive, given the limited
political influence of the Jews at that time.[59]

Moreover, after 1907, rising public support for restrictive legislation against immigrants convinced Jewish communal leaders to muf-
fle their efforts against prostitution. In the early months of the NCJW
effort, Sadie American cautioned that "Whatever work is to be done
in this direction must be done absolutely quietly and confidentially."
The NCJW's "friendly visitors" to immigrant homes were warned not
to send East European girls to state hospitals or they would be deported as "undesirables."[60] At the same time, the Federation of Jewish
Organizations pleaded for public restraint against Jewish pimps and
brothels, claiming it would use quiet influence to curb the disease.

The Federation's policy failed. It was not until 1912 that New York's Jewish public opinion was more effectively mobilized by the New York Kehillah's vigilante squad, supported by several Jewish organizations including the NCJW.[61] Ultimately, the NCJW was primarily responsible for galvanizing the Jewish community on a long-term basis.

THE NCJW'S ANTI–WHITE SLAVERY CRUSADE

Sadie American, executive secretary of the NCJW and president of the New York Section from 1902 to 1908, first learned of white slavery from Anglo-Jewish women leaders in Britain, with whom she had corresponded since 1893. As early as 1899, as NCJW delegate to the International Council of Women's (ICW) conference in London, American discussed white slavery and other social problems with Constance Rothschild Battersea and established a network to deal with social concerns with Anglo-Jewish women and other ICW delegates. Returning home, she reported to Council members about the international ramifications of white slavery and other social reform issues.[62]

In 1902, American convinced the NCJW to join England's JAPGW in protecting immigrant Jewish girls and women forced to return to Eastern Europe via England because of restrictive U.S. immigration laws.[63] This mutual cooperation lay the groundwork for the NCJW's active intervention in the anti–white slavery effort.

By 1908, reeling from the furor of journalistic exposés, investigations, and the Committee of Fifteen's actions, Sadie American was still unsure "whether we Jewish people need to concern ourselves for the sake of our own co-religionists." Nevertheless, the NCJW decided to see for itself if charges of widespread Jewish prostitution were valid, and conducted its own study of twenty-nine hundred immigrant Jewish girls. The results showed that despite poverty, brutal working conditions, and inadequate wages, the majority of immigrant Jewish girls remained chaste. Most of the girls in this study found employment, either in domestic service or in factory work. Within a year, their average weekly wage rose 25 to 50 per cent.[64] Only two immigrant girls out of the twenty-nine hundred in the study were deported as prostitutes.[65] American cited these conclusions to refute anti-Semitic charges that Jewish immigrants increased prostitution.

Yet, further NCJW research did confirm other studies that provided evidence of Jewish prostitution. Declaring that no other Jewish agency was putting extensive resources into this work, American decided to lead the Jewish community's battle against international vice and reorganized the Council to meet the new challenge. She persuaded the NCJW to integrate its work with the woman's movement, and to send delegates to the International Council of Women's forthcoming conference on the "White Slave Traffic."[66]

> No other Jewish organization is doing or is prepared to do this. Ours is the duty, ours the responsibility, and ours the sin of omission if one single person who might rise through our extended hand falls deeper for lack of it.[67]

Drawing upon the JAPGW model in England, American developed a plan for prevention and rescue that went far beyond the initial involvement of Constance Battersea and the female members of the JAPGW. The fact that many Council leaders and members were Reform or Conservative Jews used to public involvement as well as feminist activists contributed to this approach. Accustomed to more visibility in religious life than their Anglo-Jewish counterparts, the coterie around Hannah G. Solomon had not only organized the Congress of Jewish Women as early as 1893, but, as we shall see, by 1896 had also begun to wage a successful campaign for suffrage in Reform synagogues. NCJW leaders such as Hannah G. Solomon, Nina Morais Cohen, Sadie American, and Minnie D. Louis had participated in the national suffrage campaign during the 1890s. Moreover, since its founding in 1895, the National Council of Jewish Women had already begun working with girls in juvenile courts and detention homes, providing NCJW members with first-hand experience in dealing with Jewish prostitutes.[68]

By 1911, the Council's New York Section created a Department of Immigrant Aid to help East European immigrant girls and women; it developed a nationwide network of services. Middle-class women assumed prominent leadership positions. Many of the NCJW's central office and regional directors across the United States came from the ranks of middle-class professional women, such as Cecelia Razovsky, director of the Department of Immigrant Aid. The United States' relatively fluid class structure encouraged more broadly based leadership in the social purity and anti–white slavery woman's movements than in England.

The NCJW's interaction with immigrant women was complicated, however, by its members' benevolent condescension toward East Europeans, an attitude that marked all German-Jewish social service and reform efforts. Even language reflected the class gulf, noted a Jewish social worker for another organization. "Girl" was the name for a young woman of Eastern European origin, between sixteen and forty years of age, "whose parents are Orthodox, who earns wages or a small professional salary." "Woman" was the title for a "superior" "Jewess" of any age, married or unmarried, who "considers herself or is considered by the girls to be of their betters, either socially or financially."[69] At the same time, at least one Washington, D.C., Council chairwoman attempted to modify existing discrimination and insisted that Council meetings were "conducted on lines of social equality. For the Jewish immigrant does not belong in the class in which we find her, but has been forced there by untoward circumstances."[70]

Still, most Council members' attitudes toward prostitution reflected the complicated pity and class bias of the era. Like their Anglo-Jewish counterparts, NCJW members believed that anti-Semitic persecution and poverty caused Jewish immigrant girls to be "no match" for the temptations of prostitution or the deceit of white slave traffickers.[71] Yet, like their Christian peers, Council members also blamed the sexual double standard for prostitution, associating the latter exclusively with the lower classes, whom they suspected were at least susceptible to immorality.

NCJW founder Hannah Solomon was convinced that "It is rather the love of pleasure and ease, love of society and luxury and, most of all, the absence of proper maternal care."[72] Sadie American did not totally disagree, but insisted that the issue was more involved:

> it is a well-known fact that the first generation of the immigrant population produces more evil than the next generation . . . because all the old sanctions are gone and the new sanctions are not yet here.[73]

More concerned to defend the middle-class Jewish woman who becomes a prostitute, American declared that "when a woman . . . is willing to go out into the world with her babe on her arm and face that world where every man thinks that she is rightfully his prey, she needs every bit of support that we can give her."[74]

Sadie American believed that one solution to Jewish prostitution was to help immigrant girls find good jobs, homes, healthy amusements, and education in American morality to replace the "temptation" of the dance hall. As part of the NCJW's progressive education program, in 1911 Council member and physician Rosalie Morton designed and supervised a pioneering NCJW course in sex education.[75]

NATIONWIDE PROJECTS

In several cities, NCJW opened homes for "wayward girls" that provided moral and occupational training for residents. The training was so successful that the Council estimated that 75 percent of former residents of the Lakeview Home in Staten Island, for example, were living "self-respecting" lives by 1914. Forty percent of the residents of NCJW homes were of "subnormal" intelligence in an era when few institutions were willing to care for immigrants with mental problems of any kind.[76]

As in England, it was particularly difficult to help mentally ill or retarded immigrant girls, because legislation required the deportation of any immigrant who might become a public charge. However, through lobbying and protests, Council members prevented the deportation of 1,327 girls between 1908 and 1911, and attempted to ease the passage of girls who were returned to their native countries.[77] One retarded child from an immigrant family with six children was returned to Russia, where the few facilities for the mentally ill were unavailable to Jews. This girl, commented an NCJW volunteer, was "merely one of the procession . . . that are sent back to Russia, while we in this twentieth century who call ourselves civilized stand here helpless."[78]

Under Sadie American's leadership, the Council instituted a major campaign to protect immigrant girls and to "root out" the cause of Jewish prostitution, the "professional destroyers and the dens they infest."[79] In 1905 alone, 4,500 Jewish women entered Ellis Island, and 700 unmarried Jewish women arrived in Philadelphia.

Between 1906 and 1908, the "friendly visitors" from the New York Section made 4,314 visits to girls or their families. They offered "friendly aid" to 833 girls. Of these, the visitors obtained work for 262; placed 278 in English classes; placed 29 in industrial classes; provided legal, medical, or other aid for 77; and entertained and advised 1,697 girls at the weekly social evening. None asked for financial aid. By 1908, several cities were in the process of developing similar programs.[80]

In 1908 alone, New York Section agents and volunteers met 10,000 immigrant girls at Ellis Island and ensured their transportation to Council homes or other respectable lodgings. The Section's friendly visitors went to these homes and advised 1,000 girls, securing homes, employment, medical care, and English-language and job training. The Section also placed a probation officer in the courts to work with "wayward girls" and their children.[81] The Council also worked closely with the police, courts, and New York Travelers' Aid Society to develop a system of protection for unguarded immigrant Jewish women.

To deal with the nationwide ramifications of white slavery, the NCJW created a Department of Immigrant Aid headquartered in New York City, with correspondents in over three hundred American cities. Between 1908 and 1911, the reorganized Council helped 36,933 immigrants. Between 1911 and 1914, the organization assisted 41,000 immigrant girls and women between the ages of fourteen and fifty-nine. The NCJW hired three female agents who met thousands of girls and women at the docks to prevent them from falling into the hands of unscrupulous traffickers. Unused to fending for themselves, immigrant girls were easy prey to Yiddish-speaking men and women who promised to guide them to a safe destination. One young woman tricked in this way became insane before being rescued by relatives. NCJW agents made certain that most emigrés arrived safely at their destination or at secure temporary lodgings.[82] Relatively few American Jewish men joined the fight against Jewish prostitution and white slavery, despite vigorous and public efforts of B'nai B'rith and a handful of rabbis and male communal leaders. The NCJW was the only American Jewish organization to send delegates to the international white slavery conferences in London and Madrid in 1910. The men's lack of interest in white slavery may indicate that commercial vice and its anti-Semitic repercussions affected the American Jewish community, at least outside of New York and Chicago, somewhat less than they affected the more concentrated European Jewish communities. Given this situation, it was easier to perceive prostitution as "a woman's problem" not related to the Jewish community as a whole. Sadie American prophesied that unless Jewish men "waked up on this subject . . . they are going to be waked up in a way they will not like."[83]

SUCCESS

The NCJW's network of agents, rescue homes, friendly visitors, and political agitators garnered admiration from agency representatives and government officials around the world. The Hebrew Immigrant Aid Society's (HIAS) male professionals were so jealous of NCJW's success that they attempted to replace NCJW's female agents on the docks. The move was blocked by lawyer Max Kohler, chairman of the Baron de Hirsch Fund Committee on Immigrant Aid, which subsidized both the NCJW and HIAS, a communal service organization which helped bring immigrants to America.[84] The lesson was not lost on the NCJW membership, who recognized that their triumphant social reform crusade had garnered unprecedented communal political leverage for any group of women. As we shall see, NCJW members' visibility as national and even international social reformers also forged the basis for their widespread entrée into all levels of the secular woman's movement.

Sadie American earned an international reputation for guiding the anti–white slavery effort, with leaders around the world seeking her advice. When she visited Rome in 1913, the Italian secretary of immigration consulted her about what should be done to protect Italian women immigrants. NCJW lobbying convinced President Roosevelt to issue an executive order permitting Boarding Matrons to join the inspectors who boarded ships before docking. When Secretary of the Treasury Shaw and Commissioner Williams tried to ignore the order, Sadie American claimed she persuaded the gentlemen to change their minds. American often boasted, perhaps too freely and publicly, that her leadership was responsible for the Council's achievements.[85]

Jewish women were particularly drawn to the anti–white slavery issue because it involved them simultaneously in a general and Jewish nationwide crusade. They improved their own skills and found personal self-fulfillment while helping the Jewish community and the nation at large. Through this "double *mitzvah,*" NCJW activists fulfilled a major goal of acculturated American Jewry: admired and sought out by important secular personages and organizations, NCJW members also studied and preached Jewish values. Rapidly becoming invaluable to the Jewish, secular, and feminist communities, anti–white slavery activity enabled the NCJW to justify a new vision of Jewish womanhood as social reformers.

INTERNATIONAL JEWISH FEMINISM

However valuable the contributions of the NJCW and the JAPGW within their own countries, the scope of the white slavery problem extended far beyond any one nation. The Jewish Association for the Protection of Girls and Women and the National Council of Jewish Women played a pivotal role in framing an international, cooperative anti–white slavery effort among feminists, inter-faith organizations, and secular social reformers.

Beginning with Sadie American's first contact with Anglo-Jewish women social service volunteers in 1893, close ties had developed among American, Constance Rothschild Battersea, and Bertha Pappenheim, president of Germany's Jewish Feminist Organization (*Judischer Frauenbund*). The JFO sought social and economic equality for Jewish women, but eschewed national political goals because of Germany's more restrictive attitude toward Jews and women.[86] Marion Kaplan's study of Pappenheim effectively analyzes her central leadership role in attacking white slavery on an international level. Pappenheim's JFO, American's NCJW, and Battersea's JAPGW forged an anti–white slavery alliance among Jewish social reformers, their Christian counterparts, and feminists around the world.[87]

Membership in the International Council of Women proved to be decisive for Jewish women's development as feminists. Representing their individual organizations, American and Battersea attended their first ICW Congress in 1899; Pappenheim joined them in 1904. The trio continued as delegates to successive ICW Congresses and to international Jewish, inter-faith, and League of Nations anti–white slavery conferences until the rise of Hitler in 1933.[88]

In 1904, American, Pappenheim, and Battersea formed an informal caucus with other Jewish delegates to focus on issues of concern to Jewish women, including religious equality, social service, and white slavery. As we shall see, the caucus expanded its scope so greatly over the years that in 1923 it created the first World Council of Jewish women. From 1904 onward, the ICW Jewish caucus successfully lobbied the ICW to organize an international women's campaign against white slavery. ICW and inter-faith organizations' efforts convinced the League of Nations to create a special committee against the white slave traffic that achieved signal results during the 1920s.[89]

Jewish organizations focused on protective measures at the 1910 and 1927 Jewish International Conferences on White Slavery. Although the conferences achieved a measure of success, gaining enough support from Eastern European rabbis to attempt to stop *stille chuppah* was nearly impossible, and little change occurred in traditional Jewish family law during the interwar years.[90]

Jewish women's international meetings provided a forum for mutual action on white slavery and a clearinghouse through which national Jewish women's councils could acquire information relevant to other issues affecting Jewish women.[91] As a result, the conferences' value went far beyond fighting white slavery. Delegates shared ideas, brought them back to their own national Jewish women's organizations, and implemented them in social programs and legislative campaigns related to girls and women. Increasingly, Jewish women's organizations around the world focused on similar issues and methods. Anti–white slavery, social service, women's emancipation, and women's religious equality dominated the agendas of Jewish women's organizations in England, Germany, and the United States in varying degrees.

International efforts achieved limited success until World War I, primarily in western countries, by obtaining police and government cooperation, rescuing potential victims, fostering legislation to protect young women, safeguarding female travelers, limiting the exploitation of prostitutes, and providing moral education for young people. Although little was accomplished in dislodging commercial Jewish vice, thousands of girls were rescued from enforced prostitution.[92] Nevertheless, white slavery continued to flourish because of massive starvation in Eastern Europe, blackmail of young women trapped into secret religious marriages, and the immigration of traffickers and their victims to western and South American countries. The disruptions caused by World War I slowed but did not stop the white slave traffic.

After the war, national Jewish women's societies led by Sadie American, Bertha Pappenheim, Constance Rothschild Battersea, and Mme. Simon of France encouraged the formation of Jewish women's societies in Eastern Europe, particularly in Galicia, Hungary, Poland, and Rumania.[93] These organizations guarded docks and railroad stations, opened homes for women at risk, located missing husbands and deserted wives, and lobbied politicians in an attempt to stop the white slave traffic.[94] Jewish women in several countries also actively participated in national Jewish and inter-faith white slavery committees.[95]

Simultaneously with these activities, national Jewish women's groups allied with the ICW to pressure the League of Nations into enacting anti–white slavery legislation. By 1933, the international alliance, combined with national restrictions on immigration and foreign prostitutes, had significantly curbed the "great social evil."[96] After 1933, with the Nazis in power in Germany, Jewish anti–white slavery efforts in Eastern Europe were futile. The 1933 Ninth International Congress against White Slavery was held in Berlin, without Jewish delegates. A final congress was held in 1937 in Paris. By that time, Nazi persecution ended the Jewish crusade against white slavery.

There were now relatively few tasks left for white slavery opponents. Thanks to the international coalition, most countries had strict immigration restrictions, and many banned foreign prostitutes. As a result, although commercial vice remained, there was little international traffic. Restrictive legislation and social reform campaigns accelerated the postwar trend toward improving the lives of immigrants and the working classes. Yet, in countries where Jews could not escape postwar misery, the problem remained.[97]

CONCLUSION

English and American Jewish feminists' anti–white slavery campaign adapted Josephine Butler's LNA and the secular social purity crusade to fit Jewish needs. Middle- and upper-class Jewish women rescued and protected immigrant and working-class Jewish women, defended them against charges of immorality, and educated them in western attitudes of morality and civility. Nevertheless, like their Christian social purity counterparts, by asserting that only immigrant and working-class Jewish women became prostitutes, Jewish middle-class crusaders distinguished themselves as moral guardians from the unfortunate victims whom they successfully rescued. The Jewish community's rush to educate and civilize Jewish immigrants took on a new urgency with the growth of the sexual scandal.

Jewish feminists were strikingly effective. Initially faced with a hostile silence from the majority of their co-religionists, and a not-so-hidden anti-Semitism from Christian social purity reformers, female Jewish anti–white slavery activists created a new organization in England and mounted a "holy war" in the United States that spearheaded national and international campaigns limiting Jewish prostitution and the white slave traffic.

A larger core of male Jewish leaders in England than in America provided national and international leadership on the effort to rescue Jewish girls and women. Far more male Jewish leaders in America than in England either avoided the "burning scandal" or attempted to dominate women reformers' successful activities.

Men's attempts to take over the women's accomplishments failed or succeeded depending upon the stage of Jewish feminism in each country. In the United States, HIAS failed miserably in its attempt to displace NCJW on the docks. The vigorous feminism of Sadie American and the Council, beginning in 1908, reflected the freedom, social mobility, and enthusiasm of the nation. As we shall see, this same independent spirit also encouraged Jewish women's nationwide participation in other forms of feminist social reform, trade unionism, and suffrage activity.

By contrast, in England the Gentlemen's Committee took over the JAPGW's international effort. The Anglo-Jewish community, even more conservative than their Christian English peers, and fearful of anti-Semitism, were not prepared in 1885 to allow Jewish women to tackle a worldwide sexual scandal. Constance Rothschild Battersea was forced to move cautiously even as she took the radical step of creating the JAPGW. Before World War I, Battersea and her circle of women leaders focused on prevention and rescue homes, although they did participate in national lobbying efforts and international conferences to curb the white slave traffic. After the war had shattered many of England's conventions of class and society, they rejoined the

Gentlemen's Committee, making a public statement about their national and international visibility. Still, female Anglo-Jewish anti–
white slavery activists never equaled the dynamic political leadership
of their American co-religionists. As we shall see, this lack of militancy would carry over into every other feminist sphere except suffrage.

Jewish women's leadership in the anti–white slavery crusade not
only heightened fears of anti-Semitism but intensified Jewish men's
concerns about public behavior by "respectable" women that might
affect traditional family, religious, and communal norms. Jewish men
who either opposed or attempted to dominate women's involvement
in the campaign, like those who fought Josephine Butler's LNA, feared
that the anti–white slavery activists would launch Jewish women's
entry into secular and communal politics. They were correct.

Sexual politics dramatically affected Jewish communities in both
England and the United States. Jewish feminists attacked the double
standard, demanded social chastity by both sexes, and discussed intimate sexual matters in public forums. Indeed, their later social reform efforts often seemed tame after their public discussion of
bedrooms and brothels.

Moreover, Jewish anti–white slavery activists' membership in the
International Council of Women fostered an increasing, although still
relatively small, Jewish influence in worldwide secular feminist
causes.[98] From 1904 on, Jewish delegates spurred the ICW to take an
active role in international campaigns against white slavery. The creation of the ICW and the League of Nations committees significantly
influenced curbing of the traffic. International secular feminist leadership discovered that the effectiveness of socially acceptable upper-
and middle-class Jewish women provided a valuable contribution to
the woman's movement. As international feminism gathered support
to expand its base, Jewish women's participation became increasingly
welcome. Jewish feminists, on the other hand, enjoyed the increasing
acceptance, learned ICW tactics, and translated ICW policies into
programs for their own organizations. Jewish women's leadership in
international Jewish and secular anti–white slavery conferences further strengthened their feminism.

As we shall see, Jewish feminists' new organizational and political
roles generated a new self-identification as social reformers on a wide
variety of issues. They learned the lessons of sexual politics well:
incorporating their new political personas into their concept of Jewish
womanhood, they constructed the next stage in the emergence of a
Jewish woman's movement in England and the United States.

4

Settlement Reformers

By THE end of the nineteenth century, English and American upper-
and middle-class Jewish women's organizations, like their secular
counterparts, increasingly concentrated upon improving women's education, employment possibilities, and living conditions. Education
became the catalyst for improving women's lives, providing new opportunities for working- and middle-class women alike.

Higher education provided training for middle-class women in
teaching, nursing, and social service, and opened the doors to the
legal and medical professions. For the first time, a small group of
professional women enjoyed social and economic independence separately from their fathers, husbands, or brothers.[1] Yet, although thousands of working- and middle-class women in western Europe and
America were employed outside the home, the Pope, middle-class society, and even the Socialist Party denounced women's employment
or opposed equal work and equal pay for women.[2]

At the same time, the increased demand for female social workers
in England and America brought to its height the concept promoted
by Charlotte Perkins Gilman and others that women's inherent moral
superiority could reform a nation's social disorder.[3] Like their Christian peers, female Jewish social workers perceived their task as an
extension of women's moral obligation to protect the weak. Accepting
this concept, and buoyed by the success of the anti–white slavery
crusade, middle-class Jewish women flocked to join women's social
service organizations. As long as they engaged in *service* and not
reform, these women had the approval of the Jewish community,
which applauded their charitable mission and their social acceptance
by American women's organizations.

The social gospel's message of national moral reform permeated
philanthropy and the budding profession of social work.[4] Carol Christ
suggests that many women, seeking to find their own identity in a

changing world, adopted the social gospel and social service as an expression of their womanhood. As a cause larger than themselves, the social gospel spoke to their own needs and identity as women within and without the home.[5]

Along with their Gentile peers, many turn-of-the-century Jewish social activists reinterpreted the social gospel to include a combination of feminism, social service, and social reform. Female Jewish reformers were particularly influenced by Judaism's adaptation of the social gospel through synagogues, women's organizations, and, in America, Dr. Felix Adler's nonsectarian Ethical Culture Society.[6]

Jewish women increased their contact with each other and their Christian counterparts through a rapidly expanding network of women's clubs, social service organizations, and settlement houses. Banding together, Jewish women not only learned essential political skills but also strengthened their feelings of sisterhood to support their aspirations as women. Jewish women's social reform activities, like those of their Gentile colleagues, became a tool to help them obtain their own political goals and the key to developing a powerful Jewish feminist movement.[7]

ENGLAND

In England, educational opportunities for middle-class Anglo-Jewish girls quickly expanded beyond private tutors and fashionable boarding schools.[8] By the 1890s, the first generation of college-educated Jewish women served as teachers and charitable workers in the Jewish community.

Miriam Moses was one of the first group of female Jewish certified teachers. Moving from a teaching position at the charitable Jews' Free School, she was elected headmistress of Birmingham Hebrew National School. She held this post until 1874, when the boys' and girls' departments were merged under a headmaster and she was demoted to the position of teacher.[9] Although Moses taught at the school for forty years, she was never again permitted to become headmistress. Her situation was typical of women teachers at the turn of the century. As soon as teaching achieved a respected professional status, men assumed supervision of administration and policy direction. Only a few women educators continued as school principals.[10]

Women who attempted to win roles on either secular or Jewish community educational governing boards faced even more formidable obstacles. Board membership meant policy leadership, and men feared that women's presence on such councils would diminish their own power. Nevertheless, women argued that such a role would extend their moral guardianship of home and family, because it would enable them to assert "moral welfare" over public schoolchildren.[11] Franklin family wives, representatives of one of Anglo-Jewry's most socially concerned clans, broke the barriers against Jewish women's involvement in secular educational policy. Their success provided a precedent for women's further involvement in Jewish communal matters.

Carolyn Franklin (Mrs. Arthur), a friend observed, overcame considerable prejudice against both Jews and women to become the first woman on the Bucks County Education Committee. Her success in this wealthy and deeply conservative suburban district made it possible for other Anglo-Jewish women to follow her example. Like her husband, Franklin was prominent in Anglo-Jewish educational circles, particularly in organizations that focused on improving Jewish education among the Jewish working class. Influenced by her mother's work with East European immigrant women, Franklin also created an East End settlement and a "Fellowship of Jewish Women," which became the predecessor of England's Women's Institutes.[12]

Henrietta "Netta" Franklin was the sister of Lily Montagu, founder of England's first Liberal Jewish movement. Netta helped to create and promote a system of education which dominated English educational theory during the first quarter of the twentieth century. Outraged at the educational, civic, and political limitations imposed upon women, she turned, as we shall see, to suffrage agitation, eventually becoming president of the National Union of Women Suffrage Societies.[13]

By 1912, college education had become a stepping-stone for a generation of Anglo-Jewish women who branched out into new volunteer and professional positions. Several Jewish women took honors at Cambridge University in that year, while learned female Jewish authors published works reflecting a thorough knowledge of Jewish and English tradition and literature.[14] Poet and essayist Nina Davis Salaman and novelist-essayist Katie Magnus were only two among many authors who wrote on feminist and suffragist themes.[15]

UNION OF JEWISH WOMEN

Despite the prominence of a select group of female authors and a handful of elite professionals in other fields, the majority of women were educated as teachers and governesses, traditional and socially acceptable fields for women. Few women were prepared to take advantage of new employment opportunities in Britain's expanding economy. To enable more women to do so, the Union of Jewish Women devoted itself to training middle-class Jewish gentlewomen for a wide range of jobs.

By 1912, the Union boasted approximately 1,600 members throughout Great Britain and its colonies. Its employment training program placed women as social workers, teachers of domestic science, nurses, embroiderers, gardeners, kindergarten teachers, lamp-shade makers, seamstresses, printers, and photographers. Trained secretaries could always get a job. The Union even helped to train and place aspiring musicians or singers. In 1913, the Union had 503 applications for employment, 387 applications for information, and 56 candidates in training. By the eve of World War I, the Union was able to place girls as "plan-tracers," physical drill and dancing instructors, accountants, and photographers.[16]

Female Jewish physicians were rare, although Netta Franklin relied upon an Anglo-Jewish woman surgeon, a female physician supervised the health of girls in JAPGW rescue homes, and UJW correspondents reported that a Jewish "lady doctor" practiced in India.[17] Although the nursing profession in England was open to Jewish women, few took up the occupation. They resented the frequent combination of hard physical work and anti-Semitic antagonism from hospital staff and patients. Nevertheless, Jewish hospital wards and private homes desperately needed nurses. Concerned about the problem, the Union of Jewish Women established an education and training program, which graduated dozens of new Jewish nurses. To provide a hospital in which Jewish patients and staff would feel comfortable, in 1912 the UJW helped mount a communitywide campaign to build Beth Holim Hospital.[18]

At the same time, a worldwide network of Union volunteer correspondents assisted Anglo-Jewish women in several countries and represented the Union at meetings of national and international Jewish women's organizations. To avoid promoting the myth of Jewish international power or a Jewish conspiracy, the Union carefully extolled the notion that "The sun never sets over the British Empire" while emphasizing that Union members assisted the "scattered Jewish race" with "help and sympathy."[19] By drawing upon the image of loyalty to the British Empire and its traditional sympathy to the unfortunate, the Union hoped to avoid anti-Semitic attacks and justify its work in the eyes of non-Jews.

THE UJW AND THE WOMAN'S MOVEMENT

From its inception, the Union attempted to assert its influence in communal policy decisions and sought representation on the Jewish

Board of Guardians, which had never admitted women members. In 1902, its first year, the UJW leaders convinced the Board to pass a resolution adopting the principle of admitting women, but they failed to secure a vote that would turn the principle into fact. The Union then began a campaign for Board membership that, as we shall see, did not succeed until after World War I.[20]

Faced with persistent rejection by male communal leadership, the Union aligned itself with secular women's organizations. Connections with these groups not only provided female bonding and mutual support but also reinforced the UJW's connection with successful and prestigious Christian-dominated female institutions, thereby improving the Union's political leverage within the Jewish community.

Constance Lady Battersea, elected NUWW president in 1901, persuaded the Union to affiliate with a number of national and international women's organizations, including the NUWW and, in 1904, the ICW.[21] Battersea ensured that the Union was well represented by distinguished UJW members such as International Council of Women leader Lady Desart on NUWW and ICW committees and conferences. Secretary Kate Halford and other Union representatives also participated in ICW committees and attended its international conferences.[22] International Council of Women meetings clearly influenced Union policy. After the 1904 ICW conference, Halford and Countess Desart reported to the Union on ICW suffrage discussions and suggested that the UJW promote Jewish religious suffrage in England. A decade later, Union members were heavily involved in this effort. As we shall see, after World War I the UJW spearheaded the Anglo-Jewish women's campaign for synagogue voting rights throughout Great Britain.

From 1904 until 1933, Union delegates to ICW Conferences participated in the Jewish caucus initiated by Battersea, Sadie American, and Bertha Pappenheim. By 1913, Union delegates to ICW conferences had persuaded the UJW to expand its mandate to include the same goals as the international feminist community: equal employment, improved living conditions, and political and religious rights for working-class as well as middle-class Jewish women.[23] The anti–white slavery crusade appears to be the only major social feminist effort in which the Union was not ultimately involved. Indeed, the UJW cooperated in creating the World Council of Jewish Women in 1923. Membership in the International Council of Women had influenced the Union's broadening of its mandate, from assisting "necessitous gentlewomen" to seeking political, religious, and communal change along similar lines to America's NCJW and the ICW itself.[24]

WEST CENTRAL AND JEWISH GIRLS' CLUBS

By the end of the nineteenth century, a plethora of Jewish women's volunteer philanthropic and social service groups had produced charitable aid, job training, and housing for East European immigrants, but appeared less able to meet the particular needs of the vast numbers of Jewish working girls that had swelled London's East End since 1881.

To fill this gap, in 1893 Lily Montagu re-shaped and revitalized Lady Rothschild's relatively small West Central Jewish Girls Club into England's first multi-purpose Jewish girls' educational and social club and settlement house.[25] She relied heavily upon friends and family, particularly her sisters Netta and Marion, for emotional and financial support.[26] Montagu's precedents included numerous Christian-led women's social service organizations and Louise Lady Rothschild's West Central Friday Night Club. Following these examples, Montagu's club was rooted in the belief that women's role as moral saviors of the household and community imbued them with a mission to protect and educate the poor, immigrants, and the weak according to upper-class standards.[27]

The West Central Jewish Girls' Club sought to Anglicize its members and foster "an ideal of honesty of purpose, integrity and self-effacing service." At the same time, Montagu and her staff sought to teach the girls "the true meaning of Judaism" through service to the community and faith in God.[28]

Montague ran the Club according to principles of "democratic management" based upon the settlement model developed by Arnold Toynbee and put into operation by Canon Samuel Barnett at Toynbee Hall in Whitechapel. West Central achieved some success in bending England's rigid class barriers and forging warm, personal relationships between the leaders and working-class Club members.[29] Moving freely around the East End, Montagu's staff became particularly involved in the problems of women and children.

By 1896, the Club's program was teaching girls English, along with domestic skills and other marketable trades: cooking, needle-work, dress-making, basket-work, clothes-laundering, and wood-carving. Recreational activities at the Club included painting and brush-drawing, singing, and learning to play musical instruments. Over the years, the Club gradually expanded to count on its rolls more than 100,000 members spanning three generations of women. It provided a Settlement House; a Children's Section; a Married Members' Guild; the

Lily Montagu

Maud Nathan Home for Little Children; an Employment Bureau and the West Central Flower Company which employed Club members.[30]

To counteract the efforts of a "missionary Doctor" to convert the Jewish girls he treated, a Jewish physician and his wife donated a portion of their week to caring for Club girls. Emphasizing morality and Judaism, Montagu and her volunteers taught the girls Hebrew and religion and instituted Sabbath worship services at the Club.[31]

Despite the Club's emphasis on Judaism, education, and job training, it and its successors faced considerable opposition, similar to that encountered by Louise Lady Rothschild. Many veteran social workers felt that girls' clubs contributed to the deterioration of the family by taking girls away from their families during their leisure hours.[32] Still, West Central was so successful that two years after it was founded, a group of men created the Jewish Lad's Brigade. This was followed in 1896 by the Brady Street Club and in 1901 and later by the Victoria Boys' Club and several other clubs.[33]

A host of Jewish girls' clubs emulated Montagu's West Central Girls' Club, most notably the Butler Street Girls' Club, founded by Mrs. Frank Lyons in 1902. The only Jewish girls' club serving the Spitalfields district of London's East End, the club sought to "lure girls from the streets, the penny-gaffs and the music-halls." In rented premises over the Jewish Soup Kitchen, Butler Street enticed its two hundred members with twenty-seven different types of classes.[34] Major Jewish girls' clubs also included the Beatrice Club for Jewish Working Girls and the Jewish Girls' Club in Whitechapel, the latter founded by author Katie Magnus, a friend and supporter of Lily Montagu.[35]

By 1898, Jewish boys' and girls' clubs received whole-hearted communal approval. Even Mrs. Rachel Adler, wife of the Chief Rabbi, spent much of her time volunteering in an extensive network of Jewish girls' clubs and women's organizations.[36] By the time Montagu technically "retired" from her Club in 1922, she had turned the club idea into a de facto settlement house and a beloved communal institution.[37]

SETTLEMENT HOUSES

By the early twentieth century, Montagu's West Central served as the model for a profusion of settlement houses founded and managed by female professional Jewish social workers. The management of Jewish settlement houses, like their secular models, was based upon the growing professionalization of social work and, after the war, England's shift toward social welfare.[38]

In an England faced with rising unemployment and anti-alien sentiment, Jewish settlements were continually pressured to Anglicize, educate, and provide employment training for immigrants. Eastern European girls, who received less basic education than boys, desperately needed training for a gradually expanding job market. Following the example of Lily Montagu's West Central Jewish Girls' Club, the Butler Street, Leman Street, and Beatrice Girls' Clubs met the need by expanding into major settlements.[39]

Rose Henriques exemplified the dominance of upper-middle-class Anglo-Jewish gentlewomen over settlement life. She shared the management of the Bernhard Baron Settlement in St. George's District with her husband, Basil, its founder and warden. By insisting that the club include both boys and girls, Rose Henriques broke one of the major taboos of the day and helped to transform a small club into a major settlement and mission, raising many of the funds herself. She created the settlement's synagogue, developed projects for all ages, and founded a settlement Girls' Club.[40]

Henriques was a tireless, dedicated worker and born leader who alienated some of her staff and former club girls because she insisted upon an "almost unquestioning obedience and devotion." Contemporary communal leader L. L. Loewe describes her as "one of the most remarkable, difficult, capable, gifted, infuriating and generous women of her time."[41]

World War I shattered the rigidity of English social life. As men went off to war, women left the home to serve the war effort in hospitals, settlements, offices, and factories. Newly independent women of all classes, working closely together in factories, shops, civil service, and hospitals, slowly redefined class boundaries and the role of women.

The Stepney Jewish B'nai B'rith Settlement was one of the first Jewish settlements to involve working-class women in its management. Founded by the German-Jewish matron Mrs. Anna Schwab (1887–1963) and her circle, it is the only Jewish settlement remaining in Stepney today.[42] Mrs. Schwab was a devoted housewife and mother who focused much of her remarkable energy upon community service. She threw herself into refugee work during the war, then into postwar volunteer social work in London's East End. In 1925, she assumed leadership of the small Stepney Girls' Club, surrounded by an executive board that included Miriam Rothschild and Rebecca Sieff, suffragist and founder of England's Women's Zionist Organization.[43] Social worker Phyllis P. Gerson was hired as organizer in 1927, and the two women turned Stepney into a thriving settlement for men and women providing a range of educational, social service, artistic, and vocational activities.[44]

East End resident Florrie Passman, hailed by newspapers as the "Queen of the clubs" for her work at Stepney, joined the Butler Street Girls' Club as a young girl in 1903 and ten years later began her social service career. When Butler Street closed in 1953, Miss Passman joined the Stepney Jewish Settlement. She helped to organize the National Insurance scheme, which helped refugees coming to Britain, in addition to other tasks. In 1976, she was awarded an M.B.E., and in 1981, when she was ninety-two, her cheery smile continued to enliven the settlement, where she still worked three days a week.[45]

Settlement work launched a small group of Jewish women into politics. Miriam Moses, the first warden of the Brady Girls' Club and Settlement, became the first daughter of the Eastern European immigrant generation to assume political leadership. Born to Orthodox parents in the Spitalfields district of London's East End, Moses was the daughter of a master tailor who became a justice of the peace, a rare honor for an East End resident. An active member of the New Synagogue in Stamford Hill, Miss Moses became the first woman representative to the Council of the United Synagogue, still very much a male preserve. She became a liberal councillor for Stepney Borough Council and served as mayor of Stepney from 1931 to 1932.[46]

Regarded almost as royalty by her East End neighbors, she was a member of the Board of Deputies of British Jews as well as the Board of Guardians, now the Jewish Welfare Board. Appointed justice of the peace, she sat as a judge in Juvenile Court and served as governor on several state schools. She earned an O.B.E. for her relief work during World War II and undertook extensive activities during and after the war.[47]

SELF-HELP SOCIETIES

Passage of the Health Insurance Act of 1911 spurred the creation of a new generation of self-help societies, which further encouraged the involvement of Jewish immigrants in the management of their own affairs. In 1911, Lady Desart and a group of upper- and middle-class female Anglo-Jewish social workers founded a number of self-help societies to foster working-girls' independence and permit them to take advantage of the Act.[48]

English workers' societies had flourished since 1797; Jewish self-help societies boasted approximately a fifteen-hundred-year-old tradition. East End working-women's self-help organizations benefited from Jewish women's involvement in the settlement and trade union movements, and the precedent of Jewish working-men's and women's clubs, which adapted English and Jewish models to their own welfare and educational programs.[49]

Although the National Insurance Act permitted Friendly Societies to distribute workers' medical and burial benefits, Jews avoided joining English societies because most of them did not welcome Jewish immigrants. In addition, the insurance contracts signed by English societies did not allow for the seven days required for the Jewish week of mourning (shiva). Moreover, clinics or hospitals covered under English societies' medical and maternity insurance did not follow Jewish dietary restrictions.[50]

Lily Montagu, seeking to help immigrant Jews to become properly Anglicized citizens, urged Jewish working girls to join English Friendly Societies and sign up for the insurance coverage held by the National Federation of Women Workers (NFWW). The NFWW promised increased benefits to Jewish members to gain Jewish support for the Labour Party.[51]

Montagu appears to have been the only female Anglo-Jewish leader to urge Jewish working girls to join English Friendly Societies. The majority of Jewish women preferred Jewish societies, in order to remain within a familiar framework and to receive medical and burial benefits tailored to their needs. Anglo-Jewish women social workers allied with working girls to create these Friendly Societies, helping to modify class distinctions among Jewish women in England. Although social barriers still flourished, working girls appear to have had a far stronger voice in the management of these organizations than was the case in many social work ventures.

In April 1912, Mrs. Alice Model and her Sick Room Helps Society founded the first Friendly Society for Jewish Women and Girls under the 1911 National Insurance Act. Since the Act insured husbands only, subscriptions by unemployed married working-class women to the Sick Rooms Helps Society provided the women's sole support for home medical care after childbirth. Over 5,100 women contributed to the Sick Room Helps provident branch.[52]

Model's society also spawned a wave of successors staffed by Anglo-Jewish social workers well known and trusted in immigrant districts. The Anglo-Jewish community applauded these agencies because they were established and managed by the Anglo-Jewish gentry and also satisfied women workers' need to contribute toward their own insurance protection.[53]

CONCLUSION

Female Jewish social service professionals and volunteers radically changed the nature of women's work, bringing medical, educational, social, and vocational care and training into the East End. Women social workers expanded the scope of organizations like the Union of Jewish Women and founded settlement houses with a wide array of services, changing communal social service methods and policies in the process. As we shall see, a few social workers like Lily Montagu also became engaged in more radical feminist social reform and the suffrage campaign. Like Miriam Moses, some women built political careers upon the base of social service.

Immigrant Jewish women contributed only modestly to decisions made primarily by the upper- and middle-class leadership of self-help societies and settlement houses before the war. Like their secular peers, East European women began to have an effective voice in management after World War I changed English society.

As we shall see, the majority of Anglo-Jewish social workers differed from their American sisters in avoiding reformist militancy. Their caution may reflect a concern about anti-Semitic backlash. It may also indicate Jewish women's own definition of their social work careers as extensions of women's traditional role of nurturer, in both English and Jewish culture. Like their Christian peers, female Anglo-Jewish social workers had a public image as mothers to "their girls," a role that permitted them to engage in social service with a minimum of opposition from male relatives. Political militancy threatened to end the male quiescence that had freed many Jewish middle-class women from the confines of their homes. However dedicated, the majority of prewar Anglo-Jewish women settlement workers were unwilling to take that risk.

Nevertheless, these social service professionals and volunteers generated several important changes. Growing numbers of these women emerged into communal and national prominence, altering the structure of social services in the Anglo-Jewish community. Miriam Moses's political career and Florrie Passman's influence in the National Insurance scheme indicate the postwar softening of class distinctions and creation of new opportunities for Jew and Christian alike. Although upper-class Anglo-Jewish gentry still dominated the social scheme, middle-class and immigrant working-class Jews became increasingly influential in Jewish women's organizations. The rapidly growing presence of Jewish women in public life set the stage for Jewish women's wider participation in communal and national feminist activity.

UNITED STATES

Education ought to prepare [woman] . . . to be the best qualified guardian of her offspring. . . . [she] should receive instructions in all branches which will promote the physical condition of future generations.[54]

In 1895, the *American Jewess* argued that higher education would strengthen women's role as wives and mothers while preparing those who needed financial independence for professional careers.

American Jewish women were studying at women's colleges in several states, including Mount Holyoke's women's seminary and the women's annexes at Oberlin, Cornell, and Harvard.[55] College women believed that education provided the key to economic independence and improved skills as a wife and community volunteer. They were supported by progressive male educational authorities who felt that while a woman's primary task should be as a homemaker, education would prevent her from becoming frivolous, ignorant, or empty-headed.

Higher education changed women's lives as radically in the United States as in England. Peter Gay estimates that women's access to universities during this period proved more important to woman's cause than winning the vote.[56]

Annie Nathan Meyer (1867–1951) founded Barnard College in order to open new educational and occupational opportunities to women. The daughter of a distinguished Sephardi family, she rejected her father's dictum that "men hate intelligent wives." A year after her graduation from Columbia University's Collegiate Course for Women, she married a prominent New York physician and began the successful campaign to establish a women's college attached to Columbia University. She was determined that women should have the "best possible equipment that education of all kinds can furnish." When Barnard opened its doors in 1888, Meyer boasted proudly that "This course would secure for women all the advantages now enjoyed by the College men."[57]

By opening Barnard to all women, Meyer dealt simultaneously with the severely limited quota placed upon Jews at many colleges and with the fears of female competition at male universities. Given the high proportion of Jews in New York City, many of Barnard's students were Jewish women, who became anthropologists, psychologists, social workers, and teachers.[58] They opened up new professions for middle-class women, enabling them to assert control over a sphere of public life previously closed to them. The teaching profession, in particular, gained new impetus from the rapidly growing number of colleges, like Barnard, that admitted women.

Julia Richman (1855–1912) became one of the first, and certainly the most influential, female Jewish principals in New York City. Graduating from Hunter College, she taught public school on the Lower East Side and became New York's first woman district superintendent of public schools in 1903. Although an outstanding progressive educator, Richman infuriated the school's Lower East Side neighborhood by publicly speaking out against the hunger that sapped the children's energies and the crime that flourished in ghetto streets. Parents, convinced that Richman was criticizing the way they cared for their

children, petitioned the Board of Education for Richman's resignation, but she was eventually cleared of malfeasance. Unrepentant,
Richman denounced the "utter inability of creating a civic conscience in these people."[59]

Despite the controversy, Richman's educational policies made a
major contribution to the Americanization of Jewish immigrants in
the public schools. Moreover, as a member of the boards of several
major Jewish organizations, including the Educational Alliance, she
profoundly influenced the Jewish community's approach to immigrant education. The *American Hebrew* applauded her "keen insight
into conditions on the East Side and [her] experienced sense of the
practical."[60]

A member of the National Council of Jewish Women, Richman
cautiously promoted the emancipation of Jewish women, even though
she did not advocate suffrage. Part of a wave of single women dedicating themselves to teaching and social service, Richman insisted
that a single woman engaged in useful work was more valuable to
society than women trapped in one of the "horror of ill-assorted marriages" she saw "everywhere."[61]

Unlike college-educated German-Jewish teachers such as Richman, female Jewish immigrants often had to battle their husbands in
order to attend night school. One housewife's painful letter in the
Jewish Daily Forward's "Bintel Brief" column queried "whether a
married woman has the right to go to school two evenings a week."
Her "intelligent" and "educated" husband was acting "contrary to
his beliefs" by forbidding her to attend classes. Bintel Brief's editor,
Abraham Cahan, scolded the husband for enslaving his wife and
urged her to continue school.[62]

Most immigrants preferred public education to the traditional
yeshiva, since they viewed secular learning as the critical tool for
upward social and economic mobility.[63] Jewish boys learned quickly,
since they were often already literate in Hebrew or Yiddish and
trained in the religious schools of Eastern Europe. Jewish girls from
traditional families had been restricted to learning only home rituals
and household skills, yet they soon overcame this handicap and ex-
celled as students.[64] For adults, night school became the tool for entrée
into American social, economic, and political life. Thus, the classroom simultaneously became a window of opportunity both for established German-Jewish women and for Eastern European immigrant
children and adults.

As education expanded from the classroom to the meeting rooms
of synagogues and public forums, immigrants began to perceive it as

a key to social and economic mobility as well as an avenue toward social and political power. By transforming the study hall into a meeting hall, Jewish immigrants began the transformation from East European to American Jewish life. This process also gave Jewish girls and women the confidence and skills to speak out in public. Female as well as male immigrants learned that they could shape people and events, thereby becoming vital to East European Jewry's entry into secular society.[65] As we shall see, this facet of their education became particularly important to the immigrant Jewish women who used the stage of New York's Cooper Union Hall to launch the dramatic 1909 strike of 20,000 garment workers.

Conscious of the importance of adult education, German-Jewish women provided direction and staffing for vocational training as well as English-language classes for the immigrants. By 1895, women were being admitted to the Hebrew Technical Institute in New York, and Philadelphia's Young Women's Union had established a school for immigrant women in the building owned by the Hebrew Educational Society.[66]

PROFESSIONAL JEWISH WOMEN

Although teaching was vital to the Jewish community, increasing numbers of well-educated German-Jewish women branched out into other fields. Like their non-Jewish counterparts, most of them had more education, had worked in offices before marriage, or remained single and continued their careers, often achieving considerable prominence.

One hundred seventy-five Jewish women were listed in the 1928 edition of *Who's Who in American Jewry.*[67] A 1919 study undertaken by the *Jewish Tribune* discovered that the majority of prominent women were college graduates. Approximately one-third were volunteer activists with Jewish philanthropic organizations, while the rest spanned a full range of professional vocations. Nearly all maintained some type of Jewish affiliation, usually with a Jewish women's organization.[68] Leah Morton's semi-autobiographical book, *I am a Woman— and a Jew,* chronicled the vicissitudes of a Jewish woman struggling to secure a professional niche and a personal identity in this changing world.[69] In a Jewish community that still put boys' education and advancement ahead of girls', success stories such as these became important role models to a new generation of Jewish women.

Harriet B. Lowenstein became a major figure in the distribution and administration of Jewish charities as the "confidential and communal advisor" to Felix Warburg, Jacob Schiff's son-in-law and banking partner in Kuhn, Loeb & Co. As Warburg's adviser, Lowenstein helped to determine which charities should survive and to force the modernization of daily operations and fund-raising practices of War-burg's charities. Her position enabled her to influence the financial structure of two notable recipients of Warburg's largesse, Lillian Wald's Henry Street Settlement and New York Jewry's premier set-tlement house, the Educational Alliance.[70]

Lowenstein became the only American woman before World War I to be accredited as both a lawyer and a certified public accountant. After joining Warburg, she became one of the most successful busi-nesswomen in the country. An adviser to the Bank Israelite, a Jewish-owned financial institution, she was "one of the few successful professional Jewish women in the country whose income equals that of a Metropolitan bank president." Acclaimed as "the leading woman in Jewish philanthropic affairs," Lowenstein served on the boards and restructured the financial systems of several major Jewish charitable organizations. Her efficiency and business acumen awed New York's Jewish community.[71]

Lowenstein's success was an extraordinary example of the increas-ing presence of American women in the financial world. She was followed by only a handful of Jewish women such as Harriet B. Gold-stein, a lawyer and certified public accountant who served as comp-troller of the New York Federation of Jewish Charities in the late 1920s.[72]

SOCIAL SERVICE

Jewish women volunteered in the host of Jewish communal charitable institutions created or expanded in scope to meet immigrant needs. Primarily founded by the German-Jewish elite, the most distinguished of these organizations included the Baron de Hirsch Fund and the HIAS. Settlement houses such as the Educational Alliance provided aid and education to Lower East Side residents. The United Hebrew Charities provided free lodging, meals, medical care, entertainment, and lectures on subjects ranging from marriage to the dangers of socialism.[73]

NATIONAL COUNCIL OF JEWISH WOMEN

In the wake of its anti–white slavery campaign, the National Council of Jewish Women branched out from its original stress upon religious study circles and Sabbath Schools to emphasize its social service role.[74] Council workers conducted clubs and classes for immigrants, took care of sick children and their parents in homes and hospitals, and raised money for a range of other social services. Focusing on problems facing Jewish women and girls, the Council sponsored juvenile court officers, established homes for delinquent girls, and conducted night classes and vacation schools, work rooms and vocational classes. The organization cooperated wherever possible with established Jewish and nonsectarian social service organizations.[75]

The NCJW adopted the new concept of professionally directed "scientific" social work being used to clean up America's cities. This approach highlighted the tension between volunteers and professionals in social service agencies and settlement houses, spawning a conflict between generations, classes, and outlooks. The upper-class German-Jewish woman volunteer looked down upon the often-younger middle-class professional. Yet these volunteers, although experienced in the day-to-day work of the organization, lacked the new social workers' academic training.[76]

Cecelia Razovsky, a professional social worker, was secretary of the Council's Department of Immigrant Aid. She directed the Council's work with immigrants, the establishment of settlement houses, and the fight against white slavery. Razovsky wrote the standard booklet on citizenship for women, and her reports on the Immigration Act of 1924 became the standard guide for Jewish professionals attempting to fight the restrictions of the Act.[77]

Razovsky and other professionals trained Council volunteers, who undertook a formidable series of tasks. Desertion was a particularly acute problem faced by East European women. One Seattle CJW volunteer dropped in unexpectedly to visit a Russian-Jewish immigrant's family. She found that the husband

> had become tired of his wife because she would not work, had taken the rings her first husband had given her and sold them, then gave his wife a terrible beating, blackening her eyes and tearing one open, and kicked her whole body until it was black and blue, and had then run away, leaving her away out in the suburbs, without money, fuel or food and a sick baby. The woman told me afterwards that if I had not come in, she would have died.
>
> We are helping her financially through the Hebrew Benevolent Society, and as soon as she can take out her papers I feel quite sure we will be able to raise enough money to bring over [her other daughter].[78]

Grappling with the ramifications of white slavery and the health, safety, education, and employment problems of immigrants, in 1911 the Council joined a political campaign to enact social legislation as part of a coalition of feminists and social reformers that included Lillian Wald and Rabbi Stephen S. Wise. The program called for elim-

NCJW boarding matrons meeting immigrant women and girls on ships arriving at
Ellis Island. Courtesy, National Council of Jewish Women

ination of child labor and creation of a federal Children's Bureau,
decent housing for low-income families, legislation to protect women
workers, regulation and standards for midwives, and uniform marriage and divorce laws.[79]

Council women across the country proved strikingly effective.
Chicago's "Jewish Jane Addams," the NCJW leader and Jewish communal activist Jennie Franklin Purvin (1873–1958), almost single-
handedly created the city's network of public bathing beaches and
recreation facilities.[80]

William Toll contends that the Portland (Oregon) Section's women
volunteers eclipsed the men in their understanding and organization
of social welfare, thereby achieving a far larger civic role.[81] The emi-
nent Reform rabbi Stephen S. Wise and his wife, Louise Waterman
Wise, played a pivotal initial role.[82] Louise Wise also achieved a formidable reputation as a social reformer and activist in women's
causes.

Despite their valuable contributions, some Council members
aroused instant resentment for their typically German-Jewish benevolent condescension toward East Europeans. Minnie D. Louis, one of

NCJW volunteer teaching in a home. Courtesy, National Council of Jewish Women

the founders of the New York Section of the NCJW, exemplified the problem. A dedicated volunteer for numerous charities, she was founder and first president of the Hebrew Technical School for Girls in New York City and one of two women elected as vice-president of the National Conference of Jewish Charities. A talented writer, she was a prolific poet and newspaper columnist and suffrage supporter.[83] Despite her theoretical commitment to equality, she was also typical of social workers of the day who believed that moral advice was the best form of assistance. Many immigrants hated her visits to the East Side. While distributing cookies to the children, she quoted "uplifting poetry," and exhorted residents to stop speaking Yiddish and to cut off the side curls worn by East European Orthodox Jewish men. An object of suspicion to the immigrants, they spread the rumor that she was not a Jew at all but a Christian missionary, because she called her East Side center a mission school and emulated Christian missionary tactics.[84]

Despite these problems, the NCJW's social service contributions

NCJW volunteer helping rural family. Courtesy, National Council of Jewish Women

proved immensely valuable to the Jewish community. Nevertheless, female Jewish social service workers were typically rewarded only by an occasional honorary degree or award from the Jewish community. When a 1915 conference of Jewish social workers did not include any women, an infuriated Minnie D. Louis complained publicly that she was "afraid that women count for very little in this world." Embarrassed, the conference's director then placed professional social worker Belle Moskowitz on the program.[85] This incident highlighted Jewish women's communal inferiority and their growing demands for a greater role in determining the Jewish community's social policy.

EINSTEIN AND LOEB

In spite of the tensions between volunteers and professionals, a wealthy German-Jewish "grande dame," Hannah Bachman Einstein (1862–1929), and a *New York Evening World* reporter, Sophie Irene Loeb (1876–1929), formed one of the earliest cross-class alliances between German Jews and East Europeans. In her newspaper column, East European immigrant Sophie Loeb publicized the two women's campaign for welfare legislation for widowed and divorced mothers. Einstein, the first woman board member of the United Hebrew Charities, resigned her position to found the Widowed Mothers' Pension Fund.[86]

    Einstein and Loeb helped to establish a public assistance program that anticipated the federal social security system launched in the

1930s. The pair obtained pensions for thousands of widowed and divorced mothers. They also won the passage of legislation that provided funds to foster homes and a range of services to make life easier for the poor in their own neighborhoods. At the same time, they maintained their membership in a multitude of Jewish community organizations, persuading some to work for their favorite cause.[87] Their combination of support for both national issues and Jewish communal activity encouraged Jewish women to undertake political reform.[88]

SETTLEMENT WORKERS

Between 1890 and 1900, Jewish and non-Jewish leisured and professional women took the first tentative steps toward allying with working-class women in social reform organizations. Jewish women were deeply involved in the subsequent creation of feminist-oriented settlement houses, the Consumers' League, the Women's Trade Union League (WTUL), and in the introduction of working women into the suffrage movement.

By the turn of the twentieth century, America's urban middle class simultaneously attempted social reforms to help working people and feared a new wave of violence springing from the Haymarket riot and its many successors.[89] To rectify social wrongs, a wave of Jewish as well as Christian social reformers created new settlement houses and reform organizations. Professional social workers made the settlement movement even more crucial to America's future than women's clubs, however valuable their contribution.[90]

Although these women built successful careers, they resented the limitations imposed upon them and other working women because of their sex. As a result, they concentrated on helping the vast numbers of working women among whom they lived. Failing to interest society in their cause, many American Jewish and non-Jewish women settlement leaders gravitated into the feminist movement.[91] They turned to political reform and occasionally militant tactics to improve the lives of women and children. They became part of a cadre of feminists who, as Sheila Ryan Johansson notes, sustained an organized but peaceful protest against laws, institutions, and professions that excluded women.[92]

LILLIAN WALD

Lillian Wald (1867–1940) was raised in an upper-middle-class Reform German-Jewish family whose values influenced her drive for social reform. After completing her nursing training and postgraduate stud-

Visiting nurse service, Irene Kaufmann Settlement House, Pittsburgh, 1920. Courtesy, American Jewish Historical Society

ies in New York City, Wald moved into New York's College Settlement House, which was run by a group of women professionals inspired by England's Toynbee Hall. Surrounded by reformers and feminists, Wald came to envision settlement work as a place where women could demonstrate "their ability to enlarge their own sphere of activity into the life of the community."[93]

Henry Street Settlement was the result of that vision. Funded primarily by financier Jacob Schiff and his circle of German-Jewish friends, Henry Street became a center for nursing services, clubs, lectures, and classes on New York's Lower East Side. Encouraged by

Mothers bringing their babies to the Better Baby Clinic, Irene Kaufmann Settlement House, Pittsburgh. Courtesy, American Jewish Historical Society

the patronage of Schiff and other wealthy supporters, Wald gathered together a group of nurses who helped her pioneer America's public health nursing system in schools and homes, as well as the country's rural nursing service.[94] Primarily concerned for the welfare of women and girls, she brought to Henry Street social workers who became the catalysts for protective legislation, the allies of female trade unionists, and active suffragists. The "Wald circle" led a campaign for protective legislation for children at the national level, led by Henry Street resident Florence Kelley, that culminated in creation of the Federal Children's Bureau.[95] Wald's leadership in the strike movement and other social causes made her the target of attacks by trade union radicals and Henry Street's wealthy conservative supporters. Even anarchist Emma Goldman, who applauded Wald's idealism, scorned her methods.[96]

Throughout this process, Wald's involvement with the Jewish community helped to shape her career. Although she insisted that she was areligious, by the early twentieth century religious affiliation was no longer the sole determinant of Jewish identification. Many Jews, rejecting Judaism as a religion, maintained strong ties to the Jewish people and Jewish culture. It was no accident that Wald worked

Hannah G. Solomon and Jane Addams. Courtesy, National
Council of Jewish Women

on the Lower East Side, filled as it was with East European Jewish
immigrants. She argued for special legislation and social services to
protect immigrant Jewish women, contending that they faced more
hostility and exploitation than any other immigrant group.[97] To
gather support for the newcomers among the Jewish community, Wald
cited a profusion of biblical verses in a multitude of synagogue sermons and lectures to German-Jewish women's organizations.

She worked closely with Rabbi Stephen S. Wise, rabbi of New
York's Free Synagogue and American Jewry's most famous spiritual
leader involved in social reform. Wise and Wald shared many of the
crusades that made them both famous:[98] the Triangle Waist fire protest, the Women's Trade Union League, Woodrow Wilson's campaigns
for the presidency, the suffrage movement, and the peace movement's
American Union against Militarism during World War I, for which
Wald was accused of being part of the so-called Red Menace.[99]

Lillian D. Wald, ca. 1919. Painting by William Sherrill.
Courtesy, American Jewish Historical Society

Wald's connections with Jacob Schiff attracted a cadre of wealthy women volunteers to Henry Street, including Irene and Alice Lewisohn, Rita Wallach Morgenthau, and Nina Loeb Warburg.[100] These women and their friends were the wives or daughters of Wald's benefactors from the Schiff-Loeb group. Their initial motives for volunteerism may have been grounded in the relatively fashionable American obsession with social service. Their enduring commitment, however, was based upon an intense personal devotion to Lillian Wald that was shared by Henry Street's resident nurses and social workers.

The affluent volunteers admired Wald and regarded her with affection. She, in turn, nurtured and sustained them. The Lewisohns founded the Neighborhood Playhouse, supported music and dance education projects, and were co-workers in the Woman's Peace Party and the American Union against Militarism. Alice Lewisohn wrote to "Lady Light" Wald that "You know perhaps even better than I what the months of companionship with you . . . have meant. . . . Much of my heart to you." Young Rita Wallach Morgenthau was Wald's closest friend among the younger nonresidents. She wrote to Wald that "you always have been and always will be my 'Leading Lady.' "[101]

Carroll Smith-Rosenberg has documented the intensity of close female friendships in a society that sprang from the separation between women and men in the late nineteenth and early twentieth centuries. In this atmosphere, Henry Street residents and volunteers provided a support network for Lillian Wald that enabled her to pursue her grueling schedule and multiple crusades. One might argue, as does Blanche Wiesen Cook, that Wald's relationship with her circle was at least emotionally lesbian in nature. On the other hand, Allen Davis contends that the close relationship among Henry Street residents and friends was a common feature of emotional bonding among women in this era, who often expressed intimate feelings in their correspondence. The mutually nurturing support provided by these relationships proved essential in uniting the Wald circle into a dedicated group prepared to do battle for Wald's social causes.[102]

Cook suggests that the Henry Street circle's particularly strong mutual emotional support system enabled them to withstand the difficulties facing reformers in general and women reformers in particular. The full significance of their success emerged when they initiated attempts to break the pattern of class-consciousness that had led professionals to separate themselves from working-class women.[103]

Wald and her circle initiated the first serious middle-class alliance with working women, which laid the basis for cross-class cooperation in the WTUL and the 1909 garment industry strikes.[104] Wald insisted that Jewish immigrants were valuable American citizens who should be considered as equals. She invited Jewish and non-Jewish immigrant women such as Rose Schneiderman and Leonora O'Reilly to join many of her social reform strategy sessions and involved them in women's organizations such as the Women's Trade Union League, which Wald helped to establish. Wald, Schneiderman, and O'Reilly also worked together in the suffrage campaign.[105]

The Wald circle agreed with feminist social reformers' claims that women were particularly suited to undertake social reform because they were morally superior to men and were filled with a gentleness, sensitivity, and responsiveness to human needs. These characteristics obligated women to organize among themselves to help other women. Moreover, argued Wald and her supporters, because women of all classes were a disadvantaged social group, all women could empathize and should work with each other.[106]

Although the United States had its share of class snobbery and religious distinctions, freedom from the rigid social conventions and widespread anti-Jewish sentiment of England made it easier for Wald to put her ideas into practice. Wald and her settlement house colleagues shared management responsibilities with trade union leaders such as Rose Schneiderman. As a result, Wald's reform campaigns gained far wider support among all classes than if they had been led solely by middle-class women. By contrast, in England, Anglo-Jewish women became settlement workers and joined the Women's Trade Union League (WTUL), but neither settlements nor trade unions attempted to involve working women in leadership until well after World War I.

Lillian Wald's circle also initiated the first cross-class campaigns for protective legislation for women. Yet, Wald's middle-class social workers perceived working-class women as victims who must be protected at all costs, despite the fear that excluding women from certain occupations would reduce their wages. A contradiction existed whereby middle-class feminists who demanded protection for others while demanding autonomy and the vote for themselves still maintained implicit class distinctions.[107] These goals and contradictions were part of Wald's legacy and inherent in two women's organizations that attempted cross-class alliances: the Consumer's League and the WTUL.

CONCLUSION

From the West Central Jewish Girls' Club to the National Council of Jewish Women, the dynamism of professional social work revolutionized Jewish women's organizations and propelled many Jewish women into national as well as communal affairs. Lily Montagu's combination of Jewish and English values, scientific social service methods, and educational and employment training for working-class girls and women spawned many imitators in England. The National Council of Jewish Women followed similar patterns, allowing for adaptation to American values, and became this country's foremost exemplar of Jewish women's social service during this period.

The close linkage between the secular and Jewish woman's movement led to greater Jewish feminist activism. As we shall see, Montagu and several NCJW leaders were closely involved with secular as well as Jewish social reform and suffrage campaigns. Lillian Wald, primarily a national rather than a Jewish reformer, set a powerful example for Jewish women volunteers and professionals. Settlement workers who remained exclusively inside the Jewish community tended to participate less in social reform, even for Jews.

As the Union of Jewish Women expanded its secular education and employment training programs and joined the International Council of Women, it increased its campaign for representation on Jewish communal boards. As we shall see, it also intensified its drive for women's right to vote in synagogues and participate equally in religious life.

The professionalization of social work also increased Jewish women's influence in communal life in England and the United States, to a certain degree. On one hand, Jewish women were indispensable in expanding German Jewry's social service network. They could no longer be totally ignored by their male colleagues. On the other hand, male Jewish leadership prevented women from achieving policy-making status. On the eve of World War I, Jewish women influenced communal social work but were poorly represented on community-wide governing boards that determined policy. Like Lillian Wald, they were often more influential in the secular world than in their own Jewish community. In time, Jewish women's participation in secular feminism would spur them toward more powerful campaigns for reform in the Jewish and national realms.

5

Allies, Unions, and Strikes

ENGLAND

In 1885, Louisa Lady Goldsmid and Millicent Garrett Fawcett led a delegation of women coal miners to the Home Office to protest unfair wages at the mines, sponsored by the Women's Protective and Provident League (WPPL) later renamed the Women's Trade Union League (WTUL).[1] Goldsmid joined the WTUL in its formative years and spearheaded Jewish support for the organization. Her involvement ranged from subsidizing vacation trips for members to fighting against the Factory Acts, which were designed to provide better wages for men by keeping women out of higher-paying positions.[2] Similar to her leadership in higher education for women, Goldsmid's WTUL activism drew Anglo-Jewish women into employment and trade union concerns. Several Anglo-Jewish WTUL feminists later helped to spearhead national and communal suffrage activity.

In the same year that Goldsmid marched to the Home Office, Jewish communal leaders were embroiled in employment and housing issues surrounding East European Jews. The community was still reeling from W. T. Stead's white slavery exposés and accusations from nearly every segment of English society that the immigrants were causing unemployment, overcrowding, and the near-slavery of "sweated labor" in the garment industry. Inspired by studies of working conditions in the East End, angry English citizens accused immigrant Jewish employers of paying below-subsistence wages to their "greenhorn" co-religionists working in intolerable home or factory conditions. In this atmosphere, Lady Goldsmid persuaded the Jewish Board of Guardians to cooperate with the Women's Trade Union League's attempts to organize East End Jewish immigrant garment workers into trade unions.[3]

JEWISH IMMIGRANTS IN THE EAST END

The majority of immigrant Jews were particularly difficult to organize. Like their co-religionists on New York's Lower East Side, they were impelled by their persecution in Russia and their inability to speak English to minimize contact with the threatening Christian world by living and working within London's East End or similar ghettos in England's industrial northern cities. The newcomers relied upon a host of native Anglo-Jewish charitable services, ranging from the Rothschild housing complex to social service clubs and settlement houses.[4]

The prevalence of Yiddish-speaking employers among already settled German or Russian Jews, the familiarity of certain trades and the flexibility of working sites in homes and factories brought droves of Jewish immigrants into the clothing, boot- and shoemaking and furniture trades. By 1900, Jewish entrepreneurs and workers had refined the already established manufacture of ready-to-wear clothing, and Jewish workers quickly became the majority in such trades as coatmaking, vestmaking, and trousermaking. Jewish women and girls were employed as milliners and dressmakers; men were employed as tailors. Both men and women worked in the tobacco industry, but only men in the furniture trade. Other Jews were peddlers, glaziers, and suppliers to the Jewish community—bakers, butchers, and various religious functionaries.[5]

JEWISH WOMEN SWEATED WORKERS

Most immigrants worked in the "sweated" outwork system of the clothing trades. Under this system, a manufacturer would subcontract work to a small workshop or to individual "outworkers." The recently invented portable sewing machine made it possible for a semi-skilled laborer to work at home on pieces of cheap garments when supervision was unnecessary. The worker would then return the finished product to the manufacturer. Because employees were paid a very low wage by the piece rather than by the hour, they drove themselves to work twelve to fourteen hours each day in order to earn what amounted to a below-subsistence wage. Crowded into unsanitary tenement apartments or unsafe workshops, workers and small manufacturers alike sweated for long hours in virtual slavery and near-isolation.[6]

Women and children could work at home and were willing to accept lower wages than male workers. As a result, women soon dominated the sweated trades and production shifted steadily from South London centers to the bedrooms and kitchens of London's North and

East End neighborhoods. In 1901, women totaled 71 percent of all clothing workers. By 1911, employment among women in heavily Jewish districts such as Bethnal Green totaled 80 percent of those between the ages of fifteen and twenty-five. Jewish women worked as under-pressers, basting-hands or second tailors, machinists, finishers, buttonhole hands, and "plain hands." They worked on ladies' wear as well as gentlemen's coats and trousers as well as "the khaki" during World War I. It was not until after the war and the successes of the woman's movement that Jewish women moved into the formerly male, more highly paid, preserves of cutter, tailor, and presser.[7]

The largest number of both native English and immigrant Jewish female clothing workers were single women and widows. Minnie Szart was typical of the single women. Born in the Rothschild Buildings in 1893, she had left school at fourteen. She machined the lining into men's caps for five years but was forced to change trades during the strike of 1912. Finding a job in ladies' tailoring, Szart worked for an immigrant who ran a small shop with twelve workers making women's topcoats. Because she was a fast learner, her employer taught her basting, which brought her more money. Szart worked twelve hours a day, with an hour for dinner and half an hour for tea.[8] Like other single working girls, Jewish and non-Jewish, she had family responsibilities. Although Jewish single working-class girls enjoyed some independence, many lived with their parents to save money and contribute to the livelihood of siblings and parents.[9]

James Schmiechen argues that many female Jewish textile workers, especially those in the sweated outwork system, returned to work at some point during their marriage,[10] unlike women married to factory or shop workers in other trades.[11] In the heavily Jewish Hackney district of East London, 98 percent of outworkers were women, of whom 74 percent were married or widowed. Sixty-four percent of married women worked to augment their husbands' incomes. Schmiechen estimates that over 70 percent of widows in England's working-class neighborhoods were employed as outworkers in a variety of occupations. Widow Leah Katchinsky worked at different times for five employers. In addition to working as a home help for the Sick Room Helps Society, she took in washing, fur sewing, and "khaki" homework, and finished horse blankets by hand. After the war, she made dresses at home on a sewing machine she saved up to buy during the war.[12]

Sweated outworkers like Leah Katchinsky worked at home, as they had for centuries, reinforcing a traditional lifestyle and values. The only difference was that they now used a sewing machine for piecework instead of sewing an entire garment by hand.[13] Schmiechen suggests that because of these conditions, sweated women outworkers in England did not become truly modernized, but lived in a situation more similar to that of preindustrial women than historians have previously supposed.[14]

As a result, sweated women workers were especially reluctant to organize into unions. Their long hours, minimal wages, and the system of working at home generated a feeling of apathy toward politics in general and labor organizations in particular. The relatively few women who did become unionized were influenced by male unions and working women's organizations controlled by upper- and middle-class women.[15] The difficulties became apparent as the Women's Trade Union League attempted to organize women in the sweated trades.

MALE JEWISH UNIONS AND WOMEN

Male Jewish unions had been founded by East European immigrants in reaction to their exclusion by English tailors' unions, which feared Jewish business competition. The only exception was the London branch of the Amalgamated Society of Tailors, which had created an East End branch of Jewish tailors in the 1870s, hoping that unity would lead to higher wages.

Most Jewish unionists in England remained far more traditional and less inclined toward socialism and unionism than their counterparts in the United States, for several reasons. William Fishman suggests that one reason was their entrenched ghetto existence in England, maintained because Jews in London had a more clearly prescribed status than did their compatriots in major American cities. Moreover, except for Irish citizens working in England, Jews were the only significant immigrant minority in England, whereas in America they were one of many. Therefore, it was easier for them to become targets of the anti-alienist attitude held by both trade union leaders and the gentry.[16] In addition, the supervision of immigrant clubs and the Federation of Synagogues by the Anglo-Jewish establishment extended to unions as well, using these institutions to modify and Anglicize the immigrants' traditional Jewish lifestyle.[17]

Given these circumstances, the socialism many brought from Russia to the East End did little to change the mass of Jews. Although a nascent socialist Jewish trade union movement sponsored a few strikes in London, Leeds, and Manchester between 1880 and 1890, it never achieved real power. Most working-class Jewish immigrants who claimed to be socialists might pray three times a day, then hold a meeting to discuss unions and strikes. The socialism of Aaron Lieberman and his successor Morris Winchevsky was only successful when it suppressed its antireligious elements and appealed to the proletariat's need for a change in industrial conditions.[18]

Most Jewish trade unionists refused to bring women into the union. They resented women workers as rivals and insisted women belonged in the home.[19] Worse, many of them viewed women workers in the same way that Jews were viewed by Englishmen: as the source of the sweating system, because they were willing to work longer hours under worse conditions than unionized Englishmen or male Jews. Socialist Jewish working men not only opposed unionizing Jewish women, but also refused to accept them in radical governing councils despite official ideology. Therefore, Jewish working women bore the handicap of being both woman and Jew. They were resented as women by male Jewish workers and as both women and Jews by British workers. Both British and Jewish male workers blamed them for undercutting their wages. One male Jewish union organizer in Leeds complained:

> Until now you have been the right hand of the masters. Whenever the men have gone on strike, you have completed the partly finished work, and, because of this, many strikes have been lost. . . . you work for 8s0d, and the highest wages for a fellerhand are 21s0d a week.[20]

The majority of male Jewish and English trade unionists demanded that women withdraw or limit their work in industrialized occupations. However, a handful of male trade unionists gradually accepted the concept of equal pay for women, not as a principle of equal rights, but as a way to end undercutting by women workers.[21]

WOMEN'S TRADE UNION LEAGUE

The WTUL's 1884 study of sweatshop conditions, among others, impelled the Jewish Board of Guardians to ask its secretary, economist David Schloss, himself a former bootmaker, to undertake a Board survey of working conditions in East London. The report by the Board, combined with subsequent studies on sweating by government commissions and private organizations, persuaded Charles Booth to begin *Life and Labour in Britain*, his monumental study of poverty and labor in London. Connecting Jewish immigrants with sweated labor, Booth blamed Jewish employers for promoting "unsavory" Jewish practices in the sweated garment industry.[22]

Simultaneously, large numbers of native English workers protested against Jews in the sweated trades and other occupations, accusing them of stealing jobs from English laborers and creating the high unemployment that existed sporadically after the 1890s. In fact, fewer British workers suffered than contemporary publicity indicated.[23]

Responding to the pressure, a House of Lords investigation resulted in two contradictory reports. On the one hand, immigrants were commended as good citizens who were being unfairly blamed for working conditions that also existed outside of immigrant areas. On the other hand, several House of Lords committee reports declared that the growing numbers of aliens might make it necessary to restrict immigration.[24]

Concerned over the plight of sweated workers, the WTUL sought to attract middle-class Anglo-Jewish membership and support, as well as East European male union leaders and female garment workers whom it attempted to unionize. However, League members lacked sufficient time, education, or money to manage union affairs. The job of training was taken over by sympathetic men, some of whom, like David Schloss, were Jewish communal workers.[25]

Guided by Schloss and other organizers, in 1885 the WPPL founded the Pimlico Tailoresses' Union, with Jewish working women as members of its East End branch. The East London Tailoresses' Union, however, had more influence among immigrants. It had originally been organized in 1880 and 1881, when the WPPL paid a Miss Browne to organize a branch of the union in the Whitechapel district of the East End. By the mid-1880s it needed a stronger organizer, and David Schloss volunteered to serve as its treasurer for five years.[26]

Several Anglo-Jewish leaders supported the WTUL's expanding influence in the East End, since the trusted David Schloss guided the East London Tailoresses and the union itself was affiliated with the London branch of the "respectable" Amalgamated Society of Tailors. The AST was not socialist, but a welfare-oriented union that emphasized workers' independence and self-improvement through savings and educational programs and preferred peaceful negotiations with management to strikes. The union was one of the few to admit women in order to improve wages for all workers.

Because the East London Tailoresses was similarly welfare-oriented, both the WTUL and the new union were permitted to solicit membership among Jewish communal organizations such as the Westminster Jews' Free School.[27] Louise Lady Goldsmid mounted the East London Tailoresses' fund-raising effort, attracting contributions from notable Jewish leaders such as Reform theologian Claude G. Montefiore and earning the applause of the influential London *Jewish Chronicle*.[28]

WTUL's organizing among Jewish women was not confined to London. In 1885, the WTUL and the Leeds Jewish Branch of the Tailors' Society founded the Leeds Tailoresses' Society. Some LTS members also became union organizers. The results were visible in 1886, when a general strike of Leeds Jewish tailors brought out 1,700 women, apprentices, and young people in addition to the men. The strike fizzled out, however, and proved to be the last general strike of Leeds's Jewish tailors until 1911.[29]

THE WOMEN'S CAMPAIGN AGAINST SWEATED LABOR

Angered by hostility from the male unions, in 1886 the WTUL turned to the leadership of socialist and suffragist Lady Emilia Dilke, who encouraged the mass organization of lower-paid, less skilled workers.[30] Anglo-Jewish women quickly joined the WTUL's new leadership circle. Emily Routledge, half-sister of publisher Edward Routledge, held the position of league secretary for several years. May Abraham, secretary to Lady Dilke, became the organization's treasurer. After conducting a tour of working conditions in linen mills in 1891, Abraham and Routledge organized three unions of spinners, weavers, and warehouse workers. Miss Abraham organized the laundresses as well. In 1893, Abraham became one of England's first two female factory and workshop inspectors.[31]

In 1888, after the WTUL's match-makers' strike and its successors, Jewish women garment workers helped the League organize working-women's unions: the East End's Jewish Tailoresses' Union, the Society of Tailors and Tailoresses in Leeds, and the Cigarette-Makers' Union. In 1890 and 1891, the East London Tailoresses' Union organized English and Jewish women in the Spitalfields area of the East End. After undergoing the vicissitudes common to most unions during this period, in 1904 the Union became a branch of the London Tailors' and Tailoresses' Society.[32]

As economic conditions worsened, a few male Jewish organizers helped the WTUL to organize Jewish women, hoping to prevent them from undercutting men's wages. This achieved some success. By cooperating with the WTUL, the Leeds Tailoresses' Society became the Leeds Jewish Tailoresses' Union in 1896. The LJTU reached a membership of 200 members, large for an era when the number of organized women in the clothing industry totaled no more than 500.[33] Even male British locals were not much larger. In 1900, for example, approximately 1,252 English union locals cared for a membership of 1.9 million, an average of about 1,500 members per local. One hundred large unions organized over one million workers. The average membership for the remaining locals totaled 650 each; many had fewer than a hundred.[34]

Despite these figures, neither men's nor women's Jewish unions became successful during the 1890s. This was due to anti-alien sentiment combined with international dissension within the radical movement, which fragmented union organizers.[35] However, as East European Jews moved away from urban ghettos toward the suburbs, and it became more difficult for the Jewish communal leadership to mold the immigrants' thinking, they joined unions in larger numbers. World War I opened new opportunities for women in factories and shops, and allowed their entry into nursing and other professions. During and after the war, education and assimilation absorbed most radical Jewish women and men into British society and the lower-middle class. Even those who remained socialists were drawn into the English trade union movement.[36] This development encouraged more Jewish women in the suburbs and the East End alike to join unions, creating greater support for strikes and work stoppages.[37]

ANARCHISTS AND STRIKES

German anarchist Rudolf Rocker's Brenner Street Club was more successful than welfare-oriented unions in fomenting strikes of East End Jewish workers during the years between 1898 and 1914. The center for Jewish immigrant radicals' political and union activities, it was open to men and women above the age of sixteen:

> The Union has been started first of all to bring a brotherhood among toiling persons, young or old, male or female, so that it [sic] should henceforth be brothers and sisters.[38]

Brenner Street veterans Millie Sabel and "Red" Rose Robins marched in strikes with their colleagues, but they appear to have assumed traditional female roles within the Club such as cooking.[39] Their situation highlighted a critical dilemma facing turn-of-the-century socialist and anarchist feminists in every country: whether to seek equality for women and men without recognition of gender differences, or to campaign first for feminist goals and then work toward a genderless society. Both approaches involved important changes from the existing social order and both were utilized by feminists depending upon their generation or the countries in which they lived.

Perhaps mindful of the example set by the East European Bund, Jewish immigrant feminists in England decided not to risk cutting themselves off from the socialist mainstream and sought recognition

of women's rights within the context of achieving general equality
for all workers.[40] It may have seemed impossible to pit feminist goals
against the combined obstacles of England's class structure, socialist
ideology, and the relative isolation imposed by outwork, which reinforced traditional patterns.

Still, the Brenner Street Club paralyzed London in a series of massive strikes between 1906 and 1912. Inspired by Rudolf Rocker, thousands of East End women and men jammed the streets to protest
against abysmal wages and working conditions. Jews joined English
workers for the April 1912 strike, which dealt a severe blow to sweating and created a more cordial relationship between Jewish and British workers. Even after 1914, when Rocker was deported to Germany,
500 men and women struck at Schneider's Whitechapel clothing factory in October 1916. Similar strikes were held by East End men and
women throughout the war.[41]

Like their counterparts in New York, even traditional immigrant
housewives joined the protests at the neighborhood level. When the
men went on strike, mass meetings of East End women publicly
pledged support of their menfolk until the strike ended favorably. In
March 1904, when the Jewish Bakers' Union went out on strike,
Jewish women bought only bread and produce with the union label.
Grocers were left holding so much unsold bread they switched to
union-based suppliers. As a result, the masters conceded the union's
demands.[42] This type of neighborhood action exemplifies grass-roots
strike support by Jewish housewives, which occurred sporadically in
Eastern Europe and America as well as England.[43]

JEWISH FEMINISTS AND UNIONS

Only a handful of Jewish working-class women became regular union
activists before World War I, despite participation by larger numbers
of Jewish women in occasional strikes. The few durable unions of
women in the clothing trades were either assisted by men's unions
or, like the Pimlico union, emerged out of a factory system in which
women worked together. Moreover, even when women attempted to
organize, low wages made union membership nearly impossible and
made a women's union financially precarious. The East End Tailoresses' Union finally failed because the women could not afford
membership. It was not until the 1930s that Sarah Wesker led the
East End's trouser-makers in their memorable strikes.[44]

Moreover, like their non-Jewish counterparts, Jewish working
women rejected the middle-class feminist movement because the
gentlewomen did not understand and always attempted to control

them. The same pattern predominated in the East End girls' clubs and working-women's organizations. Despite their sporadic membership in tailoresses' unions, therefore, the majority of working-class Jewish women in England avoided unions and the feminist movement. Ironically, doing so did not help East End residents avoid the grasp of the gentry. Even more than other women workers, they were forced by isolation and lack of unity to rely for help upon middle- and upper-class women concerned with social service and social reform.[45] As a result, Jewish immigrant women workers gained even less of a voice in the trade union and feminist movements than their Gentile or male Jewish counterparts.[46]

PROTECTIONIST LEGISLATION

Therefore, by the 1890s, the WTUL turned to protectionist legislation for sweated women. In the process, it attracted a larger group of influential upper- and middle-class Anglo-Jewish women. Mrs. Herbert Samuel, wife of the postmaster general, and WTUL union organizer May Abraham, now Mrs. H. J. Tennant, among others, supported the WTUL's famous 1906 Sweated Industries Exhibition at Langham Place, helped create the National Anti-Sweating League, and successfully lobbied for passage of the Trades Bill, which outlawed sweating and supported a minimum wage against the opposition of the Board of Jewish Deputies. Even Jewish immigrant women supported the Trades Board Bill, bitterly opposing the Board of Deputies' claim to speak on their behalf.[47]

Through the campaign for protectionist laws, upper-class Anglo-Jewish WTUL members secured a new foothold in the politically active English feminist movement. By the eve of World War I, a small but vocal group of Anglo-Jewish WTUL members had played an important role in the WTUL's campaign for protectionist legislation for women workers. They also contributed toward founding some short-lived unions, several strikes, and one strong and lasting tailoresses' union.[48] These Anglo-Jewish WTUL members also had gained experience in political organizing, lobbying, marches, and demonstrations. They had earned their first taste of national political power when Parliament approved the Trades Bill. Above all, they perceived themselves and were viewed by growing numbers of Christian feminists as Englishwomen who were, like themselves, dedicated to achieving social reforms.

UNITED STATES

The Jewish women's movement in the United States entered a new phase when a core group of socialist East European immigrant women

banded together into unions and joined middle-class-dominated feminist organizations. The female East European union organizers' alliance with their German-Jewish and Christian "sisters" in the
Consumers' League and Women's Trade Union League ultimately
brought a small but influential core of immigrant women into the
National Woman's Suffrage Association. This coalition not only
achieved limited welfare legislation for women and children, but also
contributed to the gradual erosion of class and religious barriers in
the United States.[49]

IMMIGRANT WOMEN'S REBELLION

The majority of East European Jewish immigrants crowded into factories and tenement apartments on New York's Lower East Side and
similar urban ghettos along the East Coast. Since it was impossible
for most immigrant men to earn a decent wage, wives worked at home
in traditional female *shtetl* occupations: taking in boarders and laundry, or selling goods at market. When scholar Henry Warshavsky became blind, his wife Miriam Elizabeth (Lizzie) opened a store to
support him and their three children.[50]

As noted earlier, some immigrant wives lost their families altogether. Unable to bear their "greenhorn" status, bitter poverty, and
many children or siblings, some husbands deserted their wives and
children ran away from their parents.[51]

Immigrant daughters particularly resented their inferior status in
religious life, confinement to household tasks, and second-class status
in relation to their fathers and brothers. During the holiday of Suc-
coth, author Bella Chagall and her mother waited on her father and
brothers in the *sukkah*, but the women ate alone inside the cold apartment. Bella asked her mother, " 'Why do [the men] eat apart from
us?' " " 'Ah, my little child, they're men,' says mother, sadly, as she
eats her piece of cold meat.' "[52]

Emily Solis-Cohen, a pioneer advocate of family and social plan-
ning, served as a field worker for women's activities at the Jewish
Welfare Board and counseled girls at the Young Women's Hebrew Association (YWHA). Her attempts to teach Jewish values to immigrant
girls were constantly undermined by the behavior of rabbis and Jewish
communal leaders. Relegated to the synagogue gallery, single Jewish
working-girls were often unable to afford synagogue membership and
were turned away from congregational forums. To combat their isolation from Judaism, Solis-Cohen helped a group of girls found a Jewish history study circle. A rabbi met with the group for only three
meetings and then refused to teach them, claiming it was "a waste
of his time." Under these conditions, immigrant girls found no reason

to attend synagogue. "Why should we? What's there in synagogue for us? We're girls."

Denigrated by rabbis and male Jewish communal workers, embittered by poverty and tension at home, female Jewish factory workers rarely joined any Jewish organization and often rejected formal Jewish affiliation altogether. Jewish immigrant girls worked on the Sabbath, ate non-kosher food, and searched for other ways to give meaning to their lives.

> Girls do not count in Jewish life. What does it matter about us? It's the boys they educate first. . . . Judaism doesn't think much of women.[53]

Chafing at the restrictions of home, religion, and community, many Jewish immigrant girls eagerly turned to the socialist ideas they discovered in the garment factories and ghetto streets. Jewish union women were filled with rising expectations, seeking to turn America into the utopian *goldene medina* they envisioned in their Eastern European *shtetls*.

In a study that included fifteen Jewish women out of a total of thirty-two female radicals, Gerald Sorin found that over 90 percent of the Jewish radicals remained immersed in Jewish tradition and culture. They lived within the tradition-oriented network of Jewish homes, self-help groups, synagogues, and/or workmen's circles, and they sent their children to socialist or communist children's camps, schools, and societies. This framework provided an outlet for their idealism and desire for independence. These women affirmed their Jewish heritage by operating within a predominantly Yiddish-speaking constituency. Whether Socialist or traditionalist, their Jewish neighbors understood, if not sympathized with, their class consciousness, well-developed ethic of social justice, and the terms within which they couched the labor and political conflict.[54]

Even radical Jewish women's forms of rebellion were grounded in Jewish experience. Parents of future labor organizers like Fania Cohn used one *shtetl* tradition—education—to overcome another disability—being a woman. As a result, Cohn developed a concept of herself as a capable woman, which fostered her desire for independence.[55]

Radically inclined immigrant daughters could also find role models in the housewives who initiated several successful riots in 1902 against the high price of kosher meat[56] on New York City's Lower East Side. Paula Hyman notes that, historically, Jewish communities traditionally condoned Jewish women's participation in public protests when they were not directly related to issues involving Jewish law. Furthermore, the Jewish community had accepted Jewish women's involvement in the Jewish socialist labor and Zionist movements in Russia.[57] America's emphasis upon individual freedom reinforced the heritage of public activism by Eastern European women.

Hyman's study of several boycotts indicates that East European women expressed their political concerns and their confidence in their own abilities within the neighborhood, in contrast to the men. As Mrs. Levy, a cloakmaker's wife, shouted during the 1902 boycott: "... if *we women* make a strike, then it will be a strike." Women participating in the 1904 and 1907–08 rent strikes on the Lower East Side used similar tactics, protesting the rising cost of wholesale meat prices during neighborhood meetings. Still, even though these boycotts reduced food prices, it is difficult to assess their long-term impact. These events were brief episodes, with no direct continuation of leadership. Nevertheless, Hyman believes that they were significant because the boycotters' political awareness was communicated to younger sisters and daughters, influencing the later garment industry strikes.[58]

TRADE UNION WOMEN

Thousands of immigrant Jewish women and men in the United States worked in the garment industry, as they did in England. In America, unlike England, however, the majority of workers were employed in factories, where they were exposed to the new ideas of the secular world. Immigrants often found employment with successful German-Jewish factory owners. Although many bosses were generous to their employees, some also maintained sweatshop conditions.[59]

By the 1890s, female immigrant Jewish organizers were attempting to change this system, allying themselves with colleagues of the same class and ethnic origin.[60] Like their male Jewish counterparts, some Jewish women had been socialists or anarchists in Eastern Europe, but others turned to radicalism as a result of their experiences in America.

Pauline Newman worked at the Triangle Waist Company from 1901 until 1909. She suffered through low pay, eleven-hour days, and an eighty-hour work week sewing by the light of gas jets. In winter, only a potbellied stove heated the entire factory, and in summer, workers suffocated in rooms with closed windows and no air shafts to provide ventilation. A member of the New York Socialist Party's Women's Committee, Newman fought against these conditions as a trade union organizer and feminist leader.[61]

Radicalized immigrant women like Newman were initially drawn to male-run Jewish unions. Like their counterparts in England, Jewish

A sweatshop, Boston. Courtesy, American Jewish Historical Society

unions were founded because American craft unions rejected Jewish members, fearing that Jewish competition and long hours of work would undercut native workers.[62] Samuel Gompers (1850–1924), a Jewish emigré from London who opposed socialism and further immigration, co-founded the American Federation of Labor, approximately one-third of whose members were socialists.

Under Gompers's direction, the AFL focused on improving working conditions for its employees. The AFL claimed to defend the rights of women in the labor force, but resolutions confining women to the home continued to be debated until 1914 and many locals refused to admit women.[63] President Robert Glackling of New York's bookbinders' union even acknowledged that fact.

Like its counterparts in England, the AFL regarded women as it did unskilled labor in general: as competitors who lowered the wage scale and were unfit for organization. Nevertheless, when the anti-sweatshop campaigns began in 1891, Gompers supported the women who organized the Federal Ladies' (now Women's) Union No. 2703. In 1892, Gompers hired the first female general organizer for the AFL. The union leadership forced him to fire her, however, and rebuffed his later attempts to hire other women organizers.[64]

At the same time, Jewish socialist unions were formed that ultimately joined larger unions such as the International Ladies Garment

Workers' Union (ILGWU) or the AFL. However, schisms between radicals and moderates and skilled and unskilled workers haunted the
labor movement throughout its history.[65]

SOCIALIST WOMEN

Jewish women totaled at least one-quarter of all unionized American
women, and female Jewish garment workers joined the union in
greater numbers than their proportion in the industry as a whole. The
majority were members of the Socialist Party of America. Although
the Socialist Party was the first political party to recognize women's
rights and perceive women as an exploited class, equal rights for
women was not a Party priority. Party ideologists contended that
women would achieve equality only when rights were won for the
working class as a whole.[66]

Moreover, radical men regarded single women union organizers as
failures because they lacked emotional and sexual relationships with
men. Indeed, single women lived an isolated existence, in part because they avoided marriage as a threat to their independence. Pauline
Newman, the first woman organizer for the ILGWU, wrote to Rose
Schneiderman that "my life, and way of living is *very interesting*—
it is at the same time a very lonely life."[67]

Still, men never made the same emotional and sexual sacrifices
they demanded from union women. Although socialist men criticized
marriage as a failed bourgeois institution, most of them lived very
conventional married lives. These men insisted that their wives maintain home and children in a traditional manner, so that they would
be free to be politically active. A small minority of Jewish women
attempted to combine home and work outside the home in factories
and businesses: in 1880, 2 percent of Eastern European immigrant
women returned to work after marriage. By 1905, this figure had
dropped to 1 percent. The lack of birth control and their husbands'
demands for supportive wives made it nearly impossible for married
women to work.[68]

A few radical women attempted to combine marriage and career.
Twenty-four of thirty-two women in Gerald Sorin's study were married, and most continued to work, often in their homes.[69] However,
the Socialist Party condemned their tasks of housework and child-
rearing as "valueless" non-wage labor, and discounted the importance
of work done at home, or anywhere else except the factory. The Party
even refused to publish articles by several female Jewish radical authors that did not focus upon the value of factory labor.[70]

Because separation from men remained the only alternative for women desiring to remain in the Party, radical Jewish and non-Jewish housewives and professional women organized women's branches of the Party, while working women created female union locals, which often left them isolated and angry. "The men are afraid of the women," remarked one socialist feminist worker; "They are afraid the women will outvote them." Struggling to organize the Triangle shirtwaist factory, Pauline Newman received little assistance from male union leadership. Her efforts were primarily funded by women's locals affiliated with the AFL and ILGWU's Local 25.[71]

The ILGWU, a minority voice within the AFL, became one of the major financial supporters of the Socialist Party, and East European Jewish women provided much of the leadership for both the ILGWU and independent women's unions. A relatively powerful union by 1904, the ILGWU welcomed women organizers in the hope they would draw women into union activity and raise wages for all workers. By 1907, the ILGWU had precipitated a successful strike in the children's cloak industry, and by 1909 it began agitation against women's waist manufacturers.[72]

It was almost impossible to balance socialism and feminism. Theresa Serber Malkiel (1874–1949) believed that "the future of the world is in the workingmen's hands, and the working woman must learn to share the burden of her brothers."[73] Even so, she realized that only an autonomous institution could adequately represent socialist women, and thus in 1892 she founded the Woman's Infant Cloak Maker's Union. She also organized the Women's Progressive Society of Yonkers, later Branch No. 1 of the Socialist Women's Society of New York, to serve as a propaganda and educational outlet for socialist women. Malkiel envisioned her women's movement as a "preparatory school" that would draw women into the Socialist Party.[74]

Within the Party, Malkiel engaged as a member of its Women's Committee in campaigns for unionization of women workers, relief of the plight of foreign-born women, woman's suffrage, and the Party's commitment to sexual equality. She also pioneered methods to organize tenement women through informal networks of personal contacts. Despite her efforts, Malkiel's consistent prodding failed to convince the Socialist Party to wholeheartedly support woman's suffrage.

Despite these tensions, the common background, radical convictions, and feminist concerns of a core group of female Jewish unionists propelled them toward militant action on behalf of immigrant women. As Hutchins Hapgood discovered, the ghetto's union women were "willing to lay down their lives for an idea, or to live for one."[75]

THE GARMENT WORKERS' STRIKES

The "uprising of the twenty thousand" in 1909 galvanized the city of New York and stimulated a reexamination of unionism and social reform in America. The strike was triggered by the unbearable working conditions in the Triangle Waist Company and the Leiserson shop and spearheaded by the shirtwaist makers from Local 25 of the ILGWU. Sixty-five percent of the waist makers were Jewish; the rest included Italian, Polish, German, and other English-speaking immigrants as well as native-born Americans. Six members of Local 25's executive committee and two members of the Local's "committee of five," which organized the strike, were Jewish women.[76]

Thousands of people milled around inside Cooper Union and other New York City halls on November 22, harangued for two hours by social reformers and union leaders. Then Clara Lemlich, "a wisp of a girl, still in her teens," recalls Louis Levine, demanded the right to speak. A striker from the Leiserson shop and a member of Local 25's executive committee, she jumped onto the platform, exhorting the crowd with her "philippic in Yiddish":

> I am a working girl, one of those who are on strike against intolerable conditions. I am tired of listening to speakers talk in general terms. What we are here for is to decide whether we shall or shall not strike. I offer a resolution that a general strike be declared—now.

Instantly the gathering was on its feet, shouting and waving hats, canes, handkerchiefs. Carried away by the emotional outburst, the chairman of the meeting cried:

> "Do you mean faith? Will you take the old Jewish oath?" And up came two thousand hands, with the prayer: "If I turn traitor to the cause I now pledge, may this hand wither from the arm I now raise."[77]

The general strike that followed closed over five hundred shops throughout New York City and its boroughs for nearly a year. Fifteen thousand waist- and dressmakers walked out, precipitating a series of strikes that spotlighted the city's greatest industry. As the strike spread to other locals, sympathetic allies from the New York's Women's Trade Union League (WTUL) rallied to support the strikers and were arrested for marching on the picket lines. Strikers from the factories were arrested along with Jewish Socialist Party members Rose Pastor Stokes and Theresa Malkiel, suffrage and settlement house leaders including Lillian Wald, and Women's Trade Union League members. The arrest of dozens of workers alongside some of the city's leading social reformers made newspaper headlines around the country.[78]

Immigrant Clara Lemlich "lost everything in the struggle." Dedicating herself to the strike, Lemlich abandoned without complaint her plans for obtaining an education and a better job. Fannie Zincher had been saving for years so that she could study dentistry. While working, she took a night course in dentistry and passed the regents' examination. She gave up her hopes of a career to support the strike, believing that "only through organization could the girls get better conditions."[79]

The strike demonstrated publicly the cross-class feminist commitment between factory workers and their middle-class allies. Rose Schneiderman, Pauline Newman, and other socialist women had turned to the Women's Trade Union League out of frustration at the socialists' and unionists' lack of commitment to women.

Schneiderman, an organizer for the ILGWU and the WTUL, had begun her career as a young factory worker who organized the first women's local of the United Cloth Hat and Cap Makers' Union in 1903. Joyfully discovering as an organizer that she was "not lonely anymore," Schneiderman rejected her mother's warning that such activities were unfit for women. In 1904, she became the first trade union woman elected to the General Executive Board of the Union. Her membership in both the Socialist Party and the Manhattan Liberal Club furthered a political career that eventually led her to become President Franklin D. Roosevelt's only woman appointee to the Labor Advisory Board of the National Recovery Act.[80]

During the 1909 strike, Schneiderman organized women from the Leiserson shop and set up the picket lines. She worked almost continuously, convincing other unions to join the strike in sympathy with their colleagues.[81]

Twenty thousand waistmakers left their jobs in the first great walkout of women in American history. The strike's female leadership and cross-class alliance heralded a new tactic in the history of women's unionism, inspiring a new cooperation between feminists and workers.[82]

Labor historian Louis Lorwin credits the strike with laying the foundations of unionism in the dress and waist trade. Local 25's membership increased to over 10,000 members in 1909 alone, creating the first large-scale union local to wield unity into a successful political tool. The Jewish community learned the importance of unity as a bargaining mechanism, a lesson that would be used by United Hebrew Trades organizers, the Yiddish press, and social reformers such as Stephen S. Wise and Lillian Wald. Above all, the strike spawned a wave of successors that lasted through 1912 and resulted in concessions by manufacturers and the passage of factory legislation in Albany and Washington.[83]

The men were stung by the waistmakers' success, recalled Pauline Newman. Humiliated, they declared, "If girls can do it, why can't we?" The male cloakmakers followed the women's example, and a series of strikes by women and men continued from 1909 through 1913 within New York's garment industry. These strikes not only fundamentally altered unionism and labor relations, they pushed America toward an era of major social reform.[84]

THE AFTERMATH

Caught up in a spiral of strikes, employers and strikers negotiated the landmark 1910 "Protocol of Peace." Management agreed to give hiring preference to union men at specified wage scales and created boards for arbitration and grievances. Moreover, the Protocol ensured that men would receive the highest-paid jobs, thereby formalizing discrimination against women through a sexual division of labor in the garment industry. Indeed, the lowest-paid male would earn more than the highest-paid female. The unions not only agreed to these terms, but initiated them, despite the fact that women had led the strikes leading to the Protocol.[85] Moreover, despite the efforts of Lillian Wald and other negotiators, management forced workers to compromise on enforcement of strong safety and health regulations, with disastrous results.

On March 25, 1911, approximately five hundred young, predominantly Jewish women were working inside the Triangle Waist factory's wooden building when the upper floors caught fire. The factory's doors had been locked to keep employees from taking breaks during the long workday. Sadie Hershey and her friends

> all ran to the [other] door and the door was locked. . . . There were two elevators there and nobody can use them. . . . One girl said to me, "Sadie, let's go and jump down from the window." I said, "Marie, don't jump. Brown [the machinist] will come and he'll open the door." . . . I don't remember how she disappeared. Brown opened the door and we all ran out. . . . I came downstairs and I see that girl's body on the floor, in the gutter. And so many people on the floor. It was just like garbage. They threw one on top of the other.[86]

One hundred forty-six people died in the Triangle fire, setting off a wave of indignation throughout the country. Jewish women were well represented among the Women's Trade Union League and union organizers who spearheaded a social reform campaign that compelled the New York legislature to enact the first comprehensive legislation in America concerning labor, safety, and working conditions.[87]

In the wake of the Triangle Waist fire and continuing strikes, the Dress and Waist Manufacturers Association hired a new labor arbitrator, social worker Belle Moskowitz (1877–1933), to ensure that the terms of the Protocol would be carried out in the shops. Moskowitz had a distinguished reputation as a social worker for the Educational Alliance, New York's premier Jewish settlement house, and as a volunteer with the National Council of Jewish Women.[88] Since Manufacturers Association leaders reneged on terms and blocked her efforts to enforce the Protocol, however, Moskowitz eventually resigned in protest, effectively ending implementation of the Protocol of Peace.[89]

In 1918, Moskowitz abandoned social work to become Al Smith's confidential adviser and political strategist, bringing her industry and labor experience to government and politics. She wielded "more political power than any other woman in the United States," according to the New York Times. She was also the first Jewish woman in America to hold an important political post. Elizabeth Israels Perry, Moskowitz's granddaughter and biographer, notes that Moskowitz was "the only woman of her time to achieve political power without holding office, inheriting wealth, or moving up through a husband's career."[90]

ALLIED REFORMERS

The Consumers' League's campaign to end child labor and the exploitation of working women "aroused the public conscience."[91] It became the first national women's social reform organization to attract both "uptown" Jewish women such as President Maud Nathan and the Goldmark sisters, and East European immigrants such as Rose Schneiderman and Clara Lemlich.[92]

Pauline and Josephine Goldmark directed the fight for protective legislation for women, through lobbying, writing journal articles, and assisting Louis Brandeis in preparing the legal briefs for successful landmark cases in support of welfare legislation.[93] Proudly boasting that "the labor laws are a means toward industrial equality for women,"[94] immigrants such as Maud Schwartz and wealthy German-Jewish matrons such as Mrs. Jacob Schiff preached the League's message in synagogues, NCJW meetings, Jewish settlement houses, and the Jewish Ethical Culture Society.[95]

The Consumers' League's concept of protective legislation posed a problem for many feminists, who felt it reinforced the view of women as naturally dependent and unequal in competition with men. Two wings of the radical movement epitomized the opposition: the uncompromising East European Jewish anarchist and feminist Emma Goldman,[96] and the militant suffragist National Woman's Party (NWP). Carrying the feminist argument to its logical conclusion, they insisted that by discriminating against women, protective legislation would perpetuate women's inferior status.[97]

The Consumers' League not only made major contributions to formulating protective legislation to protect working women, but its working class and middle-class members also attempted to develop a multi-ethnic and cross-class approach to political social reform campaigns. This latter effort never really succeeded, however. Middle- and upper-class women continued to control the League's policies. Although they sympathized with trade union strikes, they did not really understand the issues. Nevertheless, the League's emphasis upon welfare legislation, its mixture of religions and classes, and the prominence of Jewish leadership provided a stepping-stone for more significant feminist action.

THE WOMEN'S TRADE UNION LEAGUE

The Women's Trade Union League of New York (WTUL) became the first organization to grapple with the problems of women in industry on a nationwide basis. Drawing women from all classes into its ranks, the League supported strikes, attempted to integrate women into unions, and promoted state and federal legislation benefiting workers.[98] Nancy Schrom Dye's meticulous study of the League elucidates the manner in which WTUL members considered themselves both feminists and trade unionists.

> As unionists, they worked to integrate women into the mainstream of the early twentieth-century labor movement. As feminists, they sought to create an egalitarian alliance of working-class and upper-class women and to make the early twentieth-century woman movement relevant to working women's concerns.[99]

The League attracted upper-class women reformers, known as "allies," as well as Socialist women who resented the way male Socialist Party and labor union leaders condescended to and neglected women. Rose Schneiderman explained that

> We were doing exactly the same work as the men . . . but our wages were much smaller and our hours much longer. On Saturdays, when the men had but a half day of work, we were obliged to stay all day. Every

time an increase in wages would be given the men, our wages were cut accordingly.

Schneiderman and other immigrant Jewish women were attracted by the WTUL's promise of mutual support through sisterhood and power through feminist collective action. Attaining these goals was reinforced by close ties with Lillian Wald's circle and cross-class personal friendships such as that between Rose Schneiderman, Mary Dreier, and Leonora O'Reilly. By the eve of World War I, working-class women such as Rose Schneiderman, Clara Lemlich, and Theresa Malkiel were assuming leadership positions within the organization.[100] Schneiderman so offended one male socialist leader that he accused her of being a traitor to the socialist cause because she put feminism ahead of socialism.[101]

Still, wealthy, well-educated women such as Ida Rauh dominated League policies until the war, often insensitive to League members who were Jewish or socialist. Despite protests from Jewish members, for example, WTUL leadership scheduled one citywide conference of working women on Yom Kippur. In stereotypical fashion, WTUL literature described Jewish women as "dark-eyed," "studious," and "revolutionary."[102]

Despite these attitudes, the New York WTUL founded several women's unions and introduced thousands of Jewish women garment workers to the labor movement. Particularly active within the garment industry where Jews predominated, the League played a central role in supporting Jewish women strikers during the 1909–13 garment workers strikes as well as backing women workers' demands in the 1913 Protocol of Peace.

Pauline Newman recalls that, in 1913, the WTUL was "practically in charge" of the underwear workers' strike. Marching columns of plainly clad Jewish teen-age girls marshaled by the WTUL paraded in the Lower East Side streets during the fateful October of 1909. The League helped to organize several ILGWU locals and to place the national union on a stable financial footing. When the strike was over, the WTUL paid for a bookkeeper to establish a financial system in Local 25.[103] Simultaneously, the WTUL maintained strong ties with the Jewish community and with other parts of the Jewish labor movement, including the ILGWU and the United Hebrew Trades.

The 1909 shirtwaist strike seemed to prove Jewish women's readiness for unionization. The WTUL praised Jewish women's militancy in labor organizing and their interest in economic conditions. During the strike years, when trade unions gave women few opportunities for leadership, the WTUL trained working women as organizers and business agents.[104]

Among the WTUL's dozens of immigrant Jewish members, Rose Schneiderman, Pauline Newman, Clara Lemlich, and Bessie Abramovitz stood out as League union and suffrage organizers. Rose Schneiderman, who joined the League in 1905, was the WTUL's strike representative from 1909 to 1913, advising strike committees and organizing support from other unions, the Consumers' League and other women's organizations, the general public, and the press. Schneiderman later became the first immigrant vice-president of the WTUL.[105]

Pauline Newman joined the League during the 1909 strike, marching with other WTUL organizers on the picket line, helping the girls, and choosing speakers. After the strike, Newman served as a League organizer in East Side neighborhoods and helped establish a WTUL branch in Philadelphia. She believed she was the only woman on the road as a union organizer at that time. Newman also worked as a sanitary inspector and organizer for the ILGWU and as a Socialist Party speaker. In 1918, she ran for Congress on the Socialist Party ticket.[106]

The WTUL's support of the strikes proved that upper-class, middle-class, and working women could unite in a politically effective alliance to deal with women's industrial concerns. Moreover, by admitting significant membership and limited leadership by immigrant as well as wealthy Jewish women, the League represented a turning point in the feminist movement. As we shall see, the presence of large numbers of experienced Jewish women unionists provided one wing of a new Jewish power base for the final phase of the American suffrage movement.

Despite some success, organizing Lower East Side women was so difficult even at the height of the garment workers' strikes, that in 1910, Rose Schneiderman asked for a special "Jewish Committee" to assist her efforts. The Committee proved temporarily effective, but it dissolved after the strikes. In the years following, the waistmakers' union steadily lost membership as manufacturers and unions agreed to lower wages for women. Disillusioned, few women challenged the union's male leadership, and Rose Schneiderman recounted progressively more serious difficulties in recruiting Jewish women for organizational work.[107]

As a result, notes Nancy Schrom Dye, WTUL members began to reassess their opinions of Jewish immigrant women who lost interest in unions that did not give them significant concessions. Tensions increased as native-born American working women resented Jewish domination of the ILGWU and union meetings conducted in Yiddish. Strained relations between the WTUL and the ILGWU further compounded the difficulties. By 1912, the WTUL shifted its organizing emphasis away from the Lower East Side and toward native-born American women. It even hired a proponent of immigration restriction to head the drive.

The League's Jewish members were infuriated. Rose Schneiderman resigned as East Side organizer. Lillian Wald resigned about the same time, although it is unclear whether this tension or her connection with the Lawrence millworkers' strike was responsible. During the 1914 contest for the WTUL's presidency, Schneiderman lost to a non-Jewish woman by four votes. Newman concluded that Schneiderman lost because she was a socialist, a Jew, and a suffragist in an organization divided between middle-class "social workers' and working-class "trade unionists."[108]

In reaction to the election, Rose Schneiderman, Clara Lemlich, and Pauline Newman temporarily left the League to work as ILGWU organizers. However, the sexism within the union was so rampant that it drove them back to the WTUL.[109]

In 1913, male labor leaders agreed to enforce the Protocol establishing inequity for women in the workplace. In despair, the WTUL shifted its stand away from unionism and toward campaigns for suffrage and protectionist legislation in order to help working women. Although by then Clara Lemlich had permanently resigned from the League, a few Jewish women remained, and they eventually overcame anti-Jewish sentiment to become WTUL leaders. Rose Schneiderman, noted for her suffrage work in both the WTUL and NAWSA, served as WTUL president from 1918 until 1949.[110]

Although the WTUL garnered more significant accomplishments in union organizing and strike support than its English counterpart, it failed to persuade unions to grant equal wages to women workers. The League was far more successful when it concentrated on feminist goals. As in England, the WTUL's alliances with the Consumers' League and other reformist organizations spurred the passage of protectionist legislation, and its coalition with suffrage groups helped to win the franchise for women.

Although immigrant Jewish women's experience in the WTUL had been mixed, they had received considerable support during the strike era, as well as a high level of organizational and political training and some leadership opportunities. The WTUL also facilitated the first serious interaction between Christian and Jewish women of all classes in any labor movement organization. Even the Consumers' League did not make such a strong attempt to bring immigrant women into leadership positions. The League also became a stepping-stone toward leadership in the suffrage movement for Rose Schneiderman, Clara Lemlich, and other Jewish working women.

At the same time, the deterioration of relations with Jewish working women demonstrated the League's difficulties in transcending differences of ethnicity, class, and political orientation. Immigrants' experiences in the WTUL intensified their consciousness of class and religious distinctions. The 1914 vote for the presidency reinforced East European women's awareness that their identity as Jews remained a liability within, as well as outside, the feminist movement, despite all the talk of "sisterhood." That knowledge strengthened their cultural self-identity, maintaining the Jewish prism through which they continued to view the feminist struggle, even as they participated in it.

CONCLUSION

Feminist trade union organizing and efforts toward protectionist legislation varied considerably in England and the United States, as did the position of Jews within those campaigns. Jewish women's ability to become accepted within the feminist trade union undertaking determined their influence not only within the feminist movement, but within the Jewish community as well.

In the United States, Jewish women reformers joined their non-Jewish colleagues in creating a cross-class and multi-ethnic feminist alliance that achieved some limited success. The garment strikes, with their extensive Jewish immigrant participation and support by middle-class allies, refocused social reform in the United States and helped to alter many Americans' picture of immigrants and Jews.

The membership of middle-class American Jewish women in the WTUL and the Consumer's League drew them into closer interaction with immigrants than ever before. One result was to provide an atmosphere in which a handful of immigrant Jewish women were drawn into leadership positions in these feminist organizations. Still, the vast majority of East European women remained merely part of the rank-and-file on the membership rolls of the WTUL and Consumers' League.

The strikes and the subsequent drive for protective legislation also helped to reshape American Jewish social policy. Middle-class women gained a degree of communal influence because of their prominence in the strikes, the Consumers' League, and the WTUL. The visibility of immigrant women activists in the meeting halls and strike demonstrations of the Lower East Side indicated a major change in the role of working women within the Jewish community. As communal social workers focused ever more intensively on the needs of immigrant women and children, selected East European Jewish women noticeably influenced Jewish social welfare policy decisions for the first time.

Women's union organizing and social reform campaigns proved insufficient in the face of opposition from male-run union, liquor, business, and industrial interests. As a result, strikes and welfare legislation campaigns radicalized many middle-class Jewish as well as non-Jewish women, turning them from social feminists into suffragists. Like their Christian peers, Jewish feminists viewed the franchise as the only means of achieving equality for themselves and social reforms for working women.[111]

Although thousands of American Jewish women engaged in the campaigns to organize women and to generate protective legislation, these activities were not specifically Jewish even though participants functioned within a local Jewish network. However, female Jewish social reformers and union leaders like the Goldmark sisters and Rose Schneiderman gained sufficient national distinction during this process that they raised Jewish women's prestige within the Jewish community. As we shall see, this enabled female Jewish activists to be strategically positioned to demand a new level of religious and communal reforms for women.

The situation in England was considerably different. A small core of Anglo-Jewish women joined the WTUL's trade union organizing effort. Like their non-Jewish counterparts, only a handful of Jewish women actively supported striking unionists. Anglo-Jewish women, as cautious as their male co-religionists and many non-Jewish social reformers, were unwilling to support socialist unions although they helped their welfare-oriented counterparts.

After the WTUL shifted toward obtaining protectionist legislation for women, a much larger group of Jewish women, like their non-Jewish peers, played a significant role in the League's legislative campaign. Defending the weak reinforced Anglo-Jewish as well as secular English feminism. Jewish women's visibility in WTUL's crusade expanded their stature within organized English feminism and laid the groundwork for their participation in the suffrage movement.

Unlike the American WTUL, however, England's League fostered little real cross-class cooperation before World War I, bringing few East European women into visibility within the organization. Although a few immigrant women's unions were organized in London and Leeds, the majority were short-lived ventures. Relatively few East European women participated in strikes, and even fewer joined the WTUL or other organizations within the feminist movement, feeling that middle-class women could not understand, let alone really improve, their lives.

Immigrant Jewish women's isolation within the sweated industry's system of outwork facilitated their traditionalism and conservatism. Coming from Eastern Europe, with its virulently anti-Semitic atmosphere, the newcomers also felt physically and emotionally threatened by the more moderate social anti-Semitism of their English neighbors and working-class competitors. Jewish immigrants in the United States, exposed to the secular factory world, were certainly reminded frequently of anti-Semitism in schools and workplace, but felt less harassed, as they lived in a country accustomed to a variety of immigrants and which prided itself on separation of church and state.

Whether they were religiously or culturally identified as Jewish, proud of being Jewish or fearful of anti-Semitism, the nature of Jewish women's participation in the English or American secular feminist movement was governed to a great degree by the way in which they saw themselves and perceived their obligations as Jews. Bound together as Jews and as women, they struggled to identify their place as *Jewish* women within a feminist movement that was not always hospitable, precisely because they were Jewish. As we shall see, the question of the identity of Jewish womanhood would finally become resolved as Jewish women joined the "votes for women" crusade.

6

"Votes for Women"

ENGLAND

THE JEWISH LEAGUE FOR WOMAN SUFFRAGE

> *May God forgive [Postmaster General] Herbert Samuel and [Attorney General] Sir Rufus Isaacs for denying freedom to women. May God forgive them for consenting to the torture of women.*

ON YOM Kippur, the Jewish Day of Atonement, in October 1913, three middle-class Anglo-Jewish women became the first women in Jewish history ever to be forcibly ejected from a synagogue. Their loudly proclaimed "heretical prayer" attacked two distinguished Anglo-Jewish ministers of the Crown who supported the imprisonment and forced feeding of English suffragists.[1]

Castigated as "blackguards in bonnets" by the Anglo-Jewish press, the trio in the synagogue were accused of "dastardly crimes" in the cause of suffrage. These "quasi-demented creatures," commented the *Jewish Chronicle*, would go to any lengths in their "madness." The women may or may not have been aware that interrupting worship to air grievances was a time-honored Jewish tradition. They were certainly, however, imitating the methods of Christian suffragists, who were, at the same time, disrupting worship at churches throughout England.[2]

The "blackguards in bonnets" and the synagogue's minister (rabbi) were members of the Jewish League for Woman Suffrage (JLWS), the only Jewish women's organization in the world devoted exclusively to obtaining both national and Jewish suffrage.[3] Neither the Jewish Feminist Organization in Germany nor the National Council of Jewish Women in America voted as a body to support the national franchise for women, although both supported communal and religious suffrage.[4]

134

Founded on November 3, 1912, by a group of distinguished communal leaders, the League publicly proclaimed twin goals:

> to demand the Parliamentary Franchise for women on the same line as it is, or may be, granted to men, and to unite Jewish Suffragists of all shades of opinion for religious and educational activities. . . .
> [It will also] strive to further the improvement of the status of women in the Community and the State.[5]

Intertwining feminist goals with Jewish loyalties, the Jewish League for Woman Suffrage couched their campaigns in Judaic terminology and feminist rhetoric. Like their non-Jewish colleagues, Jewish feminists contended that suffrage was a "necessary step" toward social reforms that men were unable to secure.[6] The biblical prophets' calls for justice, added League founders, established the "religious and moral basis for enfranchisement." Obtaining the franchise was "Holy work, and therefore Jewish work."

Deliberately speaking as Jews, League members equated their national and communal suffrage campaigns with Anglo-Jewry's efforts to obtain political emancipation, overcome continuing social discrimination, and fight repression against Jews elsewhere in the world. These tactics and language reflected the fact that by the turn of the twentieth century, upper-middle-class Anglo-Jewry felt socially and politically secure enough within the class structure to become distinctly visible, as Jews, in English political life.[7] The world's first Jewish organization to link Judaism with suffrage, the League redefined the concept of Anglo-Jewish womanhood to include secular, religious, and communal feminist goals.

The League's executive council featured a bastion of upper-middle-class Anglo-Jewish women from the Franklin extended family, Jewish community and women's organization leaders, and social reform activists. Male members included prominent Liberal and Orthodox rabbis, communal leaders, author Israel Zangwill, and Hugh Franklin, who was imprisoned twice, for horse-whipping Winston Churchill and for setting fire to a train as part of a suffragist protest.[8] The prominence of its members forced Anglo-Jewry to seriously consider the League's arguments.

Many League officers were active members of the National Union of Women's Suffrage Societies and the London Society for Woman Suffrage. Founders Laura and Leonard Franklin's closest advisers included pioneer educator Henrietta "Netta" Franklin, who would become president of the NUWSS from 1916 to 1917. A life-long feminist, Netta served as president of the National Council of Women from 1925 to 1927.[9] She was joined on the League Council by her sister Lily Montagu, founder of the West Central Jewish Girls Club and of England's first Liberal Jewish movement, who provided spiritual inspiration for the League's campaign.

LILY MONTAGU, LIBERAL JUDAISM, AND FEMINISM

Liberal Judaism undergirded the League's campaign for religious and communal, as well as secular, suffrage, by providing a theological framework for the "religious and moral basis for enfranchisement." Lily Montagu, defined in Ellen Umansky's path-breaking study as the movement's founder and lay minister, was the world's first female religious leader of a recognized Jewish movement.[10] Linking women's emancipation with Liberal Judaism, Montagu also became the spiritual guide of the Jewish League for Woman Suffrage. She preached the connection between suffrage and Judaism at League prayer meetings as well as at national suffrage events.[11]

Rejecting her father's rigid Orthodoxy and the minutiae of home and synagogue observance, Montagu bitterly resented women's second-class status in Jewish religious and communal life. As a young woman, she was deeply influenced by the movement for women's emancipation, the 1890s controversies over women's participation in religious life,[12] and the teachings of Reform theologian Claude Montefiore. He emphasized prophetic ethical teachings, the power of individual conscience, Anglicized worship services, and improving the status of women in religion.[13] Those ideals infused Montagu's commitment to social service and trade unionism,[14] as well as to "her girls" at the West Central Jewish Girls' Club.

Montagu knew of no Jewish precedents for congregational religious leadership by a woman. Ray Frank had functioned as a traveling preacher for less than a decade, and never became the permanent spiritual leader of a synagogue. Montagu knew nothing of Hannah of Ludmir in Poland, whose small community followed her to Jerusalem, or of the handful of Eastern European women unofficially termed "rabbi" for their scholarship and wisdom, although they never guided a synagogue.[15] Montagu would, however, have read in English newspapers about the growing spiral of single Christian women who became Anglican nuns or deaconesses, or missionaries for nonconformist churches.[16] Their precedent, and the concomitant emancipation of Jews and women as a group, Montagu believed, facilitated Liberal Judaism's acceptance of her as a spiritual leader.

Increasingly convinced that God called her to bring others to the service of the Divine, between 1899 and 1902 Montagu gathered support for creation of the Jewish Religious Union, an association of Orthodox, Reform, and Liberal Jews who were committed to religious change and the "reanimation of Judaism."[17] As the group moved further away from traditional Jewish law, however, and became more distinctly Liberal, Orthodox members broke away. In 1909, the remaining progressive members created Anglo-Jewry's first Liberal Jewish movement, the Jewish Religious Union for the Advancement of Liberal Judaism, and announced the opening of its first synagogue. Lily Montagu remained the institution's organizing force and spirit, Claude Montefiore assumed the presidency, and Dr. Israel I. Mattuck became the Liberal Synagogue's first minister.[18]

In speeches to her West Central Jewish Girls' Club, women's organizations, and Liberal Judaism meetings, Montagu demanded an end to the sexual double standard,[19] enforcement of equal standards of sexual chastity, and equalization of Jewish women's rights in religious marriage and divorce.[20] She called for rejection of past tradition, when a girl's place in the Jewish community was "inferior to that of the boys . . . [and] there was no place for her in the Synagogue." The woman's movement, said Montagu, empowered young women to make new kinds of decisions and seek new kinds of opportunities.[21] All aspects of religious life and leadership, suggested Montagu, were within the province of Jewish women.

Insisting that "women today in England have to become thinkers,"[22] Montagu declared that women were *obligated* to take advantage of the new religious opportunities open to them, so that they could make a distinct contribution to the "spiritual treasury of the world." Jewish women's femininity and emotional warmth enabled them to bring a more imaginative and creative approach to Judaism[23] and a "spiritual aspect" to "home life and social service." By their commitment to social work, Jewish women would endow the world with "truth and right."[24]

By 1912, Montagu was heavily involved in suffrage activities. Horrified at the forced feeding of imprisoned suffragists, she protested in vain to her brother Edwin Montagu, then Secretary for India.[25] In 1913, she became a vice-president of the Jewish League for Woman Suffrage. Functioning as spiritual adviser of the League, she frequently led the JLWS in prayer before the organization's meetings and public assemblies.[26] Montagu arranged for the League to conduct prayer meetings at denominational assemblies as part of the national suffrage movement's week of prayer, held November first through eighth of 1912.

In 1918, Montagu delivered the first sermon preached by a woman in any Anglo-Jewish synagogue. "Accepted by the congregation without any stir," the sermon triggered a lifetime career as a lay minister in Liberal synagogues, although Montagu was not formally inducted until 1944.[27] Inspired by her example, author Nina Davis Salaman preached from a Liberal pulpit in 1922, and essayist Katie Magnus delivered a sermon at Cambridge University. Eventually, a network of Liberal congregations spread across Great Britain, Western Europe, and America that culminated in creation of the World Union for Progressive Judaism in 1925.

Montagu's position in the World Union for Progressive Judaism enabled her to break some barriers. Preaching at the 1928 Conference of the World Union in Berlin, she became the first Jewish woman ever to deliver a sermon from a German synagogue pulpit. Even so, she encountered difficulty in persuading the WUPJ to recognize women as leaders. As late as 1945, she was forced to demand that "at least *one woman*" should be part of a forthcoming World Union conference.[28]

Lily Montagu's extraordinary career was due, in great part, to the interaction between English feminism, Liberal Judaism, and the emotional security provided by Montagu's upper-class status and close-knit family.[29] Nevertheless, her powerful religious vision, charismatic personality, and formidable determination ultimately forged her success. Liberal Judaism provided a spiritual center for those 10 percent of English Jews who wished to remain religious without maintaining Orthodoxy.[30] On a larger scale, through creation of the World Union for Progressive Judaism, Montagu helped to influence the growth of liberal Judaism throughout Western Europe and the United States.

Montagu was a committed suffragist. However, she, like Millicent Garrett Fawcett, was less radical than many of her colleagues. She never smashed windows or disobeyed the law; rather, she advocated "votes for women" on the basis of "moral justice." Furthermore, she sought to expand women's opportunities so that they might strengthen their primary roles as wives, mothers, and moral guardians of society. Montagu strongly believed in traditional Jewish concepts of family sanctity, Victorian virtues of the nobility of womanhood, and the responsibilities inherent in class status. This moderation may have been due to the fact that her status as a female religious leader appeared so radical that she did not wish to subject the Liberal movement to further risk. She was painfully aware that opponents of the movement speculated that it would "end in moonshine" because it was founded by a young Jewish woman.[31]

Nevertheless, Lily Montagu successfully functioned as the first official female religious leader in an organized Jewish movement. Until the 1970s, she had just one official successor in the United States. As we shall see, Tehilla Lichtenstein assumed leadership of the Jewish Science movement in the late 1930s.[32] America's Reform movement ordained its first woman rabbi, Sally Priesand, in 1972. Montagu's spiritual legacy through the Jewish League for Woman Suffrage influenced Jewish women's postwar campaign for religious suffrage. Summing up her impact, Montagu herself concluded: "I was able to prove that . . . it is not fair to deny women as a whole the opportunity to bring their contribution to the spiritual treasury of the world."[33]

LEAGUE DEMONSTRATIONS

Anglo-Jewish suffragists existed prior to formation of the League. Numbers of Jewish women had participated in the great march of 40,000 women to Albert Hall in June 1911. Like their non-Jewish colleagues, these Jewish suffragists argued that granting the franchise to women would improve the country, in the same way that women had improved local government through their participation in local elections and their service on communal, educational, and municipal boards.[34]

League members "held their banner high" marching and demonstrating for "votes for women." Carefully identifying with other suffrage organizations, the JLWS joined the Council of Federated Women's Suffrage Societies; it sent representatives to the International Congress of Suffrage Societies at Budapest in June 1913; and it signed the pro-suffrage petition of the Actresses' Franchise League, which was presented to the House of Commons in April 1913. The League joined other denominational suffrage societies in sponsoring public meetings throughout 1913 and 1914.[35]

The JLWS also attempted to organize East European Jewish immigrants by founding an East End branch in May 1913 that appealed to working-women's interests.[36] The East End branch, however, did not join Sylvia Pankhurst's East End Federation of Women's Suffrage Societies (EEF), perhaps because of Pankhurst's anti-Semitism, which Dora Montefiore had protested against earlier in the century.[37]

Despite the League's official moderation, by 1912 a number of militant Jewish suffragists, many of whom, like the Lowys of Bayswater, were League members, "boldly entered into the ranks of unrest in Woman's cause." These "Jewish martyrs" were arrested, imprisoned, and force-fed for taking part in violent demonstrations.

Thank God, there are Jewesses who are suffering the personal temporary, physical degradation . . . of prison so as thereby to save thousands

upon thousands of women from permanent degradation and permanent
constant ignominy.[38]

Simultaneously, militants at the New West End and other synagogues continued to disrupt Sabbath worship services in London
from early 1913 until the outbreak of war, demanding religious as
well as political suffrage for women. Four suffragists were removed
from Hampstead Synagogue on three occasions because they had "disturbed" the Sabbath service by "brawling" over suffrage. One woman
interrupted the worship service at Brighton Synagogue with a prayer
asking God to forgive King George and the Russian Tsar for "torture
practiced on their women subjects in and out of prison."[39] Writing in
The Westminster Review, Elizabeth de Bruin applauded the JLWS for
its attacks against traditionalism. Denouncing Anglo-Jewry's "exclusion of women from every sphere but the domestic," she contended
that even religious education for Jewish girls was only a palliative.[40]

COMMUNAL REACTION

The League terrified the majority of the Anglo-Jewish community
who feared that Jewish suffragists heralded the breakdown of the
home, a rise in anti-Semitism that seemed connected to passage of
the 1906 Aliens Act, and an end to native Jewry's social acceptance
in England.[41] Moreover, male members of the Anglo-Jewish gentry,
like English suffrage opponents of their class, dreaded the specter of
government by "irrational" and "emotional" women. Jewish working
men, like their English counterparts, were especially hostile, convinced that suffrage would give women more power to impose middle-
class reformist controls upon their lives. This fear made it even more
difficult to recruit East End women into the suffrage campaign than
it had been to organize them into unions.

The controversy filled the Anglo-Jewish press for two years. Leopold Greenberg, editor of the *Jewish Chronicle* since 1907, acknowledged that although a "large number of Jewish men and women"
were in the suffrage movement, the absence of a formal Jewish suffrage organization would seem "an invidious exception" at a time
when church-based organizations supported suffrage. However, despite Greenberg's respect for League officers' social status, the majority of his editorials protested that "suffragist aims" may "prejudice," rather than help, Jewish women's status and risked inciting
anti-Semitism against the entire Jewish community. A militant Jewish suffragist

> who splintered that plate glass . . . aroused indignation against her, not
> because she was a woman, but because she was a Jewess. That senti-

ment, once engendered . . . spreads itself . . . to all Jewesses, and it is easy to see . . . the damage we Jews must suffer.[42]

Although Jewish feminists argued that "one indignant shopkeeper" did not constitute an entire anti-Semitic British nation, their voices were drowned out by vitriolic letters to the editor that fulminated against women's emancipation as an insufferable "sex revolt" and thundered that "the idea [of suffrage] is execrable. . . . Only in the philosophy of fools can Judaism have any affinity with Woman Suffrage."[43]

"VOTES FOR WOMEN" IN THE SYNAGOGUE

Heightening the communal furor, in 1912 the League mounted a campaign for "votes for women" for female synagogue seatholders, supported by Liberal Jewish ministers who believed the synagogue should mirror social concerns. Attacking the JLWS religious campaign as "sacrilege," outraged traditional synagogue and Jewish communal leaders thundered that religious suffrage would drive men from the synagogue and destroy the institution.[44] Anti-suffragists' apologias declared that the daily prayer, "Blessed are Thou, O Lord, our God, who has not made me a woman," was not discriminatory, but merely thanked God for granting men the privilege of assuming religious obligations. Angry Jews from all classes lashed out at the "disgraceful methods adopted by women who are supposed to have a sacred cause at heart." Rowdy battles between pro- and anti-suffragist crowds broke up League meetings.[45]

Despite these attacks, support for religious suffrage increased. Even Chief Rabbi Hertz "expressed himself favorably" to a League delegation, stating that in several Orthodox synagogues in America, women seatholders "had the privilege of the vote." By 1914 two synagogues had granted partial votes to women, and five synagogues gave them an unlimited franchise. As a result, Jewish women secured a voice in synagogue management and a quasi-religious sanction for representation on Jewish communal boards. Nevertheless, despite the *Jewish Chronicle*'s support, the League failed to convince the United Synagogue to grant the vote to women throughout all United Synagogue congregations.[46]

CONCLUSION

Anglo-Jewish suffragists' upper-class social status, communal distinction, powerful extended families, and preeminence in social service enabled them to overcome hostility, gain admittance to English feminist organizations, and create a distinctively Jewish woman's movement officially identified with its English counterpart.

Gradually breaking down barriers of religion, class, and culture, by the close of World War I, a handful of elite Anglo-Jewish women achieved leadership positions in English suffragist organizations. Publicly acknowledging themselves as Jews, this select group of Jewish women created the Jewish League for Woman Suffrage. Winning "votes for women" gave Anglo-Jewish women their first taste of real political power in national, religious, and communal life. Suffrage became a vital symbol of their social acceptance as Englishwomen as well as of their political, religious, and communal emancipation.

The very existence, let alone the success, of the Jewish League for Woman Suffrage was rooted in the upper-class social status, family connections, and communal distinction of its leadership. These factors endowed Jewish feminists with self-confidence that enabled them to face the intense antagonism generated by their suffrage activities.

Conversely, the JLWS and UJW were acceptable to the Christian-dominated suffragist movement for similar reasons. Suffragists, most notably the NUWSS, welcomed the League because of its members' upper-middle-class position and the organization's identity as one "church-affiliated" group among many, even though the League's contribution was rarely acknowledged in suffragists' memoirs. Individual upper-middle-class Anglo-Jewish women such as Netta Franklin[47] even achieved leadership positions in the NUWSS.[48] The Union of Jewish Women was also appreciated for its dedication to women's social concerns.

In contrast to the United States, therefore, England's class and religious distinctions facilitated both the creation of a unique Jewish suffrage organization and Anglo-Jewish women's admittance to the English campaign for the ballot. As a result, these Jewish women's organizations sought the franchise in a very different manner from their counterparts in the United States.

UNITED STATES

"I think that I was born a suffragist," said Rose Schneiderman, "but if I hadn't been I am sure that the conditions of the working girls in New York . . . would have made me one."[49] East European immigrant Schneiderman helped lead the campaign for the vote for women in the United States, envisioning the ballot as a "tool in the hands of working women." Following Schneiderman Jewish immigrant women participated in the American suffrage movement to a far greater degree than did their Jewish sisters in England, joining a cross-class alliance launched by middle-class women that contributed significantly to the national suffrage campaign.

THE AMERICAN SUFFRAGE MOVEMENT

Like their Jewish peers in England and their Christian colleagues in both countries,[50] most American Jewish women suffragists hoped to secure their own equality and to obtain social reforms to protect working-class women. Unlike the situation in England, by 1910 the American suffrage movement was attracting significant numbers of middle- and working-class women with experience in settlements, consumers' groups, and women's trade unionist organizations. They were furious over the refusal of male businessmen and politicians to grant badly needed reforms.

This new generation of activists revitalized the suffrage movement after years of quiescence, employing the same type of skilled political organization that had gained them other legislative victories. A steady flow of progressive issues made "votes for women" appear relatively less radical and more acceptable to the popular view. Social reform became respectable after the adoption of direct election of senators and the graduated income tax, railroad regulation, workmen's compensation, and pure food and drug laws. In many states, particularly in the West, suffrage and progressive legislation went hand in hand. The interaction between women's rights and progressivism was heightened when the Progressive Party endorsed suffrage in 1912 and Jane Addams seconded Theodore Roosevelt's nomination for president on the Progressive ticket.

Progressivism's increasing respectability and Roosevelt's endorsement of suffrage reenergized NAWSA. At the same time, Harriet Stanton Blatch, daughter of Elizabeth Cady Stanton, organized the Equality League of Self-Supporting Women and drew working-class women into the American suffrage movement. Alice Paul created the more radical Congressional Union, basing it upon England's WSPU. NAWSA, although it split with Paul's organization, cooperated with the Equality League. This generated a cross-class alliance that attracted Jewish women and proved vital to the suffragist victory as a whole.[51]

After votes on a federal amendment failed in 1915, Carrie Chapman Catt was elected NAWSA's new president to revitalize the organization. She directed NAWSA in a brilliant and tenacious state-by-state campaign that achieved a referendum victory in New York in 1917 and ultimately succeeded in winning passage of the Nineteenth Amendment in 1920.[52]

MAUD NATHAN

By the time of Catt's election, America's growing religious toleration, the popularity of secularism, and the need for massive support convinced this new generation of suffragists that they needed support from women of all backgrounds. National suffrage organizations welcomed acculturated upper- and middle-class Jewish women of German origin who shared their social reform convictions.[53]

Nevertheless, only a handful of Jewish women achieved national leadership status. Maud Nathan, daughter of a distinguished Orthodox Jewish Sephardic family, became America's most prominent Jewish suffragist. Her motives and career illuminate the involvement of upper- and middle-class Jewish women in the suffragist movement. Nathan insisted that voting women would strike a blow against "vice and corruption and low standards."[54] She was furious at the male "scoffers" who sneered at women's abilities, laughed at their campaigns for social reform, and demanded that women remain at home. She joined the suffragist movement believing that it meant "the opening of prison doors."

> Women had been kept behind bars, their hands manacled, their feet tied by the ball and chain of conventionality. At last, we were summoned to go out in the open and do our share of human uplift work.[55]

Nathan's "handsome presence, fine humor and long experience" captivated her colleagues and audiences alike.[56] A leader in the National and New York Consumer Leagues, she was first vice-president of the New York City Equal Suffrage League and head of the Fifteenth Assembly District of New York's Woman Suffrage Party (WSP). Nathan led the Party's open-air rallies and marches, and she convened mass meetings of Jews in New York's Carnegie Hall, Philadelphia's Arch Street Theatre, and elsewhere.[57] She traveled across the country and to international conferences lecturing for suffrage.[58]

Under her leadership, the WSP's Fifteenth District opened a unique suffrage home and political center for permanent and transient guests. Nathan and her associate Martha Klatschken attracted numbers of Jewish women, including East European immigrants, into the Party's Fifteenth District where they participated in suffrage meetings, assemblies, and demonstrations.[59] Her speeches at synagogues, rallies on the Lower East Side, and meetings of her New York NCJW chapter turned her into a public symbol of Jewish women's suffrage activism.[60]

Nathan was expert at NAWSA's new methods of grass-roots political organizing and innovative techniques for attracting crowds and publicity. Stunts included making twenty-four speeches from auto-

A Jewish suffragist. Courtesy, National Council of Jewish
Women

mobiles stationed around the city, or giving "silent speeches" in front
of a prominent window of a vacant store. America needed a different
approach from European radicalism, said Nathan:

> The nation was hardly out of its swaddling clothes. . . . It was not hide-
> bound by tradition. Its youthful adventurous spirit, its sense of humor,
> its love of fair play, demanded a different stimulus. . . . [We] devised all
> sorts of original "stunts," anything that would give us publicity, with-
> out violating any existing law.[61]

This moderate approach attracted significant numbers of Jewish
women. Reflecting the pattern of the American suffragist movement
as a whole, few, if any, American Jewish suffragists used the violent
tactics of the Anglo-Jewish radical suffragists who threw rocks and
interrupted worship services. To an even greater degree than their
Christian counterparts, American Jewish women appear to have chosen peaceful methods. This may reflect middle-class Jewish women's
nationwide acceptance as individuals within NAWSA and the Equality League. Moreover, American Jewish women, unlike those in England, did not feel compelled to band together as an organized, church-
affiliated "sympathetic supporter" of the cause.

JEWISH SUFFRAGISTS NATIONWIDE

Perhaps as a result of American moderation, more Jewish women appear to have been involved in the American than in the English suffrage movement. Jewish women from all classes and all areas of the United States joined suffragist organizations. Yet, they never united in a distinctively Jewish suffragist organization like their co-religionists in England. Jewish feminists appeared to have felt that membership in American suffrage organizations marked their acceptance in American society. A distinctive Jewish organization seemed unnecessary in the United States, where more flexible attitudes toward class status and separation between church and state had facilitated greater Jewish social mobility than in England.

The lack of a Jewish suffrage organization, therefore, did not reflect an attempt to deny one's Jewish identity. As we shall see, most middle-class American Jewish suffragists, who composed the majority of Jewish feminists, appear to have been members of Jewish organizations. Significant numbers of immigrant or working-class Jewish suffragists lived in Jewish neighborhoods and joined socialist or labor Zionist groups whose members were predominantly Jewish.

Moreover, East European working women were labeled as Jewish in suffrage publications such as the *Woman Voter* that described their participation in parades and demonstrations. While there was no way that an immigrant Jewish woman during this period could hide her identity as a Jew, it is equally true that these women proudly identified themselves as Jews when they joined a suffrage group, relied upon Jewish friends and cultural experiences in publicizing suffrage, and marched with suffrage banners into their own Jewish communities.

Ivy Husted Harper's six-volume history of the suffrage movement and the journal *Woman Voter* list dozens of local Jewish women suffragist leaders by name and indicate that thousands more were rank-and-file members of suffrage organizations across the United States.

Suffrage platforms often included Alice and Louis Brandeis, as well as Louise and Rabbi Stephen S. Wise.[62] Louise Wise was a social reformer who founded the Child Adoption Committee of the Free Synagogue, the first Jewish agency to provide for adoption by Jewish families. In addition to a multitude of other activities, she created the Women's Division of the American Jewish Congress in 1931, which concentrated its final activities on aiding Jewish refugees from Nazi-controlled Europe.[63]

Lawyer Jennie Loitman Barron was raised by Jewish immigrant parents who encouraged her ambition to study law. While working on her law degree from 1915 to 1917, she organized Boston University's Equal Suffrage League, at the same time maintaining active membership in several Jewish organizations. Barron was one of a group of women who completed a successful tactical revitalization of the Massachusetts suffrage organization in the face of widespread anti-suffrage activities. After passage of the suffrage amendment, she represented the League of Women Voters in its effort to unify laws affecting women throughout the United States. Her prominence in civic as well as legal activities enhanced Barron's reputation as the first female associate justice of the Massachusetts Superior Court.[64]

Mary Fels, wife of Massachusetts philanthropist Joseph Fels, was one of only two honorary presidents of NAWSA. She helped spearhead the successful 1918 campaign to defeat anti-suffragist Senator John W. Weeks, and persuaded several Jewish women to join NAWSA in the process.[65] In addition to New York, Massachusetts, and Ohio, Jewish suffragists were particularly active in Pennsylvania, Oregon, Colorado, Washington, D.C., Maryland, and Nevada. Suffragists such as Sarah Platt Decker of Colorado were among "the most accomplished and forceful of women."[67]

Jewish suffragists closely connected their social reform crusades with the suffrage effort. Martha Gruening, sister of Senator Ernest Gruening, was the only prominent female Jewish member of the NAACP involved in the pre–World War I civil rights movement.[67] Dr. Rosalie S. Morton linked suffrage with her NCJW crusade advocating sex education and sexual purity for men as well as women.[68] Ohio suffragist Pauline Steinem, Gloria Steinem's grandmother, was chairperson of the NCJW's education committee, securing women's membership on both Jewish and public boards of education.[69]

JEWISH COMMUNAL REACTION

By the turn of the twentieth century, Jewish women felt they had taken great strides toward religious equality in Reform congregations, thanks to the efforts of the National Council of Jewish Women and the *American Jewess*. Reform temples in large cities gave equal seating and synagogue voting privileges to women, noted Hannah G. Solomon, freeing women to concentrate on political, rather than religious, suffrage.

However, some Jewish feminists equated suffrage with Jewish tradition and religious reform. Rebekah Kohut demanded changes in Jewish family law in the same breath that she insisted upon political suffrage. The founder and "leading spirit" of the United States Employment Service, she focused on creating new job opportunities for

Hannah G. Solomon and Susan B. Anthony at the 1904 International Council of Women conference. Courtesy, National Council of Jewish Women

women. As a leader of the NCJW, and the daughter and wife of distinguished rabbis, Kohut made speeches that linked prophetic Judaism's call for justice with her own national social reform and suffragist activities. As we shall see, she became the driving force behind the creation of the World Council of Jewish Women after World War I.[70]

Yet, although individual NCJW leaders such as Solomon, Kohut, Sadie American, and Minnie D. Louis supported national suffrage, neither the Council nor any other Jewish women's organization officially supported votes for women before the passage of the Nineteenth Amendment.[71]

The ambivalence of Jewish women's organizations reflected the concerns of male Jewish authorities. The Reform movement's Central Conference of American Rabbis avoided passing pro-suffrage resolutions for several years, despite a series of resolutions by individual rabbis.

While the CCAR hesitated, individual rabbis spoke out. Rabbi Emil Hirsch, Hannah G. Solomon's mentor, insisted that the "franchise should . . . be extended to women." During the later stages of the suffrage campaign from 1910 to 1920, Rabbi Stephen S. Wise, a founding member and vice-president of the Woman Suffrage Party, spearheaded a host of Reform rabbis who called for votes for women based upon prophetic Judaism's demands for justice. In concert with many Christian clergy, Reform rabbis advocated suffrage in newspapers, at NAWSA conferences, and at public demonstrations. However, despite several attempts, it was not until 1917 that the Reform movement's Central Conference of American Rabbis passed a pro-suffrage resolution.[72]

The growing importance of the suffrage debate affected every corner of the Jewish community. In 1915, New York *World* newspaper columnist Sophie Loeb chaired a suffrage symposium for the *American Hebrew* that was extensively reported in that newspaper. Loeb argued that suffrage was the key to correcting injustices against working women: "if only one woman wanted, needed and would use the vote, every other woman should see to it that she gets it." Lillian Wald, speaking on the same platform, added that social reform needs were responsible for suffrage's occupying "one of the first places in the social discourses of the East Side." Rebekah Kohut noted that suffrage was "a plea for justice from one-half of the human family to the other half."[73]

Arguing against Loeb at the same symposium were Mrs. Annie Nathan Meyer, the sister of Maud Nathan, and Mrs. Henry Seligman, the wife of a prominent German-Jewish banker. Their arguments were rooted in American anti-suffragists' fears of equality for themselves and empowerment for immigrants.

THE ANTI-SUFFRAGIST DEBATE

Jewish anti-suffragists reflected a nationwide concern that suffrage threatened the separate roles of men and women. Anti-suffragists claimed that voting was unwomanly because it was a public act restricted to men. Some women opposed the independence inherent in the franchise because they wanted to remain protected within the family. Meyer bitterly opposed "unrestricted equal suffrage" and complained that the franchise would enshrine the economically independent woman as an "ideal" when she should be regarded as "an exception or a misfortune."[74] Fearing the connection between social reform progressives and suffragists, American business and liquor interests feared that suffrage would bring in prohibition. Southerners worried that granting the vote to women would empower Blacks. Philanthropists suggested that if women won the vote, charitable organizations would be unnecessary, because there would be demands for "work, money, bread, leisure." To maintain the status quo, anti-suffragists demanded that legislatures should restrict suffrage to those males with education and property.[75]

Meyer and Seligman integrated America's class biases toward working and immigrant women, contending that enfranchising women would add an "inferior element" to the electorate. These speakers, both NCJW members, reflected middle-class suffragists' antagonism toward the working class, and accepted the commonly held view that immigrant working-class women, like their men, would vote for conservative political and business interests in compliance with their employers' demands. As we shall see, this attitude affected suffragists as well.

Meyer's frequently published articles on "spreadhenism," her own word satirizing the "spreading" of feminism, savaged the suffragists' claim that granting the franchise to women would cure social ills. Contending that women's character had not improved along with their education, Meyer claimed that democracy might suffer if women got the vote before they were sufficiently educated to receive it. Moreover, women, perennially on the prowl to catch men, might even be less qualified than men to attempt society's moral reform. Meyer said that she dreaded the advent of women as voters and officeholders "a little more than that of the tiger."[76]

Despite hesitation in the Jewish community by otherwise-progressive Jewish elements, as well as strong anti-suffragist outpourings, there does not seem to have been the same outraged reaction against suffrage as there was in England. This was due in great part to the popularity of suffrage among individual Jews and the social eminence of prominent suffragists like Maud Nathan. It was also caused by the moderation of Jewish suffragists and their widespread acceptance within the movement.

SUFFRAGISTS' ATTITUDE TOWARD IMMIGRANTS

Despite America's ostensibly classless society, Jewish suffragists, like their non-Jewish colleagues, ostracized working and immigrant women. The cult of separate spheres' insistence upon keeping women in the home had increased the split between women of different classes. As Alice Kessler-Harris has noted, it was particularly easy to make class distinctions when working women could be identified by appearance, dress, rough manners, and the often-brusque attitudes that reflected their daily battles for mere survival. Exacerbating class antagonisms, many native Americans, including Jews of Sephardic or

German origin, feared that if immigrants obtained the vote, they would contaminate America and destroy its traditional values. In addition to feminists who adopted these views, still others accepted these arguments as a way of countering anti-suffragism. As a result of this complex situation, notes Aileen Kraditor, immigrant women were not recruited for the suffragist movement until relatively late.[77]

Class distinctions and nativist biases powerfully affected Jewish women in the suffrage movement. Like their Gentile peers, Jewish suffragist activists such as Rebekah Kohut often couched their visceral antagonism in political terms, contending that immigrants voting according to their employers' instructions would cause a landslide victory for reactionary business interests.[78]

Middle-class Jewish women also had specifically Jewish reasons for their attitudes. Like other German Jews, Jewish suffragists argued that extending the franchise to East Europeans would trigger an increase in anti-Semitism, citing evidence that anti-Semitism had risen after the influx of Jewish immigrants.[79]

IMMIGRANT SUFFRAGISTS

Despite the anti-immigrant bias of suffragists and anti-suffragists alike, a core of German-Jewish social reform activists such as Lillian Wald and Maud Nathan were instrumental in recruiting East European women into the suffrage movement by 1907. Wald perceived suffrage as an extension of her dedication to the immigrants she served. Her Henry Street Settlement was so closely identified with suffrage work by its Lower East Side neighbors that they connected suffrage to Henry Street rather than to the Woman Suffrage Party.[80]

Wald argued that "society will be the gainer" when all women have the vote. A founding member and the honorary vice-president of the Woman Suffrage Party as well as a founder of the WTUL, she scathingly attacked those who would block woman suffrage because it would give immigrants the vote.[81]

The WTUL was particularly instrumental in forging a link, by 1910, between middle-class suffragists and women trade unionists.[82] Jewish women such as Wald, Nathan, and Rose Schneiderman joined a cross-class, nationwide suffrage coalition of social reformers, settlement workers, trade unionists, and socialists.

As noted earlier in the discussion on the WTUL, the labor movement's refusal to negotiate for equal wages and working conditions drove immigrant women toward suffrage.[83] Rose Schneiderman viewed the ballot as the only "tool" that they could use "to correct the terrible conditions existing in industry."

> It is for women to revolutionize industry, to humanize it, not only for women but for men. They can, through the power of the ballot, make a bloodless war upon the evils of industry.[84]

By 1910, Schneiderman was campaigning for NAWSA and the Equality League of Self-Supporting Women[86] in the face of opposition from male socialist trade unionists who protested that she was harming the labor movement:

> *You either work for Socialism and as a consequence for the equality of sexes, or you work for women suffrage only and neglect Socialism —* *Then you act like a bad doctor who pretends to cure his patient by remedying the symptoms instead of removing the disease itself.*[86]

Ignoring this and similar warnings, Schneiderman campaigned for the Woman Suffrage Party and joined Clara Lemlich Shavelson, heroine of the "march of the 20,000," as both a union and suffrage organizer for the Women's Trade Union League. Suffrage finally became so important to Schneiderman that she took a leave of absence from WTUL in 1912 to concentrate exclusively on the suffrage campaign.[87]

"I think that I was born a suffragist," said Rose Schneiderman, "but if I hadn't been I am sure that the conditions of the working girls in New York . . . would have made me one." Convinced that only the ballot would secure a living wage for working women, Schneiderman campaigned her way through factories, tenement houses, open parks, luxurious estates and elite colleges such as Vassar. Strong men who heard Schneiderman speak "sat with the tears rolling down their cheeks," reported a colleague. New York, she declared, owed the vote to the "1,000,000 women who work—not for pin money, but to live."[88] After teaching at "suffrage school" in Washington, D.C., she helped lead a march on the White House and argued before President Wilson that "The vote, Mr. President, is a necessity."[89]

THE NEW YORK LEADERSHIP

New York state became the focus of the campaign for a federal suffrage amendment when it passed its own suffrage amendment in 1917, making it the first large Eastern industrial state to do so.[90] New York had the largest Jewish community in the United States, with the greatest amount of Jewish suffrage activity. All economic levels of New York Jewry united to provide the "largest, strongest and most consistent support" for passage of the 1917 amendment. By 1917, 78 out of 100 pro-suffrage election districts were Jewish. Within these

Jewish districts, from 76 to 93 percent of the total vote and half of all Jewish neighborhoods were pro-suffrage, while no identifiably Jewish districts were consistently anti-suffrage.[91]

Unlike Maud Nathan and Rose Schneiderman, the majority of New York's Jewish suffragists were involved at lower levels of the party within small election districts. Significant numbers of these Jewish women participated in New York's suffrage campaign. Elinor Lerner indicates that Jewish women comprised at least 17 percent of the founding members of Women's Suffrage Party district organizations and 64 percent of the membership in predominantly Jewish assembly districts.[92] Canvassing was conducted throughout Jewish neighborhoods. Meetings and demonstrations were held in Jewish schools, homes, auditoriums, and in the streets. Jewish working women, noted the *Woman Voter*, had a reputation as "good suffragists, willing and anxious to work."[93]

They were supported by a limited cadre of Jewish socialists and trade unionists. Lawyer Meyer London, a distinguished East Side socialist leader, was elected to Congress in 1914. A consistent advocate of votes for women, London thundered in a speech to the New York State Legislature in 1917 that if a woman "is a member of the community, she has a right to vote." Even Samuel Gompers and his American Federation of Labor finally felt pressured into issuing statements approving suffrage.[94]

Nevertheless, despite immigrants' significant contributions to the suffrage victory, the vulnerability of German Jews during and after World War I increased their antagonism toward East Europeans. In the midst of America's wartime hostility to all Germans, and the postwar panic over the Bolshevik revolution, it was dangerous for German Jews to appear to be socialist sympathizers. Trapped between their own vulnerability as German Jews and the immigrants' liability as Russians, German-Jewish suffragists imitated American suffragists, who vociferously disavowed socialists' contribution to the Nineteenth Amendment.

Rosalie Loew Whitney exemplified the dilemma. As America's first practicing Jewish woman lawyer, her suffragist and social reform efforts were widely publicized. Yet, when she appeared before a house committee on suffrage in 1918 to argue for a federal suffrage amendment, she claimed that the 1917 New York state suffrage amendment victory owed nothing to socialists from the Lower East Side.[95]

JEWISH IMMIGRANTS' IMPACT

Jewish immigrant and working-class women's participation in American suffragist organizations added a dimension to the American fem-

inist movement that was unparalleled in England. A handful of
immigrant women like Rose Schneiderman and Clara Lemlich achieved
prominence. Their status as role models and their cooperation with
middle-class German-Jewish activists such as Maud Nathan attracted
significant numbers of Jewish working-class women into NAWSA, the
WTUL, the Equality League, and the Woman Suffrage Party. Their
massive demonstrations and rallies in the streets of the Lower East
Side and their efforts for Socialist candidates like Meyer London were
indispensable in garnering widespread support for votes for women.

Through membership in the WTUL and NAWSA, Schneiderman,
Lemlich, and other working-class Jewish women helped forge an alliance between working women and middle- and upper-class feminists that at least temporarily proved critical to the American suffrage
campaign. The New York victory provided a major catalyst for the
1920 federal amendment. Without the immigrants' participation, it
is doubtful if middle-class women alone could have gathered the grass-
roots political base that secured the victory.

England's Jewish immigrant women never participated in comparable numbers or achieved similar influence in the British suffrage
movement, nor did they successfully develop a cross-class feminist
alliance during this period. Even after World War I, class rigidity in
England perpetuated the social and political dominance of the upper
and middle class.

American circumstances, however, varied somewhat. Although
the upper and middle classes still retained social and political control,
the massive concentration of East Europeans on the Lower East Side
and other urban areas ensured that male immigrant property-holders
elected local politicians and congressional representatives. Therefore,
immigrant Jewish suffragists wielded limited power through their
alliances with immigrant men and middle-class suffragists.

Nevertheless, as we shall see, securing the vote did not empower
immigrant women to the degree they expected. They did not win
equal pay or equal working conditions, nor did they achieve political
power in the years after 1918. Instead, the majority left the WTUL
and sought through welfare legislation rather than political visibility
the protection they needed in their homes and workplaces.

CONCLUSION

Jewish suffragists culminated the process of forging a distinctive Jewish woman's movement that sought to redefine Jewish womanhood

in political as well as religious-communal terms. The campaign for the franchise strengthened Jewish women's identity as citizens, as Jews, and as feminist political activists, both in England and in the United States.

"Bonds of sisterhood" were forged among Jewish and Christian social-reformer suffragists in the process of their drive to win the vote. Social anti-Semitism, while it still existed, played a relatively minor part in affecting upper- and middle-class Jewish women's involvement in the later stages of the suffrage campaign. Jewish women's previous participation in social reform facilitated that welcome in the suffrage campaign.

The Jewish presence influenced the secular movement somewhat differently in each country. In England, a relatively small but powerful group of Jewish women participated in the suffrage movement, and some, like Netta Franklin and Eva Hubback, achieved distinction. Yet, Jewish suffragists remained less visible and influential as Jews in secular campaigns because the prominence of the Jewish League for Woman Suffrage established a separate Jewish suffragist presence that was perceived as only one of many church affiliates. In America, however, thousands of Jewish suffragists from all social classes participated in nearly every secular suffrage group throughout the nation. As a result, they deeply influenced the suffrage movement's methodology and tactics. Sephardic, German-Jewish, and East European Jewish women helped to initiate the cross-class alliance between middle-class and immigrant women that profoundly shaped the suffrage movement.

For Jewish suffragists, winning the ballot symbolized achieving their own national, religious, and communal equality at the same time it represented protection of working-class women through social reform.

Firmly committed to social change, Jewish feminists believed that winning the vote was essential to securing those reforms. Like Nathan, female Jewish activists were angered by male rejection of their social reform endeavors. Nathan bitterly assailed the "scoffing among certain groups of men, who asked what mere women, with no political status, could possibly accomplish to change conditions."[96] Nathan determined to secure the political power that alone could secure reform. "Until women obtained the franchise," commented Nathan, "their influence with members of the legislature would continue to be a negligible quantity."[97]

Many Jewish suffragists rooted their concerns for social reform in biblical prophetic calls for justice, or *tzedakah*. This theme runs throughout their personal memoirs, public speeches, the minutes of organizations to which they belonged, and newspaper accounts. Maud Nathan, rooted in her family's commitment to social service, declared that she became a suffragist because she simply "could not bear the thought of injustice."

Jewish women's participation in the suffrage campaign strengthened their social and political acceptance by secular feminists. Campaigning for the ballot alongside Christian women demonstrated that Jewish women were sufficiently acculturated to take public risks. Maud Nathan vividly described her cultivation of wealthy "society women" to draw them into suffrage activity. Her account not only indicates how important the money and influence of these women could be to the suffrage movement, but, perhaps unconsciously, how important they were to establishing Nathan's own status among the American elite.[98]

Still, the majority of immigrant Jewish women in both countries felt that idealistic notions of equality were irrelevant to their lives, and that their class and immigrant status formed insuperable barriers between them and middle-class suffragists.[99] Far more immigrants became suffragists in America than in England, however, joining the campaign for the ballot out of anger at the state's or trade unions' failure to improve their wages.

Jewish women became members of the American suffrage movement by the thousands. Yet, leadership of national suffrage organizations by Jewish women was limited to a few "stars" like Maud Nathan, Rose Schneiderman, or Lillian Wald,[100] who passed tests of class status or national prominence. Nevertheless, in cities across the country, middle-class Jewish suffragists appear to have been highly influential in local suffrage organizations, and working-class and immigrant Jewish women provided the backbone for many suffrage campaigns. Insofar as the suffrage movement indicates a major trend in American society, Jewish women's participation signaled their growing influence on the American social and political scene.

There were major differences in Jewish women's approach to the campaign for the franchise in the two countries. Jewish feminists' approach toward religious and political suffrage determined the manner in which they reshaped their identity as Jewish women and strikingly differentiated English and American colleagues.

In America, twentieth-century Jewish suffragists often exclaimed with Hannah Solomon that the religious battle was won. Rebekah Kohut knew better, but in an age when Reform women delivered sermons from the pulpit, religious concerns appeared secondary to the national franchise.

In England, the creation of a separate Jewish League for Woman Suffrage reflected many factors. Jewish women's difficulties in achieving religious reform made them determined to use the ballot to win equality in religious as well as in national life. Lily Montagu's Liberal Judaism was still a very small movement in 1920, and Reform Judaism had not gained a large foothold in England. Yet these movements' emphasis upon women's equality profoundly influenced the League, through the Liberal and Reform women who dominated its councils.

At the same time, English feminism's Christian-centered attitude and social anti-Semitism continued to isolate many Jews from the mainstream of the movement. The League's status as a church-related group permitted Jewish women to participate in suffrage in a socially acceptable manner. Moreover, remaining united as a Jewish group that participated in a national movement gained them some sympathy from the larger Jewish community.

Jewish suffragist leaders' upper-class status and close-knit, extended family network enabled them to face often virulent opposition from their opponents, whether Jewish or Christian. Although outwardly acculturated and socially accepted by World War I, the Anglo-Jewish community in England remained wary of anti-Semitism and as conservative as native English citizens themselves. The majority of English Jews feared that Jewish suffragists threatened not only traditional religious and British national values but also the steady process of social acceptance. The result was virulent Jewish communal hostility to suffrage, ranging from verbal attacks in newspapers to violent harangues by angry mobs outside meeting rooms of the Jewish League for Woman Suffrage.

Upper- or middle-class English Jews with a proven commitment to social reform joined the NUWSS and other national suffrage groups across England. Nevertheless, the Christian-centric attitude of the suffragist movement permitted only a selected handful of upper-class Anglo-Jewish women such as Netta Franklin and Eva Hubback to become national leaders. Despite these obstacles, the League's status as a "church"-affiliated organization strengthened its position within the suffragist movement because of England's emphasis upon the ties between church and state. Given all these factors, Anglo-Jewish suffragists felt that their acceptance into the controversial movement "proved" their status as Englishwomen, in the same way that male Anglo-Jewish communal leaders boasted that Jewish men sat on both sides of the aisle in Parliament.

Anglo-Jewish suffrage radicalism proved dramatically visible, despite the conservatism of the Jewish community. Jewish militant suffragists, feeling secure in their English class status, saw themselves as part of an historic tradition in England that witnessed riots at the coal mines in the same year that women were breaking windows. The majority of radicals were upper- and middle-class Anglo-Jewish feminists. The fragile Jewish socialism of the East End may have contributed a handful of women to this process.

In contrast, the lack of Jewish militancy in America was part of the nation's mainstream suffragist context; Alice Paul's Congressional Union proved the exception to the rule. Maud Nathan commented that Jewish and Gentile suffragists alike "set to work to keep ourselves in the public eye in a fashion that would interest and not antagonize."[101]

American Jewish women did not feel the need to create a separate Jewish suffragist organization. Middle-class Jewish women's nationwide suffrage activism indicated their extensive acculturation and their strong feeling of social acceptance. Moreover, the deep divisions in Jewish religious and communal life also affected the Jewish feminist movement, making it difficult for Jewish women to unite into one national organization.[102]

The presence of East European immigrants in the American suffrage movement indicated a cross-class alliance that marked a fundamental difference between England and the United States. Maud Nathan, Lillian Wald, and other middle-class Jewish suffragists helped to bring immigrants into the movement. Rose Schneiderman, Pauline Newman, Clara Lemlich, and others organized working women across the United States into NAWSA, the Equality League, Woman Suffrage Party, and the WTUL.[103] This coalition of middle-class and working-class Jewish women contributed significantly to the suffragist victory, influencing the direction of the American suffragist movement and the victory that led to the Nineteenth Amendment.

The numbers of East European suffragists were dramatically fewer in England than in the United States. The same isolation and resentment that made it extraordinarily difficult to unionize Jewish immigrant women in England appear to have made it even harder to draw East European women into suffrage. Given the class snobbery and anti-alien attitudes of England and the suffragist movement, it was astonishing that the East End branch of the Jewish League for Women Suffrage even existed.

When the ballots were won, Jewish women had forged a Jewish woman's movement and secured their place within national feminism, in England and the United States. The interaction between Jewish and secular feminism had helped to reshape the lives of Jewish and Christian women alike, winning the vote in the national and Jewish spheres.

7

The "New" Jewish Woman

I would much rather people did not emphasise that I am the first woman President. I have to carry out the work of the Board whether I wear petticoats or trousers.

HANNAH COHEN's election as the first woman president of England's Jewish Board of Guardians in 1930 symbolized women's postwar attainments in the Jewish community.[1] Moreover, her presidency also represented Jewish women's desire, after winning the vote, to emulate the progress of their non-Jewish colleagues in England and the United States.

As Nancy Cott has pointed out, electoral politics was not the only major consequence of winning the vote. Suffragists moved from equal rights to social welfare feminism, pursuing politics through voluntary associations that continued nineteenth-century women's tradition of exercising political influence through voluntary associations.

Some historians see the embrace of social welfare as a feminist conservative backlash that in America revived only partially toward progressivism with the advent of the New Deal.[2] Cott disagrees. The creation of thousands of women's organizations, their members' skilled political lobbying which effected political change, and their focus on health, safety, welfare and moral issues to protect women and children demonstrate that there were more similarities than differences in women's political participation before and after 1920.[3] This post-1920 approach varied somewhat in each country, depending upon when national suffrage was achieved and to what degree the aftermath of war aroused popular support for welfare legislation.[4]

Still, this emphasis on welfare and service was partly due to an interweaving of the postwar economic situation, the rise of conservatism and anti-feminism throughout Europe, and the growing threat of fascism in the early 1930s. Although the economic situation demanded that women work in order to survive, public propaganda,

159

official and unofficial, pressured women to leave their wartime jobs and return to their homes, and even accused working women of being unpatriotic by taking jobs away from returning soldiers. This anti-feminist backlash and the Depression exacerbated the employment problem for women. Only the single-issue birth control movement remained a widely supported feminist campaign, although equal rights activity persisted until World War II.[5]

In this atmosphere, suffragists, many of whom were social workers, returned to their original social concerns, believing that securing the franchise guaranteed that they could now effectively influence national priorities. Equal rights feminism did not disappear, but women who still pursued legal and economic equality were regarded as selfish and unconcerned with postwar social needs.

Jewish women's postwar activities fit this pattern. As we shall see, Mathilde Schechter's call for a "bond of unity" among Jewish women symbolized a unity within diversity among English and American Jewish women's organizations; the focus was on Jewish social welfare as well as communal and religious service. Only in England, where the campaign for full adult suffrage continued until 1928, did organized Jewish women systematically pursue communal and religious equality.

ENGLAND

By the close of World War I, Englishwomen's wartime service ended the last philosophical argument against women's suffrage and gave women a powerful political weapon with which to pursue the vote. The WSPU's successor Woman's Party gradually ceased to exist and the non-militant NUWSS survived as Britain's most important suffrage organization, leading the successful drive for limited suffrage in 1918.

The Representation of the People Bill gave men universal manhood suffrage. It restricted the vote to women householders or the wives of householders who were at least thirty years of age, enfranchising six out of eleven million adult women. Although the bill abandoned the principle of sex equality, the NUWSS accepted the bill because they did not want to risk this partial success by holding out for more.[6]

In 1919, the NUWSS was renamed the National Union of Societies for Equal Citizenship (NUSEC). For the next decade, it led the campaign for full adult suffrage, which was finally achieved in 1928.[7] Yet, although NUSEC and other women's organizations successfully lobbied for improvements in the legal, political, economic, and social position of women during the interwar period, NUSEC never achieved its prewar size or status.

Feminists' postwar drive for universal woman suffrage sustained a vibrant equal rights–oriented feminist movement in England for ten years after its drastic decline in the United States. English feminists forged an alliance between women and welfare, often supported by women trade unionists, the Labour Party, and the Fabian Society; this coalition shaped the manner in which the woman's movement was to develop in the interwar years.[8] Elizabeth Wilson notes that women's organizations protested against discrimination against women in employment and social services and urged legislation which strengthened the ties between social work, welfare, and feminism.[9] As we shall see, Anglo-Jewish women helped to lead those activities and undertook a drive for equal rights in Jewish communal and religious life.

POSTWAR JEWISH FEMINISM

Anglo-Jewish feminists' activities paralleled those of their English peers in nearly all aspects of life. Jewish women's dramatic advances in education, employment, and volunteer opportunities prompted the *Jewish Guardian* newspaper's special supplement, *The Jewish Woman*, to feature articles on Jewish women's professional and political accomplishments more prominently than it did traditional articles on fashion and diet.[10]

Active in the national and international woman's movement, Jewish women were highly visible in NUSEC, the International Council of Women, international peace organizations, and the League of Nations.[11] Eva Hubback was especially prominent in both equal rights and welfare feminism. Hubback, a Franklin cousin, became a suffragist while a student member of Cambridge University's Fabian Society. After the death of her husband in 1917, she threw herself even more intensely into suffragist politics, combining "pertinacious attack with friendly and reasonable cooperation." She and her cousin Netta Franklin were particularly close throughout the campaign.[12]

By 1919, Hubback had become the parliamentary secretary of NUSEC and worked closely with its president, Eleanor Rathbone, to obtain a series of successful equal rights laws that granted women eligibility to professions and Parliament, as well as equality in child protection and divorce. Like her non-Jewish colleagues, Hubback perceived the ballot as the key to a larger goal:

> The vote alone is valueless, but it is the key to citizenship. It unlocks the door to the real equality of liberties, status and opportunities which should exist between men and women in every well-ordered community.[13]

After full adult suffrage was granted in 1928, Hubback, like her non-Jewish colleagues, devoted herself to promoting welfare legislation for women in alliance with the Labour Party. Active in the birth control movement, Hubback helped lead NUSEC's effort to persuade the Ministry of Health to give birth control advice at their maternity clinics. She worked for passage of legislation granting equality for women in wages and child custody divorce cases as well as for a widow's pension plan and access by women to professional societies and boards.

Hubback worked particularly hard for Eleanor Rathbone's "new feminism" concept, which suggested that mothers should receive a stipend from the state for each child. Women who had to work to support their families should receive equal pay with men. This idea was never implemented, although it was popular among social welfare feminists.[14]

Still, the "new feminism" was anathema to equal rights advocates like Millicent Garrett Fawcett, who viewed these ideas as a return to anti-feminist arguments of the nineteenth and earlier centuries. She and her followers left NUSEC in 1926, and the woman's movement split over the issue.[15]

Hubback, like the majority of women reformers, continued to focus on education and family health care legislation as a member of the London County Council during the 1930s and 1940s, helping to create national women's organizations devoted to these concerns.[16] Through much of her career, the large house, given to her as principal of Morely College (Kennington), an adult education institute, served as a meeting point of feminists and female academics from England, the Commonwealth, and the United States.[17]

Netta Franklin's postwar activities reflected a similar shift toward social welfare. After stepping down from the presidency of the NUWSS, she became president of the National Council of Women (NCW). Under her leadership, the NCW lobbied for national and international social welfare programs that resulted in legislation protecting women and children.[18]

THE JEWISH COMMUNITY

Feminists' renewed emphasis upon protective legislation to strengthen the maternal role and the family meshed perfectly with the Anglo-

Jewish community's need for new forms of health care and other social services. Immigration virtually ceased after 1915, so economics alone determined the volume of applicants to Jewish social service agencies. The increase in welfare legislation and the dispersal of Jews from the East End to the London suburbs meant that, although poverty increased as a result of wartime deprivations and the 1929 Depression, social services also had to disperse and reorient themselves to meet new types of clients.[19]

All of these conditions forced Jewish agencies to expand health programs and create new services intended to be of permanent, rather than temporary, benefit. In response to health needs, Anglo-Jewish women financed beds in a women's hospital, helped to found the London Jewish Hospital in 1919, created more women's "friendly societies" with their insurance benefits, and expanded the services of cooperative organizations like Alice Model's Sick Room Helps Society.[20]

Outside of England, the vast social service needs of the newly founded Jewish Homeland in Palestine attracted thousands of volunteers. In 1918, suffragist Rebecca Sieff founded the Federation of Women Zionists, which later became the Women's International Zionist Organization (WIZO). Focusing upon the dearth of decent health care, food, and housing, FWZ established a network of welfare services that supported the English Zionist Federation's political efforts.[21]

Faced with the combination of communal and Zionist exigency at the same time that English feminists were turning toward social welfare, postwar Anglo-Jewish women flocked to public service in even greater numbers than before the war. Once again, Franklin women proved instrumental inside and outside the Anglo-Jewish community.

Nettie Adler, the elder daughter of Chief Rabbi and Mrs. Herman Adler, served as a member of the London County Council, where she devoted herself mainly to the education, job training, and employment of young people. Her scheme to rejuvenate Jewish communal service in the East End by training Jewish women as social workers was adopted by the Anglo-Jewish community. She inspired and partly directed the special Jewish War Memorial education project for the East End. Adler was idolized by the Jewish community, and her prominence made her a role model for Jewish women who assumed professional roles or moved into public service, such as her cousin, crystallographer Rosalind Franklin. In 1922, when Adler was elected deputy chairman of the London County Council, the *Jewish Guardian* exulted in

Helen Bentwich. Courtesy, Greater
London Photographic Library

the "striking tribute to her efficient public service," which was "particularly gratifying to her many friends in the Anglo-Jewish community."[22]

Helen Bentwich was the daughter of publisher Arthur Franklin
and his wife Beatrice, a founder of the Union of Jewish Women. As a
forewoman in a munitions factory at Woolwich arsenal during World
War I, Bentwich was so horrified at working conditions that she attempted to organize workers into a trade union and joined the Labour
Party, rapidly rising to a leadership position. In 1937, she joined the
London County Council as a Labour Party representative. There she
focused on securing welfare legislation sponsored by a coalition of
feminists and the Labour Party. Actively engaged in Jewish communal
service in England and abroad, she lived for a decade in Palestine with

her husband, Zionist leader Norman Bentwich, who served as attorney-general for Palestine from 1920 to 1931.[23]

Beginning with Carolyn Franklin, the first Jewish woman on the Bucks County school board, the Franklin "Cousinhood"—Laura, Leonard, and Hugh Franklin, Netta Franklin and her sister Lily Montagu, Eva Hubback, Helen Bentwich, and Nettie Adler—reveal an extraordinary family involvement in both the equal rights and social welfare aspects of Anglo-Jewish feminism during the first half of the twentieth century.

At the same time, the Franklin cousins helped to shape the postwar ideal of Anglo-Jewish womanhood through their combination of English and Anglo-Jewish politics, public service and social work. To a Jewish community still wary of the "new woman," they proved that feminism could strengthen Jewish home life, values, and the synagogue. Indeed, the Anglo-Jewish community applauded the prominence of these "new" Jewish women as exemplars of Jewish acculturation and the possibilities for Jewish women in public life.[24] To the English feminist movement, which had hesitated over accepting Anglo-Jewish women into its ranks, these cousins personified the class status, personal commitment, social reform credentials, and organizational skills that made Anglo-Jewish women welcome in its ranks in ever-greater numbers.

THE UNION OF JEWISH WOMEN

The Union of Jewish Women typified the manner in which Anglo-Jewish women applied equal rights and welfare feminism in the Jewish community. During the war, Union members had concentrated on helping refugees and finding employment for Jewish gentlewomen. The Union even persuaded some Jewish women to work as farmers, thus freeing men for the army.[25]

Wartime changes forced the Union to expand its services and open up its leadership, however. New employment and business opportunities had stimulated the rising influence of the middle class. Distinctions between the middle and lower classes became blurred as fewer servants worked in middle-class homes and women sought new occupational opportunities.[26]

Many Eastern European immigrants had become "respectable" members of the middle class after they opened their own businesses. Retailing, the radio industry, scrap metal, textiles, clothes, jewelry, and foodstuffs provided the key to success. The postwar generation of Jewish immigrants and their children were educated, English-speaking, and acculturated. Its members moved out of the East End to comfortable suburbs. They not only climbed the ladder to financial comfort but attained a certain amount of social and political influence as well.[27]

The rising influence of middle- and working-class women forced the postwar Union to expand its governing council to include middle-class women. In addition to educating teachers and nurses, the Union trained Jewish women as social workers, dentists, and even police-women, who worked in the East End with young women. Going beyond its traditional mandate, the UJW added affiliate social service organizations concerned with Jewish women and children.[28]

Involved in a mixture of English social feminist and Jewish projects, the Union worked closely with Millicent Garrett Fawcett and affiliated with the Fabian Women's Group. It insisted that Jewish women "with their recently acquired political power, have greater responsibilities to face, and there are many special problems before the Jewish Community." To deal with these concerns, the Union lobbied for improved social services and protective legislation for working-class women and children and helped to build the Jewish community's War Memorial, with its emphasis on Jewish education for the East End.[29]

Although social welfare was important to the Jewish community, the Union realized that it would never achieve significant political influence in Jewish life until it improved women's religious and communal rights. Helen Bentwich, for example, exercised more political influence in English than in Jewish affairs. As a result, the UJW undertook a campaign for equality in all aspects of Jewish religious and communal life.

The Union won confirmation of girls and mixed seating in the synagogues that still did not permit them, and obtained votes for women in several independent synagogues. Arguing that confirmation of girls was not prohibited in Jewish law and had precedents in both the United States and England, the Union persuaded seven synagogues to pass resolutions in favor of confirmation classes for girls by 1923. The Union's campaign for mixed synagogue seating also began in the same year at the West London Synagogue.[30]

The *Jewish Guardian* supported the confirmation effort but opposed the UJW's campaign for mixed seating, although it had been sympathetic to other measures equalizing women's role in the synagogue. Unlike proposals dealing with confirmation of children and votes in the synagogue, the editors argued, the practice of separate seating was firmly embedded in Jewish tradition and changing it

would split the Jewish community by softening the distinction between a church and a synagogue. Despite this argument, sympathetic
Jewish ministers noted that mixed seating was a step that followed
logically from confirmation for boys and girls.

> You go to an "orthodox" Synagogue on the occasion of a marriage, and
> you find men and women sitting together quite indiscriminately. Girls
> and boys have been . . . confirmed . . . together. All this in the Chief
> Rabbi's Synagogue! If this defiance of Tradition is right on these occa-
> sions, it cannot be wrong on others.[31]

At the same time, England's Liberal and Reform synagogues began
to democratize synagogue management and made major innovations
in ritual, including calling women to the pulpit to read the Torah
blessings.[32]

However thorny were these questions of ritual, the immigration
of thousands of highly traditional Eastern European Jews and the publicity about white slavery publicized equally difficult religious issues
affecting marriage and divorce. Some East European rabbis perform-
ing religious marriages and divorces, for example, did not realize that
they must also conform to England's civil code. One woman who was
charged with bigamy in the Thames Police Court explained that she
had received a Jewish divorce at the house of a rabbi and believed
herself free to remarry.[33] To address these problems, in 1920 the *Jewish
Guardian* ran a series of articles entitled "Some Legal Difficulties
which beset the Jewess," written by a Miss Hands, a communal
worker. The series called for an international conference of Orthodox
rabbinical authorities to meet and issue edicts modifying Jewish law.[34]
No conference of this type was held before World War II.

Liberal and Reform Judaism solved the many problems surrounding religious divorce by abrogating religious divorce altogether and
declaring that divorce was a civil matter. Orthodox Jewry made no
attempt to change family law, but preferred individual counseling
wherever possible.

The changes promoting Jewish study and confirmation for girls in
Orthodox as well as Liberal and Reform synagogues, and the growing
popularity of mixed seating in progressive synagogues, strengthened
the case for granting voting rights to women. The Union had not taken
a formal position on suffrage during the prewar battle for the vote,
because it believed its functions were limited. After the war, its broad-
ened membership base of primarily middle-class women demanded
that the Union participate in the national campaign for universal

woman suffrage, and undertake a campaign for Jewish religious and communal equality.

As a result, the UJW affiliated with several English suffrage groups, publicly identifying itself as the representative of Anglo-Jewish women in the continuing political drive for the vote.[35] The Union also revived the prewar campaign by the Jewish League for Woman Suffrage to secure the franchise for women seatholders in all congregations affiliated with the United Synagogue, supported by the *Jewish Guardian*.[36] As noted earlier, the JLWS had dissolved during the war so that its members could focus on the war effort. After the war, many of its members joined or reactivated their membership in the Union of Jewish Women, spearheading the ensuing project.

By 1918, as a result of work by the now-defunct Jewish League for Woman Suffrage, seven synagogues had granted the franchise to women in whole or in part. By 1920, due to the UJW's efforts, sixteen out of eighteen constituent synagogues in the United Synagogue voted in favor of granting the franchise to women seatholders.[37]

The Union then placed a motion for religious suffrage before the United Synagogue to grant the vote to women seatholders in all its constituent synagogues. Recognizing the precedents established by Christian churches and the desperate need to revivify Jewish religious life, the *Jewish Guardian* supported the measure. Despite much sympathy, however, the issue was defeated in 1922.[38]

The UJW failed in its efforts to obtain the vote throughout the United Synagogue during the interwar period. Many leaders of the United Synagogue were among the most conservative men in Anglo-Jewish leadership, and they maintained the status quo until World War II. Despite this, the Union succeeded in obtaining the ballot in a number of individual synagogues whose leadership was prepared to act independently of the Chief Rabbi and the United Synagogue.

Wartime changes and the need to bring young English Jews back into the synagogues had already fostered a movement toward religious equality in the synagogue. Women in the Liberal movement had been permitted to lead the reading of prayers and psalms during services ever since the Jewish Religious Union's first worship service in 1902. As already noted, Lily Montagu gave her first sermon in 1918, others followed after the war, and, by early 1920, women were preaching frequently in the Liberal Jewish Synagogue.[39]

The logical next step was triggered by information from America. In September 1920, the Anglo-Jewish newspapers carried reports that Martha Neumark had entered Hebrew Union College in Cincinnati, Ohio, to study for the rabbinate. The Liberal Synagogue soon passed a motion approving "the principle of admitting women into the ministry" and, despite the ensuing furor, established a search committee to find a suitable candidate. By 1926, Lily Montagu was functioning as a lay minister.[40]

By the late 1920s, Anglo-Jewish women's progress in the synagogue had increased their communal political influence. Jewish women were admitted to membership on the boards of many Anglo-Jewish synagogues and communal institutions, and were involved in decisions affecting internal communal life.

COMMUNAL AND RELIGIOUS LEADERSHIP

The limited victories in the synagogue established a quasi-religious sanction for seeking membership on communal boards. By 1919, the UJW had won three voting seats for Union representatives on the Board of Guardians. This "great step forward" permitted Union members to influence all matters affecting the internal affairs of British Jews.[41] In addition to its Board seats, the Union also gained representation on the Jewish War Memorial Council, which dealt with postwar reconstruction.[42]

For Hannah F. Cohen, prominence in English and Anglo-Jewish women's concerns served as a springboard to power within the postwar Jewish community. Before assuming the presidency of the Board of Guardians, she had served on the governing bodies of two women's colleges and as an officer of the University Women's Club. During World War I, she worked for the government, in both the Home Office and Treasury. Cohen also found time to write two books and volunteer for a wide range of Jewish charitable and Zionist activities.[43]

In 1930, Cohen became the Board of Guardians' first woman president, and she held that post until 1940. The niece, daughter, and first cousin of successive Board presidents, and a leader of the Union of Jewish Women, she had been active on the Board for several years. As president, she was a brilliant administrator, focusing on the developing progressive projects in social services and preventive health care.[44] Cohen's unique position empowered her to dominate the Board's communal welfare policy until World War II, but she insisted that ability, not sex, was the determining issue.

Hannah Cohen's election symbolized Anglo-Jewish women's growing communal influence. By 1933, Jewish women's social service and political leadership had a significant impact upon the Jewish community. Jewish women's membership on the Jewish Board of Deputies, the Board of Guardians, and the boards of nearly every communal social service agency gave them a voice in deciding communal

Hannah F. Cohen. Courtesy, Jewish Welfare Board

policy. Their postwar activism, like that of their Christian peers,[45] contributed to bringing the needs of women and children to the forefront of the national political agenda.

Nonetheless, Jewish women's communal and religious influence between 1914 and 1933 remained somewhat limited, since official communal deputations to the British government usually consisted entirely of males. Orthodox synagogues occasionally allowed confirmation of girls, but they did not otherwise extend women's rights in religious life. Women still worshiped from the women's gallery and took no part in leading worship services. Reform and Liberal synagogues permitted women to preach occasionally in the pulpit and take a more equal part in religious life, but only Lily Montagu acted as a lay preacher, and she was not formally inducted as a lay minister until 1944. Progressive Judaism formally ordained men as rabbis in the late 1950s, but women did not achieve the same status until the

1970s. The era between the wars witnessed progress for Anglo-Jewish women that was severely tempered by the conservative reaction that affected all of Britain, including its Jewish community.

UNITED STATES

The Nineteenth Amendment, which passed in 1920, granted universal suffrage to women and men throughout the United States. Feminists assumed the great victory would lead to a massive outpouring of women into electoral politics. Instead, because America did not experience England's continuing suffrage effort, which lasted until 1928, American women activists turned almost immediately to social welfare volunteerism. Feminists encountered the same postwar phenomena—conservatism, anti-feminism, economic depression, and, by the 1930s, the rise of fascism—that had transformed the woman's movement in England. The defeat of the child labor amendment after 1924 signaled the end of an era.[46]

Nevertheless, as Nancy Cott has noted, although there was a considerable decline in the membership of women's organizations solely devoted to women's interests, women avidly joined single-purpose groups that were enlisting both women and men in an effort to solve their prewar community concerns.

Wooed by political party organizations, women left the League of Women Voters and joined the Democratic and Republican parties. Membership in the General Federation of Women's Clubs declined, but thousands of women joined the Parent-Teacher Association, where they continued their efforts for their children's welfare. Equal rights organizations declined drastically, particularly the National Consumers' League and the National Women's Trade Union League. Professional staff members in labor unions, their work absorbed by government or more formal private institutions, now tackled other objectives.[47]

JEWISH WOMEN'S ORGANIZATIONS

After passage of the Nineteenth Amendment, some Jewish feminists, such as Ray Frank and Jennie Loitman Barron, joined the League of Women Voters (formerly NAWSA), concentrating on its education programs and protective legislation for women.[48] They were among the thousands of Jewish women who participated in the explosion of volunteerism by American women and the rise in group consciousness by minority women, Black as well as Jewish. Dozens of new Jewish

NCJW conference delegates visit the White House. Courtesy, National Council of
Jewish Women

women's organizations sprang up during the 1920s: Junior Hadassah
(1921), the Conference Group of National Jewish Women's Organizations (1923), the Women's Branch of the Union of Orthodox Jewish
Congregations of America (1924), the women's organization of the
Pioneer Women of Palestine (1925).[49]

Older organizations of Jewish women expanded considerably during this same period. The National Council of Jewish Women multiplied its community services and lobbying efforts for welfare legislation.[50] Joan Dash's study of Henrietta Szold examines the manner
in which Szold brilliantly forged Hadassah into an effective fund-
raising and social welfare organization in support of the Jewish Homeland in Palestine before the war.[51] By 1930, the NCJW and Hadassah
each claimed between forty and fifty thousand members. By 1935,
half a dozen new Jewish women's organizations had been founded.

RELIGIOUS CHOICES

Women's groups affiliated with the Reform and Conservative movements, founded just before or just after the war, now increased wom-
en's participation in religious life. To varying degrees, depending upon
the particular movement, women assumed positions on synagogue
school boards and executive committees, attended classes in Judaism,

and participated more fully in religious ritual. Women's attempts to assert leadership in national religious movements, though limited in scope, proved vitally important. Nationwide sisterhoods brought thousands of women into religious life, providing a climate that, as we shall see, encouraged some women to seek rabbinical ordination or other forms of religious leadership, and leading Mordecai Kaplan's new Reconstructionist movement to assert women's equality as intrinsic to its theological structure.

Once again, a trend among American women—in this case, massive volunteerism—formed the essential prerequisite for attracting the large numbers of women who joined national sisterhoods' membership rolls. The organizations' development was also due to the declining influence of Reform, and the rising star of the Conservative movement.

The Reform movement faced a major crisis. Jewish Eastern European immigrants now vastly outnumbered the population of native American Jews of German-Jewish descent. Most of these newcomers preferred traditional Orthodoxy to Reform's abrogation of tradition. Moreover, even those Jews of Eastern European origin who rejected Orthodoxy did not become Reform. Some remained staunchly socialist; others joined the burgeoning Conservative movement, which allowed them a moderate degree of traditionalism while retaining a strong sense of Jewish law and custom. As a result, the Reform movement had to scramble for members in order to strengthen its ranks.[52]

Aware of the effectiveness of Jewish women's organizations, Reform leaders hoped that a Reform women's organization would help rejuvenate the movement. Like Anglo-Jewish author and suffrage advocate Israel Zangwill, many Reform rabbis believed that women would revitalize the synagogues threatened by the decline in men's attendance.[53]

To attract women otherwise engaged in social service and Zionist organizations, J. Walter Freiberg, president of the Union of American Hebrew Congregations (UAHC), invited all temple sisterhoods to send delegates to a conference that would create a federation of temple sisterhoods affiliated with the UAHC. The conference opened on January 21, 1913, in Cincinnati, home of the UAHC and its rabbinical seminary, Hebrew Union College. In his opening address, Rabbi David Philipson defined the task of the new federation as a "religious and congregational organization" that would be "the counterpart" of the UAHC. As an auxiliary of the synagogue, the National Federation of Temple Sisterhoods (NFTS) would "lift it out of the formalism into which it is lapsing." However, warned one rabbinical speaker, the role of women was not to initiate or change, but to "maintain" an organization. The synagogue was "a man's society," and women's role was to sustain and help improve it through the "inspiration" of the home life generated by women's superior "moral personality."[54]

The first constitution of the NFTS defined its task as furthering "the religious and moral development of Israel" by "cooperation" with Reform congregations. Carrie Obendorfer Simon, the NFTS's first president (1913–19) and secretary of the Cincinnati section of the NCJW, had been involved with the woman's movement since she joined the Council in the 1890s.[55] Far from agreeing that the synagogue was a "man's society," Simon defended feminism's equal rights aspirations as the basis for women's modern role in religious life.

> Is there any connection between the renaissance of Religion and the rise of the Women's Movement? I think there is. And I believe there will be a still more intimate and positive relationship between the Synagogue and the American Jewess. The Synagog [sic] shall hear the call of the Sister. The Synagog is not a masculine institution; it must provide a place of equal *privilege, prayer, activity* and *responsibility* for the Jewess. Must *she* not be the creator of the new enthusiasm in Israel?[56]

Local temple sisterhoods in conjunction with the NFTS, suggested Simon, would encourage women to extend their religious influence to both home and synagogue. " '*Forward with synagog*' is now our ruling passion." NFTS's format mirrored that of similar American volunteer organizations. Like the NCJW or Hadassah, the NFTS was rooted in the Jewish community. Unlike them, however, the NFTS concentrated on fostering religious commitment in home and synagogue. Although the group also supported local charitable causes,[57] it emphasized activities that strengthened Reform Judaism.[58]

In cooperation with local sisterhoods, Federation attempted to foster improvement in Reform congregational life for both women and men. They introduced congregational singing, helped to sponsor a new Reform prayerbook, raised money to beautify and improve synagogue buildings, and provided scholarships and a dormitory for rabbinical students. Primarily concerned with women's needs, NFTS taught ritual to women, created women's study circles in Judaism, improved synagogue religious schools, and instituted parent teacher associations for them.[59]

NFTS affirmed its "commitment to women's equality" and "full participation in society." To that end, they affiliated with the National Conference of Jewish Women's Organizations, the NCJW, and similar groups. In 1928, however, NFTS resigned from Council, asserting that the basic aims of the two groups were different.[60] Determined to place women in influential positions within the Reform religious establishment, NFTS secured membership for women on synagogue school boards and on temple boards of trustees.[61] After steady lobbying by NFTS, the UAHC Board in 1923 declared women eligible for membership on the Executive Board. By 1932, Board membership included three NFTS representatives.[62]

Arguing that women "are naturally fitted to develop and understand the religious life," Sisterhood leadership urged their members to participate fully in all aspects of synagogue life, especially ritual worship. Some NFTS leaders asserted that women's capabilities would soon lead them into the rabbinate and applauded Lily Montagu's spiritual leadership in England.[63]

In theory, the Reform movement permitted women's ordination. However, no one had tested the proposition, either as a traveling preacher like Ray Frank or as a congregational leader, until Martha Neumark entered Hebrew Union College's undergraduate program at the age of fourteen. The daughter of Rabbi David Neumark, a professor at Hebrew Union College (HUC), she received her B.H.L. (Bachelor of Hebrew Letters) in 1921 and was formally admitted into the rabbinical program. To Neumark, ordination seemed the natural outcome of her father's influence, the woman's movement, the ferment created by Jewish women's organizations, Reform women's increasing influence in the UAHC, and the example of Lily Montagu in England, who by 1921 was beginning her career as a lay minister. Newspaper publicity and the close connections between England's Liberal Judaism and America's Reform movement ensured that Neumark and Montagu knew about each other's activities.

In the fall of 1921, soon after her acceptance into the rabbinical program, Neumark requested permission to conduct High Holiday services at HUC. Concerned about the request's larger implications, the faculty split over the issue but finally voted in her favor. At the recommendation of Rabbi Kaufmann Kohler, who supported Neumark's petition, the Board of Governors of the college formed a committee to study the question of women's ordination. Concluding that women should be discouraged from entering the rabbinate, the committee sent the question to the annual conference of the Central Conference of American Rabbis (CCAR) during the summer of 1922.[64]

At the conference, Dr. Jacob Lauterbach, HUC's distinguished professor of Talmud, issued a legal opinion (*responsum*) opposing women's ordination on the basis of Jewish legal precedent. He further contended that ordaining women would not justify creating further distinctions between Reform and other rabbis.[65] Lauterbach's regard for Jewish law and fears of a split in Judaism's ranks constituted two major reasons for the Reform movement's delay in ordaining women until 1972. Conservative Judaism hesitated to ordain women for similar reasons until 1986. Orthodox Judaism today has not yet ordained women. Orthodox Jewish feminists continue to struggle today with legal limitations placed upon women's role in synagogue ritual and certain aspects of religious life.

Lauterbach represented the minority among his colleagues in 1922. The majority argued that the Reform movement "broke with tradition long ago" when they granted equality to women. Three wives of rabbis, invited to speak on the issue, urged the rabbis to pass the measure, based on Reform's emphasis upon women's involvement with the movement. Rabbi David Neumark, Martha's father, argued in support of his daughter:

> The woman rabbi who will remain single will not be more, in fact less, of a problem than the bachelor rabbi. If she marries and chooses to remain a rabbi, and God blesses her, she will retire for a few months and provide a substitute, as rabbis generally do when they are sick or meet with an automobile accident. When she comes back, she will be a better rabbi for the experience.[66]

The CCAR conference overwhelmingly voted in favor of the ordination of women. However, the Board of Governors of Hebrew Union College refused to accept its decision. At the Board's February 1923 meeting, the Board's two rabbis voted yes, and the six laymen no. In outvoting the rabbis, HUC's laymen had decided that "no change should be made in the present practice of limiting to males" the right to enter the rabbinate.[67]

A stunned Martha Neumark bitterly commented that men who knew nothing of rabbinical duties had voted against her, whereas the majority of Reform rabbis supported her. Fear, wrote Neumark, underlay the Board's rejection: "a struggle ensues each time that a woman threatens to break up man's monopoly upon any . . . province." Neumark remained in her classes for two years, hoping unsuccessfully that she could convince Board members to change their minds. Finally resigning herself to the inevitable, she left Hebrew Union College in 1925 and watched from the audience as her class became ordained the next year.[68]

The National Federation of Temple Sisterhoods remained officially silent during Neumark's struggle, although three wives of rabbis spoke in favor of Neumark's ordination during the CCAR Conference. NFTS's large financial contributions to Hebrew Union College and the three seats on the UAHC Board of Directors only endowed it with a limited political influence by 1923. Despite Carrie Simon's equal-rights feminism, the organization as a whole emphasized *service* to the wider Reform movement. Thus NFTS saw itself within Judaism's traditional view of women as enablers, as well as within modern women's volunteer activities. Eager to be accepted as partners within the Reform movement, NFTS subsumed women's singular interests into the larger goal of benefiting Reform as a whole. Since the lay leaders and not the rabbis on the HUC Board set College policy, NFTS loyally accepted their decisions regarding ordination.

Two other women followed Martha Neumark and unsuccessfully sought ordination in the years before World War II. Irma Levy (Lindheim) was a Zionist leader who entered Hebrew Union College in 1922, at the height of the controversy over Martha Neumark. Levy was accepted as a candidate for a rabbinical degree but was never ordained.[69] Helen Levinthal completed the entire rabbinical course at the Reform movement's Jewish Institute of Religion in New York in 1939. According to Rabbi Stephen S. Wise, the Hebrew Union College faculty seriously debated the matter but concluded that ordaining women was not yet practical. Levinthal was granted an M.H.L. (Master of Hebrew Letters) degree and a diploma written in Hebrew that recognized her scholarship.[70]

Without political support from NFTS or the winning votes from their rabbinical supporters, Neumark, Levy, and Levinthal could not muster sufficient political organization to defeat the laymen on the HUC board. Women's ordination was defeated by fears of women's intrusion into a "male" sphere and women's postwar emphasis upon service rather than equality, which made NFTS reluctant to tackle male authority. The question of women's ordination would not arise again until 1972, when Hebrew Union College ordained Sally Priesand as its first female rabbi.

THE CONSERVATIVE MOVEMENT

Founded at the end of the nineteenth century by Zechariah Frankel, the Conservative movement asserts that Jewish law, while not immutable, has become part of Jewish consciousness and constitutes the Jewish way of expressing religious feeling. Therefore, while Jewish law may be amended to reflect new historical situations, these changes should be gradual so as not to destroy the fabric of the community.[71]

In this spirit, the American Conservative movement authorized mixed seating,[72] but severely restricted ritual participation by women. Instead, Conservative rabbis encouraged women to play a greater role in synagogue religious schools and a supportive role in congregational life.

Adopting this mandate, Mathilde Schechter, the wife of Solomon Schechter, president of the Jewish Theological Seminary, launched the Women's League of the United Synagogue in 1918. A learned, warm, and sympathetic woman, Mrs. Schechter envisioned the League as serving "the cause of Judaism by strengthening the bond of unity among Jewish women, and by learning to appreciate everything fine in Jewish life and literature."[73]

Founded to assist the male leaders of the United Synagogue, the League saw its role as extending the Jewish home into the synagogue.[74] To fulfill this goal, the League taught Jewish members basic Judaism, which they were encouraged to reinforce through home rituals. The League carried on fund-raising for the Jewish Theological Seminary and Conservative synagogues, assisted students, and engaged in charitable activities. Like the founders of NFTS, its organizers decided not to replicate the social service functions of the Council of Jewish Women or the Young Women's Hebrew Association.[75] The women were welcomed with enthusiasm and warmth throughout the Conservative movement.

Yet, despite the need for the League's services, neither rabbis nor laymen in the mainstream Conservative movement even considered easing restrictions that hampered women's participation in ritual during this period. The League reflected postwar women's emphasis upon service, and based itself upon Conservative Judaism's acceptance of the traditional attitude that women were ancillary worshipers and primarily supporters of synagogue life.

Conservative rabbi and theologian Mordecai Kaplan, however, rejected Conservative Judaism's approach, contending that women's emancipation made it impossible for the home to continue on a quasi-patriarchal basis.[76] His views on women developed organically from his concept of Judaism as a total civilization and a result of historical and sociological forces, rather than a religion centered around a personalized God. Kaplan attracted a core of rabbinical students who later split off from Conservative Judaism to found the Reconstructionist movement.

Balancing ethics and pragmatism, his Americanized theology included the notion that women must be equal in the synagogue. In 1922, his daughter became the first Conservative girl ever to read from the Torah as a *bat mitzvah* during a Sabbath morning service. By the 1950s, synagogues based on Kaplan's philosophy of Judaism practiced equality of the sexes. In the early 1970s, the newly created Reconstructionist Rabbinical College graduated women in its first class.

Despite women's growing participation in synagogue life, neither the Reform nor the not-yet-formalized Reconstructionist movement encouraged women's religious leadership during the 1920s and 1930s. Both movements permitted women to give occasional sermons from the pulpit, but guiding the spiritual life of a congregation was deemed a task suitable only for men. Jewish Science, which radically separated itself from Jewish law and tradition, took another view.

Founded by Rabbi Morris and Tehilla Lichtenstein in 1922, in many ways Jewish Science was based on Mary Baker Eddy's Christian Science. It taught that God was the source of all healing, and that faith and prayer can lead to health and peace of mind. Worship services loosely followed a Jewishly oriented ritual and language.[77]

Tehilla Lichtenstein became the religious leader of this small movement in 1938 after her husband's death. Her sermons and publications fostered the growth of Jewish Science and delineate her insistence upon women's equality. Lichtenstein's Mother's Day sermons, for example, emphasize women's abilities, influence, and natural authority.

Jewish Science never gained the stature of a major movement. Ellen Umansky estimates that it probably never had more than five hundred members, although far more subscribed to the *Jewish Science Interpreter*. Today, there are approximately between one hundred and two hundred members.[78] Still, even though membership dwindled drastically in recent years, weekly services are maintained by a few regular worshipers to this day.[79]

The size of Jewish Science and the radical nature of its teachings ensured that Lichtenstein's religious leadership would directly affect relatively few people. Still, her role as spiritual guide indirectly influenced the larger trend toward non-traditional Jewish movements such as Jewish Humanism and the burgeoning Reconstructionism, which were attracting thousands of followers in the twenties and thirties and sustain rapid growth today. Jewish women boast equality in each of these movements, functioning as religious leaders, conducting worship services, and sharing in management responsibilities. As already noted, Reconstructionism ordained women rabbis in the first seminary graduating class. As these and other non-traditional movements expanded, their emphasis upon women's religious equality would ultimately influence Reform and Conservative Judaism during the second Jewish women's movement in the sixties, seventies, and eighties.

Still, American Jewish women did not seek religious equality as avidly as their English sisters in the years between the wars. Several factors—the immediate decline in equal rights feminism after passage of the Nineteenth Amendment, the turn toward social service volunteerism, and the post-suffrage eagerness to be part of a wider framework that finally included men—inhibited American women from seeking equality or leadership in mainstream Judaism. Judaism's emphasis upon tradition undergirded their reluctance. Reform Judaism, fighting to regain its preeminence among Jews inclining toward more traditional Conservative or Orthodox Judaism, was reluctant to totally abandon a heritage that prohibited women from assuming religious leadership or ascending the *bimah* (pulpit) to deliver a sermon. Conservative Judaism, although not committed to the same concept of immutable law as Orthodox Judaism, was certainly not prepared to admit women upon the *bimah*. Only small, non-traditional Jewish movements such as Reconstructionism, Jewish Science, and Jewish Humanism put fully into practice the theory of women's religious equality in the years before World War II.

WORLD COUNCIL OF JEWISH WOMEN

Jewish women's organizations in England, the United States, and Germany had been cooperating since 1904, when Hannah Solomon, Constance Battersea, and Bertha Pappenheim met at the International Council of Women conference in Berlin. The need for formal interaction became apparent over the years as these groups exchanged information and suggestions for grappling with the anti–white slavery furor, social reform, trade unionism, and religious and communal equality. Plans for formation of a World Council of Jewish Women (WCJW) began at the 1914 ICW conference, but had to be shelved because of the war.[80]

Jewish women's postwar social service volunteerism and their involvement in religious issues triggered a new interest in an international institution. NCJW leader Rebekah Kohut spearheaded the creation of the World Council. Kohut, by now a noted suffragist, simultaneously campaigned for women to be admitted to the U.S. Congress and for rabbis to equalize Jewish religious laws affecting marriage and divorce.[81]

Kohut convinced the NCJW to organize the World Council of Jewish Women's first Congress in Vienna in 1923. Attracting worldwide publicity, the Congress drew two hundred Jewish women from over seventy countries. At the last minute, anti-Semitic demonstrations in Vienna almost canceled the Congress, but it soon proceeded, with a covey of reporters jostling participants for seats.

With Rebekah Kohut as chairman, the Congress focused on a range of social and religious problems affecting Jewish women. Participants primarily concerned themselves with ensuring communal and religious equality, insisting that until Judaism viewed women as equal to men, women would remain susceptible to "victimization" in all spheres of Jewish life.[82] Dealing with "social justice and social righteousness" vis-à-vis Jewish women, the Congress established committees to deal with the issues of protection of women and girls, migration, child and maternity welfare, religious education, public health, and international relations.[83]

World Council founders envisioned it as an international clearinghouse through which national Jewish women's councils could acquire information relevant to Jewish women's issues.[84] Delegates communicated policy decisions and committee resolutions to their own national Jewish women's councils, helping them to formulate objectives for their organizations. Enthusiastic about the WCJW's success and its potential for uniting Jewish women, Rebekah Kohut declared that the Council would increase women's social and political influence in every Jewish community around the globe.

The WCJW held a second Congress in 1929, and in 1930 the National Federation of Temple Sisterhoods accepted a membership invitation. By the late 1920s and early 1930s, World Jewish Council congresses anguished over the problem facing German Jewish women with the rise of Hitler but were powerless to help them. Like other international Jewish organizations such as the JAPGW, the WCJW halted its operations at the outbreak of World War II.[85] Reviving after the war, the WCJW today is a thriving international institution claiming membership from Jewish women's national organizations in every part of the world.

The WCJW generated a feeling of international sisterhood among Jewish women. Its approach to social and religious issues influenced decisions by individual national Jewish women's groups. Nevertheless, the Council's strongest effect lay in its psychological influence upon its delegates. Like its parent body, the International Council of Women, it provided an invaluable support structure and advisory system for Jewish women's organizational leaders who pioneered work in social causes and Jewish women's rights.

The Council's formation highlights the process by which the interaction of Jewish women with the wider feminist movement shaped the Jewish women's movement and defined its impact upon the Jewish community. As noted earlier, the seeds of WCJW were planted at an ICW meeting in 1904 and fostered at subsequent conferences. WCJW leaders were grounded in the secular as well as the Jewish feminist movements, and active in anti–white slavery, social reform, and national suffrage causes. The resulting intersection between secular and Jewish feminism typified the Jewish woman's movement in England and the United States.

CONCLUSION

For both Jewish women and their non-Jewish peers in England and America, the tension between adherence to equal rights and social welfare feminism dominated their activities in the interwar period. Nancy Cott asserts that although feminists did not coalesce into one movement, their post-suffrage diversity represents a vital ambivalence that should be "embraced rather than avoided under the name *feminism*" and set the stage for the vitality of the 1960s and 1970s.[86]

Her comments apply to Jewish feminists as well. Unprecedented numbers of Jewish women flooded into a host of Jewish and secular women's organizations in the 1920s and 1930s. Barriers against Jewish membership in national women's organizations that were gradually eroding before the war tumbled down in the wake of Jewish women's war effort and the suffrage victory. Middle-class Jewish women's widespread participation in national life indicated how close they were coming to acculturation and social acceptance.

Jewish women advocated a plethora of causes, from Zionism to religious leadership. Non-traditional Judaism encouraged Lily Montagu and Tehilla Lichtenstein to assume religious leadership, although in movements that greatly differed in size and scope.

Hailing their "bonds of unity," Jewish women volunteered for a vast number of Jewish women's communal and religious organizations. These groups became a springboard for a limited number of women such as Hannah Cohen to assume communal leadership in dealing with social welfare concerns.

. Jewish membership in the International Council of Women continued to influence ICW policies and programs as well as the further expansion of the Jewish woman's movement. The founding of the World Council of Jewish Women in 1923 provided an organized basis for the international cooperation between Jewish women's groups that flowered after World War II.

Nevertheless, Jewish women's hopes for communal and religious equality remained severely limited. In the communal sphere, despite their leadership in communal social welfare, Jewish women exercised scant influence upon the Jewish community's political relationships with the non-Jewish world. In the religious sphere, mainstream Judaism, including Reform, still perceived women's role as primarily supportive of the synagogue and its rabbi.

No major Jewish movement ordained a woman during this era. Tehilla Lichtenstein functioned as leader of a relatively small Jewish movement. Lily Montagu, inducted as lay leader in 1944, was over eighty years old in the 1950s when English Jewry began to ordain women. While Reform and Conservative Judaism permitted women's involvement in ritual in varying degrees, the Conservative movement's primary innovation was restricted to mixed seating in some synagogues. Orthodoxy still placed women in the gallery or behind the *mechitza*, the curtain dividing women and men in the synagogue. Religious law affecting family life persisted unchanged.

Nevertheless, the manner in which Jewish women integrated themselves into the spheres of religious life and communal social welfare provided a vision of full participation in Jewish life that laid the groundwork for a resurgence of Jewish feminism in the early 1970s. It is not inconsequential that the "bond of unity" among Jewish women ultimately transcended the dissensions of Jewish life to coalesce in a struggle for social welfare and religious equality.

Conclusion

THE "BOND of sisterhood" forged by Jewish women's interaction with their Christian peers altered and enriched both the Jewish and the general feminist movements. Secular feminism's precedent encouraged Jewish women to emerge from the home and the constraints of their traditional role in the Jewish community. It activated Jewish women's involvement in feminist issues and inspired the creation of a distinctive Jewish woman's movement. Christian women's increased participation in the ritual and management of their churches established a precedent for Jewish women's demands for religious equality. National feminist organizations and the International Council of Women reinforced Jewish women's crusade against white slavery, influenced the policies of Jewish women's social service and reform organizations, and became the catalyst for creation of the World Council of Jewish Women.

In turn, American and Anglo-Jewish feminists participated in and influenced nearly every aspect of the woman movement in the twentieth century, although the pace varied in each country. As members, and occasionally leaders, of feminist organizations, Jewish women helped to formulate policies, methods, and tactics of the woman's movement in England and the United States. Jewish women and their organizations joined or became affiliates of a plethora of national and international women's organizations that affected social services, settlement house-led reform, trade unionism, suffrage, and protectionist welfare legislation affecting women and children:

> 1. national women's social service organizations, such as England's National Council of Women or America's General Federation of Women's Clubs;
> 2. national social reform organizations supporting working-class women, such as the Consumer's League and the Women's Trade Union Leagues;
> 3. socialist organizations, including the Socialist parties of England and America, the Labour Party, and the Fabian Society;
> 4. national suffrage organizations, primarily the National Union of Women's Suffrage Societies, the London Society for Woman Suffrage,

National American Woman's Suffrage Association, Equality League, and Woman's Suffrage Party.

The Jewish woman's movement developed from experience in these organizations. Jewish feminist organizations that affiliated with their secular national and international counterparts strengthened the grass-roots base that was so crucial to the success of feminist campaigns.

Jewish feminism focused most intensely on Jewish concerns, improving Jewish women's status in religious and communal life. Jewish feminists modified the Jewish community's approach to social services and pressured prominent male-run community institutions into supporting campaigns for nationwide social reforms related to the protection of immigrant and working-class women and children. In the process, feminists helped somewhat to erode traditional Jewish attitudes toward women.[1] This development extended further in America than in England, but cooperation between English and Jewish women through a common language, shared social service, and shared feminist goals ensured that the basic process developed similarly in both countries. Several Jewish women's organizations became the vehicles for this process:

1. Jewish social feminist organizations such as the NCJW and UJW, which concentrated on social service and reform but also sought religious and communal equality;
2. Jewish equal rights publications and groups like the *American Jewess* and the Jewish League for Woman Suffrage, which sought the national franchise as well as equal religious and communal rights.

These organizations redefined the vision of Jewish womanhood within a feminist political context. The new Jewish women who emerged, like many of their non-Jewish peers, maintained the sanctity of marriage and motherhood but expanded their parameters to include a public activist role. At the same time, single Jewish women became accepted as guardians of the extended Jewish family, that is, the Jewish community. Their protection of less fortunate Jewish women and children garnered religious and communal acceptance. Nevertheless, they still remained outside Jewry's family orientation. With more free time than their married peers, and more painfully aware of their exclusion from male bastions of power, single Jewish women like Lily Montagu, Rebecca Gratz, Sadie American, Lillian Wald, and Rose Schneiderman devoted themselves to changing secular, religious, and communal life.

JUDAISM AND FEMINISM

Jewish feminists' greatest challenge lay in resolving the tension between Judaism and feminism. Jewish tradition and communal society remained the fundamental basis of Jewish feminists' lives, demanding mediation between the past and the present. In England, Jewish emancipation functioned as a model for Louisa Lady Goldsmid and her followers, demonstrating the manner in which Jewish women could maintain Jewish values while demanding social and political equality in English life. In America, civil religion and the separation of church and state simultaneously encouraged loyalty to Judaism as well as the state, fostering a diversity of religious groups. Jewish women interwove their Judaism with feminism accordingly, developing a bastion of women's organizations from Maine to California.

Asserting religious equality based upon prophetic calls for "justice," Jewish women and sympathetic rabbis urged mixed seating, mixed choirs and confirmation for girls which launched women into active synagogue life, particularly in progressive Judaism. Rosa Sonneschein's demand for women's equality "in the pulpit and the pew" reinforced Ray Frank's preaching career and echoed Lily Montagu's message across the Atlantic. Women's new visibility in the synagogue appeared to sanction the empowerment of Jewish women in communal life as well. Women's ritual participation led to membership on synagogue and communal boards which, in turn, laid the basis for Jewish women's pulpit sermons and increased women's impact upon synagogue and communal policies. The Jewish League for Woman Suffrage's more than three hundred members insisted that Judaism's traditional stress on prophetic "justice" made "votes for women" a "holy cause and therefore a Jewish cause."

The Jewish woman's movement's emphasis upon religious equality triggered Lily Montagu's career as a lay minister and Martha Neumark's quest to become ordained as a Reform rabbi. The failure of both women to become rabbis is rooted in the impact of patriarchal Judaism and secular society. Moreover, the majority of early twentieth-century Jewish women, like their non-Jewish peers, believed in the separation of roles between women and men. This created less pressure among Jewish feminists to seek formal ordination. Montagu's prominence as a lay minister and Neumark's admission to a formal program of study represent the first steps toward women's religious leadership in England and the United States.

Despite partial success, Jewish women's religious influence from 1914 to 1933 remained limited. Lily Montagu remained the world's

only female spiritual leader of a synagogue and major religious movement. Tehilla Lichtenstein became the leader of a relatively small
Jewish sect, but she did not begin her career until 1938, after the
scope of this study. The Conservative movement encouraged mixed
seating, female religious educators, and an auxiliary Women's League,
but did not further extend women's rights during this period. Orthodox synagogues also modernized and adopted women's auxiliaries,
but rabbis did not modify family and religious law to accommodate
women's needs.

JEWISH COMMUNAL LIFE

Winning the vote in the national arena as well as the religious-communal sphere gave Jewish women a major political victory and indicated their growing political, religious, and communal emancipation.
In secular life, the franchise symbolized Jewish women's acceptance
into the majority culture. In Jewish life, the ballot empowered women
to join communal, synagogue, and Reform movement governing
boards in large numbers. Hannah Cohen's presidency of England's
Jewish Board of Guardians epitomized the dramatic impact of women
upon communal policies.

Postwar Jewish feminists in both England and America, like their
Christian peers, turned toward an emphasis upon welfare, demanding
protective legislation for women and children. Anglo-Jewish feminists
like Eva Hubback and Helen Bentwich often allied with the Labour
Party, and American Jewish feminists joined progressive political parties to lobby for protective legislation to help women and children.
Welfare feminism empowered Jewish women to expand and consoli-
date their communal political strength, and to play a significant role
in communal decisions affecting Jewish social services. At the same
time, upper- and middle-class Jewish women's increasing educational,
professional, and social opportunities enabled them to exercise new
influence upon many aspects of secular and Jewish life.

A BOND OF SISTERHOOD

Jewish women's "bond of sisterhood" enabled the personal to become
political. Family relationships and individual friendships formed the
basis for Jewish women's participation in the secular and Jewish feminist movements. Parents, siblings, and cousins[2] established a framework that reinforced women as they branched out from the home to
public life. Constance Rothschild Battersea's venerated mother, Louise
Lady Rothschild, trained her daughter to a lifetime of "duty" for her
"less fortunate sisters." Battersea's suffragist friend Fanny Morgan

brought her into the feminist movement, and a temperance colleague and missionary friend introduced her to the misery of Jewish prostitutes.

Without the "Cousinhood," Jewish feminism would never have survived in England. An intimate network of primarily female cousins formed the core of prewar governing councils for Louise Lady Rothschild's benevolent societies, Constance Lady Battersea's Jewish Association for the Protection of Girls and Women, the Cohens and Rothschilds' Union of Jewish Women, the Franklins' Jewish League for Woman Suffrage, and Lily Montagu's West Central Jewish Girls Club and Jewish Religious Union.

Close friends often formed highly integrated networks that held communities together, notes Carroll Smith-Rosenberg. The Wald circle, with its loving friendships, provided emotional support for Lillian Wald and brought wealthy Lewisohn, Morgenthau, and Warburg women into social service.[3] Years of shared trade union organizing and anger at male unionists kept Rose Schneiderman, Pauline Newman, and Clara Lemlich together at the Women's Trade Union League, fearful of bourgeois feminism but prepared to use it as a weapon for equal wages.

The political, communal, and religious organizations founded by these women emerged from the close personal networks that surrounded them. Support by family and friends made it possible for Jewish women to overcome the difficulties and occasional hostility emanating from traditional Jewish attitudes toward women, the Christian bias of nineteenth-century feminists, anti-immigrant sentiment, and the anti-feminism that pervaded Jewish and secular culture.

CONTRASTS

Although patterns are similar, Jewish feminism varied in timing and vigor at different times and situations in England and the United States, reflecting the social and political context. England's established Anglican Church maintained an official connection with the English crown totally unlike America's separation of church and state. Anti-Jewish sentiment based on church teachings never completely disappeared, while racial anti-Semitism swept through Western Europe and America.

England's social hierarchy remained more rigid than America's nominally classless society, protecting upper- and middle-class Anglo-Jewry as English citizens, but making it nearly impossible for East European immigrants to feel economically, socially, or politically secure before World War I. England's xenophobia, combined with religious and social restrictions, caused all Jews to feel particularly vulnerable to social exclusions and the anti-Semitic harangues, cartoons, and articles that increased dramatically with the onset of immigration from Eastern Europe.

In this atmosphere, feminism posed greater risks for Anglo-Jewish women than for their sisters in the United States. Jewish antifeminists accused Jewish suffragists of destroying the family and exposing the community to a new wave of anti-Semitism. At the same time, Christian feminists often ignored or stereotyped middle-class Jewish women. But the sense of security that stemmed from Anglo-Jewish feminists' upper-class social status and powerful extended family network enabled feminists from Constance Rothschild Battersea to the Franklin cousins to withstand criticism from Jew and Gentile alike.

England's Jewish League for Woman Suffrage highlights two of the differences between England and the United States: (1) The JLWS was one of many church-related suffrage organizations in a country where church institutions were extremely important; (2) England's emphasis upon religion and the persistent, subtle English anti-Semitism forced Anglo-Jewry to develop many institutions like the League that paralleled existing English organizations.

Still, American Jewish feminists faced anti-Semitism and class snobbery as well. Henry Ford's *Dearborn Independent* and his dissemination of the bogus *Protocols of the Elders of Zion* was only one of the most blatant among a rising host of anti-Semitic publications in the early twentieth century.[4] German-Jewish social reformers, like their Christian peers, often looked down upon the East European immigrants they sought to help.[5] Nevertheless, America's political flexibility and economic and educational opportunities provided a tolerant atmosphere that encouraged Jewish feminism among middle-class as well as East European immigrant women.

By the turn of the century, anti-Semitism declined in secular feminist organizations, particularly in relation to acculturated German-Jewish social reformers. Class mobility and religious freedom encouraged large numbers of American Jewish women to join women's social reform and suffragist organizations.

American Jewish women never united into organizations for the sole purpose of promoting both Jewish and political suffrage, as had England's JLWS. "Universal suffrage" seemed a goal more attainable through American than through Jewish suffrage organizations. This situation does not appear to reflect a denial of Jewish identity by some Jewish suffragists. Rather, a distinctively Jewish organization appeared simply unnecessary in the more tolerant American climate, where class status and church-state relationships were less structured than in England.

Jewish feminists never denied or attempted to hide their identity, even if that would have been possible during this era. Sadie American, Maud Nathan, and Rebekah Kohut typified Jewish suffragists who publicly linked themselves to their people during the campaign for the vote through their public statements and through leadership in the National Council of Jewish Women. *The American Jewess* made a connection in its campaigns for Jewish religious and communal suffrage with the "universal sisterhood" seeking the national franchise. Because of the prominence of Reform Judaism in the United States, American Jewish women's drive for religious and communal equality ultimately affected a larger group of synagogues and Jewish communities than did that of their Anglo-Jewish counterparts, despite Anglo-Jewish feminists' separate organization and greater militancy.

Immigrant Jewish women in America participated in the suffrage movement far more widely than did their peers in England. Campaigning within the circle of their family and friends, immigrant women marched in rallies, held meetings, and organized torchlight parades through their own neighborhoods, publicly asserting their identity as Jews and feminists.

Working-class women in England faced even greater difficulties than their upper-class sisters. Feminism touched fewer East European immigrant women in England than in the United States. Their harsh existence and England's rigid class barriers turned the concept of equality into a bourgeois issue totally irrelevant to their lives. Only a handful of Jewish immigrant women joined trade unions and even fewer joined the WTUL.

Despite their differences, the English and American Jewish feminist movements shared similarities that had far-reaching implications for Jewish women. On both sides of the Atlantic, Jewish feminism revitalized a vital, durable, and active Jewish woman's movement. For English and American Jewish women alike, participation in the feminist movement reflected their belief in their own acculturation and emancipation as well as their convictions about social reform. By the time Hitler came to power in 1933, a growing number of Jewish women were influencing social welfare communal decisions, were deeply involved in synagogue life within Judaism's progressive wing, and were beginning to modestly affect Conservative and even Orthodox Judaism in varying degrees. Jewish feminists maintained their international activity through the World Council of Jewish Women and the ICW. Through all these activities, the first Jewish feminist movement from 1881 to 1933 laid the groundwork for the resurgence of Jewish equal rights feminism in the early 1970s.

Notes

INTRODUCTION

1. Martha Vicinus, ed., *Suffer and Be Still: Women in the Victorian Age* (Bloomington and London: Indiana University Press, 1973); Nancy F. Cott, *The Bonds of Womanhood* (New Haven and London: Yale University Press, 1977), p. 9; Barbara Welter, "The Cult of True Womanhood," *American Quarterly* 18 (1966): 151–74; William O'Neill, *The Woman Movement: Feminism in the United States and England* (London: George Allen & Unwin; New York: Barnes & Noble, 1969), p. 13; Anne Firor Scott, *Making the Invisible Woman Visible* (Urbana and Chicago: University of Illinois Press, 1984), p. 37.

2. Olive Banks, *Faces of Feminism: A Study of Feminism as a Social Movement* (New York: St. Martin's Press, 1981), passim; Banks, *Becoming a Feminist: The Social Origins of 'First Wave' Feminism* (Brighton: Wheatsheaf Books, 1986), p. 7.

3. In addition to Olive Banks's *Faces of Feminism* and *Becoming a Feminist*, cited above, see also O'Neill, *The Woman Movement*, Ross Evans Paulson, *Women's Suffrage and Prohibition: A Comparative Study of Equality and Social Control* (Glenview, Ill.: Scott Foresman & Co., 1973); Richard Evans, *The Feminists: Women's Emancipation Movements in Europe, America and Australasia 1840–1920* (London: Croom Helm; New York: Barnes & Noble, 1977).

4. Mary P. Ryan, "The Power of Women's Networks," in *Sex and Class in Women's History*, ed. Judith L. Newton, Mary P. Ryan, and Judith R. Walkowitz (London, Boston, Melbourne, and Henley: Routledge & Kegan Paul, 1982), p. 170.

5. Cott, *Bonds of Womanhood*, p. 9; Welter, "Cult of True Womanhood," pp. 151–74.

6. Gerda Lerner, "Placing Women in History: A 1975 Perspective," in *Liberating Women's History*, ed. Berenice Carroll (Urbana: University of Illinois Press, 1976), p. 357.

7. William O'Neill, *Everyone Was Brave: The Rise and Fall of Feminism in America* (New York: Quadrangle, 1969), p. x.

8. Banks, *Faces of Feminism*, p. 3; see also Cott, *Bonds of Womanhood*, p. 9; Paula Hyman, "The Volunteer Organizations: Vanguard or Rear Guard?" *Lilith* no. 5 (1978): 17; Constance Rover, *Women's Suffrage and Party Politics in Britain, 1866–1914* (London: Routledge & Kegan Paul, 1967), p. 470; Geof-

frey Alderman, *The Jewish Community in British Politics* (Oxford: Clarendon Press, 1983), p. 77.

9. Hyman, "Volunteer Organizations," p. 17.

10. O'Neill, *The Woman Movement*, p. 13; O'Neill, *Everyone Was Brave*, p. x; Scott, *Making the Invisible Woman Visible*, p. 37; Banks, *Faces of Feminism*, p. 3; Mary Wollstonecraft, *A Vindication of the Rights of Woman*, Carol H. Poston, ed. (New York and London: W. W. Norton, 1975); Eleanor Flexner, *Century of Struggle: The Woman's Rights Movement in the United States* (New York: Atheneum, 1974), p. 208; Aileen Kraditor, *Up from the Pedestal: Selected Writings in the History of American Feminism* (Chicago: Quadrangle, 1968), pp. 184–86.

11. Deborah Grand Golumb, "The 1893 Congress of Jewish Women: Evolution or Revolution in American Jewish Women's History?" *AJH* 70 (Sept. 1980): 55–56, 66.

12. George L. Berlin, "Solomon Jackson's *The Jew*: An Early American Jewish Response to the Missionaries," *AJH* 71 (Sept. 1981): 10–28; Jeffrey S. Gurock, "Jacob A. Riis: Christian Friend or Missionary Foe? Two Jewish Views," ibid., pp. 29–47.

13. Paula Hyman, "The Other Half: Women in the Jewish Tradition," in *The Jewish Woman: New Perspectives*, ed. Elizabeth Koltun (New York: Schocken, 1976), p. 106; Norma Fain Pratt, "Culture and Radical Politics: Yiddish Women Writers, 1890–1940," *AJH* 70 (Sept. 1980): 68; Myra Shoub, "Jewish Women's History: Development of a Critical Methodology," *Conservative Judaism* (Winter 1982): 39; *Genesis Rabbah* 71:5 (New York: Soncino, 1939); Linda Gordon Kuzmack, "Aggadic Approaches to Biblical Women," in Koltun, *Jewish Woman*, p. 252; Steven M. Cohen and Paula Hyman, eds., *The Jewish Family: Myths and Reality* (New York and London: Holmes & Meier, 1986), passim.

14. Rachel Adler, "The Jew Who Wasn't There: Halacha and the Jewish Woman," *Response* 7 (Summer 1973): 77; Hilda Smith, "Feminism and the Methodology of Women's History," in *Liberating Women's History*, ed. Berenice Carroll (Urbana: University of Illinois Press, 1976), p. 371; Joan Kelly, "The Social Relation of the Sexes: Methodological Implications of Women's History," in idem, *Women, History and Theory: The Essays of Joan Kelly* (Chicago and London: University of Chicago Press, 1984), pp. 5–6.

15. Rachel Biale, *Women and Jewish Law* (New York: Schocken, 1984), pp. 21–24; Gail B. Shulman, "View from the Back of the Synagogue," in *Sexist Religion and Women in the Church*, ed. Alice L. Hageman (New York: Association Press, 1974), p. 145; Susan Weidman Schneider, *Jewish and Female* (New York: Simon & Schuster, 1984), p. 60; Leonard Swidler, *Women in Judaism: The Status of Women in Formative Judaism* (Metuchen, N.J.: Scarecrow Press, 1976), pp. 88–89; Judith R. Wegner, *Chattel or Person? The Status of Women in Mishnah* (New York and London: Oxford University Press, 1978), pp. 152–53.

16. Judith Hauptman, "Women in the Talmud," in *Religion and Sexism:*

Images of Woman in the Jewish and Christian Traditions, ed. Rosemary Radford Ruether (New York: Simon & Schuster, 1974), pp. 191–92; Hyman, "The Other Half," pp. 105–13; Saul Berman, "The Status of Women in Halakhic Judaism," in Koltun, *Jewish Woman*, pp. 114–28; Adler, "The Jew Who Wasn't There," pp. 77–82; Blu Greenberg, "Judaism and Feminism," in Koltun, *Jewish Woman*, pp. 184–85.

17. Judith Hauptman, "Women in the Talmud," p. 203; Israel Abrahams, *Jewish Life in the Middle Ages* (New York: Atheneum, 1973), p. 26; Sonya Henry and Emily Taitz, *Written Out of History* (New York: Bloch, 1978), pp. 178–90; "Hannah of Ludmir," *Menorah Journal*, n.d.; Charles Raddock, "Hannah of Ludmir," *Spectator* (April 1948).

18. Linda Gordon Kuzmack, "Jewish Working Women as Agents of Change," *Humanistic Judaism* (Autumn 1984): 24–26.

CHAPTER 1

1. Judith Montefiore, *Diary*, in Lucien Wolf, "Judith Montefiore," *Essays in Jewish History* (London: Jewish Historical Society of England, 1934), p. 241; *Diaries of Sir Moses and Lady Montefiore*, ed. L. Loewe (London: Griffiths, Farran, Okeden, & Welsh, 1890), pp. 8–9; cited in Wolf, *Essays*, pp. 241–58; Chaim Bermant, *The Cousinhood* (London: Eyre & Spottiswoode, 1971), p. 110. William B. Wilcox, *The Age of Aristocracy, 1688 to 1830* (Lexington, Mass.: D. C. Heath & Co., 1976), pp. 262–63. Richard Davis, *The English Rothschilds* (Chapel Hill: University of North Carolina Press, 1983), p. 24.

2. See Cecil Roth, *A History of the Jews in England* (Oxford: Clarendon Press, 1967), p. 158; Roth, "The Resettlement of the Jews in England in 1656," in *Three Centuries of Anglo-Jewish History*, ed. V. D. Lipman (London: Jewish Historical Society of England, 1961), pp. 1–26; Roth, "The European Age in Jewish History," in *The Jews*, ed. Louis Finkelstein (New York: Schocken, 1970), pp. 225–58; Edward H. Flannery, *The Anguish of the Jews* (New York: Macmillan; London: Collier-Macmillan, 1964), pp. 47–50; Jacob Katz, *Exclusiveness and Tolerance: Jewish and Gentile Relations in Medieval and Modern Times* (New York, Schocken, 1962), chaps. 1–4; Howard M. Sachar, *The Course of Modern Jewish History* (New York: Dell, 1958), p. 63; Sachar, *Diaspora: An Inquiry into the Contemporary Jewish World* (New York: Harper & Row, 1985), p. 142.

3. Roth, *History*, pp. 228–29.

4. Israel Finestein, "Post-Emancipation Jewry: The Anglo-Jewish Experience" (Oxford: Oxford Centre for Postgraduate Hebrew Studies, 1980), p. 8; Todd Endelman, *The Jews of Georgian England, 1714–1830: Tradition and Change in a Liberal Society* (Philadelphia: Jewish Publication Society, 1979), pp. xi, 10; Walter L. Arnstein, *Britain Yesterday and Today: 1830 to the Present* (Boston: D. C. Heath, 1976), chap. 1; G. M. Trevelyan, *A Shortened History of England* (Baltimore: Pelican, 1960), chap. 3.

5. Harold Pekin, *The Origins of Modern English Society, 1780–1880*

(London: Routledge & Kegan Paul; Toronto: University of Toronto Press, 1969), pp. 38–39; Bermant, *Cousinhood*, p. 3.

6. Sachar, *Course of Modern Jewish History*, pp. 40–41, 115; V. D. Lipman, "The Age of Emancipation," in Lipman, *Three Centuries*, p. 77.

7. Judith Montefiore, *Private Journal of a Visit to Egypt and Palestine, 1827*, intro. by I. Bartal, photocopy of the unpublished 1836 London ed. (Jerusalem: Hebrew University), pp. 71–72; Sonia L. Lipman, "Judith Montefiore—First Lady of Anglo-Jewry," *Transactions of the Jewish Historical Society of England* 21 (1968): 287; Helen Rosenau, "Montefiore and the Visual Arts," in *The Century of Moses Montefiore*, ed. Sonia Lipman and V. D. Lipman (London: Published for the Littman Library of Jewish Civilization in association with the Jewish Historical Society of England by Oxford University Press, 1985), pp. 118–19; Bermant, *Cousinhood*, p. 111; Barbara Corrado Pope, "Angels in the Devil's Workshop: Leisured and Charitable Women in Nineteenth-Century England and France," in *Becoming Visible: Women in European History*, ed. Renate Bridenthal and Claudia Koonz (Boston: Houghton Mifflin, 1977), p. 310; Endelman, *Georgian England*, p. 126.

8. Jacob Katz, *Out of the Ghetto* (Cambridge, Mass.: Harvard University Press, 1973), p. 84; Hannah Arendt, *Rachel Varnhagen: The Life of a Jewess* (London: East and West Library, 1957); Michael Meyer, *The Origins of the Modern Jew: Jewish Identity and European Culture in Germany, 1749–1824* (Detroit: Wayne State University Press, 1967), p. 91.

9. Judith Montefiore, *Notes of a Private Journey* (London: Lea & Co., 1885), p. 74. Cited in Bermant, *Cousinhood*, pp. 110–11.

10. Amalie M. Kass, "Friends and Philanthropists: Montefiore and Dr. Hodgkin," in Lipman and Lipman, *Century of Moses Montefiore*, p. 87.

11. Rosemary Skinner Keller, "Women, Civil Religion, and the American Revolution," in *Women and Religion in America*, ed. Rosemary Radford Ruether and Rosemary Skinner Keller, vol. 2 (San Francisco: Harper & Row, 1983), p. 376; Patricia Branca, *Silent Sisterhood: Middle Class Women in the Victorian Home* (Pittsburgh: Carnegie-Mellon University Press, 1975), p. 7; Deborah Gorham, *The Victorian Girl and the Feminine Ideal* (Bloomington: Indiana University Press, 1982), p. 4; Jill Conway, "Stereotypes of Femininity in a Theory of Sexual Evolution," *Victorian Studies* 14 (Sept. 1970): 61; Steven Mintz, *A Prison of Expectations: The Family in Victorian Culture* (New York and London: New York University Press, 1983), pp. 22–23, 51; Carl Degler, *At Odds: Women and the Family in America from the Revolution to the Present* (New York: Oxford University Press, 1980), pp. 42–43.

12. Welter, "Cult of True Womanhood," pp. 151–74; Cott, *Bonds of Womanhood*, p. 2; Alice Kessler-Harris, *Women Have Always Worked* (Old Westbury, N.Y.: Feminist Press; New York, St. Louis, San Francisco: McGraw-Hill Book Co., 1981), p. 15.

13. Cott, *Bonds of Womanhood*, p. 201.

14. Lucy Cohen, *Lady de Rothschild and Her Daughters, 1821–1931* (London, 1935), p. 26. Anthony was the son of the "king" of the stock ex-

change, Nathan Mayer Rothschild. Nathan's will (d. 1836) sheds light on the control that a Victorian patriarch had over his daughters. Nathan specified that if his daughters married without the consent of their mother and brothers they would forfeit their entire inheritance, complete with interest.

15. Charlotte Montefiore to Rev. D. A. de Sola, n.d., Montefiore Papers, Spanish and Portuguese Synagogue, London; Bermant, *Cousinhood*, pp. 139, 142; see Constance Rothschild Battersea, ed., *Lady de Rothschild: Extracts from Her Notebooks* (London: Arthur L. Humphreys, 1912), p. 4 and passim.

16. Lucy Cohen, *Lady de Rothschild*, pp. 7–8.

17. Constance Rothschild Battersea, "Preface," in Rothschild, *Notebooks*, p. 5.

18. Ibid., pp. 12, 14, 16, 22.

19. V. D. Lipman, *Three Centuries*, p. 179; Robert Kenny to Linda Gordon Kuzmack, personal communication, May 1985; David Owen, *English Philanthropy 1660–1960* (Cambridge, Mass.: Belknap Press, Harvard University Press, 1964), p. 157.

20. Lloyd P. Gartner, *The Jewish Immigrant in England, 1870–1914* (Detroit: Wayne State University Press, 1960), pp. 19–20; Sachar, *Diaspora*, p. 142.

21. "1902 Conference of Jewish Women," *JC*, May 16, 1902, p. 10.

22. V. D. Lipman, *Social History of the Jews in England, 1850–1950* (London: Watts, 1954), p. 18; Endelman, *Georgian England*, pp. 237, 239–40.

23. V. D. Lipman, *Social Service*, p. 115; Owen, *English Philanthropy*, pp. 222, 421; Gareth Stedman Jones, *Outcast London* (Oxford: Clarendon Press, 1971), p. 268; Elizabeth Wilson, *Women and the Welfare State* (London: Tavistock, 1977), pp. 50–51.

24. V. D. Lipman, *Social Service*, p. 115; Owen, *English Philanthropy*, pp. 222, 421; Jones, *Outcast London*, p. 268; Wilson, *Women and the Welfare State*, pp. 50–51.

25. Carroll Smith-Rosenberg, "The Female World of Love and Ritual: Relations between Women in Nineteenth-Century America," *Signs* 1 (Autumn 1975): 319.

26. *JC*, Apr. 24, 1885, p. 9; May 26, 1896, p. 14; Aug. 23, 1912, p. 8; Battersea, "Preface," in Rothschild, *Notebooks*, p. 16; Ronald G. Walton, *Women in Social Work* (London and Boston: Routledge & Kegan Paul, 1975), p. 24; Finestein, "Post-Emancipation Jewry," p. 6.

27. Constance Battersea, *Reminiscences* (London, 1922), pp. 414–17.

28. *JC*, Jan. 9, 1885, p. 15; Feb. 3, 1888, pp. 7–8; June 12, 1896, p. 6; May 19, 1896, p. 6; May 26, 1896, p. 8; Battersea, "Preface," in Rothschild, *Notebooks*, p. 15; L. L. Loewe, *Basil Henriques* (London: Henley, and Boston: Routledge & Kegan Paul, 1976), p. 191; Battersea, *Reminiscences*, p. 412.

29. *JC*, Feb. 3, 1888, pp. 7–8; Jan. 11, 1935; Battersea, *Reminiscences*, p. 412.

30. Alice S. Rossi, ed., *The Feminist Papers* (New York and London: Columbia University Press, 1973), pp. 47–49; F. K. Prochaska, *Women and*

Philanthropy in Nineteenth-Century England (Oxford: Clarendon Press, 1980), pp. 8–17, 97–103.

31. Kathryn Kish Sklar, *Catherine Beecher: A Study in American Domesticity* (New Haven: Yale University Press, 1973); cited in Anne M. Boylan, "Evangelical Womanhood in the Nineteenth Century: The Role of Women in Sunday Schools," *FS* 4 (Oct. 1978): 63.

32. Gorham, *Victorian Girl*, pp. 18–29; Horton Davies, *Worship and Theology in England: The Ecumenical Century, 1900–1965* (Princeton: Princeton University Press, 1965), p. 209; Lee Virginia Chambers-Schiller, *Liberty, a Better Husband: Single Women in America: The Generations of 1780–1840* (New Haven and London: Yale University Press, 1984), pp. 2–4, 19; Branca, *Silent Sisterhood*, p. 145.

33. Smith-Rosenberg, "The Female World of Love and Ritual," pp. 1–29; Estelle Freedman, "Separatism as Strategy: Female Institution Building and American Feminism, 1870–1930," *FS* 5 (Fall 1979): 513.

34. Cott, *Bonds of Womanhood*, pp. 200–201.

35. See Eleanor Flexner, "Ideas in 'A Vindication of the Rights of Woman,'" in Wollstonecraft, *A Vindication of the Rights of Woman*, p. 232; Evans, *The Feminists*, pp. 22–24; See Evelyn Gordon Bodek, "Salonieres and Bluestockings: Educated Obsolescence and Germinating Feminism," *FS* 3 (Spring–Summer 1976): 185–97; Banks, *Faces of Feminism*, pp. 29–32.

36. O'Neill, *The Woman Movement*, p. 29; Julia O'Faolain and Lauro Martines, eds., *Not in God's Image* (New York: Harper, 1973), p. 330; Lee Holcombe, "Victorian Wives and Property," in *A Widening Sphere: Changing Roles of Victorian Women*, ed. Martha Vicinus (Bloomington and London: Indiana University Press, 1980), pp. 3–28.

37. Banks, *Faces of Feminism*, pp. 25, 40; O'Neill, *The Woman Movement*, pp. 16–17.

38. Anne Aresty Naman, *The Jew in the Victorian Novel* (New York: AMS Press, 1980), pp. 40–42; Irving Howe, "Introduction," George Eliot, *Daniel Deronda* (New York and Scarborough, Ontario: Signet New American Library, 1979), p. xiii.

39. Patricia Robertson, *An Experience of Women: Pattern and Change in Nineteenth-Century Europe* (Philadelphia: Temple University Press, 1982), p. 502; Linda Gertner Zatlin, *The Nineteenth-Century Anglo-Jewish Novel* (Boston: Twayne, 1981), p. 27 and passim; Karen Halttunen, "The Domestic Drama of Louisa May Alcott," *FS* 10 (Summer 1984): 233–54.

40. Grace Aguilar, *Women of Israel*, 2 vols. (New York: D. Appleton & Co., 1854), cited in Henry and Taitz, *Written Out of History*, p. 238; *Encyclopedia Judaica*, vol. 2 (Jerusalem: Keter, 1972), s.v. "Aguilar, Grace," p. 427; Gustav Karpeles, "Women in Jewish Literature," *Jewish Literature and Other Essays* (Philadelphia: Jewish Publication Society, 1895), cited in Henry and Taitz, *Written Out of History*, p. 238.

41. Beth-Zion Lask Abrahams, "Grace Aguilar: A Centenary Tribute," *Transactions of the Jewish Historical Society of England* 16 (1952): 137–48;

Correspondence nos. 67, 73, 74, Charlotte Montefiore to David de Sola, editor of the *Voice of Jacob,* n.d.; Correspondence no. 69, Grace Aguilar to David de Sola, n.d., Montefiore Papers, Spanish and Portuguese Synagogue, London.

42. Endelman, *Georgian England,* p. 154.

43. Bermant, *Cousinhood,* p. 76; David Philipson, *The Reform Movement in Judaism,* rev. ed. (New York: Ktav, 1967), p. 402.

44. Sara Delamont, "The Contradictions in Ladies' Education," in *The Nineteenth-Century Woman: Her Cultural and Physical World,* ed. Sara Delamont and Lorna Duffin (London: Croom Helm, 1978), pp. 139–46.

45. Rita McWilliams-Tullberg, "Women and Degrees at Cambridge University 1862–1897," in Vicinus, *A Widening Sphere,* p. 119; Barbara Welter, "Anti-Intellectualism and the American Woman, 1800–1860," in *Dimity Convictions: The American Woman in the Nineteenth Century* (Athens, Ohio: Ohio University Press, 1976), pp. 71–82; Ray Strachey, *The Cause: A Short History of the Women's Movement in Great Britain* (London: Bell & Sons, 1928), p. 146.

46. Emily Davies to Barbara Bodichon, March 3, 1867, Girton Archives. Cited in McWilliams-Tullberg, "Cambridge University," p. 294n. 6.

47. Lee Holcombe, *Wives and Property: Reform of the Married Women's Property Law in Nineteenth-Century England* (Toronto and Buffalo: University of Toronto Press, 1983), pp. 133, 140–41, McWilliams-Tullberg, "Cambridge University," p. 294n. 6.

48. Holcombe, *Wives and Property,* p. 211.

49. Sara Delamont, "The Domestic Ideology and Women's Education," in Delamont and Duffin, *The Nineteenth-Century Woman,* p. 174.

50. Sachar, *Modern Jewish History,* pp. 9, 11, 144; Jonathan Sarna, ed., *People Walk on their Heads: Moses Weinberger's "Jews and Judaism in New York"* (New York and London: Holmes & Meier, 1981), p. 7.

51. Richard Wiebe, *The Search for Order* (New York: Hill & Wang, 1967), pp. 2–4; Naomi W. Cohen, *Encounter with Emancipation: The German Jews in the United States, 1830–1914* (Philadelphia: Jewish Publication Society, 1984), pp. 39–43; Robert M. Healey, "Jefferson on Judaism and the Jews: 'Divided We Stand, United, We Fall!'" *AJH* 73 (June 1984): 360; Robert N. Bellah, *The Broken Covenant: American Civil Religion in Time of Trial* (New York: Seabury Press, 1975), p. 45; Jonathan S. Woocher, "'Civil Judaism' in the United States," p. 2, AJA.

52. Wiebe, *Search for Order,* p. 58; Jonathan D. Sarna, *Jacksonian Jew: The Two Worlds of Mordecai Noah* (New York and London: Holmes & Meier, 1981), p. 54; Jacob Katz, *From Prejudice to Destruction: Anti-Semitism, 1700–1933* (Cambridge: Harvard University Press, 1980), p. 8; Leo P. Ribuffo, "Henry Ford and *The International Jew,*" *AJH* 69 (June 1980): 439; Sachar, *Modern Jewish History,* p. 162; Cohen, *Encounter with Emancipation,* p. 109.

53. Sarna, *Jacksonian Jew,* p. 24; Sarna, *People Walk on Their Heads,* p. 9.

54. Yosef Hayim Yerushalmi, *Zakhor: Jewish History and Jewish Mem-*

ory (Seattle and London: University of Washington Press, 1982), p. 94; Salo Baron, "American Jewish Communal Pioneering," *PAJHS* 43 (1954): 56; Steven M. Cohen, *American Modernity and Jewish Identity* (New York and London: Tavistock, 1983), p. 21.

55. *Devotional Exercises, for the use of the Daughters of Israel,* ed. Rev. M. J. Raphall (New York: L. Joachimssen, 1852), p. 115.

56. *The Jewish Messenger* (Mar. 7, 1884), p. 4.

57. Rosemary Keller, "Civil Religion," in Ruether and Keller, *Women and Religion in America,* vol. 2, p. 370; Abigail Adams to John Adams, Mar. 31, 1776, cited in Rossi, *The Feminist Papers,* pp. 10–11.

58. Henry and Taitz, *Written Out of History,* pp. 220–21.

59. Banks, *Faces of Feminism,* p. 27; Prochaska, *Women and Philanthropy,* p. 6.

60. Degler, *At Odds,* p. 160. Chambers-Schiller, *Liberty, a Better Husband,* pp. 4, 16, 46; Evans, *The Feminists,* p. 25; Banks, *Becoming a Feminist,* p. 35.

61. Quoted in Degler, *At Odds,* p. 160; Chambers-Schiller, *Liberty, a Better Husband,* pp. 46, 49, 15.

62. Dianne Ashton, "Building Ethnicity: Rebecca Gratz and Jewish Women in Philadelphia, 1780–1880" (Ph.D. diss., Philadelphia: Temple University), chap. 2, pp. 8–10; Ann Braude, "The Jewish Woman's Encounter with American Culture," in Ruether and Skinner, *Women and Religion in America,* p. 154; Henry and Taitz, *Written Out of History,* pp. 55, 226; David Philipson, *Letters of Rebecca Gratz* (Philadelphia: Jewish Publication Society, 1929), p. 238.

63. Sol Liptzin, *The Jew in American Literature* (New York, Bloch, 1966), p. 59; Braude, "Jewish Woman's Encounter with American Culture," p. 155; Henry and Taitz, *Written Out of History,* p. 230.

64. "Epigram," in Jacob Rader Marcus, *The American Jewish Woman: A Documentary History* (New York: Ktav; Cincinnati: American Jewish Archives, 1981), p. 126.

65. Rufus Learsi, *The Jews in America* (New York, 1972), pp. 120–21; Moshe Davis, *The Emergence of Conservative Judaism: The Historical School in 19th Century America* (Philadelphia: Jewish Publication Society, 1963), p. 16.

66. *Occident,* 2 (1844), 245; 4 (1846), 226; 13 (1856), 537–42; 23 (1856), 144; 1 (1843), 435–36; 3 (1845), 415; 3 (1846), 571; 6 (1848), 213; 9 (1851), 382; 13 (1854), 229; 12 (1854), 258–59; 13 (1855), 3a; 13 (1855), 183; 13 (1855), 245; 17 (1859), 167; 26 (1868), 427–28; 15:175–80, cited in Clifford M. Kulwin, "The American Jewish Woman as Reflected in Leeser's *Occident,* 1843–1869," unpublished term paper (Cincinnati: Hebrew Union College, 1980), p. 7.

67. Degler, *At Odds,* pp. 299–300; Barbara Welter, "The Feminization of American Religion: 1800–1860," in *Clio's Consciousness Raised,* ed. Mary Hartman and Lois W. Banner (New York, Hagerstown, San Francisco, London: Harper Colophon Books, 1974), pp. 138–39.

68. Ashton, "Building Ethnicity," pp. 7–8, 11–14.

69. Garry Loeb, "Jewish Women and the Reform Movement in America" (M.H.L. thesis, Hebrew Union College-Jewish Institute of Religion, 1981), p. 51; Ashton, "Building Ethnicity," p. 24; Philipson, *Letters of Rebecca Gratz*, pp. 244–45; and Henry and Taitz, *Written Out of History*, pp. 235–46; Evelyn Bodek, "Making Do: Jewish Women and Philanthropy," in *Jewish Life in Philadelphia: 1830–1940*, ed. Murray Friedman (Philadelphia: ISHI Press, 1983), p. 149.

70. Ernestine Rose, "On Legal Discrimination," Second Worcester Convention, 1851, in *History of Woman Suffrage*, ed. Ida Husted Harper, vol. 1 (Indianapolis, 1902), pp. 237–41.

71. Marcus, *Documentary History*, p. 162.

72. Flexner, *Century of Struggle*, pp. 41–55.

73. Anne Firor Scott and Andrew MacKay Scott, *One Half the People: The Fight for Woman Suffrage* (Urbana, Chicago, London: University of Illinois Press, 1982), pp. 8–11.

74. Naomi Cohen, *Encounter with Emancipation*, p. 9.

75. Jonathan Sarna to Linda Gordon Kuzmack, June 15, 1989.

76. Jonathan Sarna, "The 'Mythical Jew' and the 'Jew Next Door' in Nineteenth Century America" (Cincinnati: HUC-JIR, 1983), typescript, pp. 6–7.

77. *Deborah*, 25 (Nov. 7, 1889), 3; 7 (Aug. 9, 1861), 22.

78. Michael Meyer, *Origins*, pp. 86–87.

79. Abraham Geiger, "Die Stellung des Weiblichen Geschlechts in dem Judenthume unserer Zeit," *Wissenschaftliche Zeitschrift für Jüdische Theologie* 3 (1837): 1–14, quoted in Philipson, *Reform Movement*, p. 473.

80. *A. Z. d. J.*, 11, 28, cited in Philipson, *Reform Movement*, p. 473; *Voice of Jacob*, 6, 123; in Philipson, *Reform Movement*, p. 473; Gunther Plaut, *The Rise of Reform Judaism: A Sourcebook of Its European Origins* (New York: World Union for Progressive Judaism, 1963), p. 254.

81. Michael A. Meyer, "German-Jewish Identity in Nineteenth-Century America," in *The American Jewish Experience*, ed. Jonathan D. Sarna (New York and London: Holmes & Meier, 1986), p. 52; Joseph L. Blau and Salo W. Baron, *The Jews of the United States, 1790–1840*, vol. 1 (New York: Columbia University Press, 1963), p. xxix; Bernard D. Weinryb, "Jewish Immigration and Accommodation to America," in *The Jews: Social Patterns of an American Group*, ed. Marshall Sklare (New York: Free Press; London: Collier-Macmillan, 1958), pp. 4–5; Anita L. Lebeson, *Recall to Life* (New York: Thomas Yoseloff, 1970), pp. 66–67; *Letters of the Franks Family, 1733–1748*, the Lee Max Friedman Collection of American Jewish Colonial Correspondence, Studies in American History, no. 5 (Waltham, Mass.: American Jewish Historical Society, 1968), pp. 116–17; Gerson D. Cohen, "The Meaning of Liberty in American Tradition," in *Jewish Life in America: Historical Perspectives*, ed. Gladys Rosen, Institute of Human Relations Press of the American Jewish Committee (New York: Ktav, 1978), p. 6; Woocher, "Civil Judaism," p. 13.

82. Nathan Glazer, *American Judaism* (Chicago and London: University of Chicago Press, 1972), p. 35, 342–55.

83. Isaac M. Wise, *Reminiscences* (New York: Ayer, 1945), pp. 56, 258–60; *Deborah*, 40 (Aug. 16, 1894), 4; 6 (Sept. 14, 1860), 46.

84. *The Israelite* (Aug. 17, 1855), p. 45.

85. *Deborah*, 35 (Nov. 7, 1889), 3; 7 (Aug. 9, 1861), 22; *Occident* (Jan. 1856), p. 496, and Feb. 1856, p. 541; *Israelite* (Aug. 10, 1855), p. 36; *Deborah*, 12 (Mar. 1, 1867), 134; 12 (Mar. 8, 1867), 139; 12 (Mar. 15, 1867), 142; 12 (Mar. 22, 1867), 146; 12 (Mar. 29, 1867), 150; 12 (Apr. 5, 1867), 155; 12 (Apr. 12, 1867), 158; 12 (Apr. 19, 1867), 162–63; 12 (Apr. 16, 1867), 167; Wise, *Reminiscences*, p. 117; Loeb, "Jewish Women," pp. 86–87; *Deborah*, 40 (Aug. 16, 1894), p. 4; *Deborah*, 12 (Mar. 22, 1867), 146.

86. Wise, *Reminiscences*, p. 212; *Deborah*, 1 (Apr. 11, 1856), 278.

87. Kaufmann Kohler, "Origin and Function of Ceremonies in Judaism," *Central Conference of American Rabbis Journal*, pp. 78, 226, cited in Loeb, "Jewish Women," p. 97; *Sinai*, 2 (1858), 792; 4 (1859), 219; and *Deborah*, 7 (Sept. 13, 1861), 42; *Deborah*, 10 (June 9, 1865), 199; 10 (June 23, 1865), 206; see "Confirmation," *Encyclopedia Judaica* (Jerusalem: Keter, 1971). D. Philipson and L. Grossman, *Selected Writings of Isaac M. Wise* (New York: 1969), pp. 68, 106; J. G. Heller, *Isaac M. Wise: His Life, Work and Thought* (New York: 1965), p. 254, both works cited in Loeb, "Jewish Women," p. 97.

88. Michael Meyer, "German-Jewish Identity," pp. 56–57; Sefton Temkin, *The New World of Reform* (Bridgeport, 1974), p. 52; Philipson, *Reform Movement*, pp. 483–84.

89. Glazer, *American Judaism*, pp. 36–42; *Deborah*, 2 (Aug. 24, 1855), 1; and 2 (Aug. 22, 1856), 1; "On Women's Work," by Isaac M. Wise, *Deborah*, 2 (Sept. 26, 1856), 47.

90. *Deborah*, 2 (Oct. 3, 1856), 49; 24 (May 16, 1879), 4 (Dec. 3, 1858), 126; 10 (Apr. 7, 1865), 164; 29 (Nov. 23, 1877), 2; 32 (Feb. 21, 1897), 3; 7 (May 30, 1862), 190; 10 (May 26, 1865), 191; 32 (June 6, 1879), 2; *Sinai*, 4 (1859), 27; 2 (1857), 502; 2 (1857), 433; 7 (1862), 230–31; 7 (1862), 172, AJA.

91. *Deborah*, 26 (Apr. 28, 1876), 2–3; 8 (May 15, 1863), 178.

92. Cott, *Bonds of Womanhood*, p. 134.

93. *Sinai*, 3 (1858), 818–20, AJA; *Deborah*, 1 (Aug. 24, 1855), and Jan. 18, 1856); 11 (Aug. 18, 1865), 26–27; 11 (Aug. 18, 1865), 26; 1 (Jan. 18, 1856), 169; for Wise's curriculum, see *Deborah*, 1 (Mar. 14, 1856), 241; 11 (July 7, 1865), 2; *Israelite* (Jan. 8, 1856), p. 58, cited in Loeb, "Jewish Women," p. 92.

94. Jeffrey S. Gurock, *When Harlem Was Jewish, 1870–1930* (New York: Columbia University Press, 1979), pp. 10–11.

95. *Deborah*, 2 (Dec. 12, 1856), 134; 2 (Jan. 30, 1857), 187; 2 (Jan. 30, 1857), 186–87; 2 (Mar. 6, 1857), 228; 2 (Aug. 14, 1857), 414; *Deborah*, 2 (Dec. 12, 1856), 134; 2 (Jan. 30, 1857), 187.

96. *Deborah*, 12 (Apr. 5, 1867), 154; 13 (Jan. 17, 1868), 111; 6 (Feb. 8,

1861), 127; cited in Jacob Marcus, *The American Jewish Woman, 1654–1980* (New York: Ktav, Cincinnati: American Jewish Archives, 1981), p. 34; see Wise's article, in *Deborah*, 38 (Mar. 9, 1893), 5; also Judah Wechsler's letter, *Deborah*, 8 (Mar. 27, 1863), 150.

97. *Deborah*, 2 (Jan. 30, 1857), 186–87; 2 (Mar. 6, 1857), 228; 2 (Aug. 14, 1857), 414.

98. Battersea, *Rothschild Notebooks*, pp. 15, 17.

CHAPTER 2

1. Sklare, *The Jews*, p. 5.
2. Wiebe, *Search for Order*, p. 111.
3. *JC*, Jan. 14, 1881, p. 6; Marshall Sklare, *America's Jews* (New York: Random House, 1971), pp. 14–15.
4. Pamela S. Nadell, "The Journey to America by Steam: The Jews of Eastern Europe in Transition," *AJH* 71 (Dec. 1981): 269–84; Thomas Kessner, *The Golden Door: Italian and Jewish Immigrant Mobility in New York City, 1880–1915* (New York: Oxford University Press, 1977), p. 32; Irving Howe, *World of Our Fathers* (New York and London: Harcourt Brace Jovanovich, 1976), p. 20; Henry L. Feingold, "Introduction," *AJH* 71 (Dec. 1981): 182–83; Wiebe, *Search for Order*, p. 60.
5. *Deborah*, 44 (Feb. 23, 1899), 7; 44 (Mar. 23, 1899), 3.
6. Deborah Dash Moore, *B'nai B'rith and the Challenge of Ethnic Leadership* (Albany: State University of New York Press, 1981), p. xiii; *A History of B'nai B'rith Women* (pamphlet, Washington, D.C.: B'nai B'rith Women, 1984).
7. Benjamin Rabinowitz, *The Young Men's Hebrew Associations (1854–1913)* (New York: National Jewish Welfare Board, 1948), pp. 37–38.
8. *Deborah*, 27 (Dec. 3, 1891), 6–7; 39 (Apr. 19, 1894); 43 (Nov. 25, 1897), 4.
9. *Notable American Women, 1607–1950*, p. 566; *Deborah*, 43 (Nov. 25, 1897), 4.
10. Anne L. Kuhn, *The Mother's Role in Childhood Education: New England Concepts, 1830–1860* (London: Yale University Press, 1947), pp. 43–45; William O'Neill, "Feminism as a Radical Ideology," in *Dissent: History of American Radicalism*, ed. A. F. Young (De Kalb, Ill.: Northern Illinois University Press, 1968), p. 287; Cott, *The Bonds of Womanhood*, p. 205; O'Neill, *Everyone Was Brave*, p. 43.
11. Cott, *Bonds of Womanhood*, p. 201; Smith-Rosenberg, "Female World," pp. 1–29.
12. O'Neill, *The Woman Movement*, p. 47.
13. Ibid., p. 49; Inez Haynes Irwin, *Angels and Amazons: A Hundred Years of American Women* (Garden City, N.Y.: Doubleday, Doran & Co., 1933), p. 232; Karen Blair, "The Clubwoman as Feminist: The Woman's Culture Club Movement in the United States, 1868–1914" (Ph.D. diss., State

University of New York at Buffalo, 1976), p. 55. Cited in Ellen Sue Levi Elwell, "The Founding and Early Programs of the National Council of Jewish Women: Study and Practice as Jewish Women's Religious Expression," (Ph.D. diss., Indiana University, 1982), pp. 16–17. See also pp. 19–20.

14. Golumb, "1893 Congress," p. 57. See also Rudolf Glanz, "The Rise of the Jewish Club in America," *Jewish Social Studies* 31 (Apr. 1969): 82–89.

15. Mildred L. Braun, *A History of Johanna No. 9, United Order of True Sisters: 1874–1955* (authorized 2nd ed., rev., and supplement covering mid-1949–55), p. 9, AJA. A note on this page indicates that philanthropy was also part of the original purpose. Dr. Michel was a member of B'nai B'rith, and he advised the formation of a secret society. It was to be "secret in the sense that material assistance should be rendered without humiliation to the recipient and that a moral obligation could be imposed in both heart and mind of the giver to observe such integrity."

16. Braun, *History,* pp. 9–12; Golumb, "1893 Congress," p. 54. For secondary source material on the Order, Golumb recommends Hyman Grinstein, *The Rise of the Jewish Community in New York* (Philadelphia: Jewish Publication Society, 1945); and Rebekah Kohut, "Jewish Women's Organizations," *American Jewish Yearbook* 33 (1932), p. 170.

17. Hannah Greenbaum Solomon, *Fabric of My Life: The Story of a Social Pioneer* (1946; reprint, New York: Bloch & the National Council of Jewish Women, 1974), p. 109. William Cameron, *The World's Fair: Being a Pictorial History of the Columbian Exposition* (Philadelphia: National Publishing Co., 1893), p. 449, cited in Elwell, "Founding," p. 54.

18. Hannah Greenbaum Solomon, *A Sheaf of Leaves* (privately printed, 1911), p. 127.

19. *AJ,* July 1895, pp. 10–11; Emil G. Hirsch, *My Religion* (New York: 1925), pp. 369–71. Cited in Golumb, "1893 Congress," p. 59.

20. *Papers of the Jewish Women's Congress* (Philadelphia: Jewish Publication Society, 1894), pp. 61–62.

21. For a list of speeches, see Mary Kavanaugh Oldham Eagle, ed., *The Congress of Women* (1894; reprint, New York: Arno Press, 1974), p. 77.

22. *The American Israelite,* Sept. 7, 1893, p. 6. Cited in Golumb, "1893 Congress," p. 52.

23. *Papers of the Jewish Women's Congress,* p. 223.

24. Ibid., p. 190.

25. Ibid., pp. 218–62.

26. Elwell, "NCJW," pp. 100–101.

27. National Council of Jewish Women, *The First Fifty Years,* p. 22.

28. Hyman, "Volunteer Organizations," p. 17. Faith Rogow, "'Gone to Another Meeting': A History of the National Council of Jewish Women" (Ph.D. dissertation, Binghamton: State University of New York, 1988), pp. 36–38.

29. Ray Frank to Rev. S. J. Willis, Dec. 15, 1896, Ray Frank Litman Papers, AJHS; *Oakland Times,* Sept. 5, 1902; *Town Talk,* 1897, Litman Papers, AJHS.

30. *San Francisco Examiner*, Feb. 1893, Nov. 13, 1896, Ray Frank Litman Papers, AJHS; Ray Frank to Rev. S. J. Willis, Dec. 15, 1896, Litman Papers, AJHS; for information about frontier Jews, see "Harry Redinger—A Jew of the Old West," in *To Make a Dream Come True: Stories of the Residents of the Hebrew Home of Greater Washington*, ed. Linda Gordon Kuzmack and Shulamith Weisman (Rockville, Md.: Hebrew Home of Greater Washington, 1983), pp. 26–32; Moses Rischin, ed., *The Jews of the West: The Metropolitan Years* (Waltham, Mass.: AJHS, 1979), p. 6.

31. Mary Daly, *The Church and the Second Sex* (New York: Harper, 1975), p. 61.

32. Barbara Brown Zikmund, "The Struggle for the Right to Preach," in Ruether and Keller, *Women and Religion in America*, vol. 1, pp. 194–95.

33. Zikmund, "Struggle," p. 200; Rosemary Radford Ruether, "Women in Utopian Movements," in Ruether and Keller, *Women and Religion in America*, vol. 1, pp. 50–53.

34. *Stockton Mail*, Mar. 22, 189——, Litman Papers, AJHS.

35. Stockton *Jewish Progress*, n.d., Litman Papers, AJHS; Ray Frank to Rev. S. J. Willis, Dec. 15, 1896, Litman Papers, AJHS.

36. Simon Litman, *Ray Frank Litman: A Memoir* (New York: AJHS, 1957), p. 35.

37. Ray Frank, "Women in the Synagogue," in *Papers of the Jewish Woman's Congress* (Philadelphia: Jewish Publication Society, 1894), pp. 8, 52–65.

38. Ray Frank to Charlotte Perkins Stetson, Sept. 14, 1894, Litman Papers, AJHS.

39. Litman, *Ray Frank Litman*, p. 127.

40. Ibid., p. 55.

41. *Post*, n.d., Litman Papers, AJHS.

42. *Oakland Enquirer*, Sept. 18——; San Francisco *Bulletin*, Nov. 1895, Litman Papers, AJHS; *AJ*, Apr. 1898, p. 22.

43. Litman, *Ray Frank Litman*, pp. 161–62.

44. Ibid., p. 145.

45. For a study of the conflicts facing women during a personal spiritual quest, see Carol P. Christ, *Diving Deep and Surfacing: Women Writers on a Spiritual Quest* (Boston: Beacon Press, 1980), p. 5.

46. Litman, *Ray Frank Litman*, p. 5.

47. Lily H. Montagu to Ray Frank, Mar. 24, 1901, cited in ibid., pp. 137–38; Nina Davis to Ray Frank, Jan. 25, 1899, Litman Papers, AJHS; Nina Davis to Ray Frank, May 30, 1899, Litman Papers, AJHS; Nettie Adler to Ray Frank, Jan. 28, 1899, Dec. 27, 1899, Apr. 2, 1901, cited in Litman, *Ray Frank Litman*, pp. 134–37.

48. Ambrose Bierce to Ray Frank, May 5, 1895; Feb. 23, 1896, Litman Papers, AJHS, The Litman Papers include several years' correspondence between Ambrose Bierce and Ray Frank.

49. Jonathan Sarna, "The Daughters of Rabbis," AJA; "Nina Morais Cohen: 1893–1907," NCJW Papers, AJA; Stanton excerpts cited in Golumb, "1893 Congress," p. 56.

50. Golumb, "1893 Congress," p. 56.

51. *AJ*, Nov. 1895, p. 101.

52. Golumb, "1893 Congress," p. 56; Elizabeth Cady Stanton et al., *The Woman's Bible*, part 1 (New York, 1895), p. 8.

53. Flexner, *Century of Struggle*, p. 316.

54. Golumb, "1893 Congress," p. 56.

55. *AJ*, May 1896, p. 438.

56. *AJ*, July 1897, pp. 156–59; Oct. 1897, pp. 13–14; July–Aug. 1898, p. 54; Sept. 1898, pp. 5–6, 60; Aug. 1899; Jan. 1896, p. 221; Aug. 1897, p. 236.

57. Robert Singerman, "The American Jewish Press, 1823–1983: A Bibliographic Survey of Research and Studies," *AJH* 73 (June 1984): 422–44.

58. David Loth, "The *American Jewess*" and supplemental "Notes on the Marital Discord of Solomon and Rosa Sonneschein," unpublished paper, Rosa Sonneschein Papers, AJA, n.d., p. 1 and passim. Loth is Rosa Sonneschein's grandson; Anita Liebman Lebeson, *Recall to Life—The Jewish Woman in America* (New York: Thomas Yoseloff, 1970), p. 229; Albie Sachs and Joan Hoff Wilson, *Sexism and the Law: A Study of Male Beliefs and the Law* (New York: Free Press, 1978), p. 78; June Sochen, *Herstory: A Woman's View of American History*, p. 202.

59. Banks, *Becoming a Feminist*, p. 38.

60. Loth, "*American Jewess*," pp. 5–6.

61. *AJ*, Apr. 1898, p. 22; Jan. 1899, p. 4; Apr. 1898, p. 22; May 1896, p. 438.

62. *AJ*, Jan. 1899, p. 4; Apr. 1897, p. 27; Apr. 1897, p. 28; Jan. 1899, pp. 3–5; Mar. 1897, p. 273; Sochen, *Herstory*, p. 201.

63. *AJ*, July–Aug. 1898, p. 52; Nov. 1897, p. 94; Dec. 1895, p. 165; Apr. 1897, p. 45; *AJ*, Oct. 1896, p. 11; Aug. 1896, pp. 474–75; Dec. 1898, pp. 27–28; Apr. 1897, p. 45; Oct. 1896, p. 97; May 1897, p. 85; Dec. 1895, p. 176; May 1895, pp. 67–69; Dec. 1895, p. 24; Oct. 1896, p. 43; June 1895, p. 175; Mar. 1897, p. 291.

64. *AJ*, June 1895, p. 171; Jan. 1897, p. 164; Nov. 1897, p. 95.

65. *AJ*, Jan. 1899, p. 5.

66. *AJ*, Nov. 1895, p. 112; Oct. 1896, p. 12; Apr. 1898, pp. 19, 22; *San Francisco Examiner*, Feb. 1893; Ray Frank to Rev. S. J. Willis, Dec. 15, 1896, Litman Papers, AJHS.

67. Emil G. Hirsch, "The Modern Jewess," *AJ*, July 1895, p. 10; *AJ*, Oct. 1895, p. 64; May 1897, p. 96; July 1896, p. 24; June 1895, pp. 114–15; July 1895, p. 18; May 1895, pp. 63–65.

68. Isaac M. Wise, "The Principles and Achievements of the Central Conference of American Rabbis, 1889–1913," in *Centenary Papers and Others*, ed. David Philipson, p. 213.

69. *AJ*, Nov. 1895, p. 112.

70. *AJ*, Dec. 1897, p. 147.

71. *AJ*, May 1895, pp. 82–83; June 1895, pp. 129–32, 176; July 1895, pp. 47, 27–31; Oct. 1895, pp. 48–51; Aug. 1895, pp. 248–49; Dec. 1895,

pp. 177–85; Jan. 1896, pp. 191–96, 277–82, 221–22, 225; Apr. 1896, pp. 380–81, 383–85; May 1896, p. 414; June 1896, pp. 498–500; July 1896, p. 561; Nov. 1896, pp. 68–69; Dec. 1896, pp. 122–24, 125–30, 141; Jan. 1897, p. 179; Mar. 1897, p. 295; May 1897, p. 65; Nov. 1897, pp. 83–84; Feb. 1898, p. 301; Mar. 1898, p. 274; Apr. 1899, pp. 40–42; Oct. 1896, p. 28; Nov. 1895, p. 115; June 1895, p. 19.

72. *AJ*, Dec. 1896, pp. 137–38.

73. *AJ*, Nov. 1895, p. 12; Feb. 1898, p. 224; Dec. 1897, p. 147; Sept. 1896, p. 638; Jan. 1897, p. 187; June 1895, pp. 180, 204–07; July 1895, p. 34; Aug. 1895, pp. 262–66; Dec. 1895, pp. 145–47; Jan. 1896, pp. 196–97, 210–12; May 1896, pp. 404–05; Aug. 1896, pp. 589–93, 606; Oct. 1896, p. 49; Nov. 1896, p. 94; Apr. 1897, p. 46; Jan. 1898, p. 158; Jan. 1898, p. 180; Sept. 1898, p. 57; Sept. 1898, p. 62.

74. *AJ*, Feb. 1897, pp. 233–34; Jan. 1899, p. 44; Marcus, *The American Jewish Woman, 1654–1980*, p. 76; *AJ*, Aug. 1899.

75. *AJ*, Dec. 1896, pp. 137–38; Apr. 1898, p. 22; May 1895, p. 101; Dec. 1895, p. 138.

76. *JC*, Jan. 14, 1881; Sachar, *Diaspora*, p. 141; V. D. Lipman, "Age of Emancipation," in Lipman, *Three Centuries*, pp. 70–72.

77. Sachar, *Course of Modern Jewish History*, pp. 243–45; Gartner, *Jewish Immigrant in England*, p. 43; Roth, *History of the Jews in England*, p. 269.

78. Bernard Gainer, *The Alien Invasion: The Origins of the Aliens Act of 1905* (New York: Crane, Russak & Co., 1972), p. 12; Richard Davis, *The English Rothschilds*, p. 117.

79. Gainer, *Alien Invasion*, p. 75; Beatrice Webb, "The Jewish Community (East London)," in *Life and Labour of the People in London*, ed. Charles Booth (New York and London, 1902–04; reprint ed. New York: AMS Press, 1970), p. 181.

80. Israel Finestein, "The New Community, 1880–1918," in V. D. Lipman, *Three Centuries*, p. 112; Israel Finestein, "Jewish Immigration in British Party Politics in the 1890's," in *Migration and Settlement: Proceedings of the Anglo-American Jewish Historical Conference*, ed. Aubrey Newman (London: Jewish Historical Society of England, 1971), p. 128.

81. Gartner, *Jewish Immigrant in England*, p. 49; *JC*, Jan. 16, 1885, p. 11; Mar. 13, 1885, p. 3; *JC*, 1881, in William J. Fishman, *East End Jewish Radicals, 1875–1914* (London: Duckworth, 1975), pp. 67–68; *JC*, Jan. 12, 1912, p. 13.

82. *JC*, Jan. 7, 1910, p. 7; Mar. 29, 1912, pp. 11–12.

83. *JC*, Jan. 1, 1904, pp. 10, 11; Mar. 15, 1912; Feb. 9, 1912, p. 16; Jan. 9, 1885, p. 5; Aug. 14, 1896, p. 5; Aug. 21, 1896, p. 5; Jan. 5, 1883; Mar. 16, 1883, p. 5; May 18, 1883, p. 7.

84. *JC*, May 26, 1896, p. 14.

85. *JC*, May 26, 1885, p. 7; May 16, 1902, p. 10; Jan. 19, 1883; Jan. 16, 1885, p. 7; Jan. 14, 1898, p. 13. Freedman, "Separatism as Strategy," p. 521;

Harriet W. Schupf, "Single Women and Social Reform in Mid-Nineteenth Century England: The Case of Mary Carpenter," *Victorian Studies* 27 (Mar. 1974).

86. *JC*, Feb. 13, 1885, p. 8; Feb. 20, 1885, p. 6; Jan. 30, 1885, pp. 6–7, 11–12; Feb. 29, 1885, p. 13; Jan. 30, 1885, p. 7; Jan. 30, 1885, p. 5; Jan. 16, 1885, p. 6; Jan. 23, 1885, p. 3; Mar. 13, 1885, p. 5. See *Annual Reports* of the Union of Jewish Women, beginning with *First Annual Report*, 1913, p. 7.

87. *JC*, May 3, 1912, p. 35; *JC*, May 16, 1902, p. 11; "Conference of Jewish Women," *JC*, May 16, 1902, p. 12.

88. *JC*, 1896: Jan. 10; Mar. 13, p. 9; Mar. 27, pp. 9–10; Apr. 17, pp. 6, 7, 10; Apr. 24, pp. 16, 17; Apr. 19, p. 22. Editorials, May 8, p. 14; May 26, p. 14. See controversial letters between Rev. Spiers and Rev. Stern, 1896. From Spiers, *JC*, Apr. 24, p. 17; Stern, May 5; Spiers, May 6; Stern, May 16, p. 7.

89. Alfred G. Henriques, "Why I Do Not Go to Synagogue," *JQR* (1901): 64, 73–74; G. Kitson-Clark, *The Making of Victorian England* (New York: Atheneum, 1969), p. 296.

90. Walton, *Women in Social Work*, p. 24; Branca, *Silent Sisterhood*, p. 22; *JC*, July 10, 1885, p. 5; July 17, 1885, p. 4.

91. *JC*, May 19, 1896, p. 15; Apr. 24, 1896, p. 7; May 17, 1896, p. 6.

92. *JC*, May 8, 1896, p. 9; May 13, 1896, p. 9; June 10, 1898, p. 8; Mar. 23, 1888, p. 7; Mar. 30, 1888, p. 5; Apr. 6, 1888, pp. 8–9; Apr. 6, 1888, p. 6; Apr. 20; Apr. 17, 1896, p. 7.

93. *JC*, June 1, 1888, p. 5; Apr. 6, 1888, p. 10; May 10, 1888, pp. 5, 63; *Jewish Guardian*, June 30, 1922, p. 4; Kitson-Clark, *Victorian England*, p. 158; Stephen S. Sharot, "Religious Change in Native Orthodoxy in London, 1870–1914: Rabbinate and Clergy," *JSS* 15 (Dec. 1973): 171; Steven Bayme, "Claude Montefiore, Lily Montagu and the Origins of the Jewish Religious Union," *Transactions of the Jewish Historical Society of England* 27 (1982): 62.

94. *JC*, Jan. 3, 1896, p. 6; Olga Lazarus, *Liberal Judaism and Its Standpoint* (London: Macmillan, 1937), pp. 90, 94; Oswald Simon,"Reformed Judaism," *JQR* (1894): 265, 271, 276; Simon, "The Mission of Judaism," *JQR* 9 (1897): 77; Simon, "Jews and Modern Thought," *JQR* 9 (1899): 387–99.

95. *JC*, Feb. 24, 1922, pp. 11–12.

96. "Conference of Jewish Women," *JC*, May 16, 1902, pp. 10, 12–15, 17.

97. Ibid., pp. 10–12, 14. Philanthropic Section speakers included Lily Montagu, founder of the West Central Girls' Club; Netta Adler, daughter of the Chief Rabbi; Mrs. Morris Joseph (Frances) and Miss Kate Halford, who became secretary of the Union of Jewish Women. Constance Lady Battersea pleaded for help in prevention and rescue of white slavery victims here and in her work with the National Union of Women Workers. Representatives from Manchester included Miss Mosely, Miss Hilda Joseph and Miss Schlesinger. Several women presented papers to younger women, hoping to inspire them to volunteer for philanthropic work. These speakers included Mrs. Mor-

ris Joseph (Frances), Mrs. Benjamin Elkin, and Mrs. Bingen. Speakers on nursing and sanitation included Mrs. Lionel Lucas from the Board of Guardians' Ladies' Visiting Committee; Miss Hannah Hyam of the Charity Organization Society; Mrs. H. Lazarus, nursing matron; Mrs. Horatio Lucas, visitor to Whitechapel Infirmary; Mrs. Rosenthal, visitor at the German Hospital; Miss Salinger, superintendent of the Convalescent Home, Brighton; and Mrs. Salis Simon of the Jewish Ladies' Visiting Association of Manchester.

98. Ibid., p. 15. Eugene C. Black, *The Social Politics of Anglo-Jewry, 1880–1920* (Oxford: Basil Blackwell, 1988), pp. 222–23.

99. *First Annual Report* of the Union of Jewish Women (1903), pp. 2–4, ML. The honorary secretary was Hannah Cohen, who would later become president of the Jewish Board of Guardians. Her daughter Lucy Cohen took on the same post in 1915. The list of chairmen included Mrs. Adler and Mrs. Meyer Spielmann. Other major officers included Mrs. Morris Joseph, Mrs. Claude G. Montefiore, Miss Netta Adler, and Mrs. Arthur Franklin. In 1903, Mrs. Alice Model assumed the position of honorary secretary and held it until 1914. Rothschild women included Louise Lady de Rothschild, who remained active until her death, her daughter Constance Lady Battersea, and Louise's daughters-in-law Lady Charlotte Rothschild and Charlotte (Mrs. Lionel) de Rothschild.

100. UJW *Report*, 1905, p. 9, ML.

101. Ibid., p. 5.

102. *JC*, Jan. 12, 1912, p. 38.

103. UJW *Report*, 1911, p. 13; 1912, pp. 11, 17; 1908, p. 25; 1906, p. 6, ML.

104. UJW *Report*, 1911, p. 14; 1908, pp. 12, 13; 1911, pp. 10–11, 14; 1913, p. 20; Ellen Desart, "Union of Jewish Women," UJW *Report*, 1911, p. 7; UJW *Report*, 1912, pp. 13–14; 1913, pp. 16–17, ML; *JC*, Jan. 15, 1904, p. 17.

105. June Sochen, "Jewish Volunteers," *American Jewish History* 70 (Sept. 1980): 23.

CHAPTER 3

1. William J. Fishman, *The Streets of East London* (London: Duckworth, 1979), p. 64.

2. Battersea, *Reminiscences*, p. 409; Richard Davis, *The English Rothschilds*, p. 164; Lucy Cohen, *Lady de Rothschild*, pp. 75, 180, 201, 215, 268, 279; Bermant, *Cousinhood*, pp. 142–44, 146.

3. Battersea, *Reminiscences*, p. 409; Richard Davis, *The English Rothschilds*, p. 164; Lucy Cohen, *Lady de Rothschild*, pp. 75, 180, 201, 215, 268, 279; Bermant, *Cousinhood*, pp. 142–44, 146.

4. Lucy Cohen, *Lady de Rothschild*, pp. 198–200.

5. Battersea, *Reminiscences*, pp. 428, 433–37, 439, 446; International Council of Women, *Women in a Changing World: The Dynamic Story of the International Council of Women since 1888* (London: Routledge & Kegan

Paul, 1966), p. 45; Paulson, *Women's Suffrage and Prohibition*, p. 182; Banks, *Faces of Feminism*, pp. 79–80; Lucy Cohen, *Lady de Rothschild*, pp. 198–200; Prochaska, *Women and Philanthropy*, p. 139; Norbert C. Soldon, *Women in British Trade Unions, 1874–1976* (New York and London: Gill & Macmillan, 1978), p. 58.

6. Battersea, *Reminiscences*, p. 441; "Conference of Jewish Women," *JC*, May 16, 1902, pp. 10–17, and Jan. 12, 1912; Union of Jewish Women, *First Annual Report* (1903), pp. 2–4, ML.

7. Lucy Cohen, *Lady de Rothschild*, p. 204; Fishman, *Streets of East London*, p. 64.

8. Lucy Cohen, *Lady de Rothschild*, p. 204.

9. Ruth Rosen, *The Lost Sisterhood: Prostitution in America, 1900–1918* (Baltimore and London: Johns Hopkins University Press, 1982), p. 10.

10. W. T. Stead, *The Maiden Tribute of Modern Babylon (The Report of the "Pall Mall Gazette's" Secret Commission)* (London, 1885).

11. Edward Bristow, *Prostitution and Prejudice: The Jewish Fight against White Slavery 1870–1939* (Oxford: Clarendon Press, 1982), p. 45; Colin Holmes, *Anti-Semitism in British Society, 1876–1939* (New York: Holmes & Meier, 1979), p. 45; Gainer, *Alien Invasion*, pp. 36–40.

12. Judith Walkowitz, "Jack the Ripper and the Myth of Male Violence," *FS* 8 (Fall 1982): 555–56; Colin Holmes, "East End Crime and the Jewish Community, 1887–1911," in *The Jewish East End 1840–1939*, ed. Aubrey Newman (London: Jewish Historical Society of England, 1981), pp. 110, 112–15; Fishman, *Streets of East London*, pp. 56–57.

13. Webb, "Jewish Community," p. 190; V. D. Lipman, "The Booth and New London Surveys as Source Material," in Newman, *The Jewish East End*, pp. 41–50; William Fishman, *Jewish Radicals* (New York: Pantheon, 1974), p. 54.

14. Webb, "Jewish Community," p. 191; Gartner, *Jewish Immigrant in England*, pp. 64–65.

15. Jewish International Conference On the Suppression of the Traffic in Girls and Women, *Official Report* (London, 1910), pp. 93ff.; Jewish Association for the Protection of Girls and Women, *Annual Report* (1911), p. 113, JAPGW Papers, LL.

16. Marion Kaplan, *The Jewish Feminist Movement in Germany: The Campaigns of the Jüdischer Frauenbund, 1904–1938* (Wesport, Conn., and London: Greenwood, 1979), pp. 3, 10–11, 31–32, 34.

17. Ibid., pp. 3, 115–17; Jewish International Conference, *Official Report* (1910), p. 150, LL.

18. JAPGW *Report* (1908), p. 19, LL; *Protokoll der . . . Weltbundes Jüdischer Frauen* (1929), pp. 16–24; both cited in Bristow, *Prostitution and Prejudice*, p. 103.

19. JAPGW *Report* (1898), p. 24; (1905), pp. 23–25; (1910), pp. 33–35, LL; Jewish International Conference, *Official Report* (1910), pp. 101, 154–55; Jewish International Conference, *Official Report* (1927), pp. 24–25; J. David Bleich, *Contemporary Halakhic Problems* (New York: Ktav and Yeshiva Uni-

versity Press, 1977), pp. 151–59; Marion Kaplan, *Jewish Feminist Movement*, pp. 115–17.

20. Jewish International Conference, *Official Report* (1910), pp. 126–27.

21. JAPGW *Report* (1912), pp. 15–16, LL.

22. Battersea, *Reminiscences*, p. 422; Lucy Cohen, *Lady de Rothschild*, p. 205.

23. Linda Gordon and Ellen Dubois, "Seeking Ecstasy on the Battlefield: Danger and Pleasure in Nineteenth-Century Feminist Sexual Thought," *FS* 9 (Spring 1983): 7–10; Judith Walkowitz, *Prostitution and Victorian Society: Women, Class, and the State* (Cambridge: Cambridge University Press, 1980), pp. 87–88; Ruth Rosen, *Lost Sisterhood*, p. 6; Bristow, *Vice and Vigilance*, pp. 52–53; Paul McHugh, *Prostitution and Victorian Social Reform* (New York: St. Martin's Press, 1980), p. 17.

24. Susan Kingsley Kent, *Sex and Suffrage in Britain, 1860–1914* (Princeton, N.J.: Princeton University Press, 1987), pp. 142–43; Banks, *Faces of Feminism*, pp. 68, 81; Prochaska, *Women and Philanthropy*, pp. 186, 192; Walkowitz, *Prostitution*, pp. 88, 117; McHugh, *Prostitution*, p. 117; Strachey, *Cause*, p. 266–69.

25. JAPGW *Report* (1910), p. 61, LL.

26. JAPGW *Report* (1898), pp. 56–57; (1905), pp. 64–65; (1912), p. 79, LL.

27. JAPGW *Report* (1898), p. 32; (1905), p. 38; (1912), p. 59; (1908), p. 41, LL.

28. Battersea, *Reminiscences*, p. 422.

29. JAPGW *Report* (1898), p. 33; (1911), p. 66; (1904), p. 35; (1908), p. 40; (1912), pp. 57–58, LL.

30. JAPGW *Report* (1898), pp. 46–47; (1905), pp. 51–52; (1908), p. 53, LL.

31. JAPGW *Report* (1908), pp. 47, 50; (1908), p. 8, LL.

32. JAPGW *Report* (1898), pp. 50–51, LL.

33. JAPGW *Report* (1910), pp. 44–45; (1911), p. 64; (1914), pp. 17, 49–53, LL.

34. The school was first named the Stamford Hill Industrial Training School. In 1906, its name was changed to the Montefiore House Certified School for Jewish Girls. See JAPGW *Report* (1912), p. 93; (1905), pp. 70, 74–75; (1908), pp. 72–73; (1910), p. 79, LL.

35. JAPGW *Report* (1906), p. 71; (1912), pp. 93, 98; (1914), p. 103; (1925), p. 54, LL.

36. JAPGW *Report* (1905), pp. 77–78; (1911), p. 40; (1912), p. 40, LL.

37. JAPGW *Report* (1898), pp. 58–60; (1908), p. 67; (1906), pp. 63–66; (1907), p. 71; (1908), pp. 66–67; (1912), p. 84; (1912), pp. 17–18, LL.

38. *JC*, May 17, 1896, p. 17; May 3, 1912, p. 30; Nov. 1, 1912, p. 8; Nov. 15, 1912, p. 12; JAPGW *Report* (1912), p. 12; JAPGW *Report* (1914), pp. 16–21, pp. 86–87, LL.

39. JAPGW *Report* (1912), pp. 30–31, LL.

40. Bristow, *Prostitution and Prejudice*, p. 280.

41. Ruth Rosen, *Lost Sisterhood*, pp. 8, 11; Degler, *At Odds*, pp. 280–81, 286–87; Banks, *Faces of Feminism*, p. 69; Kuhn, *The Mother's Role*, pp. 56–57, 180–84.

42. Hasia R. Diner, *In the Almost Promised Land: American Jews and Blacks, 1915–1935* (Westport, Conn., London: Greenwood Press, 1977); *Proceedings of the Triennial Conventions of the National Council of Jewish Women* (1908) (Chicago, Toby Rubovits) (hereafter cited as CJW *Proceedings*), pp. 156–57.

43. Lucy S. Dawidowicz, *On Equal Terms: Jews in America, 1880–1981* (New York: Holt, Rinehart & Winston, 1982), p. 45; Jenna Weissman Joselit, *Our Gang: Jewish Crime and the New York Jewish Community, 1900–1940* (Bloomington: Indiana University Press, 1983), p. 29.

44. Wiebe, *Search for Order*, pp. 65–70.

45. Naomi Cohen, *Encounter with Emancipation*, pp. 266–67.

46. CJW *Proceedings* (1908), pp. 268–69; Naomi Cohen, *Encounter with Emancipation*, pp. 272–80.

47. Bristow, *Prostitution and Prejudice*, p. 161; Ribuffo, "Henry Ford," p. 440.

48. Joselit, *Our Gang*, pp. 48–49; CJW *Proceedings* (1911), pp. 85–86; JAPGW *Report* (1911), p. 37, LL.

49. Ruth Rosen, *Lost Sisterhood*, p. 15; Joselit, *Our Gang*, p. 49.

50. Ruth Rosen, *Lost Sisterhood*, pp. 14–15, 58.

51. Joselit, *Our Gang*, pp. 40–41; Henry L. Feingold, *A Midrash on American Jewish History* (Albany: State University of New York Press, 1982), p. 74.

52. Bristow, *Prostitution and Prejudice*, pp. 162–63.

53. Joselit, *Our Gang*, p. 47.

54. Charlotte Baum et al., *The Jewish Woman in America* (New York: Dial, 1976), p. 175; Bristow, *Prostitution and Prejudice*, p. 179.

55. Moses Rischin, *The Promised City: New York's Jews, 1870–1914* (Cambridge, Mass., and London: Harvard University Press, 1977), p. 70.

56. Susan Estabrook Kennedy, *If All We Did Was to Weep at Home: A History of White Working-Class Women in America* (Bloomington: Indiana University Press, 1979), p. 145; Baum et al., *Jewish Woman*, p. 119.

57. Letter from Mamie Pinzer to Fanny Quincy Howe, Dec. 9, 1910, cited in Ruth Rosen and Sue Davidson, eds., *The Mamie Papers* (Cambridge: The Feminist Press and Schlesinger Library of Radcliffe College, 1977), p. 4 and passim.

58. Joselit, *Our Gang*, pp. 52–55; Bristow, *Prostitution and Prejudice*, pp. 160–62; Baum et al., *Jewish Woman*, p. 174.

59. Joselit, *Our Gang*, p. 2; Jewish International Conference, *Official Report* (1927), p. 48; Bristow, *Prostitution and Prejudice*, pp. 220–23.

60. CJW *Proceedings* (1911), p. 40; (1908), p. 160.

61. Bristow, *Prostitution and Prejudice*, pp. 222–21.

62. CJW *Proceedings* (1902), p. 57; Solomon, *A Sheaf of Leaves*, p. 155.

63. CJW *Proceedings* (1902), p. 58.

64. Ibid. (1908), p. 27.

65. Ibid. (1908), p. 51.

66. Ibid. (1908), p. 27.

67. Ibid. (1905), p. 17.

68. Ibid. (1902), pp. 150–59.

69. Emily Solis-Cohen, untitled speech at national convention of United Synagogue, n.d., p. 2, Emily Solis-Cohen Papers, AJHS.

70. CJW *Proceedings* (1908), p. 157.

71. Ibid. (1902), p. 14; (1908), p. 153.

72. Kessler-Harris, *Women Have Always Worked*, p. 69; Solomon, *A Sheaf of Leaves*, p. 253.

73. CJW *Proceedings* (1911), pp. 67–68, 87.

74. Ibid. (1911), pp. 40, 69.

75. Ibid. (1914), p. 115; Baum et al., *Jewish Woman*, p. 50.

76. CJW *Proceedings* (1905), pp. 15, 17–18; (1911), p. 69; (1914), p. 121.

77. Zosa Szajkowski, "Deportation of Jewish Immigrants and Returnees before World War I," *AJHQ* 67, no. 4 (June 1978): 297; CJW *Proceedings* (1908), pp. 146–47, 151–52; (1911), pp. 24, 38, 78.

78. CJW *Proceedings* (1911), pp. 24–25, 37.

79. Solomon, *A Sheaf of Leaves*, p. 198.

80. CJW *Proceedings* (1908), pp. 147–48, 154–55, 161.

81. Ibid. (1908), pp. 208–09.

82. Ibid. (1911), pp. 33–34, 37, 39, 75; (1908), p. 77; (1914), p. 120.

83. Ibid. (1911), pp. 69, 83, 84.

84. Letter from Max J. Kohler to Mrs. Joseph E. Friend, President, NCJW, Nov. 26, 1929, NCJW papers, AJHS.

85. CJW *Proceedings* (1911), pp. 17, 39; (1914), pp. 119–20.

86. Marion Kaplan, *Jewish Feminist Movement*, p. 93.

87. JAPGW *Report* (1905), p. 34, LL.

88. Sadie American, "Organization," in *Papers of the Jewish Women's Congress* (Philadelphia: Jewish Publication Society, 1894); CJW *Proceedings*, p. 57; (1905), pp. 25, 169; Solomon, *A Sheaf of Leaves*, p. 155.

89. Battersea, *Reminiscences*, p. 441; Lucy Cohen, *Lady de Rothschild*, pp. 268, 276–77.

90. JAPGW *Report* (1911), pp. 14–15; Jewish International Conference, *Official Report* (1910), p. 101; JAPGW *Report* (1910), p. 75, LL; CJW *Proceedings* (1911), pp. 85–86; *JC*, May 22, 1914, p. 12.

91. World Conference of Jewish Women, *Report*, 1923, p. 11, AJA.

92. Bristow, *Prostitution and Prejudice*, pp. 279–80.

93. Ibid., pp. 302–03, 305–07; WCJW, *Report*, 1923, p. 53.

94. Marion Kaplan, *Jewish Feminist Movement*, p. 119; JAPGW *Report* (1911), pp. 27, 29–30; (1912), pp. 30–31, LL.

95. CJW *Proceedings* (1911), pp. 32–34; (1912), pp. 32–36.

96. Jewish International Conference, *Official Report* (1910), p. 101; JAPGW *Report* (1910), p. 75, LL; WCJW, *Report*, 1923, p. 11, AJA; Bristow, *Prostitution and Prejudice*, pp. 279–80, 302–5.

97. Sachar, *Diaspora*, p. 283; Bristow, *Prostitution and Prejudice*, pp. 320–21.

98. International Council of Women, *Women in a Changing World*, p. 45; Battersea, *Reminiscences*, p. 441.

CHAPTER 4

1. Wiebe, *Search for Order*, p. 122; Degler, *At Odds*, p. 376.

2. Eric Richards, "Women in the British Economy since About 1700: An Interpretation," *History* 59 (October 1974): 337–57; Sheila Lewenhak, *Women and Work* (New York: St. Martin's Press, 1980), p. 188.

3. Mary A. Hill, *Charlotte Perkins Gilman: The Making of a Radical Feminist, 1860–1896* (Philadelphia: Temple University Press, 1960), p. 264.

4. Carolyn de Swarte Gifford, "Women in Social Reform Movements," in Ruether and Keller, *Women and Religion in America*, vol. 1, p. 301.

5. Christ, *Diving Deep and Surfacing*, p. 11.

6. Rischin, *The Promised City*, p. 201.

7. Margaret Gibbons Wilson, *The American Woman in Transition: The Urban Influence, 1879–1920* (London: Greenwood Press, 1979), p. 86; Ann D. Gordon and Mari Jo Buhle, "Sex and Class in Colonial and Nineteenth-Century America," in Carroll, *Liberating Women's History*, pp. 286–87.

8. *JC*, Jan. 8, 1881, pp. 1, 15; Jan. 7, 1881, p. 15.

9. *JC*, Sept. 30, 1910, p. 11.

10. *JC*, Nov. 1, 1912, p. 22.

11. Walton, *Women in Social Work*, p. 64.

12. *Carolyn Franklin: An Appreciation* (privately printed, 1936), pp. 29, 39, 41, 43–45, 55, David Franklin Collection.

13. Monk Gibbon, *Netta* (London: Routledge & Kegan Paul, 1960), pp. 88, 121–22.

14. The library of the Union of Jewish Women had extensive publications by Jewish women authors. UJW *Report*, 1903, pp. 9–10; 1912, p. 19; 1913, p. 24, ML.

15. *JC*, June 21, 1912; Herbert M. Loewe, "Nina Salaman, 1877–1925," *Transactions of the Jewish Historical Society of England* 11 (1928): 228–32.

16. *JC*, Feb. 2, 1912, pp. 26–27; UJW *Report*, 1905, p. 20, ML; *JC*, Jan. 5, 1912, p. 20; UJW *Report*, 1911, p. 12; 1903, pp. 9, 10; 1904, p. 1; 1903, p. 8; 1910, p. 16; 1908, p. 10; 1913, pp. 21, 24, ML.

17. UJW *Report*, 1905, p. 20, ML.

18. UJW *Report*, 1904, p. 14; 1905, p. 13; 1910, p. 13, ML; *JC*, Jan. 19, 1912, p. 29; Feb. 9, 1912; Feb. 16, 1912, pp. 16–17; June 28, 1912, p. 21.

19. UJW *Report*, 1905, pp. 14, 25; 1910, p. 10, ML.

20. UJW *Report*, 1903, p. 13, ML.

21. UJW *Report*, 1904, p. 10, ML. Hannah Hyam, a leading communal worker, was the Union representative to the NUWW for many years.

22. UJW *Report*, 1904, p. 11, ML. For Union representation to other NUWW conferences, see UJW *Report*, 1906, p. 13; 1908, p. 15; 1911, pp. 19–20; 1912, p. 11. Official Union representatives in that year were Mrs. Meyer Spielman, Mrs. C. Q. Henriques, and Miss Kate Halford; UJW *Report*, 1913, p. 14; 1915, p. 7; 1904, p. 11, ML.

23. ICW, *Women in a Changing World*, p. 27.

24. UJW *Report*, 1913, ML; ICW, *Women in a Changing World*, p. 221; UJW *Report*, 1913, p. 2, ML.

25. Ellen M. Umansky to Linda Gordon Kuzmack, July 11, 1989.

26. Montagu, "Short Paper with Outline of what I want done with regard to my work if I pass away," Sept. 1, 1939, Montagu Papers, AJA; Lily H. Montagu, *My Club and I: The Story of the West Central Girls Club*, 2nd ed. (London: Neville Spearman & Herbert Joseph, 1954), p. 154; Gibbon, *Netta*, pp. 56–60, 64, 66.

27. Walton, *Women in Social Work*, p. 64; Banks, *Faces of Feminism*, p. 92.

28. *JC*, Mar. 25, 1898, p. 27; Nellie G. Levy, "Lily Montagu and the West Central Club," in *Liberal Jewish Monthly Memorial Supplement*, p. 13; Stephen S. Sharot, "Native Jewry and the Religious Anglicization of Immigrants in London, 1870–1905," *JJS* 16 (June 1974): 51; Montagu, *My Club and I*, p. 52; Montagu, "Last Club Letter," *Memorial Supplement*, pp. 15–16; Montagu, "Cast me not away from Thy Presence . . . ," sermon, May 8, 1920, Montagu Papers, AJA.

29. Montagu, "Wishes for my work after my death," June 15, 1940, Montagu Papers, AJA; Nellie Levy, "West Central Club," p. 13; L. L. Loewe, *Henriques*, p. 174n. 2.

30. *JC*, Jan. 24, 1896, p. 19; May 15, 1896, p. 16; Jan. 7, 1898, p. 8; *Minutes* of the West Central Flower Company, Mar. 13, 19——, Montagu Papers, AJA; Ellen M. Umansky, "Lily H. Montagu: Religious Leader, Organizer and Prophet," *Conservative Judaism* 34, no. 6: 70.

31. Eric Conrad, *Lily H. Montagu: Prophet of a Living Judaism* (New York: National Federation of Temple Sisterhoods, 1953), p. 18; Lily Montagu to Israel Mattuck, Dec. 10, 1922, Montagu Papers, AJA; *JC*, Mar. 25, 1898, p. 27.

32. Basil Henriques to Lily Montagu, Feb. 15, 1921, Montagu Papers, AJA; *JC*, Jan. 24, 1896, p. 19.

33. L. L. Loewe, *Henriques*, p. 20.

34. *JC*, May 3, 1912, p. 18; Jerry White, *Rothschild Buildings: Life in an East End Tenement Block 1887–1920* (London: Routledge & Kegan Paul, 1980), p. 190.

35. *JC*, May 19, 1912, p. 28; Feb. 2, 1912, pp. 13, 30; Mar. 25, 1898, p. 27; Jan. 12, 1912, pp. 14, 18; Jan. 19, 1912, p. 18.

36. For descriptions of the wide range of Jewish women's charitable organizations, see also *JC*, Jan. 8, 1904, p. 12; Jan. 5, 1912, p. 35; May 3, 1912, p. 18; Mar. 1, 1912, p. 22; Feb. 2, 1912, p. 30.

37. Letter to Lily Montagu from the Clerk to England's Lord Chancellor, Aug. 27, 1920, Montagu Papers, AJA; Conrad, *Montagu*, pp. 30–31; Letter from Lily Montagu to Israel Mattuck, Dec. 16, 1922, Montagu Papers, AJA; Bermant, *Cousinhood*, p. 214.

38. Walton, *Women in Social Work*, pp. 142–48.

39. *JG*, Nov. 14, 1919, pp. 14–15; Dec. 26, 1919, pp. 1, 12; Jan. 23, 1920, p. 6; May 14, 1920, p. 9; Feb. 27, 1920, p. 3; Mar. 18, 1921.

40. L. L. Loewe, *Henriques*, pp. 56, 59, 61, 66–67, 155–56; Rose Henriques, *Fifty Years in Stepney* (privately printed, 1966), pp. 13, 17. The same incident is recorded in Phyllis Gerson's letter to Linda Gordon Kuzmack, Mar. 29, 1982.

41. L. L. Loewe, *Henriques*, pp. 172–73.

42. The Brady and Bernhard Baron settlements were closed a few years ago. Phyllis J. Gerson to Linda Gordon Kuzmack, personal communication, Jan. 19, 1982.

43. Walter M. Schwab to Linda Gordon Kuzmack, personal communication, May 27, 1982; "In Memoriam—Mrs. Anna Schwab," *AJR Information*, May 1963, Walter M. Schwab Collection; *East London Advertiser*, Apr. 26, 1963, Gerson Collection; "Some of the things you should know about the success of the Stepney Jewish Community Center," Gerson Collection; "Scroll of Events," Stepney Jewish B'nai B'rith Clubs and Settlement, Gerson Collection; Phyllis J. Gerson to Linda Gordon Kuzmack, personal communication, Sept. 3, 1982.

44. "Stepney Jewish Girls' Club," *JC*, Jan. 25, 1935, Gerson Collection; Phyllis J. Gerson to Linda Kuzmack, personal communication, Mar. 9 and Mar. 18, 1982; *Our House*, Stepney Jewish (B'nai B'rith) Clubs and Settlement newsletter, May 1974, Gerson Collection; *Order of Proceedings* at official opening of the Beaumont Hall Day and Community Centre by Her Majesty, Queen Elizabeth, the Queen Mother, May 29, 1974, Gerson Collection; Gerson, "Scroll of Events." Miss Gerson also holds several important offices in the Jewish and general community. See *Bulletin* of Liberal Jewish Synagogue, N.W.B., n.d., Gerson Collection.

45. "Flowers—and a Gong—for Florrie," newspaper clipping, Jan. 1976, Gerson Collection; "Florrie: 'Queen' of the Clubs," newspaper clipping (1981?), Gerson Collection; "MBE for Community Worker Born in 1888," *Mackney Gazette*, Jan. 1976, Gerson Collection.

46. Dr. I. Sidney Gold to Linda Gordon Kuzmack, personal communications, June 19 and 29, 1983. The description below of Miss Moses' life and work comes primarily from these letters.

47. Dr. I. Sidney Gold to Linda Gordon Kuzmack, personal communication, June 29, 1983. I am grateful to Dr. Gold for his extensive portrayal of Miriam Moses and her era. During and after the war, Miss Moses also served

as an officer of two other major women's organizations: the Friendship Club, devoted to care of the elderly, and the League of Jewish Women, whose members volunteer in hospitals, clinics, and programs for the elderly.

48. James A. Schmiechen, *Sweated Industries and Sweated Labor: The London Clothing Trades, 1860–1914* (Urbana and Chicago: University of Illinois Press, 1984), p. 179; Sheila Lewenhak, *Women and Trade Unions: An Outline History of Women in the British Trade Union Movement* (New York: St. Martin's Press, 1977), pp. 80–81; Paul R. Thompson, *The Edwardians: The Remaking of British Society* (Bloomington and London: Indiana University Press, 1975), p. 247; Soldon, *Women in British Trade Unions*, p. 68.

49. V. D. Lipman, *Social Service*, p. 20; Harold Pollins, "East End Jewish Working Men's Clubs Affiliated to the Working Men's Club and Institute Union: 1870–1914," in Newman, *The Jewish East End*, p. 173, 177–87.

50. V. D. Lipman, *Social Service*, p. 87.

51. *JC*, Apr. 19, 1912, p. 28; Apr. 26, 1912; May 10, 1912, p. 42.

52. *JC*, Apr. 19, 1912, p. 27.

53. *JC*, Apr. 19, 1912, pp. 10, 28; May 26, 1912, p. 27; Apr. 19, 1912, p. 27.

54. *AJ*, Aug. 1895, p. 260.

55. Adele Simmons, "Education and Ideology in Nineteenth-Century America: The Response of Educational Institutions to the Changing Role of Women," in Carroll, *Liberating Women's History*, pp. 116–18; Sochen, *Herstory*, p. 17; Chambers-Schiller, *Liberty, a Better Husband*, p. 4; Sarah Drukker in *AJ*, Jan. 1899, p. 4.

56. Peter Gay, *The Bourgeois Experience, Victoria to Freud*, vol. 1, *Education of the Senses* (New York and Oxford: Oxford University Press, 1984), p. 182.

57. Annie Nathan Meyer, *It's Been Fun* (1951); Baum et al., *Jewish Woman*, p. 47; D. Askowith, *Three Outstanding Women* (1941); brief descriptions of Meyer in the *Encyclopedia Judaica*, vol. 11, s.v. "Meyer, Annie Nathan"; Marcus, *Documentary History*, p. 386; Annie Nathan Meyer, "Petition to the Hon. Hamilton Fish, Chairman of the Board of Trustees of Columbia College," ca. 1888, AJA.

58. Simmons, "Education," p. 122; Rosalind Rosenberg, *Beyond Separate Spheres: Intellectual Roots of Modern Feminism* (New Haven and London: Yale University Press, 1982), p. 86.

59. *American Hebrew*, 1912, Richman Papers, AJA; Petition "To the Board of Education, New York City," n.d., Richman Papers, AJA; "Julia Richmond's [sic] Defeat in the Board of Education," Richman Papers, AJA; *New York Times*, cited in *American Hebrew*, 1912, Richman Papers, AJA; Letter from Julia Richman to Felix Warburg, chairman of the Board of Education, Apr. 25, 1912, Richman Papers, AJA.

60. Richman became the first president of the Young Women's Hebrew Association in New York City, a member of the Jewish Chautauqua Society's Educational Council, and a director of the Hebrew Free School Association.

Marcus, *American Jewish Woman, 1654–1980*, p. 28; *American Hebrew,* 1912, Richman Papers, AJA.

61. Julia Richman, "Women Wage-Workers: With Reference to Directing Immigrants," *Papers of the Jewish Women's Congress.*

62. Isaac Metzker, ed., *A Bintel Brief: Sixty Years of Letters from the Lower East Side to the Jewish Daily Forward,* foreword and notes by Harry Golden (Garden City, N.Y.: Doubleday, 1971), pp. 109–10.

63. Arthur A. Goren, *New York Jews and the Quest for Community* (New York: Columbia University Press, 1970), pp. 96–98; Thomas Kessner, "Jobs, Ghettos and the Urban Economy, 1880–1935," *AJH* 71 (Dec. 1981): 229–30.

64. Selma Cantor Berrol, "Immigrants at School: New York City, 1898–1914" (Ph.D. diss., City University of New York, 1967), pp. 51–63.

65. Sarna, *People Walk on Their Heads*, p. 8.

66. *Deborah*, 40 (Feb. 14, 1895), p. 3; 35 (Apr. 15, 1889), p. 6; 37 (Dec. 31, 1891), p. 5; see also 36 (Feb. 12, 1891), p. 5.

67. Sochen, *Herstory*, p. 260.

68. "Jewish Girl Collegian," *Jewish Tribune,* Nov. 15, 1919, p. 9. Jennie Manheimer Papers, AJA.

69. Leah Morton, *I am a Woman—and a Jew,* rev. ed., Masterworks of Modern Jewish Writing Series, ed. Jonathan D. Sarna, intro. by Ellen M. Umansky (New York: Markus Wiener, 1986), passim.

70. David Farrer, *The Warburgs: The Story of a Family* (New York: Stein & Day, 1975), p. 70; *American Hebrew,* May 31, 1918, Harriet Lowenstein Papers, AJHS.

71. *Home News,* April 7, 1918; *Bank Israelite* (Chicago), July 27, 19——; *American Hebrew,* May 31, 1918; Dec. 6, 1919; all in Lowenstein Papers, AJHS.

72. "The Jewish Girl Collegian," *Jewish Tribune,* Nov. 15, 1919, Jennie Manheimer Papers, AJA.

73. Stephen Birmingham, *Our Crowd: The Great Jewish Families of New York* (New York, Evanston, and London: Harper & Row, 1967), p. 293.

74. NCJW *Proceedings* (1896), p. 23, NCJW Papers, AJA.

75. NCJW *Proceedings* (1914), p. 118; Chicago Section, "Record of Progress, 1894–1908," NCJW Papers, AJA; Brooklyn Section, "History," pp. 3, 6, NCJW Papers, AJA.

76. June Sochen, *Consecrete Every Day: The Public Lives of Jewish American Women, 1880–1980* (Albany: State University of New York, 1981), p. 50.

77. Cecelia Razovsky, "A Report on the Work of the Bureau of International Service of the National Council of Jewish Women" (1927), p. 1; Cecelia Razovsky, "Humanitarian Effects of the Immigration Law" (1927); *Jewish Exponent,* Nov. 26, 1926; all in NCJW Papers, AJHS.

78. Metzker, *Bintel Brief*, p. 83; letter to Cecelia Razovsky from Mrs. Abe Krudel, chairman, Seattle Section CJW, Feb. 16, 1926, NCJW Papers, AJHS.

79. NCJW, "A Brief Summary of Investigations and Inquiries made between the Years of 1905 and 1915 by Government and Private Agencies into Typical Industries Prevalent in the State of New York and Affording Work to Large Numbers of Women" (New York: 1916); CJW *Proceedings* (1911), pp. 646–49, AJA; NCJW, *First Fifty Years*, p. 35.

80. *The Reform Advocate*, May 21, 1921; Jennie F. Purvin, untitled paper; Jennie F. Purvin, *Diary*, Nov. 27, 1933; Jennie F. Purvin, "Who will be our Champion?" *The Reform Advocate*, May 27, 1916, p. 582; *Chicago Tribune*, May 19, 1923, p. 1, all in Jennie F. Purvin Papers, AJA. Neil Kominsky, "Jennie Franklin Purvin: A Study in Womanpower," term paper (Cincinnati: HUC-JIR, 1968), p. 8, AJA; *Hyde Park Herald*, Dec. 29, 1939, Purvin Papers, AJA; *Sunday-Midwest*, Nov. 3, 1957, p. 9; cited in Kominsky, "Purvin," p. 12.

81. William Toll, *The Making of an Ethnic Middle Class: Portland Jewry over Four Generations*, Modern Jewish History Series (Albany: State University of New York, 1982), pp. 57, 59–61; CJW *Proceedings* (1911), p. 66; "Sadie Ascheim Kantrowitz, 1919–1924," NCJW Papers, AJA; Minneapolis Section CJW, "Reference Information Continued"; "Bertha Weiskopf, 1907–1915"; "Annalee Weiskopf Wolf, 1918–19," NCJW Papers, AJA; NCJW, *First Fifty Years*, p. 27; letter from William Toll to Linda Gordon Kuzmack, Jan. 24, 1983.

82. Naomi Cohen, *Encounter with Emancipation*, p. 201.

83. Rebekah Kohut, *My Portion* (New York: Boni & Liveright, 1925), p. 201; Marcus, *The American Jewish Woman, 1654–1980*, p. 98.

84. Birmingham, *Our Crowd*, p. 294; Jonathan D. Sarna to Linda Gordon Kuzmack, June 15, 1989.

85. Sochen, *Consecrate Every Day*, p. 50; Baum et al., *Jewish Woman*, pp. 176, 177.

86. *Notable American Women*, "Sophie Irene Simon Loeb" by Ellen Malino James, p. 417. Sophie Irene Loeb, "Johnny Doe, His Mother and the State," *Harper's Weekly*, Jan. 31, 1914, p. 24; Sophie Irene Loeb, *Everyman's Child* (New York: Century, 1920); *The Survey*, Feb. 12, 1921, p. 707; *The Survey*, Feb. 15, 1929, p. 653, all in Loeb Papers, AJA.

87. *NAW*, "Hannah Einstein" by Roy Lubove, pp. 566–68; *The Survey*, Feb. 15, 1929, p. 653, Loeb Papers, AJA; Morris Waldron, *Nor by Power* (New York: International Universities Press, 1953), p. 379; postcard from Hannah Einstein to Dr. Gustav Gottheil, Oct. 10, 1902, AJA.

88. *Dictionary of American Biography*, vol. 11, s.v. "Loeb, Sophie Irene Simon"; *NAW*, "Hannah Einstein," pp. 567–68; Gerald Sorin, *The Prophetic Minority: American Jewish Immigrant Radicals 1880–1920* (Bloomington: Indiana University Press, 1985), p. 231.

89. Rischin, *The Promised City*, p. 119.

90. Irwin, *Angels and Amazons*, p. 188; Banks, *Faces of Feminism*, p. 92.

91. Flexner, *Century of Struggle*, p. 214.

92. Banks, *Faces of Feminism*, p. 114; Sheila Ryan Johansson, "'Her-

story' as History: A New Field or Another Fad?" in Carroll, *Liberating Women's History*, p. 400.

93. Flexner, *Century of Struggle*, p. 216; Allen Davis, *Spearheads for Reform: The Social Settlements and the Progressive Movement, 1890–1914* (New York: Oxford University Press, 1967), pp. 9–12; Lillian Wald, "What Business are Women About," New York State Nursing Association Convention, Oct. 20, 1915, Wald Papers, NYPL.

94. Lillian Wald, *The House on Henry Street* (New York: Henry Holt, 1915), p. 109; Wald, "Some Social Values of the Settlement," n.d., Wald Papers, NYPL; Wald, "Rural Nursing and the American Red Cross," Wald Papers, NYPL; Robert Duffus, *Lillian Wald, Neighbor and Crusader* (New York: Macmillan, 1938), pp. 113, 115.

95. Walter I. Trattner, *From Poor Law to Welfare State: A History of Social Welfare in America* (New York: Free Press; London: Collier, 1974), p. 150; Lillian Wald, "Children's Bureau," 1905, Wald Papers, NYPL.

96. Emma Goldman, *Living My Life* (1931), pp. 158–60; Beatrice Siegel, *Lillian Wald of Henry Street* (New York and London: Macmillan, 1983), p. 72.

97. Lillian Wald, "Immigrant Women in New York," Wald Papers, NYPL.

98. Lillian Wald, "The Immigrant," Free Synagogue, New York City, 1907, Wald Papers, NYPL; Melvin I. Urofsky, *A Voice That Spoke for Justice: The Life and Times of Stephen S. Wise* (Albany: State University of New York Press, 1982), pp. 110, 138, 140.

99. Lillian Wald, "Preparedness for War," 1914, Wald Papers, NYPL; Siegel, *Lillian Wald*, pp. 119–20.

100. Lillian Wald, "Speech to the Council of Jewish Women," Feb. 26, 1911, Wald Papers, NYPL; see Ellen Condliffe Lagemann, *A Generation of Women: Education in the Lives of Progressive Reformers* (Cambridge: Harvard University Press, 1979), p. 80; Allan Edward Reznick, "Lillian D. Wald: The Years at Henry Street" (Ph.D. diss., University of Wisconsin, 1973).

101. Blanche Wiesen Cook, *Women and Support Networks* (New York: Out and Out Books), pp. 22–23; Siegel, *Lillian Wald*, pp. 83, 84, 87.

102. Smith-Rosenberg, "Female World," p. 27 and passim; Cook, *Women and Support Networks*, pp. 20–28; Allen Davis, *American Heroine: The Life and Legend of Jane Addams* (New York: Peter Smith, 1983), p. 187; Siegel, *Lillian Wald*, pp. 83, 84, 87.

103. Cook, *Women and Support Networks*, pp. 19–21; Gordon and Buhle, "Sex and Class," p. 290.

104. Wald, "Immigrant Women in New York," Wald Papers, NYPL; Wald, *House on Henry Street*, p. 119.

105. Wald, "The Utilization of the Immigrant," Free Synagogue, New York City, 1907; Wald, "Dangers Surrounding the Young Immigrant Girl," speech in Buffalo, New York, 1909, both in Wald Papers, NYPL. Meredith Tax, *The Rising of the Women* (New York: Monthly Review Press, 1980), pp. 97–100; Philip S. Foner, *Women and the American Labor Movement:*

From Colonial Times to the Eve of World War I (New York: The Free Press; London: Collier Macmillan, 1979), p. 293; Lillian Wald, "Speech to the Council of Jewish Women," Feb. 26, 1911, Wald Papers, NYPL; Mary M. Roberts, "Lavinia Lloyd Dock—Nurse, Feminist, Internationalist," *American Journal of Nursing* 56 (Jan.–June 1956): 176–79.

106. Allen Davis, *American Heroine*, p. 187.

107. Banks, *Faces of Feminism*, p. 115.

CHAPTER 5

1. Beatrice Webb, "Women and the Factory Acts," *Fabian Tract No. 67*, 1896, cited in *Women in Public: The Women's Movement, 1850–1900*, ed. Patricia Hollis (London: George Allen & Unwin, 1979), p. 129; Wilson, *Women and the Welfare State*, pp. 7, 19–20; Soldon, *Women in British Trade Unions*, p. 18; Lewenhak, *Women and Trade Unions*, p. 74; Strachey, *Cause*, p. 236; Schmiechen, *Sweated Industries*, p. 85.

2. Webb, "Women and the Factory Acts," p. 129; Wilson, *Women and the Welfare State*, pp. 7, 19–20; Soldon, *Women in British Trade Unions*, p. 18.

3. *JC*, July 3, 1885, p. 7; Thompson, *The Edwardians*, p. 15; Lewenhak, *Women and Trade Unions*, p. 68; Schmiechen, *Sweated Industries*, p. 135; Gartner, *Jewish Immigrant in England*, pp. 64–65; Webb, "Jewish Community," p. 191; Soldon, *Women in British Trade Unions*, p. 25.

4. Sachar, *Diaspora*, p. 141; Raymond Kalman, "The Jewish East End— Where Was It?," in Newman, *The Jewish East End*, pp. 11–12; Pollins, *Economic History*, p. 142; Lipman, *Social History*, pp. 120–27; White, *Rothschild Buildings*, pp. 25–29, 50; John Cooper, "Two East End Jewish Families: The Bloomsteins and the Isenbergs," in Newman, *The Jewish East End*, pp. 59–63.

5. Gartner, *Jewish Immigrant in England*, p. 63; Gainer, *Alien Invasion*, pp. 23–24, 26–28; Pollins, *Economic History*, pp. 144–46.

6. Pollins, *Economic History*, pp. 67–68, 121–22.

7. Schmiechen, *Sweated Industries*, p. 70; White, *Rothschild Buildings*, p. 210.

8. White, *Rothschild Buildings*, pp. 212–13.

9. Schmiechen, *Sweated Industries*, p. 70.

10. Ibid., pp. 67–69.

11. Patricia Branca, *Women in Europe since 1750* (London, 1978), pp. 32–33; Peter Stearns, "Working-Class Women in Britain, 1890–1914," in Vicinus, *Suffer and Be Still*, pp. 113–14; Laura Oren, "The Welfare of Women in Laboring Families: England, 1860–1950," in Hartman and Banner, *Clio's Consciousness Raised*, p. 227.

12. Schmiechen, *Sweated Industries*, pp. 69, 70; White, *Rothschild Buildings*, pp. 236–37.

13. Kuzmack, "Jewish Working Women," p. 24; Banks, *Faces of Feminism*, p. 103.

14. Many historians assume that all working women enjoyed a situation leading to the organizing found among factory workers in the industrial north of England. Schmiechen cites the theories of E. P. Thompson, *The Making of the English Working Class* (New York, 1963), pp. 414–16; Edward Shorter, *The Making of the Modern Family* (New York, 1975), pp. 259–62. See also Ivy Pinchbeck, *Women Workers and the Industrial Revolution, 1750–1858*, 2nd rev. ed. (F. Cass & Co., 1969), pp. 198–99; Robert P. Neuman, "Working Class Sexuality," in Mary Lynn McDouglass, ed., *The Working Class in Modern Europe* (Lexington, Mass., 1975), pp. 157–68; Joan Scott and Louise Tilly, "Women's Work and the Family in Nineteenth-Century Europe," in *Family in History*, ed. Charles Rosenberg (Philadelphia, 1975), pp. 151, 172.

15. Pollins, *Economic History*, pp. 146–47; Lewenhak, *Women and Trade Unions*, p. 52; Schmiechen, *Sweated Industries*, pp. 97–103.

16. Fishman, *Jewish Radicals*, p. xii.

17. Ibid., p. 181; Jerry White, "Jewish Landlords, Jewish Tenants: An Aspect of Class Struggle within the Jewish East End, 1881–1914," in Newman, *The Jewish East End*, pp. 212–13; Lewenhak, *Women and Trade Unions*, pp. 119, 138; Gartner, *Jewish Immigrant in England*, p. 118.

18. Pollins, *Economic History*, p. 155; Alderman, *The Jewish Community*, pp. 54–55, 62.

19. Barbara Taylor, " 'The Men are as Bad as Their Masters . . .': Socialism, Feminism and Sexual Antagonism in the London Tailoring Trade in the 1830's," in *Sex and Class in Women's History*, ed. Judith L. Newton, Mary P. Ryan, and Judith R. Walkowitz (London, Boston, Melbourne, and Henley: Routledge & Kegan Paul, 1983), pp. 204–05.

20. Joseph Buckman, *Immigrants and the Class Struggle: The Jewish Immigrant in Leeds 1880–1914* (Manchester: Manchester University Press, 1983), pp. 92–93.

21. Banks, *Faces of Feminism*, p. 103.

22. Schmiechen, *Sweated Industries*, p. 135; Gartner, *Jewish Immigrant in England*, pp. 64–65; Webb, "Jewish Community," p. 191.

23. Gainer, *Alien Invasion*, p. 25; Pollins, *Economic History*, p. 147.

24. Aubrey Newman, ed., *Migration and Settlement: Proceedings of the Anglo-Jewish Historical Conference* (London: Jewish Historical Society of England, 1981), pp. 129–30.

25. Soldon, *Women in British Trade Unions*, p. 25.

26. Schmiechen, *Sweated Industries*, pp. 86, 92; Soldon, *Women in British Trade Unions*, pp. 70–71.

27. *JC*, July 17, 1885, p. 5.

28. Ibid., July 3, 1885, p. 7.

29. Ibid., July 17, 1885, p. 5; Pollins, *Economic History*, p. 161. Pollins gives the founding date of the Leeds Tailoresses' Union as 1896. He does not mention its founding under the earlier title of a "Society" in 1885 as described in the *Jewish Chronicle* of that year.

30. Soldon, *Women in British Trade Unions*, p. 9; Sheila Lochhead, "Introduction," in *Women in the Labour Movement: The British Experience*, ed. Lucy Middleton (London: Croom Helm, 1977), pp. 17–18.

31. Soldon, *Women in British Trade Unions*, pp. 35, 43, 54.

32. Anne Godwin, "Early Years in the Trade Unions," in Middleton, *Women in the Labour Movement*, pp. 96–100; Lewenhak, *Women and Trade Unions*, pp. 118–19; Schmiechen, *Sweated Industries*, p. 92.

33. Buckman, *Immigrants and the Class Struggle*, pp. 92–93; Pollins, *Economic History*, p. 161.

34. Pollins, *Economic History*, pp. 163–64.

35. Ibid., pp. 156–57.

36. Alderman, *Jewish Community*, pp. 56–57; Sachar, *Diaspora*, p. 141.

37. White, *Rothschild Buildings*, p. 260.

38. Fishman, *Jewish Radicals*, p. 297; Pollins, *Economic History*, p. 156.

39. Pollins, *Economic History*, pp. 255–56n. 4; 297 and n. 2; Fishman, *Jewish Radicals*, pp. 53, 264.

40. Jonathan Sarna to Linda Gordon Kuzmack, personal communication.

41. Gartner, *Jewish Immigrant in England*, pp. 136–37; Alderman, *Jewish Community*, p. 64; William J. Fishman, "Jewish Immigrant Anarchists in East London," in Newman, *The Jewish East End*, pp. 247–49; White, *Rothschild Buildings*, pp. 213, 215.

42. Fishman, *Jewish Radicals*, pp. 253, 297.

43. Ibid., p. 253; Paula Hyman, "Immigrant Women and Consumer Protest: New York City Kosher Meat Boycott of 1902," *AJH* 70 (Sept. 1980): 91–105.

44. Schmiechen, *Sweated Industries*, p. 103; White, *Rothschild Buildings*, pp. 213, 215.

45. Thompson, *The Edwardians*, pp. 13–14.

46. Ibid.

47. "Conference of Jewish Women," *JC*, May 16, 1902, pp. 10–17; Schmiechen, *Sweated Industries*, pp. 140–44, 163, 174–75; Banks, *Faces of Feminism*, pp. 116–17; *JC*, May 16, 1902, pp. 173–74; Lewenhak, *Women and Trade Unions*, pp. 80–81, 120–21.

48. It was not unusual for workers to create new branches, even where unions already existed within an industry or occupation. Pollins, *Economic History*, pp. 163–64.

49. Banks, *Faces of Feminism*, p. 104.

50. Kessner, *Golden Door*, pp. 75–76, 100; Kuzmack, "Jewish Working Women," p. 24; Jessie W. Bernstein, "The Grateful Thread," *American Jewish Archives* 33 (Apr. 1981): 108.

51. Bernard Martin, "Yiddish Literature in the United States," *American Jewish Archives* 33 (Nov. 1981): 184–209; Singerman, "American Jewish Press," p. 435; Metzker, *Bintel Brief*, pp. 78–79.

52. Baum et al., *Jewish Woman*, p. 60.

53. Emily Solis-Cohen, untitled speech, pp. 2–4, Emily Solis-Cohen Papers, AJHS.

54. Sorin, *Prophetic Minority,* pp. 139–40, 163–64.

55. Ibid., pp. 8, 12, 14.

56. "Kosher" meat, prepared according to Jewish ritual law, is the only meat that Orthodox Jews are permitted to eat.

57. Hyman, "Immigrant Women and Consumer Protest," p. 103.

58. Ibid., pp. 92–93, 105.

59. Kessner, "Jobs, Ghettos and the Urban Economy," p. 225; Arthur A. Goren, "The Promises of *The Promised City*: Moses Rischin, American History, and the Jews," *AJH* 73 (Dec. 1983): 179.

60. Gordon and Buhle, "Sex and Class," p. 291.

61. Jacob Riis, *How the Other Half Lives: Studies among the Tenements of New York* (New York: Charles Scribner's Sons, 1890; reprint ed. New York: Dover, 1971), p. 186; "Transcript of an Interview with Pauline Newman," Appendix B, Pauline Newman Papers, Schlesinger Library, Radcliffe College.

62. Elias Tcherikower, *The Early Jewish Labor Movement in the United States* (New York: YIVO, 1961), pp. 81–84; Irwin Yellowitz, "Jewish Immigrants and the American Labor Movement, 1900–1920," *AJH* 71 (Dec. 1981): 188–89, 192.

63. Tcherikower, *Early Jewish Labor Movement,* pp. 83–85; Flexner, *Century of Struggle,* pp. 195–202.

64. Foner, *Women and the American Labor Movement,* pp. 229–32.

65. Rischin, *The Promised City,* pp. 234–45; Louis Levine, *The Women's Garment Workers: A History of the International Ladies' Garment Workers' Union* (New York: B. W. Huebsch Inc., 1924), pp. 134–66.

66. Alice Kessler-Harris, "Organizing the Unorganizable: Three Jewish Women and Their Unions," *Labor History* 17 (Winter 1976): 102; Stephen J. Whitfield, "The Radical Persuasion in American Jewish History," *Judaism* 32 (Spring 1983): 136; Rischin, *The Promised City,* p. 149.

67. Pauline Newman to Rose Schneiderman, Nov. 7, 1911, Schneiderman Papers, Tamiment Institute Library, New York University.

68. Whitfield, "Radical Persuasion," p. 138; Sochen, *Herstory,* p. 236; Sorin, *Prophetic Minority,* p. 130; Sydney Stahl Weinberg, *The World of Our Mothers: The Lives of Jewish Immigrant Women* (Chapel Hill and London: University of North Carolina Press, 1988), p. 197.

69. Sorin, *Prophetic Minority,* p. 131.

70. Mari Jo Buhle, *Women and American Socialism, 1870–1920* (Urbana, Chicago, London: University of Illinois Press, 1981), pp. 182–84; Pratt, "Culture and Radical Politics," pp. 73, 77, 86.

71. Buhle, *Women and American Socialism,* p. 185; Milton Cantor and Bruce Laurie, eds., *Class, Sex, and the Woman Worker* (Westport, Conn., London: Greenwood Press, 1977), p. 204; Yellowitz, "Jewish Immigrants," p. 204; "Transcript," pp. xivff, Newman Papers, Schlesinger Library.

72. Rischin, *The Promised City,* pp. 190, 246–47.

73. Pratt, "Culture and Radical Politics," pp. 73, 77, 86.

74. Whitfield, "Radical Persuasion," p. 138; Sally M. Miller, "From Sweatshop Worker to Labor Leader: Theresa Malkiel, a Case Study," *AJH* 68 (Dec. 1978): 194, 197, 199.

75. Hutchings Hapgood, *The Spirit of the Ghetto: Studies of the Jewish Quarter of New York City*, rev. ed. (New York: Schocken, 1976), p. 78.

76. Levine, *Women's Garment Workers*, p. 152; Baum et al., *Jewish Woman*, pp. 140–41.

77. Reported in the *New York World*, Nov. 23, 1909, cited in Levine, *Women's Garment Workers*, p. 154.

78. Levine, *Women's Garment Workers*, p. 159.

79. Lillian Wald, "Immigrant Women in New York," speech at Dr. Stimson's Church, Dec. 4, 1910, Wald Papers, NYPL.

80. Buhle, *Women and American Socialism*, p. 188; Rose Schneiderman, *All for One* (New York: Paul S. Eriksson, Inc., 1967), pp. 49–58.

81. "Minutes of the Executive Board of the WTUL," Jan. 26, 1909, pp. 1–6; Feb. 16, 1910, p. 1, WTUL Papers, microfilm records from the New York State Dept. of Labor Library, Schlesinger Library, Radcliffe College.

82. Rischin, *The Promised City*, pp. 247–48.

83. Levine, *Women's Garment Workers*, pp. 155–56.

84. "Transcript," p. xi, Newman Papers, Schlesinger Library; Levine, *Women's Garment Workers*, p. 166.

85. Foner, *Women and the Labor Movement*, p. 349; Baum et al., *Jewish Woman*, pp. 147–48.

86. Rischin, *The Promised City*, p. 252; Linda Gordon Kuzmack and Shulamith Weisman, "Sadie Hershey," in *To Make a Dream Come True: Stories of the Residents of the Hebrew Home of Greater Washington*, ed. Kuzmack and Weisman (Rockville, Md.: Hebrew Home of Greater Washington, 1983), pp. 23–24.

87. Alice Henry, *Women and the Labor Movement* (New York: Arno and New York Times, 1971), p. 121.

88. Marcus, *American Jewish Woman, 1654–1980*, p. 120.

89. Levine, *Women's Garment Workers*, pp. 229–31.

90. Elisabeth Israels Perry, "'Doing Good': The German-Jewish Experience and the Career of Belle Moskowitz" (paper presented at Association for Jewish Studies Annual Conference, Boston, Dec. 1980), p. 1; Perry, *Belle Moskowitz: Feminine Politics and the Exercise of Power in the Age of Alfred E. Smith* (New York: Oxford University Press, 1987), pp. 83–97.

91. *Dry Goods Economist*, n.d., Nathan Papers, Schlesinger Library; Irwin, *Angels and Amazons*, p. 190; Maud Nathan, *Story of an Epoch-Making Movement*, p. 119. Boston newspaper (no title), Mar. 19, 1897; New York *Advertizer* (sic), Feb. 29, 1897; *Harper's Magazine*, n.d.; *News Letter*, Apr. 1, 1905, all in Nathan Papers, Schlesinger Library, Radcliffe College.

92. Sochen, *Herstory*, p. 245; *Woman Voter*, Sept. 1912, p. 17.

93. *Woman Voter*, Sept. 1912, p. 17; Alice Henry, *The Trade Union*

Woman (New York, Burt Franklin), pp. 44–45; Nathan, *Epoch-Making Movement*, p. 106.

94. *Dry Goods Economist*, Nathan Papers, Schlesinger Library, Radcliffe College; Horace Friess and Clifford Vessey, eds., *Memorial Service for Josephine Goldmark*, Dec. 18, 1950, Schlesinger Library, Radcliffe College; Robin Miller Jacoby, "Feminism and Class Consciousness in the British and American Women's Trade Union Leagues, 1890–1925," in Carroll, *Liberating Women's History*, p. 142.

95. *Morning Journal*, Oct. 2——; *Jewish Exponent*, Feb. 24, 1899; *American Hebrew*, Oct. 26, 1900, all in Nathan Papers, Schlesinger Library.

96. Whitfield, "Radical Persuasion," p. 139.

97. Jacoby, "Feminism and Class Consciousness," p. 142.

98. Henry, *Trade Union Woman*, p. 59; Cantor and Laurie, *Class, Sex, and the Woman Worker*, p. 205.

99. Nancy Schrom Dye, *As Equals and as Sisters: Feminism, the Labor Movement, and the Women's Trade Union League of New York* (Columbia and London: University of Missouri Press, 1980), p. 1.

100. Nancy Schrom Dye, "Creating a Feminist Alliance: Sisterhood and Class Conflict in the New York Women's Trade Union League, 1902–1914," *FS* 2 (1975): 26; Dye, *As Equals and as Sisters*, p. 56.

101. Sorin, *Prophetic Minority*, p. 135; letter from Max Fruchter [?] to Rose Schneiderman, Mar. 5, 191——; "Immigrant Girl Now Heads Union," untitled newspaper clipping, n.d., both in Schneiderman Papers, Tamiment Library.

102. Dye, *As Equals and as Sisters*, p. 54.

103. "Transcript," pp. xx, xxi, Newman Papers, Schlesinger Library; Rischin, *The Promised City*, p. 247; Henry, *Trade Union Woman*, pp. 64–68.

104. James J. Kenneally, *Women and American Trade Unions*, Monographs in Women's Studies (St. Albans, Vt.: Eden Press, 1978), pp. 61–65, 78; Dye, *As Equals and as Sisters*, p. 129.

105. "Secretary's Report to the Executive Board," Feb. 27, 1913, p. 1, and Jan. 23, 1913, pp. 1–2; "Minutes of the Meeting of the Strike Council," pp. 1–4; "Minutes of the Executive Board," Mar. 23, 1910, pp. 4–6, all in WTUL Papers, Schlesinger Library; Henry, *Women and the Labor Movement*, p. 121.

106. "Transcript," pp. xx, xxi, xviii, Newman Papers, Schlesinger Library.

107. "Minutes of the Executive Board meeting," Mar. 23, 1910, pp. 4–6, WTUL Papers, Schlesinger Library.

108. Dye, *As Equals and as Sisters*, p. 117.

109. Baum et al., *Jewish Woman*, p. 147.

110. "What is Feminism?," announcement of the first and second feminist mass meetings, Cooper Union Hall, February 17 and 20, 1914, Schneiderman Papers, Tamiment Library; *Encyclopedia Judaica*, "Schneiderman, Rose"; Jacoby, "Feminism and Class Consciousness," p. 148.

111. Flexner, *Century of Struggle*, p. 304.

CHAPTER 6

1. *JC,* Oct. 17, 1913, p. 10, reprinting a story from the *Jewish World* of Oct. 1913. Also quoted by Charles Landstone, in "Blackguards in Bonnets: The Jewish Suffragettes Revived," *JC,* Aug. 29, 1969.

2. *Jewish World,* Oct. 15, 1913; *JC,* Oct. 17, 1913; Rover, *Women's Suffrage,* p. 470.

3. Jewish religious leaders were called "minister" in the English fashion, except for the Chief Rabbi; see *Constitution* (London: 1912), p. 1, Jewish League for Woman Suffrage Papers, Klau Library, HUC-JIR.

4. Marion Kaplan, *Jewish Feminist Movement in Germany,* p. 63. Kaplan emphasizes that the Jüdischer Frauenbund was concerned with suffrage along with other social causes affecting women. The political situation and voting structure in Germany made it impossible for any women's organization, particularly one whose membership was Jewish, to survive as only a suffragist group.

5. *Constitution* (London: 1912), p. 1, JLWS Papers, Klau Library, HUC-JIR.

6. JLWS, *Annual Report* (1913), p. 9, JLWS Papers, Klau Library, HUC-JIR; *JC,* Mar 29, 1912, p. 35; Nov. 23, 1912, pp. 9–10; Mar. 7, 1913, p. 35.

7. Finestein, "Post-Emancipation Jewry," p. 8.

8. *JC,* Feb. 28, 1913, p. 29; Mar. 14, 1913, p. 28.

9. Gibbon, *Netta,* pp. 88, 121–22; H. Pearl Adam, ed., *Women in Council* (London, New York, Toronto: Oxford University Press, 1945), p. 32.

10. Umansky, *Lily Montagu.*

11. *Constitution,* JLWS Papers, Klau Library, HUC-JIR; *Anglo-Jewish Yearbook,* 1921, p. 189; *JC,* Nov. 7, 1913, p. 33; letter from Lily Montagu to Edwin Montagu, 1912, Montagu Papers, AJA; *Annual Report,* 1913, pp. 11–12, Jewish League for Woman Suffrage Papers, Klau Library, HUC-JIR. Rabbis Morris Joseph, Israel Mattuck, C. G. Montefiore, and W. Lewin all joined Lily Montagu at such meetings.

12. Lily Montagu, "O Worship the Lord in the Beauty of Holiness," sermon, Aug. 12, 1916, Montagu Papers, AJA; Frances Joseph, "The Dietary Laws From a Woman's Point of View," *JQR* 20 (1908): 643–45; Umansky, "Lily H. Montagu," p. 18.

13. Lucy Cohen, *Some Recollections of Claude Goldsmid Montefiore, 1858–1938* (London: Faber & Faber, 1940), pp. 25, 27–30, 37–48; Claude G. Montefiore, "Religious Teaching of Jowett," *JQR* 12 (1900): 377; Walter Jacob, "Claude G. Montefiore's Reappraisal of Christianity," *Judaism* 19, no. 3 (Summer 1970): 328–32; Claude G. Montefiore, "Liberal Judaism in England: Its Difficulties and Its Duties," *JQR* (1900): 631; Montefiore, "Judaism, Unitarianism, and Theism," *Papers for Jewish People* (London: Jewish Religious Union, 1908), p. 5; Joshua B. Stein, "The Contribution of C. G. Montefiore to the Establishment of Liberal Judaism in England," paper given at Association for Jewish Studies Annual Conference, Boston, Dec. 1982, p. 8; Frederick C. Schwartz, "Claude Montefiore on Law and Tradition," *JQR* 55

(July 1964): 23, 25; Montefiore, *Liberal Judaism* (London: Macmillan, 1903), pp. 87–88, 89, 97, 120–33, 144–45; Leslie I. Edgar, "Claude Montefiore's Thought and the Present Religious Situation," Claude Montefiore Lecture (London: Liberal Jewish Synagogue, 1966), pp. 4–5, 6, 16; letter from Claude G. Montefiore to Lily Montagu, Apr. 12, 1899, Montagu Papers, AJA; Claude G. Montefiore, *The Old Testament and After* (London: Macmillan, 1923), p. 556; Montefiore, "The Question of Authority in Liberal Judaism," *Papers for Jewish People,* no. 33 (London: Jewish Religious Union, 1936), pp. 2, 20.

14. Conrad, *Montagu,* p. 9.

15. Henry and Taitz, *Written Out of History,* pp. 212–14.

16. L. E. Elliott-Binns, *The Early Evangelicals: A Religious and Social Study* (Greenwich, Conn.: Seabury Press, 1953), pp. 134–36, 337; Michael Hill, *The Religious Order* (London: Heinemann, 1973), pp. 151, 153, 271, 277–78, 280–83; Janet Whitney, *Elizabeth Fry* (London: Harrap, 1937), pp. 240–41; Keith Melder, *Beginnings of Sisterhood: The American Woman's Rights Movement 1800–1850* (New York: Schocken, 1977), pp. 116–17; Robertson, *Experience of Women,* pp. 289–90, 300, 484, 519–20.

17. Lily H. Montagu, *Faith of a Jewish Woman* (Keighly: Wadsworth & Co., 1943), p. 28. Lily Montagu to Claude Montefiore, Nov. 13, 1913; Montagu to unknown recipient, Nov. 13, 1913, Montagu Papers, AJA.

18. Lily Montagu to Israel Mattuck, May 13, 1918; Apr. 21, 1920; May 10, 1949, Montagu Papers, AJA.

19. Robertson, *Experience of Women,* p. 534.

20. Montagu, "Divinity in Freedom," sermon, May 4, 1929; Montagu, "Home Worship and its Influence on Social Work," address at the Conference of Jewish Women, May 1902; Lily Montagu to Israel Mattuck, Mar. 7, 1947; Lily Montagu to Julian Morgenstern, Mar. 20, 1930; all in Montagu Papers, AJA.

21. Montagu, "Jewish Women's Contribution to the Spiritual Life of Humanity," n.d., sermon; Montagu, "O Worship the Lord in the Beauty of Holiness," Club sermon, Aug. 12, 1916; both in Montagu Papers, AJA. Montagu, *Faith of a Jewish Woman,* p. 23. See also "Loneliness," Montagu's Club sermon, Dec. 2, 1916, Montagu Papers, AJA.

22. Montagu, "Man's Ambition and God's Law," sermon, Jan. 18, 1919, Montagu Papers, AJA.

23. Montagu, "Progress in Life and Religion," sermon, Apr. 11, 1925; Montagu, "Cast me not away from Thy Presence . . . ," sermon, May 8, 1920, both in Montagu Papers, AJA. Conrad, *Montagu,* p. 9. Montagu, "Joy of Service," sermon, June 22, 1921; Montagu, "Why Do We Bother?" sermon, Feb. 21, 1925; Montagu, "Modern Woman's Greatest Duty," sermon, Apr. 30, 1938; Montagu, "The Spiritual Contribution of Women as Women," address, Nov. 26, 1948; all in Montagu Papers, AJA.

24. Montagu, "Modern Woman's Greatest Duty"; Montagu, "Address to the National Federation of Temple Sisterhoods," New York City, Nov. 7, 1948, Montagu Papers, AJA.

25. Edwin Montagu to Lily Montagu, Apr. 24, 1912, Montagu Papers, AJA.

26. *JC*, Nov. 7, 1913, p. 33; *Annual Report*, 1913, pp. 11–12, Jewish League for Woman Suffrage Papers, Klau Library, HUC-JIR.

27. Joseph Ascher, "Lily Montagu and the West Central Synagogue," in *Memorial Supplement*, p. 10; Montagu to Israel Mattuck, 1926, Montagu Papers, AJA; Montagu, *Faith of a Jewish Woman*, p. 42; Aubrey Newman, *The United Synagogue, 1870–1970* (London, Henley, and Boston: Routledge & Kegan Paul, 1976), pp. 81–82, 87; Umansky, *Lily Montagu*, pp. 160, 163, 176–77; Lily Montagu to Jack Levy, Apr. 9, 1947, Montagu Papers, AJA; Alan Mintz, *George Eliot and the Novel of Vocation* (Cambridge: Harvard University Press, 1978). Montagu, "Unfinished Man," June 13, 1925; Montagu, "The Sun as Preacher," May 23, 1925; Montagu, "Faith in this World and the Next," unpublished sermon, Dec. 12, 1925; Montagu, "Who is Self-Made?" sermon, June 13, 1925; see also her "Backwards and Forwards," sermon, Mar. 29, 1924; Montagu, "The Ten Commandments," sermon, Jan. 24, 1926; Montagu, "The Sacrifices of God are a broken spirit: a broken and a contrite heart, O God, Thou wilt not despise," sermon, Nov. 26, 1911; Montagu, "Religion and Private Possessions," sermon, Jan. 10, 1925; Montagu, "Evidences of God in Everyday Life," sermon, Nov. 14, 1925; all in Montagu Papers, AJA.

28. Montagu to Mattuck, Dec. 8, 1949; July 10, 1953; Aug. 1928; Montagu, "How to Give the Message of Liberal Judaism in the Home" (Berlin: World Union for Progressive Judaism, 1928). Montagu to Mattuck, Dec. 7, 1945; all in Montagu Papers, AJA.

29. Lily Montagu, "The Spiritual Possibilities of Judaism Today," *JQR* 11 (Jan. 1899): 217, 225–26; Umansky, *Lily Montagu*, p. 150.

30. "A Unique Personality," in *Memorial Supplement*, p. 17. In 1929, Montagu received an honorary degree of Doctor of Hebrew Law from Hebrew Union College in Cincinnati. Julian Morgenstern to Montagu, Mar. 4, 1929, Montagu Papers, AJA.

31. Conrad, "Lily Montagu's Life and Work," in *Memorial Supplement*, p. 16.

32. Paula Ackerman functioned as the lay rabbi of the Reform movement's Mississippi congregation from 1951 to 1953 and of Temple Beth El in Pensacola, Florida, Ellen Umansky to Linda Gordon Kuzmack, personal communication, July 11, 1989.

33. Conrad, *In Memory of Lily Montagu*, p. 16.

34. *JC*, Mar. 22, 1912, pp. 33, 40; Nov. 7, 1913, p. 33; Mar. 14, 1913, p. 28; Feb. 28, 1913, p. 29; Nov. 8, 1912, p. 10; Millicent Garrett Fawcett, *Women's Suffrage* (London, T. C. & E. C. Jack, 1912, reprint ed., New York: Source Book Press, 1970), p. 86.

35. Elizabeth de Bruin, "Judaism and Womanhood," *Westminster Review* (Aug. 1913): 130–31; *Annual Report*, 1913, pp. 11, 15, JLWS Papers, Klau Library, HUC-JIR.

36. *Annual Report,* 1914, p. 10, JLWS Papers, Klau Library, HUC-JIR.

37. David Morgan, *Suffragists and Liberals: The Politics of Woman Suffrage in England* (Totowa, N.J.: Rowman & Littlefield, 1975), pp. 131–32; Andrew Rosen, *Rise Up, Women!: The Militant Campaign of the Women's Social and Political Union 1903–1914* (London and Boston: Routledge & Kegan Paul, 1974), pp. 217–18.

38. *JC,* Mar. 15, 1912, pp. 17–18.

39. *JC,* July 10, 1914, p. 35; June 5, 1914, p. 25.

40. *JC,* Mar. 15, 1912, pp. 17–18; Mar. 22, 1912, pp. 40, 43; Mar. 29, 1912, p. 35; Nov. 28, 1913, p. 34; "Blackguards in Bonnets: The Jewish Suffragettes Revisited," *JC,* Aug. 29, 1969; *JC,* July 10, 1914, p. 35; June 5, 1914, p. 25; de Bruin, "Judaism and Womanhood," pp. 130–31.

41. Brian Harrison, *Separate Spheres: The Opposition to Women's Suffrage in Britain* (London: Croom Helm, 1978), pp. 138–40; Banks, *Faces of Feminism,* p. 131; Percy Cohen, "Jews and Feminism," *Westminster Review* (October 1913), pp. 457, 461; Alderman, *Jewish Community,* pp. 72–74; Fishman, *Jewish Radicals,* pp. 246–47.

42. *JC,* Nov. 15, 1912, p. 10; Feb. 28, 1913, p. 29, Nov. 15, 1912, p. 19.

43. Alderman, *Jewish Community,* p. 77; *Annual Report,* 1914, p. 9, JLWS Papers, Klau Library, HUC-JIR; *JC,* Nov. 8, 1912, p. 10.

44. *JC,* Nov. 15, 1912, p. 19; Feb. 21, 1913, p. 43; May 16, 1913, p. 10; Feb. 7, 1913, p. 35; Jan. 24, 1913; May 2, 1913, p. 32.

45. *JC,* May 2, 1913, p. 32; Nov. 21, 1913, p. 19; May 16, 1913, p. 18.

46. *Annual Report,* 1914, p. 11, JLWS Papers, Klau Library, HUC-JIR; *JC,* July 3, 1914, p. 10; July 10, 1914, p. 9; July 3, 1914, p. 9; July 10, 1914, p. 19. Synagogues granting unlimited franchise included the Great, Borough, North London, and Hampstead synagogues.

47. Gibbon, *Netta,* pp. 121–22; *Constitution,* 1912, p. 7, JLWS Papers, Klau Library, HUC-JIR; *JC,* Feb. 28, 1913, p. 29; Mar. 14, 1913, p. 28.

48. Arthur Marwick, *The Deluge: British Society and the First World War* (New York: W. W. Norton & Co., 1970), pp. 87–98, 95–100; O'Neill, *The Woman Movement,* p. 31; Bernard Wasserstein to Linda Gordon Kuzmack, personal communication, June 2, 1984; Morgan, *Suffragists and Liberals,* pp. 41, 93, 139; Jill Liddington and Jill Norris, *One Hand Tied behind Us: The Rise of the Women's Suffrage Movement* (London: Virago, 1978), pp. 180–83; Bermant, *Cousinhood,* pp. 271–73; Banks, *Faces of Feminism,* p. 123.

49. "Factory Girl Urges Shopmen to Give Women the Ballot," untitled newspaper, Rose Schneiderman Papers, Tamiment Library, New York University.

50. William H. Chafee, *The American Woman: Her Changing Social, Economic, and Political Role, 1920–1970* (London, Oxford, New York: Oxford University Press, 1972), p. 17.

51. Scott and Scott, *One Half the People,* pp. 28–29; Flexner, *Century of Struggle,* p. 271.

52. Sochen, *Herstory,* p. 271.

53. Aileen Kraditor, *Ideas of the Suffrage Movement, 1890–1920* (New York and London: Columbia University Press, 1967), pp. 77–86; Flexner, *Century of Struggle*, pp. 211–35.

54. Harper, *History,* vol. 5, p. 95. See also pp. 96, 110, 181; vol. 6, p. 702.

55. Maud Nathan, *Once Upon a Time and Today* (New York: Arno, 1974), p. 107.

56. Harper, *History,* vol. 5, p. 97; Flexner, *Century of Struggle*, p. 211.

57. New York *Tribune*, 1913; *Philadelphia Record*, [1915?]; *New York Times*, Dec. 3, 1906, p. 59; *Woman's Journal*, Sept. 13, 1913; *Rochester Herald*, Feb. 14, 1914; all in Nathan Papers, Schlesinger Library, Radcliffe College.

58. Nathan was also a member of the Equal Franchise Society (see *Notable American Women*, pp. 608–09). She was a delegate to the 1913 convention of the International Woman Suffrage Alliance in Budapest (Harper, *History,* vol. 6, pp. 843, 857) and the 1918 meeting of the Women's Peace Commission in New York (*Woman Citizen*, Nov. 23, 1918, p. 531, Nathan Papers, Schlesinger Library, Radcliffe College).

59. *Woman Voter,* July 1911, pp. 12–13; for lists of Jewish women participants, see *Woman Voter,* Sept. 1912, p. 34; Sept. 1911, p. 19; Oct. 1911, p. 19.

60. "Jewish Women in Public Affairs," *The American Citizen*, May 1913, Nathan Papers, Schlesinger Library, Radcliffe College; Harper, *History,* vol. 5, p. 97.

61. Nathan, *Once upon a Time and Today*, p. 183.

62. Alice Brandeis to Carrie Chapman Catt, Jan. 24, 1919, Louis Brandeis Papers, AJA; Harper, *History,* vol. 6, pp. 288, 298, 484, 569, 858.

63. *Notable American Women*, s.v. "Wise, Louise Waterman," *Encyclopedia Judaica*, s.v. "Wise, Stephen Samuel," p. 567.

64. *Boston Globe*, n.d., Jennie L. Barron Papers, Schlesinger Library; interview with Dr. Clara Loitman Smith, Sept. 1982. Polly Welts Kaufman, "Jennie Loitman Barron," introduction to the Barron Papers; *Chelsea Evening Record*, April, 19———, Barron Papers, Schlesinger Library. Sharon Hartman Strom, "Leadership and Tactics in the American Woman Suffrage Movement: A New Perspective from Massachusetts," *Journal of American History* 62, no. 2 (Sept. 1975): 297, 315; "Mrs. Barron Wages New Kind of Campaign for School Committee," newspaper clipping, n.d., Barron Papers, Schlesinger Library.

65. Harper, *History,* vol. 6, pp. 300, 387; *Woman Citizen*, Nov. 16, 1918, p. 507, Nathan Papers, Schlesinger Library.

66. *New York Times*, 1915, Nathan Papers, Schlesinger Library; Harper, *History,* vol. 6, pp. 60, 106, 265, 291, 385, 547–48.

67. *Woman Voter,* May 1911, p. 3; Apr. 1982 conversation with Hasia Diener, author of *In the Almost Promised Land: American Jews and Blacks, 1915–1935.*

68. Harper, *History,* vol. 5, p. 224; Baum et al., *Jewish Woman*, p. 50.

69. Harper, *History,* vol. 5, pp. 187–88, 224, 260, 263, 286, 321.

70. "Mrs. Kohut, Leader of Her Sex and Race, Wants Jewish Law

Changed," clipping from untitled newspaper, 19——; "A Dollar-a-Year Woman," *American Hebrew,* Aug. 23, 1918, both in Rebekah Kohut Papers, AJA.

71. Shoub, "Jewish Women's History," p. 41; Golumb, "1893 Congress," pp. 52–67; *AJ,* Apr. 1898, p. 22; May 1895, p. 101; Dec. 1895, p. 138; Dec. 1896, pp. 137–38; Harper, *History,* vol. 4, p. 1083.

72. *Woman Voter,* Sept. 1915, pp. 9, 11–15, includes pro-suffrage statements by ten Reform rabbis; Harper, *History,* vol. 5, pp. 141, 289; vol. 6, pp. 276, 484, 569, 858; *Central Conference of American Rabbis Yearbook* 13 (1913), p. 133; 25 (1915), p. 133; 27 (1917), p. 175.

73. "Shall Women Vote? A Symposium Prepared by Sophie Irene Loeb," *American Hebrew,* Sept. 10, 1915, pp. 458–61, Sophie I. Loeb Papers, AJA. Pro-suffragist speakers in the symposium included Maud Nathan.

74. Degler, *At Odds,* p. 349; Annie Nathan Meyer, in Loeb, "Shall Women Vote?" p. 458.

75. Flexner, *Century of Struggle,* p. 309; Kraditor, *Ideas of the Woman Suffrage Movement,* p. 20.

76. Annie Nathan Meyer, "Again Spreadhenism," letter to the editor, *Herald Tribune,* Jan. 16, 1938; Untitled speech on Spreadhenism, n.d.; both in Annie Nathan Meyer Papers, AJA. "Shall Women Vote?" Loeb Papers, AJA. *Evening World,* May 19——; Meyer, "Woman's Assumption of Sex Superiority," *North American Review,* Jan. 1904, pp. 1, 4; both in Meyer Papers, AJA.

77. Kessler-Harris, "Women, Work, and the Social Order," pp. 335–36; Gordon and Buhle, "Sex and Class," p. 292; Kraditor, *Ideas of the Woman Suffrage Movement,* pp. 20–22.

78. "Home and the Vote according to Mrs. Kohut," *American Hebrew,* n.d., Nathan Papers, Schlesinger Library.

79. Steven Cohen, *American Modernity,* p. 41.

80. Elinor Lerner, "Jewish Involvement in the New York City Woman Suffrage Movement," *AJH* 70, no. 4 (June 1981): 455; Wald, "What Business are Women About," Wald Papers, NYPL; Duffus, *Lillian Wald,* pp. 113–14; Flexner, *Century of Struggle,* p. 217.

81. Wald, "Speech at the New York State Suffrage Convention," Rochester, N.Y., Oct. 15, 1914, p. 14; Wald, "Speech at the New York State Suffrage League"; both in Wald Papers, NYPL; Flexner, *Century of Struggle,* pp. 216, 224.

82. Robin M. Jacoby, "The Women's Trade Union League and American Feminism," in Cantor and Laurie, *Class, Sex, and the Woman Worker,* pp. 213–15.

83. Harper, *History,* vol. 5, p. 705; Sorin, *Prophetic Minority,* p. 138; Baum et al., *Jewish Woman,* pp. 144–45.

84. *Youngstown Vindicator,* 1912; Rose Schneiderman, "Suffrage School Address," no. 1, Dec. 1913; both in Rose Schneiderman Papers, Tamiment Library.

85. Schneiderman, *All for One,* p. 121. Schneiderman spoke on the same

theme at the 1910 and 1914 NAWSA conventions. In 1917, Schneiderman was proxy for the chairwoman of the Industrial Section of the State Departmental Work Committee of NAWSA. Harper, *History*, vol. 5, pp. 286, 409. Letter from Harriet Taylor Upton to Schneiderman, May 6, 1910; letter from Harriet Stanton Blatch to Schneiderman, May 2, 1910; both in Schneiderman Papers, Tamiment Library.

86. Emphasis in text. Letter from Max Fruchter to Rose Schneiderman, Mar. 5, 191——, Schneiderman Papers, Tamiment Library.

87. Letter from M. W. Suffren, Woman Suffrage Party, to Rose Schneiderman, Nov. 18, 1911, Schneiderman Papers, Tamiment Library; *Woman Voter*, Sept. 1915, p. 23; Baum et al., *Jewish Woman*, pp. 142–43.

88. "Factory Girl Urges Shopmen to Give Women the Ballot," untitled newspaper; article by Rose C. Tillotson, untitled newspaper; M. A. Sherwood to Mrs. Upton, July 15, 1912; Jamestown *Morning Post*, n.d.; all in Schneiderman Papers, Tamiment Library.

89. "Wilson Rejects Suffrage Plea," untitled newspaper, n.d., Schneiderman Papers, Tamiment Library.

90. Elinor Lerner, "Jewish Involvement," p. 442.

91. Ibid., p. 443.

92. Ibid., p. 449. Comparable figures are not available for the rest of the country.

93. *Woman Voter*, Jan. 1915, pp. 10, 20; Aug. 1915, p. 25; May 1911, p. 3; July 1911, p. 14; Sept. 1915, p. 23.

94. Harper, *History*, vol. 5, pp. 205, 249, 301, 638; Sachar, *Modern Jewish History*, p. 324; Rischin, *The Promised City*, p. 235; Meyer London, speech in the New York House of Representatives [*sic*], Sept. 24, 1917, Lillian Wald Papers, NYPL; *Woman Voter*, July 1915, p. 9.

95. Rosalie Loew (later Mrs. Whitney) was admitted to the New York Bar in May 1895, three years after women were first accepted. In 1896, at the age of twenty-two, she became assistant professor of law at Rutgers Medical College for Women. *AJ*, Aug. 1896, pp. 474–75; see also Dec. 1898, pp. 27–28; Harper, *History*, vol. 5, p. 580. See also the Deutsch Catalog at the AJA, which cites the following references to Rosalie Loew: *Die Neuzeit*, 1896, no. 31, p. 321; *Die Welt*, 1899, no. 47, p. 11; *Allgemeine Zeitung des Judenthums*, 1897, no. 9, appendix, p. 4; *Hayehudi*, 1908, no. 43, p. 13; Dr. Bloch's *Wochenschrift*, 1897, p. 833.

96. Nathan, *Once upon a Time and Today*, p. 107.

97. Ibid., pp. 175, 176, 305.

98. Ibid., pp. 178–79.

99. "Minutes of the Strike Council," Apr. 2, 1911, WTUL Papers, Schlesinger Library; Rose Scheneiderman, "Suffrage School Address," no. 2, Dec. 16, 1913, Schneiderman Papers, Tamiment Library.

100. Duffus, *Lillian Wald*, p. 114.

101. Nathan, *Once upon a Time and Today*, p. 183.

102. NCJW *Proceedings* (1896), pp. 184, 195.

103. Lillian Wald, address at New York State Suffrage Convention, Rochester, New York, Oct. 15, 1914, Wald Papers, NYPL; Duffus, *Lillian Wald*, p. 114.

CHAPTER 7

1. Finestein, "New Community," p. 114; V. D. Lipman, *Social Service*, p. 178.

2. J. Stanley Lemons, *The Woman Citizen: Social Feminism in the 1920's* (Urbana, Chicago, London: University of Illinois Press, 1973), pp. 58, 186–96; Kenneally, *Women and American Trade Unions*, p. 161; Lewis L. Lorwin, *The American Federation of Labor* (Washington: Brookings Institution, 1933), pp. 174, 221.

3. Nancy F. Cott, *The Grounding of Modern Feminism* (New Haven and London: Yale University Press, 1987), pp. 85–86.

4. Ibid., p. 85; Sochen, *Herstory*, pp. 267, 309; Banks, *Faces of Feminism*, pp. 153–62.

5. Kent, *Sex and Suffrage in Britain*, pp. 223–24; Cott, *Grounding of Modern Feminism*, pp. 184–85.

6. Kent, *Sex and Suffrage in Britain*, p. 221; Marwick, *The Deluge*, pp. 95–99.

7. Banks, *Faces of Feminism*, p. 123.

8. O'Neill, *The Woman Movement*, p. 31; Liddington and Norris, *One Hand Tied behind Us*, pp. 180–83.

9. Wilson, *Women and the Welfare State*, pp. 119–20; Mary MacArthur, "The Women Trade-Unionists' Point of View," in *Women and the Labour Party*, ed. Marion Phillips (New York: B. W. Huebsch, 1918), pp. 22–23.

10. Flora Sassoon, "Address Delivered on Speech Day at Jews' College," 1924; *The Jewish Woman*, *JG* supplement, Jan. 1926, pp. 42, 47, 53; Frances Rubens to Linda Gordon Kuzmack, Apr. 1983. An active member of the Union of Jewish Women's Executive Council, Mrs. Rubens was also a Union delegate to the International Council of Women, attending conventions and serving as council president in 1963. Her service on other Jewish communal boards exemplifies the continued activism of Jewish women in communal affairs.

11. *JG*, Oct. 10, 1919, p. 18; July 11, 1919, pp. 3–4; Dec. 19, 1919, p. 3; Aug. 20, 1920, p. 1; Mar. 3, 1921, p. 12; June 30, 1922, p. 7; Feb. 23, 1923, pp. 3–4; Apr. 6, 1923, p. 5; Apr. 27, 1923, p. 4. Jean Gaffin, "Women and Cooperation," in Middleton, *Women in the Labour Movement*, p. 137; Ralph Rooper, "Women Enfranchised," in *The Making of Women*, ed. Victor Gollancz (London: George Allen & Unwin; New York: Macmillan, 1918), pp. 95–96.

12. *JG*, May 14, 1920, p. 5; Diana Hopkinson, *Family Inheritance: A Life of Eva Hubback* (London and New York: Staples Press, 1954), pp. 23, 44–45, 95–96, 183; Bermant, *Cousinhood*, pp. 271–73.

13. Hopkinson, *Family Inheritance*, p. 91.

14. Wilson, *Women and the Welfare State*, p. 121; A. Maude Royden, "The Woman's Movement of the Future," in Gollancz, *Making of Women*, pp. 138–43; Hopkinson, *Family Inheritance*, p. 160; Victor Gollancz, "Conclusion," in Gollancz, *Making of Women*, p. 176.

15. Kent, *Sex and Suffrage in Britain*, p. 226.

16. Marion L. Davies, "The Claims of Mothers and Children," in Phillips, *Women and the Labour Party*, pp. 29–38; Hopkinson, *Family Inheritance*, pp. 95–96, 166–67; Wilson, *Women and the Welfare State*, p. 123.

17. Bermant, *Cousinhood*, p. 273; interview with David Franklin conducted by Shirley Winterbotham, Sept. 28, 1983.

18. Gibbon, *Netta*, pp. 148, 153; ICW *Report*, 1912–13, pp. 61–63.

19. V. D. Lipman, *Social Service*, pp. 144–53.

20. *JG*, Oct. 31, 1919, p. 3; Nov. 7, 1919, p. 8; April 20, 1923, p. 7; May 14, 1920, pp. 5, 22; May 1921, p. 5; May 5, 1922, p. 5; *JG* Supplement, Sept. 17, 1920, pp. vi–vii; Oct. [ ], 1920, p. iii.

21. Rosalie Gassman-Sher, *The Story of the Federation of Women Zionists of Great Britain and Ireland, 1918–1968* (London: Federation of Women Zionists, 1918), pp. 7–8; "Women in the Zionist World" (Tel Aviv: WIZO, 1931).

22. *JG*, Feb. 25, 1921, p. 16; Mar. 23, 1923, p. 4; Oct. [ ], 1920, p. 3; Feb. [ ], 1921, p. 3; Mar. 17, 1922, p. 3. Adler's younger cousin Rosalind Franklin, a crystallographer, was a member of the team that defined the properties of DNA, deoxyribonucleic acid. Franklin's contribution was not acknowledged when her teammates, Crick, Watson, and Wilkins won the Nobel Prize for their work on DNA in 1958, four years after Rosalind Franklin's death.

23. Arthur Franklin was president of Routledge & Kegan Paul publishing company; Bermant, *Cousinhood*, p. 273; interview with David Franklin conducted by Shirley Winterbotham, Sept. 28, 1983; Middleton, *Women in the Labour Movement*, pp. 23–24.

24. *JG*, July 23, 1920, p. 10; May 17, 1922, p. 3; Mrs. F. C. Stern, "Women in Politics," in *The Jewish Woman*, *JG* supplement, Dec. 1925, Klau Library, JUC-JIR.

25. UJW *Report*, p. 1; UJW *Leaflet*, pp. 1–2; UJW *Report*, 1915, pp. 9, 10–11; 1917, p. 1, all in ML.

26. UJW *Leaflet*, 1914, p. 1, ML. To save money in wartime, the 1914 *Report* was printed as a *Leaflet*; UJW *Report*, 1915, pp. 2, 6; 1916, p. 2, ML; Marwick, *The Deluge*, pp. 295–96; 300–304.

27. Sachar, *Diaspora*, pp. 146–47, 150–53.

28. UJW *Report*, 1918, pp. 5, 8, 10, 16; 1919, p. 7, ML.

29. UJW *Report*, 1918, p. 14, ML; *JG*, Feb. 24, 1922, p. 12; Nov. 21, 1919, p. 5; Apr. 15, 1921, p. 1; Nov. 6, 1920, p. 6; July 2, 1920, p. 5; Feb. 3, 1922, p. 3; Feb. 25, 1921, p. 16.

30. *JG*, Jan. 30, 1920; Feb. 24, 1922, pp. 11, 12; June 30, 1922, p. 4; June 23, 1922, p. 8; UJW *Report*, Feb. 3, 1923, p. 11, ML; *JG*, Feb. 1, 1920, p. 13; Mar. 30, 1923, p. 21; Mar. 23, 1923, p. 3.

31. *JG*, Feb. 13, 1920, p. 1; Mar. 23, 1923, p. 3; Apr. 7, 1923, p. 3; May 4, 1923, pp. 1, 11.

32. *JG*, Jan. 16, 1920, p. 3; Jan. 2, 1920, p. 8. Jacob Sarna, letter in "Curiosities" section of untitled newspaper, June 20, 1924, July 4, 1924, private collection of Jonathan Sarna; Zusman Hodes, letter in "Curiosities" section of untitled newspaper, June 27, 1924, private collection of Jonathan Sarna.

33. *JG*, Aug. 6, 1920, p. 9; Isaac Klein, *A Guide to Jewish Religious Practice* (New York: Jewish Theological Seminary of America, 1979), pp. 465–73; "Some Legal Difficulties which beset the Jewess," *JG*, July 30, 1920, p. 9; Sept. 19, 1920, p. 10, and n.

34. *JG*, Feb. [ ], 1921; Dec. 19, 1920; Dec. 12, 1920.

35. UJW *Report*, 1918, p. 8, ML. The Union sent representatives to the Conference of the Central Committee for the Formation of Women Voters and Citizens Associations, and the National Political League.

36. *JG*, Feb. 13, 1930, p. 1.

37. UJW *Report*, 1919, p. 8, ML; *JG*, May 19, 1922, pp. 8–9; May 7, 1920, p. 8; May 18 (?), 1920, p. 16.

38. *JG*, Feb. 13, 1920, p. 1; May 18 (?), 1920, p. 16; May (25?), 1920; Feb. 24, 1922, p. 11.

39. *JG*, Dec. 19, 1919, p. 12; Dec. 26, 1919, p. 8; Jan. 2, 1920, p. 13. Miss Alice Moses read Psalm 16 at the first service.

40. *JG*, Sept. 3, 1920; Mar. 19, 1920, pp. 1, 11; Feb. 6, 1920, p. 4; Mar. 26, 1920, p. 3; Sept. 24, 1920, p. 9; Oct. [ ], 1919, p. 9; Jan. 19, 1923, p. 9.

41. UJW, *Report*, 1919, p. 5, ML.

42. *JG*, Feb. 13, 1920, p. 12.

43. V. D. Lipman, *Social Service*, p. 261; *JG*, Jan. 5, 1923, p. 23; Apr. 28, 1922, p. 3.

44. Lipman, *Social Service*, p. 179.

45. Banks, *Faces of Feminism*, p. 177.

46. Lemons, *Woman Citizen*, pp. 186–96.

47. Cott, *Grounding of Modern Feminism*, pp. 87–88.

48. *Hebrew Standard*, Aug. 6, 1915, pp. 1–3; Oct. 1, 1915, pp. 1, 13; Banks, *Faces of Feminism*, p. 154.

49. Cott, *Grounding of Modern Feminism*, p. 92.

50. Sochen, *Herstory*, p. 292.

51. Joan Dash, *Summoned to Jerusalem: The Life of Henrietta Szold* (New York, Hagerstown, San Francisco, London: Harper & Row, 1979), p. 113.

52. Loeb, "Jewish Women," p. 127.

53. Quoted by Rabbi Jacob Mielziner, in National Federation of Temple Sisterhoods *Proceedings*, 1 (1913–15), pp. 27–28, NFTS Papers, AJA.

54. Ibid., p. 45; 2 (1917), pp. 13, 22–24, 29, 47.

55. *AJ* 2 (July 1896): 548–49.

56. Chicago *Sentinel*, Jan. 15, 1915, cited in Loeb, "Jewish Women," p. 130.

57. NFTS *Proceedings*, 1 (1913–15), pp. 36–37, 49–50; 2 (1917), pp. 12, 15; 4 (1921), p. 50; 5 (1923), p. 102; 6 (1925), pp. 12, 109–10; 7 (1927), p. 25; 8 (1928), pp. 28, 47, 86, NFTS Papers, AJA.

58. Loeb, "Jewish Women," p. 132; Sochen, *Consecrate Every Day*, p. 68; *American Hebrew*, Jan. 6, 1928, p. 309.

59. *Proceedings*, 1 (1913–15), pp. 49–50; 2 (1917), pp. 13, 14, 26; 3 (1919), pp. 14, 45, 46; 3 (1923), pp. 17, 105; 4 (1921), pp. 22, 58; 4 (1923), pp. 23, 65; 5 (1923), pp. 66–67; 6 (1925), pp. 28, 111; 7 (1927), p. 28, NFTS Papers, AJA.

60. Ibid., 3 (1919), pp. 18, 30–31, 58–59; 4 (1921), pp. 50, 72, 100–101; 5 (1923), pp. 69–70, 105; 6 (1925), pp. 24, 77; 8 (1928), p. 99; 9 (1929), pp. 16–17; 10 (1930), p. 89; 13 (1932), p. 22.

61. Ibid., 8 (1928), p. 17; 10 (1930), p. 18; 6 (1925), p. 14; 1 (1923), p. 90.

62. 1923 Report of UAHC Committee on Legislation, in Marcus, *Documentary History*, pp. 296–97; *Proceedings*, 12 (1932), p. 25, NFTS Papers, AJA.

63. *Proceedings*, 4 (1921), p. 58; 5 (1923), p. 90; 11 (1931), p. 24.

64. Loeb, "Jewish Women," p. 138.

65. Jacob Z. Lauterbach, "Responsum on Question, 'Shall Women be ordained Rabbis?'" Central Conference of American Rabbis, 1922, pp. 156–62.

66. CCAR *Yearbook* (1922), pp. 169, 177.

67. Minutes of the Board of Governors, HUC-JIR, Feb. 27, 1923, Martha Neumark Papers, AJA.

68. Marcus, *Documentary History*, p. 739. "The Woman Rabbi," *Jewish Tribune*, Apr. 17, 1925, p. 5, Neumark Papers, AJA.

69. *Universal Jewish Encyclopedia*, s.v. "Lindheim, Irma L."; *Encyclopedia Judaica*, s.v. "Lindheim, Irma Levy."

70. Israel H. Levinthal to Jacob Marcus, Apr. 14, 1972; Earl S. Stone to Alfred Gottschalk, May 10, 1971; Earl S. Stone to Sally Priesand, June 3, 1971; *Time*, Oct. 2, 1939, p. 48; all in Neumark Papers, AJA.

71. Seymour Siegel, ed., *Conservative Judaism and Jewish Law*, Studies in Conservative Jewish Thought, vol. 1 (New York: The Rabbinical Assembly, 1977), pp. xvii–xix.

72. *American Israelite*, Jan. 16, 1913, p. 4; cited in Loeb, "Jewish Women," p. 229, n. 152.

73. Mathilde Schechter, "A Task for Jewish Women," Address to United Synagogue women, reprinted from the *American Jewish Chronicle*, Feb. 1, 1918, AJA.

74. Henrietta Szold, "The Lineaments of Mathilde Roth Schechter," in *Services in Memory of Mrs. Solomon Schechter*, Temple Ansche Chesed, Nov. 13, 1924, p. 14, Henrietta Szold Papers, AJA.

75. Schechter, "A Task for Jewish Women," AJA.

76. Mordecai Kaplan, *Judaism as a Civilization* (New York: Schocken, 1972), p. 421.

77. "Jewish Science," Tehilla Lichtenstein Papers, AJA.

78. Ellen M. Umansky to Linda Gordon Kuzmack, July 11, 1989.

79. Tehilla Lichtenstein, "The Heart of a Mother," May 14, 1933; "A Mother's Concern," May 13, 1934; "Great Mother," May 9, 1937; all in Lichtenstein Papers, AJA.

80. World Council of Jewish Women, *Report* (1923), p. 1, WCJW Papers, AJA; Rebekah Kohut, untitled speech, 1923; *New York Times*, Aug. 12, 1951; both in Rebekah Kohut Papers, AJA.

81. Kohut, "Pratt"; *American Hebrew,* Aug. 23, 1918; *Jewish Quarterly Review,* n.d., p. 478; all in Kohut papers, AJA; Marcus, *The American Jewish Woman, 1654–1980*, p. 71. Kohut, untitled speech; unnamed newspaper article; both in Kohut papers, AJA.

82. *JG*, May 18, 1923, p. 3; *American Hebrew,* May 1923, p. 798; Kohut, untitled speech, AJA; *New York Times*, May 13, 1923; all in Kohut papers, AJA. WCJW *Report*, pp. 24–25, WCJW Papers, AJA.

83. CJW *Proceedings* (1923), p. 92; WCJW *Report*, p. 7, WCJW Papers, AJA.

84. WCJW *Report*, p. 11, WCJW Papers, AJA.

85. NFTS *Proceedings* 5 (1923), p. 104, NFTS Papers, AJA. Rebekah Kohut to Estelle Sternberger, June 5, 1933; Eileen van Noorden to Estelle Sternberger, n.d. (1933); both in Rebekah Kohut Papers, AJA.

86. Cott, *Grounding of Modern Feminism*, pp. 282–83.

CONCLUSION

1. June Sochen, "Jewish Volunteers," *American Jewish History* 70 (Sept. 1980): 23.

2. Banks, *Becoming a Feminist*, chap. 3.

3. Smith-Rosenberg, "Female World," in Cott, *Heritage of Her Own*, p. 319; Cook, *Women and Support Networks*.

4. Ribuffo, "Henry Ford," pp. 437–77.

5. Naomi Cohen, *Encounter with Emancipation*, pp. 325–26.

Bibliography

ARCHIVAL PAPERS

AMERICAN JEWISH ARCHIVES, CINCINNATI, OHIO

Rebekah Kohut

Rebekah Kohut. "Pratt."
——. Untitled speech, 1923.
Rebekah Kohut to Estelle Sternberger. June 5, 1933.
Eileen van Noorden to Estelle Sternberger. 1933.
"A Dollar-a-Year Woman." *American Hebrew.* Aug. 23, 1918.
"Mrs. Kohut, Leader of Her Sex and Race, Wants Jewish Law Changed." Clipping from untitled newspaper, 19——.
American Hebrew. Aug. 23, 1918; May 1923.
Jewish Quarterly Review. N.d., p. 478.
New York Times. Aug. 12, 1951.
Untitled newspaper article. N.d.
JG. May 18, 1923.

Tehilla Lichtenstein

Lichtenstein, Tehilla. "The Heart of a Mother." Sermon, May 14, 1933.
——. "A Mother's Concern." May 13, 1934.
——. "Great Mother." Sermon, May 9, 1937.
Jewish Science. Pamphlet.

Sophie Irene Loeb

Evening World. May 19——.
Loeb, Sophie Irene. *Everyman's Child.* New York: Century, 1920.
——. "Johnny Doe, His Mother and the State." *Harper's Weekly.* Jan. 31, 1914.
Postcard from Hannah Einstein to Dr. Gustav Gottheil. Oct. 10, 1902.
"Shall Women Vote? A Symposium Prepared by Sophie Irene Loeb." *American Hebrew.* Sept. 10, 1915, pp. 458–61.
The Survey. Untitled articles about Sophie Irene Loeb. Feb. 12, 1921; Feb. 15, 1929.

Annie Nathan Meyer

Meyer, Annie Nathan. "Petition to the Hon. Hamilton Fish, Chairman of the Board of Trustees of Columbia College." Ca. 1888.

———. "Again Spreadhenism." Letter to the editor, *Herald-Tribune*. Jan. 16, 1938.

———. Untitled speech on Spreadhenism. N.d.

———. "Woman's Assumption of Sex Superiority." *North American Review* (Jan. 1904).

Lily Montagu: Ellen M. Umansky Microfilm Collection

LETTERS

Basil Henriques to Lily Montegu. Feb. 15, 1921.

Lily Montagu to Susan ———. May 28, 19———.

——— to Claude G. Montefiore. Nov. 13, 1913.

——— to unknown recipient. Nov. 13, 1913.

——— to Israel Mattuck. May 13, 1918; Dec. 16, 1922; Jan. 28, 1953; Mar. 7,
1947; Apr. 21, 1920; May 10, 1949; Dec. 1953; Apr. 15, 1919; Oct. 4, 1922; Feb. 4, 1923; Sept. 20, 1923; Feb. 15, 1928; Apr. 15, 1928; July 20, 1929; Dec. 24, 1953; Mar. 21 and 25, 1922; Apr. 24, 1947; Nov. 26, 1945; Apr. 4, 1946; Apr. 21, 1920; Oct. 13, 1921; Mar. 1, 1944; Sept. 27, 1944; June 3, 19———; July 20, 1949; Feb. 2, 1953; Jan. 20, 1948; Sept. 9, 1920; Oct. 9, 1929; Dec. 8, 1949; July 10, 1953; Aug. 1928; Dec. 7, 1945.

——— to Jack Levy. Apr. 9, 1947.

——— to Julian Morgenstern. Mar. 5, 1958.

——— to Mr. Goldstein. July 21, 1903 (?).

To Lily Montagu from the Clerk to England's Lord Chancellor. Aug. 27, 1920.

Claude G. Montefiore to Lily Montagu. Apr. 12, 1899.

——— to Lily Montagu. Apr. 29, 19———; Sept. 26, 19———.

Lily Montagu to Edwin Montagu. 1912.

Edwin Montagu to Lily Montagu. Apr. 24, 1912.

Dr. Max Dienemann to Lily Montagu. 1934–39.

Netta Franklin to Lily Montagu. (Dec.?) 20, 1952.

SERMONS AND ADDRESSES

Montagu, Lily. "Address to the National Federation of Temple Sisterhoods." New York City. Nov. 7, 1948.

———. "Backwards and Forwards." Mar. 29, 1924.

———. "Cast me not away from Thy Presence . . ." Sermon. May 8, 1920.

———. "Divinity in Freedom." Sermon. May 4, 1929.

———. "Evidences of God in Everyday Life." Nov. 14, 1925.

———. "Faith in this World and the Next." Dec. 12, 1925.

———. "Home Worship and its Influence on Social Work." Address at the Conference of Jewish Women. May 1902.

———. "How to Give the Message of Liberal Judaism in the Home." Berlin: World Union for Progressive Judaism, 1928.

———. "Jewish Women's Contribution to the Spiritual Life of Humanity." Sermon. N.d.

———. "Joy of Service." June 22, 1921.

———. "Last Club Letter." *Liberal Jewish Monthly Memorial Supplement.* 1963, pp. 15–16.

———. "Loneliness." Club sermon. Dec. 2, 1916.

———. "Man's Ambition and God's Law." Sermon. Jan. 18, 1919.

———. "Modern Woman's Greatest Duty." Apr. 30, 1938.

———. "O Worship the Lord in the Beauty of Holiness." Sermon. Aug. 12, 1916.

———. "Progress in Life and Religion." Apr. 11, 1925.

———. "Religion and Private Possessions." Jan. 10, 1925.

———. "The Sacrifices of God are a broken spirit: a broken and a contrite heart, O God, Thou wilt not despise." Nov. 26, 1911.

———. "Short Paper with Outline of what I want done with regard to my work if I pass away." Sept. 1, 1939.

———. "The Spiritual Contribution of Women as Women." Nov. 26, 1948.

———. Statement. N.d.

———. "The Sun as Preacher." May 23, 1925.

———. "The Ten Commandments." Jan. 24, 1926.

———. "Unfinished Man." June 13, 1925.

———. "Who is Self-Made?" June 13, 1925.

———. "Why *Do* We Bother?" Feb. 21, 1925.

———. "Wishes for my work after my death." June 15, 1940.

Minutes of the West Central Flower Company. Mar. 13, 19——.

Martha Neumark

Minutes of the Hebrew Union College Board of Governors. Feb. 27, 1923.

"The Woman Rabbi." *Jewish Tribune.* Apr. 17, 1925.

Israel H. Levinthal to Jacob Marcus. Apr. 14, 1972.

Earl S. Stone to Alfred Gottschalk. May 10, 1971.

——— to Sally Priesand. June 3, 1971.

Jennie Franklin Purvin

Hyde Park Herald. Dec. 29, 1939.

The Reform Advocate. May 21, 1921.

Purvin, Jennie F. *Diary.* Nov. 27, 1933.

———. "Who will be our Champion?" *Reform Advocate.* May 27, 1916, p. 582.

Chicago Tribune. May 19, 1923, p. 1.

Julia Richman

American Hebrew. 1912.

"Julia Richmond's [sic] Defeat in the Board of Education."

Julia Richman to Felix Warburg. Apr. 25, 1912.

Petition "To the Board of Education, New York City." N.d.

Rosa Sonneschein

Loth, David. "The *American Jewess*." N.d. Typescript.

———. "The *American Jewess*, Supplemental 'Notes on the Marital Discord of Solomon and Rosa Sonneschein.'"

National Council of Jewish Women

Jewish Exponent. Nov. 26, 1926.

Proceedings. 1894–1933.

———. Brooklyn Section. "History."

———. Chicago Section. "Record of Progress, 1894–1908."

———. "Nina Morais Cohen, 1893–1907."

———. "Sadie Ascheim Kantrowitz, 1919–1924."

———. "Bertha Weiskopf, 1907–1915."

———. "Annalee Weiskopf Wolf, 1918–19."

———. Minneapolis Section. "Reference Information Continued."

National Federation of Temple Sisterhoods

Proceedings. 1913–33.

World Council of Jewish Women

Report. World Council of Jewish Women. 1923.

Deutsch Catalog

References to Rosalie Loew: *Die Neuzeit* (1896); *Die Welt* (1899); *Allgemeine Zeitung des Judenthums* (1897); *Hayehudi* (1908); Dr. Bloch's *Wochenschrift* (1897).

The catalog has several listings concerning the activities of Jewish women around the world.

Miscellaneous Papers

Alice Brandeis to Carrie Chapman Catt. Jan. 24, 1919. Louis Brandeis Papers.

"Jewish Girl Collegian." *Jewish Tribune*. Nov. 15, 1919. Jennie Mannheimer Papers.

Sarna, Jonathan D. "The Daughters of Rabbis."

Schechter, Mathilde. "A Task for Jewish Women." Address to United Synagogue Women, reprinted from the *American Jewish Chronicle*. Feb. 1, 1918.

Szold, Henrietta. "The Lineaments of Mathilde Roth Schechter." In *Services in Memory of Mrs. Solomon Schechter*. Temple Ansche Chesed. Nov. 13, 1924. Henrietta Szold Papers.

Woocher, Jonathan. "'Civil Judaism' in the United States," unpublished paper for HUC-JIR.

For references to printed material related to the following women, refer to list of secondary sources:

Hannah Einstein

Sophie Irene Loeb
Jennie Mannheimer
Jessie Sampter
Rosa Sonneschein
Henrietta Szold

NEWSPAPERS
Deborah Index.
Occident and Jewish Advocate.
Sinai Index.

AMERICAN JEWISH HISTORICAL SOCIETY, WALTHAM, MASSACHUSETTS

Emily Solis-Cohen

Solis-Cohen, Emily. Untitled speech at the national convention of the United
    Synagogue, n.d.
Emily Solis-Cohen to Deborah Kallen. Jan. 16, 1924.

Ray Frank Litman

San Francisco Examiner. Feb. 1893; Nov. 13, 1896.
Oakland Enquirer. Sept. 18——.
Oakland Times, Sept. 5, 1902.
Town Talk. 1897.
Post. N.d.
San Francisco *Bulletin.* Nov. 1895.
Stockton Mail. Mar. 22, 189——.
Stockton *Jewish Progress.* N.d.
Ray Frank Litman to Rev. S. J. Willis. Dec. 15, 1896.
Ray Frank Litman to Charlotte Perkins Stetson. Sept. 14, 1894.
Ambrose Bierce to Ray Frank Litman. May 5, 1895; Feb. 23, 1896.
Lily H. Montagu to Ray Frank Litman. Mar. 24, 1901. Cited in *Ray Frank
    Litman: A Memoir.* By Simon Litman. New York: AJHS, 1957.
Nina Davis to Ray Frank Litman. Jan. 25, 1899; May 30, 1899.
Nettie Adler to Ray Frank Litman. Jan. 28, 1899; Dec. 27, 1899; Apr. 2, 1901.
    Cited in *Ray Frank Litman: A Memoir.* By Simon Litman.

Harriet B. Lowenstein

Home News. Apr. 7, 1918.
Bank Israelite (Chicago). July 27, 19——.
American Hebrew. May 31, 1918; Dec. 6, 1919.

National Council of Jewish Women

Mrs. Abe Krudel to Cecelia Razovsky. Feb. 16, 1926.
Max J. Kohler to Mrs. Joseph E. Friend. Nov. 26, 1929.

KLAU LIBRARY, HEBREW UNION COLLEGE-JEWISH INSTITUTE OF RELIGION

Jewish League for Woman Suffrage
Constitution. 1912.
Annual Reports. 1912–14.

World Union for Progressive Judaism
Minutes of the Governing Body of the World Union for Progressive Judaism. London: Sept. 7, 1927.
See secondary sources for complete list.

Jewish Guardian
The Jewish Woman Supplement to the Jewish Guardian. 1925–26.

LONDON LIBRARY, LONDON

Jewish Association for the Protection of Girls and Women. *Annual Reports.* 1895–1933.
Jewish International Conference on the Suppression of the Traffic in Girls and Women, *Official Reports.* 1910, 1927.

MOCATTA LIBRARY, LONDON

Union of Jewish Women. *Annual Reports.* 1903–33.
———. *Leaflet.* 1914.

NEW YORK PUBLIC LIBRARY, RARE BOOKS AND MANUSCRIPT DIVISION, NEW YORK CITY

Lillian Wald
Wald, Lillian. "Children's Bureau." 1905.
———. "Dangers Surrounding the Young Immigrant Girl." Speech in Buffalo, New York, 1909.
———. "The Immigrant." Free Synagogue. New York City, 1907.
———. "Immigrant Women in New York." Speech in Dr. Stimson's Church. Dec. 4, 1910.
———. "Preparedness for War." 1914.
———. "Rural Nursing and the American Red Cross."
———. "Some Social Values of the Settlement." N.d.
———. "Speech to the Council of Jewish Women." Feb. 26, 1911.
———. "Speech at the New York House of Representatives." Sept. 24, 1917.
———. "Speech at the New York State Suffrage Convention." Rochester, N.Y. Oct. 15, 1914.
———. "Speech at the New York State Suffrage League." 1917.
———. "The Utilization of the Immigrant." Free Synagogue. New York City, 1907.
———. "What Business are Women About." New York State Nursing Association Convention. Oct. 20, 1915.

London, Meyer. Speech in the New York House of Representatives. Sept. 24, 1917.

SCHLESINGER LIBRARY, RADCLIFFE COLLEGE, CAMBRIDGE, MASSACHUSETTS

Jennie Loitman Barron

Boston Globe. N.d.
Chelsea Evening Record. April 19——.
"Mrs. Barron Wages New Kind of Campaign for School Committee." Untitled newspaper clipping. N.d.
Kaufman, Polly Welts. "Jennie Loitman Barron." Introduction to the Jennie L. Barron Collection.

Maud Nathan

American Hebrew. Oct. 26, 1900.
Boston newspaper (no title). Mar. 19, 1897.
Dry Goods Economist. N.d.
Harper's Magazine. N.d.
"Home and the Vote according to Mrs. Kohut." *American Hebrew.* N.d.
Jewish Exponent. Feb. 24, 1899.
"Jewish Women in Public Affairs." *The American Citizen.* May 1913.
Morning Journal. Oct. 2, 19——.
New York *Advertizer* (sic). Feb. 19, 1897.
News Letter. Apr. 1, 1905.
New York Times. Dec. 3, 1906, p. 59; (?), 1915.
New York *Tribune.* (?), 1913.
Philadelphia Record. 1915 (?).
Rochester Herald. Feb. 14, 1914.
Woman Citizen. Nov. 23, 1918.
Woman's Journal. Sept. 13, 1913.

Pauline Newman

"Transcript of an Interview with Pauline Newman." Interview and Appendix B.

Women's Trade Union League, Microfilm Records from New York State Dept. of Labor Library

"Minutes of the Executive Board of the WTUL of New York." Jan. 13, 1905; Jan. 26, 1909; Mar. 23, 1910.
"Minutes of the Meeting of the Strike Council." 1909; 1911; 1912; 1913.
"Secretary's Report to the Executive Board." Feb. 27, 1913.

SPANISH AND PORTUGUESE SYNAGOGUE, LONDON

David De Sola
Charlotte Montefiore to Rev. D. A. de Sola. Letters. N.d.
Charlotte Montefiore to Grace Aguilar. Letters. N.d.
Grace Aguilar to David de Sola. N.d.

TAMIMENT INSTITUTE LIBRARY, NEW YORK UNIVERSITY, NEW YORK CITY

Rose Schneiderman
"Suffrage School Address." No. 1. Dec. 1913.
"Suffrage School Address." No. 2. Dec. 16, 1913.

NEWSPAPER ARTICLES
"Factory Girl Urges Shopmen to Give Women the Ballot." Untitled newspaper.
    N.d.
Rose C. Tillotson. Untitled article in newspaper.
"Immigrant Girl Now Heads Union." Untitled newspaper clipping. N.d.
"What is Feminism?" Announcement of the first and second feminist mass
    meetings. Cooper Union Hall. Feb. 17 and 20, 1914.
Jamestown *Morning Post.* N.d.
"Wilson Rejects Suffrage Plea." Untitled newspaper. N.d.
Youngstown Vindicator. 1912.

LETTERS
Max Fruchter [?] to Rose Schneiderman. Mar. 5, 191——.
Pauline Newman to Rose Schneiderman. Nov. 7, 1911.
Harriet Stanton Blatch to Rose Schneiderman. May 2, 1910.
Harriet Taylor Upton to Rose Scheiderman. May 6, 1910.
M. W. Suffren to Rose Schneiderman. Nov. 18, 1911.
M. A. Sherwood to Mrs. Upton. July 15, 1912.

Note: Published materials from all archives listed above are cited in second-
    ary sources.

NEWSPAPERS

American Hebrew
American Jewess
Deborah
Hebrew Standard
Israelite
Jewish Chronicle
Jewish Exponent
Jewish Guardian

Jewish Messenger
Jewish World
Occident and Jewish Advocate. Edited by Isaac Leeser.
Sinai
Woman Voter. 1905–18.

PRIVATE COLLECTIONS

David Franklin (England)
Carolyn Franklin: An Appreciation. Privately printed, 1936.

Phyllis Gerson (England)
Bulletin. Liberal Jewish Synagogue. N.W.B. N.d.
East London Advertiser, Apr. 26, 1963.
"Flowers—and a Gong—for Florrie." Newspaper clipping. Jan. 1976.
"Florrie: 'Queen' of the Clubs." Newspaper clipping. (1981?).
"MBE for Community Worker Born in 1888." *Mackney Gazette.* Jan. 1976.
Order of Proceedings at official opening of the Beaumont Hall Day and Community Centre by Her Majesty Queen Elizabeth, the Queen Mother. May 19, 1974.
Our House. Stepney Jewish (B'nai B'rith) Clubs and Settlement newsletter. May 1974.
"Some of the things you should know about the success of the Stepney Jewish Community Center."
"Scroll of Events." Stepney Jewish B'nai B'rith Clubs and Settlement.
"Stepney Jewish Girls' Club." *JC.* Jan. 25, 1935.

Jonathan Sarna (United States)
Letters in "Curiosities" section of untitled newspaper by Jacob Sarna; by Zusman Hodes. June 20, 1924.

Walter S. Schwab (England)
"In Memoriam—Mrs. Anna Schwab," *AJR Information.* May 1963.

INTERVIEWS

David Franklin. Interview conducted by Shirley Winterbotham. Sept. 28, 1983.
Dr. Clara Loitman Smith. Sept. 1982.
Conversation with Professor Hasia Diener. Apr. 1982.
Conversations with Professor Jonathan Sarna. Dec. 1983; Sept. 1984.

CORRESPONDENCE

The following people have kindly supplied information for this book:
Beth-Zion Lask Abrahams. June 3, 1982.
R. D. Barnett. Dec. 4, 1981; Mar. 3, 1983; Mar. 24, 1983.
Chaim Bermant. Sept. 25, 1983.
Richard W. Davis. Oct. 21, 1983.
Hannah Feldman, Mar. 11, 1982.
William J. Fishman. Mar. 2, 1983.
David Franklin. Aug. 8, 1983.
Phyllis J. Gerson. Jan. 19, 1982; Mar. 9, 1982; Mar. 18, 1982; Sept. 3, 1982.
Lily Glass. Nov. 4, 1981.
Dr. I. Sidney Gold. June 19 and 29, 1983.
Trude Levi. May 10, 1983.
Jane E. Levy. Mar. 15, 1982.
V. D. Lipman. Oct. 25, 1981.
Ann Loewe. Feb. 21, 1982; May 17, 1982.
Hyam Manoby. Sept. 10, 1981.
Gwen and Jeremy Montagu. Feb. 10, 1982.
Alan Montefiore. Nov. 22, 1983.
Joseph Munk. Mar. 10, 1983.
Claire Rayner. Nov. 26, 1982.
Frances Rubens. Apr. 1983.
Jonathan D. Sarna. June 15, 1989.
Walter M. Schwab. May 27, 1982.
Dr. Clara Loitman Smith.
Rabbi Jacqueline Tabick.
John J. Tepfer. Nov. 18, 1981.
Ellen M. Umansky. Feb. 11, 1985; July 11, 1989.
William Toll. Jan. 24, 1983.
Bernard Wasserstein. July 31, 1984.
Ruth Winston-Fox. Feb. 24, 1982.

SECONDARY SOURCES

GENERAL BACKGROUND

Abrahams, Israel. *Jewish Life in the Middle Ages.* New York: Atheneum, 1973.
Adler, Rachel. "The Jew Who Wasn't There: Halacha and the Jewish Woman."
     Response 7 (Summer 1973).
Arendt, Hannah. *Rachel Varnhagen: The Life of a Jewess.* London: East and
     West Library, 1957.
Banks, Olive. *Faces of Feminism: A Study of Feminism as a Social Move-
     ment.* New York: St. Martin's Press, 1981.
Berman, Saul. "The Status of Women in Halakhic Judaism." In *The Jewish*

Woman: New Perspectives. Edited by Elizabeth Koltun. New York: Schocken, 1976.

Biale, Rachel. *Women and Jewish Law.* New York: Schocken, 1984.

Bleich, J. David. *Contemporary Halakhic Problems.* New York: Ktav and Yeshiva University Press, 1977.

Carroll, Berenice, ed. *Liberating Women's History.* Urbana: University of Illinois Press, 1976.

Davidowicz, Lucy S. *On Equal Terms: Jews in America, 1881–1981.* New York: Holt, Rinehart & Winston, 1982.

Dubnow, Simon. *History of the Jews in Russia and Poland.* 3 vols. Philadelphia: Jewish Publication Society, 1946.

Encyclopedia Judaica. Jerusalem: Keter, 1971.

Feingold, Henry L. *A Midrash on American Jewish History.* Albany: State University of New York Press, 1982.

Feldman, David M. *Birth Control in Jewish Law.* New York: New York University Press, 1968.

Flannery, Edward. *The Anguish of the Jews.* New York: Macmillan; London: Collier-Macmillan, 1964.

Gay, Peter. *The Bourgeois Experience, Victoria to Freud.* Vol. 1. *Education of the Senses.* New York and Oxford: Oxford University Press, 1984.

Geiger, Abraham. "Die Stellung des weiblichen Geschlechts in dem Judenthume unserer Zeit." *Wissenschaftliche Zeitschrif für Jüdische Theologie* 3 (1837). In *The Reform Movement in Judaism.* Edited by David Philipson. Rev. ed. New York: Ktav, 1967.

Genesis Rabbah. New York: Soncino, 1939. 71:5.

Greenberg, Blu. "Judaism and Feminism." In *The Jewish Woman: New Perspectives.* Edited by Elizabeth Koltun. New York: Schocken, 1976.

Greenberg, Louis. *The Jews in Russia.* 2 vols. New Haven: Yale University Press, 1951.

Hauptman, Judith. "Women in the Talmud." In *Religion and Sexism: Images of Woman in the Jewish and Christian Traditions.* Edited by Rosemary Radford Ruether. New York: Simon & Schuster, 1974.

Henry, Sonya, and Taitz, Emily, eds. *Written Out of History.* New York: Bloch, 1978.

Hyman, Paula. "The Other Half: Women in the Jewish Tradition." In *The Jewish Woman: New Perspectives.* Edited by Elizabeth Koltun. New York: Schocken, 1976.

International Council of Women. *Reports.* 1888–1933.

Johansson, Sheila Ryan. " 'Herstory' as History: A New Field or Another Fad?" In *Liberating Women's History.* Edited by Berenice Carroll. Urbana: University of Illinois Press, 1976.

Kaplan, Marion. *The Jewish Feminist Movement in Germany: The Campaigns of the Jüdischer Frauenbund, 1904–1938.* Westport, Conn., and London: Greenwood Press, 1979.

Katz, Jacob. *Exclusiveness and Tolerance: Jewish and Gentile Relations in Medieval and Modern Times.* New York: Schocken, 1962.

————. *From Prejudice to Destruction: Anti-Semitism, 1700–1933.* Cambridge: Harvard University Press, 1980.

————. *Out of the Ghetto.* Cambridge, Mass.: Harvard University Press, 1973.

Kelly, Joan. "The Social Relation of the Sexes: Methodological Implications of Women's History." In *Women, History and Theory: The Essays of Joan Kelly.* Edited by Joan Kelly. Chicago and London: University of Chicago Press, 1984.

Klein, Isaac. *A Guide to Jewish Religious Practice.* New York: Jewish Theological Seminary of America, 1979.

Kuzmack, Linda Gordon. "Aggadic Approaches to Biblical Women." In *The Jewish Woman: New Perspectives.* Edited by Elizabeth Koltun. New York: Schocken, 1976.

————. "Jewish Working Women as Agents of Change." *Humanistic Judaism* (Autumn 1984): 24–26.

————. "Rabbinic Interpretations of Biblical Women." M.A. thesis, Baltimore Hebrew College, 1975.

Lerner, Gerda. "Placing Women in History: A 1975 Perspective." In *Liberating Women's History.* Edited by Berenice Carroll. Urbana: University of Illinois Press, 1976.

Meiselman, Moshe. *Jewish Woman in Jewish Law.* New York: Ktav, Yeshiva University Press, 1978.

Meyer, Michael. *The Origins of the Modern Jew: Jewish Identity and European Culture in Germany, 1749–1824.* Detroit: Wayne State University Press, 1967.

O'Faolain, Julia, and Martines, Lauro, eds. *Not in God's Image.* New York: Harper, 1973.

Philipson, David. *The Reform Movement in Judaism.* Rev. ed. New York: Ktav, 1967.

Plaut, Gunther. *The Rise of Reform Judaism: A Sourcebook of Its European Origins.* New York: World Union for Progressive Judaism, 1963.

Raddock, Charles. "Hannah of Ludmir." *Spectator.* April 1948.

Robertson, Patricia. *An Experience of Women: Pattern and Change in Nineteenth-Century Europe.* Philadelphia: Temple University Press, 1982.

Rosenberg, Rosalind. *Beyond Separate Spheres: Intellectual Roots of Modern Feminism.* New Haven and London: Yale University Press, 1982.

Sachar, Howard M. *The Course of Modern Jewish History.* New York: Dell, 1958.

————. *Diaspora: An Inquiry into the Contemporary Jewish World.* New York: Harper & Row, 1985.

————. *A History of Israel.* New York: Knopf, 1979.

Sachs, Albie, and Wilson, Joan Hoff. *Sexism and the Law: A Study of Male Beliefs and Judicial Bias.* New York: Free Press; Oxford: Martin Robertson, 1978.

Schneider, Susan Weidman. *Jewish and Female.* New York: Simon & Schuster, 1984.

Shoub, Myra. "Jewish Women's History: Development of a Critical Methodology." *Conservative Judaism* (Winter 1982).

————. *Diaspora: An Inquiry into the Contemporary Jewish World.* New York: Harper & Row, 1985.

Shulman, Gail B. "View from the Back of the Synagogue." In *Sexist Religion and Women in the Church.* Edited by Alice L. Hageman. New York: Association Press, 1974.

Siegel, Seymour, ed. *Conservative Judaism and Jewish Law.* Studies in Conservative Jewish Thought. Vol. 1. New York: The Rabbinical Assembly, 1977.

Smith, Hilda. "Feminism and the Methodology of Women's History." In *Liberating Women's History.* Edited by Berenice Carroll. Urbana: University of Illinois Press, 1976.

Swidler, Leonard. *Women in Judaism: The Status of Women in Formative Judaism.* Metuchen, N.J.: Scarecrow Press, 1976.

Voice of Jacob VI, 123. In David Philipson, *The Reform Movement in Judaism.* Rev. ed. New York: Ktav, 1967.

Weber, Max. *From Max Weber: Essays in Sociology.* Translated and edited by H. H. Gerth and C. Wright Mills. New York: Oxford University Press, 1946.

————. *The Sociology of Religion.* Intro. by Talcott Parsons. 4th ed., paperback. Boston: Beacon Press, 1964.

Wegner, Judith Romney. *Chattel or Person? The Status of Women in the Mishnah.* Oxford, New York and London: Oxford University Press, 1988.

Wollstonecraft, Mary. *A Vindication of the Rights of Woman.* Edited by Carol H. Poston. New York and London: W. W. Norton, 1975.

Yerushalmi, Yosef Hayim. *Zakhor: Jewish History and Jewish Memory.* Seattle and London: University of Washington Press, 1982.

ENGLAND

Abrahams, Beth-Zion Lask. "Grace Aguilar: A Centenary Tribute." *Transactions of the Jewish Historical Society of England* 16 (1952): 137–48.

Adam, H. Pearl, ed. *Women in Council.* London, New York, Toronto: Oxford University Press, 1945.

Aguilar, Grace. *Women of Israel.* 2 vols. New York: D. Appleton & Co., 1854. Cited in *Written Out of History.* Edited by Sonya Henry and Emily Taitz. New York: Block, 1978.

Alderman, Geoffrey. *The Jewish Community in British Politics.* Oxford: Clarendon Press, 1983.

Anglo-Jewish Yearbooks. 1881–1933.

Arnstein, Walter L. *Britain Yesterday and Today: 1830 to the Present.* Boston: D. C. Heath, 1976.

Ascher, Joseph. "Lily Montagu and the West Central Synagogue." In *Liberal Jewish Monthly Memorial Supplement.* 1963, p. 12.

Banks, Olive. *Becoming a Feminist: The Social Origins of 'First Wave' Feminism.* Brighton: Wheatsheaf Books, 1986.

Barnett, R. D. "Anglo-Jewry in the Eighteenth Century." In *Three Centuries of Anglo-Jewish History.* Edited by V. D. Lipman. London: Jewish Historical Society, 1961.

Battersea, Constance. *Reminiscences.* London, 1922.

Bayme, Steven. "Claude Montefiore, Lily Montagu and the Origins of the Jewish Religious Union." *Transactions of the Jewish Historical Society of England* 27 (1982).

———. "Jewish Leadership and Anti-Semitism in Britain, 1870–1918." Ph.D. diss., Columbia University, 1977.

Bermant, Chaim. *The Cousinhood.* London: Eyre & Spottiswoode, 1971.

"Blackguards in Bonnets: The Jewish Suffragettes Revived." *JC* Aug. 29, 1969.

Black, Eugene. *The Social Politics of Anglo-Jewry, 1880–1920.* Oxford: Basil Blackwell, 1988.

Bodek, Evelyn Gordon. "Salonieres and Bluestockings: Educated Obsolescence and Germinating Feminism." *FS* 3 (Spring–Summer 1976): 185–97.

Booth, Charles, ed. *Life and Labour of the People in London.* New York and London, 1902–04. Reprint ed. New York: AMS Press, 1970.

Branca, Patricia. *Silent Sisterhood: Middle Class Women in the Victorian Home.* Pittsburgh: Carnegie-Mellon University Press, 1975.

———. *Women in Europe Since 1750.* London, 1978.

Bristow, Edward. *Prostitution and Prejudice: The Jewish Fight against White Slavery 1870–1939.* Oxford: Clarendon Press, 1982.

———. *Vice and Vigilance: Purity Movements in Britain since 1700.* Dublin: Gill & Macmillan, 1977.

Bruin, Elizabeth de. "Judaism and Womanhood." *Westminster Review* (August 1913): 124–32.

Buckman, Joseph. *Immigrants and the Class Struggle: The Jewish Immigrant in Leeds 1880–1914.* Manchester: Manchester University Press, 1983.

Carolyn Franklin: An Appreciation. Privately printed. London, 1936. David Franklin collection.

Cohen, Lucy. *Lady de Rothschild and Her Daughters, 1821–1931.* London, 1935.

———. *Some Recollections of Claude Goldsmid Montefiore, 1858–1938.* London: Faber & Faber, 1940.

Cohen, Percy. "Jews and Feminism." *Westminster Review* (October 1913).

Cohen, Stuart A. "The Reception of Political Zionism in England: Patterns of Alignment among the Clergy and Rabbinate, 1895–1904." *JJS* 2 (Dec. 1974).

———. "The Zionists and the Board of Deputies in 1917." *JJS* 9 (Dec. 1977): 157–83.

"Conference of Jewish Women." *JC* (May 16, 1902): 10–15.

Conrad, Eric. "Lily Montagu's Life and Work." In *Lily Montagu: 1873–1963. Liberal Jewish Monthly Memorial Supplement,* 1963.

———. *Lily H. Montagu: Prophet of a Living Judaism.* New York: National Federation of Temple Sisterhoods, 1953.

Conway, Jill. "Stereotypes of Femininity in a Theory of Sexual Evolution." *Victorian Studies* 14 (Sept. 1970).

Davidoff, Lenore. "Sex and Gender in Victorian England." In *Sex and Class in Women's History.* Edited by Judith L. Newton, Mary P. Ryan, and Judith R. Walkowitz. London, Boston, Melbourne, and Henley: Routledge & Kegan Paul, 1983.

Davies, Emily, to Barbara Bodichon. Letter. March 3, 1867. Girton Archives. Cited in Rita McWilliams-Tullberg, "Women and Degrees at Cambridge University." In *A Widening Sphere.* Edited by Martha Vicinus. Bloomington and London: Indiana University Press, p. 294.

Davies, Horton. *Worship and Theology in England: From Newman to Martineau, 1850–1900.* Princeton: Princeton University Press, 1962.

———. *Worship and Theology in England: The Ecumenical Century, 1900–1965.* Princeton: Princeton University Press, 1965.

Davies, Marion L. "The Claims of Mothers and Children." In *Women and the Labour Party.* Edited by Marion Phillips. New York: B. W. Huebsch, 1918.

Davis, Richard. *The English Rothschilds.* Chapel Hill: University of North Carolina Press, 1983.

Delamont, Sara. "The Contradictions in Ladies' Education." In *The Nineteenth-Century Woman: Her Cultural and Physical World.* Edited by Sara Delamont and Lorna Duffin. London: Croom Helm, 1978.

Delamont, Sara, and Duffin, Lorna, eds. *The Nineteenth-Century Woman: Her Cultural and Physical World.* London: Croom Helm, 1978.

Edgar, Leslie I. "Claude Montefiore's Thought and the Present Religious Situation." Claude Montefiore Lecture. London: Liberal Jewish Synagogue, 1966.

———. "Memorial Tribute." In *Lily Montagu: 1873–1963. Liberal Jewish Monthly Memorial Supplement,* 1963.

Elliot-Binns, L. E. *The Early Evangelicals: A Religious and Social Study.* Greenwich, Conn.: Seabury Press, 1953.

Emden, Paul H. *Jews of Britain: A Series of Biographies.* London: Sampson Low, Marston & Co., 1944.

Endelman, Todd. *The Jews of Georgian England, 1714–1830: Tradition and Change in a Liberal Society.* Philadelphia: Jewish Publication Society, 1979.

Evans, Richard. *The Feminists: Women's Emancipation Movements in Europe, America and Australasia 1840–1920.* London: Croom Helm; New York: Barnes & Noble, 1977.

Fawcett, Millicent Garrett. *Women's Suffrage.* London: T. C. & E. C. Jack, 1912. Reprint ed. New York: Source Book Press, 1970.

Finestein, Israel. "The New Community, 1880–1918." In *Three Centuries of Anglo-Jewish History.* Edited by V. D. Lipman. London: Jewish Historical Society of England, 1961.

———. "Jewish Immigration in British Party Politics in the 1890's." In *Migration and Settlement: Proceedings of the Anglo-American Jewish His-*

torical Conference. Edited by Aubrey Newman. London: Jewish Historical Society of England, 1971.

———. "Post-Emancipation Jewry: The Anglo-Jewish Experience." Oxford: Oxford Centre for Postgraduate Hebrew Studies, 1980.

Finkelstein, Louis, ed. *The Jews*. New York: Schocken, 1970.

Fishman, William J. *East End Jewish Radicals, 1875–1914*. London: Duckworth, 1975.

———. "Jewish Immigrant Anarchists in East London." In *The Jewish East End 1840–1939*. Edited by Aubrey Newman. London: Jewish Historical Society of England, 1981.

———. *Jewish Radicals*. New York: Pantheon, 1974.

———. *The Streets of East London*. London: Duckworth, 1979.

Flexner, Eleanor. "Ideas in 'A Vindication of the Rights of Woman.'" In Mary Wollstonecraft, *A Vindication of the Rights of Woman*. Edited by Carol H. Poston. New York: W. W. Norton, 1975.

Gainer, Bernard. *The Alien Invasion: The Origins of the Aliens Act of 1905*. New York: Crane, Russak & Co., 1972.

Gartner, Lloyd P. *The Jewish Immigrant in England, 1870–1913*. Detroit: Wayne State University Press, 1960.

Gassman-Sher, Rosalie. *The Story of the Federation of Women Zionists of Great Britain and Ireland, 1918–1968*. London: Federation of Women Zionists, 1918.

Gibbon, Monk. *Netta*. London: Routledge & Kegan Paul, 1960.

Godwin, Anne. "Early Years in the Trade Unions." In *Women in the Labour Movement: The British Experience*. Edited by Lucy Middleton. London: Croom Helm, 1977.

Gollancz, Victor, ed. *The Making of Women*. Oxford Essays in Feminism. London: George Allen & Unwin; New York: Macmillan, 1918.

Gordon, Linda, and Dubois, Ellen. "Seeking Ecstasy on the Battlefield: Danger and Pleasure in Nineteenth-Century Feminist Sexual Thought." *FS* 9 (Spring 1983).

Gorham, Deborah. *The Victorian Girl and the Feminine Ideal*. Bloomington: Indiana University Press, 1982.

Harrison, Brian. *Separate Spheres: The Opposition to Women's Suffrage in Britain*. London: Croom Helm, 1978.

Henriques, Alfred G. "Why I Do Not Go to Synagogue." *JQR* (1901).

Henriques, Rose L. *Fifty Years in Stepney*. Privately printed, 1966.

Hill, Michael. *The Religious Order*. London: Heinemann, 1973.

Holcombe, Lee. "Victorian Wives and Property." In *A Widening Sphere: Changing Roles of Victorian Women*. Edited by Martha Vicinus. Bloomington and London: Indiana University Press, 1980.

———. *Wives and Property: Reform of the Married Women's Property Law in Nineteenth-Century England*. Toronto and Buffalo: University of Toronto Press, 1983.

Hollis, Patricia. *Women in Public: The Women's Movement, 1850–1900*. London: George Allen & Unwin, 1979.

Holmes, Colin. *Anti-Semitism in British Society, 1876–1939.* New York: Holmes & Meier, 1979.

———. "East End Crime and the Jewish Community, 1887–1911." In *The Jewish East End, 1840–1939.* Edited by Aubrey Newman. London: Jewish Historical Society of England, 1981.

Hooker, Bernard. "Lily Montagu and the World Union." In *Lily Montagu: 1873–1963. Liberal Jewish Monthly Memorial Supplement,* 1963, p. 9.

Hopkinson, Diana. *Family Inheritance: A Life of Eva Hubback.* London and New York: Staples Press, 1954.

Howe, Irving. "Introduction." *Daniel Deronda.* By George Eliot. New York and Scarborough, Ontario: Signet New American Library, 1979.

International Council of Women. *Women in a Changing World: The Dynamic Story of the International Council of Women since 1888.* London: Routledge & Kegan Paul, 1966.

Jacob, Walter. "Claude G. Montefiore's Reappraisal of Christianity." *Judaism* 19 (Summer 1970): 328–29.

Jones, Gareth Stedman. *Outcast London.* Oxford: Clarendon Press, 1971.

Joseph, Frances. "The Dietary Laws from a Woman's Point of View." *JQR* 20 (1908): 643–45.

Kalman, Raymond. "The Jewish East End—Where Was It?" In *The Jewish East End, 1840–1939.* Edited by Aubrey Newman. London: Jewish Historical Society of England, 1981.

Kanner, Barbara, ed. *The Women of England: From Anglo-Saxon Times to the Present.* Hamden, Conn.: Archon, 1979.

Karpeles, Gustav. *Jewish Literature and Other Essays.* Philadelphia: Jewish Publication Society, 1895. Cited in *Written Out of History.* Edited by Sonya Henry and Emily Taitz. New York: Bloch, 1978, p. 238.

Kass, Amalie M. "Friends and Philanthropists: Montefiore and Dr. Hodgkin." In *The Century of Moses Montefiore.* Edited by Sonia and V. D. Lipman. Oxford and New York: Littman Library and Jewish Historical Society of England and Oxford University Press, 1985.

Kent, Susan Kingsley. *Sex and Suffrage in Britain, 1860–1914.* Princeton: Princeton University Press, 1987.

Kitson-Clark, G. *The Making of Victorian England.* New York: Atheneum, 1969.

Kokosalakis, N. *Ethnic Identity and Religion: Tradition and Change in Liverpool Jewry.* Washington, D.C.: University Press of America, 1982.

Lazarus, Olga. *Liberal Judaism and Its Standpoint.* London: Macmillan, 1937.

Levy, Nellie G. "Lily Montagu and the West Central Club." In *Lily Montagu: 1873–1963. Liberal Jewish Monthly Memorial Supplement,* 1963, p. 13.

Lewenhak, Sheila. *Women and Trade Unions: An Outline History of Women in the British Trade Union Movement.* New York: St. Martin's Press, 1977.

———. *Women and Work.* New York: St. Martin's Press, 1980.

Liddington, Jill, and Norris, Jill. *One Hand Tied behind Us: The Rise of the Women's Suffrage Movement.* London: Virago, 1978.

Lipman, Sonia, and V. D. Lipman, eds. *The Century of Moses Montefiore.* Oxford, New York: Published for the Littman Library of Jewish Civilization in association with the Jewish Historical Society of England by Oxford University Press, 1985.

Lipman, V. D. "The Booth and New London Surveys as Source Material." In *The Jewish East End, 1840–1939.* Edited by Aubrey Newman. London: Jewish Historical Society of England, 1981.

———. *Social History of the Jews in England, 1850–1950.* London: Watts, 1954.

———. "Synagogal Organization in Anglo-Jewry." *JJS* 1 (Apr. 1959): 80–93.

———, ed. *Three Centuries of Anglo-Jewish History.* London: Jewish Historical Society of England, 1961.

———. "The Age of Emancipation." In *Three Centuries of Anglo-Jewish History.* Edited by V. D. Lipman. London: Jewish Historical Society of England, 1961.

Lochhead, Sheila. "Introduction." In *Women in the Labour Movement: The British Experience.* Edited by Lucy Middleton. London: Croom Helm, 1977.

Loewe, Herbert M. "Nina Salaman, 1877–1925." *Transactions of the Jewish Historical Society of England* 11 (1928): 228–32.

Loewe, L. L. *Basil Henriques.* London, Henley, and Boston: Routledge & Kegan Paul, 1976.

Lorwin, Louis. *The Women's Garment Workers: A History of the International Ladies' Garment Workers' Union.* New York: B. W. Huebsch Inc., 1924.

MacArthur, Mary. "The Women Trade-Unionists' Point of View." In *Women and the Labour Party.* Edited by Marion Phillips. New York: B. W. Huebsch, 1918.

McHugh, Paul. *Prostitution and Victorian Social Reform.* New York: St. Martin's Press, 1980.

McWilliams-Tullberg, Rita. "Women and Degrees at Cambridge University 1862–1897." In *A Widening Sphere: Changing Roles of Victorian Women.* Edited by Martha Vicinus. Bloomington and London: Indiana University Press, 1977.

Magnus, Katie. "The National Idea in Judaism." *JQR* 1 (1889): 353–58.

Marwick, Arthur. *The Deluge: British Society and the First World War.* New York: W. W. Norton & Co., 1970.

Mayhew, Henry. *London Labour and the London Poor,* vol. 2. London: Frank Cass & Co., 1851. Reprint ed. New York: Augustus Kelley, 1967.

Middleton, Lucy, ed. *Women in the Labour Movement: The British Experience.* London: Croom Helm, 1977.

Mintz, Alan. *George Eliot and the Novel of Vocation.* Cambridge: Harvard University Press, 1978.

Mintz, Steven. *A Prison of Expectations: The Family in Victorian Culture.* New York and London: New York University Press, 1983.

Montagu, Lily H. *Faith of a Jewish Woman.* Keighly: Wadworth & Co., 1943.

———. *My Club and I: The Story of the West Central Girls Club.* 2nd ed. London: Neville Spearman & Herbert Joseph, 1954.

———. "The Spiritual Possibilities of Judaism Today." *JQR* 11 (Jan. 1899).

———. *Thoughts on Judaism.* London, 1904.

Montefiore, Claude G. "Judaism, Unitarianism, and Theism." In *Papers for Jewish People.* London: Jewish Religious Union, 1908.

———. *Liberal Judaism.* London: Macmillan, 1903.

———. "Liberal Judaism in England: Its Difficulties and Its Duties." *JQR* 12 (1900).

———. "Mr. Smith: A Possibility." *JQR* 5 (Oct. 1893).

———. *The Question of Authority in Liberal Judaism.* Papers for Jewish People, no. 33. London: Jewish Religious Union, 1936.

———. *The Old Testament and After.* London: Macmillan, 1923.

Montefiore, Claude G., and Loewe, H. *A Rabbinic Anthology.* Cleveland and New York: Meridian Books, World Publishing; Philadelphia: Jewish Publication Society, 1963.

Montefiore, Dora. *From a Victorian to a Modern.* London: E. Archer, 1927.

Montefiore, Judith. *Private Journal of a Visit to Egypt and Palestine, 1827.* Introduction by I. Bartal. Photocopy of the unpublished 1836 London edition. Jerusalem: Hebrew University.

———. *Notes of a Private Journey.* London: Lea & Co., 1885.

Montefiore, Sir Moses, and Montefiore, Lady Judith. *Diaries.* Edited by L. Loewe. London: Griffiths, Farran, Okeden, & Welsh, 1890.

Morgan, David. *Suffragists and Liberals: The Politics of Woman Suffrage in England.* Totowa, N.J.: Rowman & Littlefield, 1975.

Naman, Anne Aresty. *The Jew in the Victorian Novel.* New York: AMS Press, 1980.

Newman, Aubrey. *The United Synagogue, 1870–1970.* London, Henley, and Boston: Routledge & Kegan Paul, 1976.

———, ed. *The Jewish East End 1840–1939.* London: Jewish Historical Society of England, 1981.

———, ed. *Migration and Settlement: Proceedings of the Anglo-American Jewish Historical Conference.* London: Jewish Historical Society of England, 1971.

O'Neill, William. *The Woman Movement: Feminism in the United States and England.* London: George Allen & Unwin; New York: Barnes & Noble, 1969.

Oren, Laura. "The Welfare of Women in Laboring Families: England, 1860–1950." In *Clio's Consciousness Raised.* Edited by Mary Hartman and Lois W. Banner. New York, Hagerstown, San Francisco, London: Harper Colophon Books, 1974.

Owen, David. *English Philanthropy 1660–1960.* Cambridge, Mass.: Belknap Press, Harvard University Press, 1964.

Pankhurst, Sylvia. *The Suffragette Movement.* London: Longmans, 1931.

Paulson, Ross Evans. *Women's Suffrage and Prohibition: A Comparative*

Study of Equality and Social Control. Glenview, Ill.: Scott Foresman & Co., 1973.

Pekin, Harold. *The Origins of Modern English Society, 1780–1880.* London: Routledge & Kegan Paul; Toronto: University of Toronto Press, 1969.

Pethick-Lawrence, Emmeline. *My Part in a Changing World.* London: Gollancz, 1928.

Phillips, Marion. *Women and the Labour Party.* New York: B. W. Huebsch, 1918.

Pinchbeck, Ivy. *Women Workers and the Industrial Revolution, 1750–1858.* 2nd rev. ed. London: F. Cass & Co., 1969.

Pollins, Harold. "East End Jewish Working Men's Clubs Affiliated to the Working Men's Club and Institute Union: 1870–1914." In *The Jewish East End.* Edited by Aubrey Newman. London: Jewish Historical Society of England, 1981.

———. *Economic History of the Jews in England.* Rutherford, Madison, Teaneck: Fairleigh Dickinson University Press; London and Toronto: Associated University Press, 1982.

Pope, Barbara Corrado. "Angels in the Devil's Workshop: Leisured and Charitable Women in Nineteenth-Century England and France." In *Becoming Visible: Women in European History.* Edited by Renate Bridenthal and Claudia Koonz. Boston: Houghton Mifflin, 1977.

Prochaska, F. K. *Women and Philanthropy in Nineteenth-Century England.* Oxford: Clarendon Press, 1980.

"Programme of the International Conference of Liberal Jews." London: Jewish Religious Union, 1926. WUPJ Papers, Klau Library, HUC-JIR.

Richards, Eric. "Women in the British Economy since About 1700: An Interpretation." *History* 59 (Oct. 1974): 137–57.

Rooper, Ralph. "Women Enfranchised." In *The Making of Women.* Edited by Victor Gollancz. Oxford Essays in Feminism. London: George Allen & Unwin; New York: Macmillan, 1918.

Rosen, Andrew. *Rise Up, Women!: The Militant Campaign of the Women's Social and Political Union 1903–1914.* London and Boston: Routledge & Kegan Paul, 1974.

Rosenau, Helen. "Montefiore and the Visual Arts." In *The Century of Moses Montefiore.* Edited by Sonia and V. D. Lipman.

Roth, Cecil. *A History of the Jews in England.* Oxford: Clarendon Press, 1967.

———. "The European Age in Jewish History." In *The Jews.* Edited by Louis Finkelstein. New York: Schocken, 1970.

———. "The Resettlement of the Jews in England in 1656." In *Three Centuries of Anglo-Jewish History.* Edited by V. D. Lipman. London: Jewish Historical Society of England, 1961.

Rothschild, Constance, and Rothschild, Anne. *History and Literature of the Israelites.* 2 vols. London: Longmans, Green, Reader & Dyer, 1870.

Rothschild, Louise. *Lady de Rothschild: Extracts from Her Notebooks.* Edited by Constance Battersea. London: Arthur L. Humphreys, 1912.

Rover, Constance. *Women's Suffrage and Party Politics in Britain, 1866–1914.* London: Routledge & Kegan Paul, 1967.

Royden, A. Maude. "The Woman's Movement of the Future." In *The Making of Women.* Edited by Victor Gollancz. London: George Allen & Unwin; New York: Macmillan, 1918.

Sassoon, Flora. "Address Delivered on Speech Day at Jews' College." 1924.

Schmiechen, James A. *Sweated Industries and Sweated Labor: The London Clothing Trades, 1860–1914.* Urbana and Chicago: University of Illinois Press, 1984.

Schupf, Harriet W. "Single Women and Social Reform in Mid-Nineteenth Century England: The Case of Mary Carpenter." *Victorian Studies* 27 (Mar. 1974).

Schwartz, Frederick C. "Claude Montefiore on Law and Tradition." *JQR* 55 (July 1964).

Sharot, Stephen S. "Native Jewry and the Religious Anglicization of Immigrants in London, 1870–1905." *JJS* 16 (June 1974).

———. "Religious Change in Native Orthodoxy in London, 1870–1914: Rabbinate and Clergy." *JJS* 15 (Dec. 1973).

Shorter, Edward. *The Making of the Modern Family.* New York, 1975.

Simmons, Vivian G. *The Path of Life: A Study of the Background Faith and Practice of Liberal Judaism.* London: Vallentine Mitchell, 1961.

Simon, Oswald. "Jews and Modern Thought." *JQR* 11 (1899): 387–99.

———. "The Mission of Judaism." *JQR* 9 (1897).

———. "Reformed Judaism." *JQR* 6 (1894).

Soldon, Norbert C. *Women in British Trade Unions, 1874–1976.* New York and London: Gill & Macmillan, 1978.

"Some Legal Difficulties which beset the Jewess." By Miss Hands. *JG,* July 30, 1920, p. 9; Sept. 19, 1920, p. 10.

Stead, W. T. *The Maiden Tribute of Modern Babylon (The Report of the "Pall Mall Gazette"'s Secret Commission).* London, 1885.

Stearns, Peter. "Working-Class Women in Britain, 1890–1914." In *Suffer and Be Still: Women in the Victorian Age.* Edited by Martha Vicinus. Bloomington and London: Indiana University Press, 1973.

Stein, Joshua B. "The Contribution of C. G. Montefiore to the Establishment of Liberal Judaism in England." Paper delivered at the Association for Jewish Studies Annual Conference, Boston, December 1982.

Stern, Mrs. F. C. "Women in Politics." In *The Jewish Woman. JG* Supplement. Dec. 1925, Klau Library, HUC-JIR.

Strachey, Ray. *The Cause: A Short History of the Women's Movement in Great Britain.* London: Bell & Sons, 1928.

Strauss, Sylvia. "Josephine Butler and Her Opposition to the Contagious Diseases Acts." Unpublished paper delivered at the American Historical Association Annual Conference, Washington, D.C., 1982.

Szajkowski, Zosa. "Deportation of Jewish Immigrants and Returnees before World War I." *AJHQ* 67, no. 4 (June 1978): 297.

Taylor, Barbara. " 'The Men are as Bad as Their Masters . . .': Socialism, Feminism and Sexual Antagonism in the London Tailoring Trade in the 1830's." In *Sex and Class in Women's History.* Edited by Judith L. Newton, Mary P. Ryan, and Judith R. Walkowitz. History Workshop Series. London, Boston, Melbourne, and Henley: Routledge & Kegan Paul.

Thompson, Paul R. *The Edwardians: The Remaking of British Society.* Bloomington and London: Indiana University Press, 1975.

Trevelyan, G. M. *A Shortened History of England.* Baltimore: Pelican, 1960.

Umansky, Ellen M. *Lily Montagu and the Advancement of Liberal Judaism: From Vision to Vocation.* Studies in Women and Religion, vol. 12. New York and Toronto: Edwin Mellen Press, 1983.

———. "Lily H. Montagu: Religious Leader, Organizer, and Prophet." *Conservative Judaism* 34, no. 6.

Vicinus, Martha, ed. *Suffer and Be Still: Women in the Victorian Age.* Bloomington and London: Indiana University Press, 1973.

———. *A Widening Sphere: Changing Roles of Victorian Women.* Bloomington and London: Indiana University Press, 1980.

Walkowitz, Judith. "Jack the Ripper and the Myth of Male Violence." *FS* 8 (Fall 1982).

———. "The Making of an Outcast Group: Prostitutes and Working Women in Nineteenth-Century Plymouth and Southampton." In *A Widening Sphere.* Edited by Martha Vicinus. Bloomington and London: Indiana University Press, 1980.

———. *Prostitution and Victorian Society: Women, Class and the State.* Cambridge: Cambridge University Press, 1980.

Walton, Ronald G. *Women in Social Work.* London and Boston: Routledge & Kegan Paul, 1975.

Webb, Beatrice. "The Jewish Community (East London)." In *Life and Labour of the People in London.* Edited by Charles Booth. New York and London, 1902–04. Reprint ed. New York: AMS Press, 1970.

———. "Women and the Factory Acts." *Fabian Tract No. 67,* 1896. Cited in *Women in Public: The Women's Movement, 1850–1900.* Edited by Patricia Hollis. London: George Allen & Unwin, 1979.

Weizmann, Chaim. *Trial and Error.* New York: Harper, 1949.

White, Jerry. "Jewish Landlords, Jewish Tenants: An Aspect of Class Struggle within the Jewish East End, 1881–1914." In *The Jewish East End.* Edited by Aubrey Newman. London: Jewish Historical Society of England, 1981.

———. *The Rothschild Buildings: Life in an East End Tenement Block 1887–1920.* London: Routledge & Kegan Paul, 1980.

Whitney, Janet. *Elizabeth Fry.* London: Harrap, 1937.

Wilcox, William B. *The Age of Aristocracy, 1688 to 1830.* Lexington, Mass.: D. C. Heath & Co., 1976.

Wilson, Elizabeth. *Women and the Welfare State.* London: Tavistock, 1977.

Wolf, Lucien. *Essays in Jewish History.* London: Jewish Historical Society of England, 1934.

Wollstonecraft, Mary. *A Vindication of the Rights of Woman*. Edited by Carol H. Poston. New York: W. W. Norton, 1975.

Youdovin, Ira S. "The World Union for Progressive Judaism: The First Fifty Years." World Union for Progressive Judaism, WUPJ Papers, 1930. Klau Library, HUC-JIR.

Zatlin, Linda Gertner. *The Nineteenth-Century Anglo-Jewish Novel*. Boston: Twayne, 1981.

UNITED STATES

Abel, Elizabeth, and Abel, Emily K., eds. *The Signs Reader: Women, Gender and Scholarship*. Chicago: University of Chicago Press, 1983.

American, Sadie. "Organization." In *Papers of the Jewish Women's Congress*. Philadelphia: Jewish Publication Society, 1894.

Ashton, Dianne. "Building Ethnicity: Rebecca Gratz and Jewish Women in Philadelphia, 1780–1880." Ph.D. diss., draft. Temple University.

Askowith, D. *Three Outstanding Women*. 1941.

Baron, Salo. "American Jewish Communal Pioneering." *PAJHS* 43 (1954).

Baum, Charlotte; Hyman, Paula; and Michel, Sonya. *The Jewish Woman in America*. New York: Dial, 1976.

Bellah, Robert M. *The Broken Covenant: American Civil Religion in Time of Trial*. New York: Seabury Press, 1975.

Berlin, George L. "Solomon Jackson's *The Jew*: An Early American Jewish Response to the Missionaries." *AJH* 71 (Sept. 1981): 10–28.

Bernstein, Jessie W. "The Grateful Thread." *American Jewish Archives* 33 (Apr. 1981).

Berrol, Selma Cantor. "Immigrants at School: New York City, 1898–1914." Ph.D. diss., City University of New York, 1967.

Birmingham, Stephen. *Our Crowd: The Great Jewish Families of New York*. New York, Evanston, and London: Harper & Row, 1967.

Blair, Karen. "The Clubwoman as Feminist: The Woman's Culture Club Movement in the United States, 1868–1914." Ph.D. diss., State University of New York at Buffalo, 1976.

Blau, Joseph L., and Baron, Salo W. *The Jews of the United States, 1790–1840*. Vol. 1. New York: Columbia University Press, 1963.

Bodek, Evelyn. "Making Do: Jewish Women and Philanthropy." In *Jewish Life in Philadelphia: 1830–1940*. Edited by Murray Friedman. Philadelphia: ISHI Press, 1983.

Boylan, Anne M. "Evangelical Womanhood in the Nineteenth Century: The Role of Women in Sunday Schools." *FS* 4 (Oct. 1978).

Braude, Ann. "Jewish Woman's Encounter with American Culture." In *Women and Religion in America*. Edited by Rosemary Radford Ruether and Rosemary Skinner Keller. Vol. 1. San Francisco: Harper & Row, 1981.

Braun, Mildred L. *A History of Johanna No. 9, United Order of True Sisters: 1874–1955*. Authorized 2nd ed., rev., and suppl. covering mid-1949–55. AJA.

Buhle, Mari Jo. *Women and American Socialism, 1870–1920*. Urbana, Chicago, London: University of Illinois Press, 1981.

Cameron, William. *The World's Fair: Being a Pictorial History of the Columbian Exposition*. Philadelphia: National Publishing Co., 1893.

Cantor, Milton, and Laurie, Bruce, eds. *Class, Sex, and the Woman Worker*. Westport, Conn., and London: Greenwood Press, 1977.

Carroll, Berenice, ed. *Liberating Women's History*. Urbana: University of Illinois Press, 1976.

Central Conference of American Rabbis. *Yearbooks*. New York, 1913–25.

Chafee, William H. *The American Woman: Her Changing Social, Economic, and Political Role, 1920–1970*. London, Oxford, New York: Oxford University Press, 1972.

Chambers-Schiller, Lee Virginia. *Liberty, a Better Husband: Single Women in America: The Generations of 1780–1840*. New Haven and London: Yale University Press, 1984.

Christ, Carol P. *Diving Deep and Surfacing: Women Writers on a Spiritual Quest*. Boston: Beacon Press, 1980.

Cohen, Gerson D. "The Meaning of Liberty in American Tradition." In *Jewish Life in America: Historical Perspectives*. Edited by Gladys Rosen. Institute of Human Relations Press of the American Jewish Committee. New York: Ktav, 1978.

Cohen, Naomi W. *Encounter with Emancipation: The German Jews in the United States, 1830–1914*. Philadelphia: Jewish Publication Society, 1984.

Cohen, Steven M. *American Modernity and Jewish Identity*. New York and London: Tavistock, 1983.

Cohen, Steven M., and Hyman, Paula A., eds. *The Jewish Family: Myth and Reality*. New York and London: Holmes & Meier, 1976.

Conway, Jill. "Stereotypes of Femininity in a Theory of Sexual Evolution." *Victorian Studies* 14 (Sept. 1970): 47–55.

Cook, Blanche Wiesen. *Women and Support Networks*. New York: Out and Out Books.

Cott, Nancy F. *The Bonds of Womanhood*. New Haven and London: Yale University Press, 1977.

———. *The Grounding of Modern Feminism*. New Haven and London: Yale University Press, 1987.

Cott, Nancy F., and Pleck, Elizabeth H. *A Heritage of Her Own*. New York: Simon & Schuster, 1979.

Daly, Mary. *The Church and the Second Sex*. New York: Harper, 1975.

Davis, Allen. *Spearheads for Reform: The Social Settlement and the Progressive Movement, 1890–1914*. New York: Oxford University Press, 1967.

———. *American Heroine: The Life and Legend of Jane Addams*. New York: Peter Smith Press, 1983.

Davis, Moshe. *The Emergence of Conservative Judaism: The Historical School in 19th Century America*. Philadelphia: Jewish Publication Society, 1963.

Dash, Joan. *Summoned to Jerusalem: The Life of Henrietta Szold*. New York, Hagerstown, San Francisco, London: Harper & Row, 1979.

Degler, Carl. *At Odds: Women and the Family in America from the Revolution to the Present.* New York: Oxford University Press, 1980.

Devotional Exercises, for the use of the Daughters of Israel. Edited by Rev. M. J. Raphall. New York: L. Joachimssen, 1852.

Dictionary of American Biography. Vol. 11, s.v. "Loeb, Sophie Irene Simon."

Diener, Hasia R. *In the Almost Promised Land: American Jews and Blacks, 1915–1935.* Westport, Conn., London: Greenwood Press, 1977.

Dinnerstein, Leonard. *Uneasy at Home: Antisemitism and the American Jewish Experience.* New York: Columbia University Press, 1987.

Donovan, Josephine. *Feminist Theory: The Intellectual Traditions of American Feminism.* New York: Frederick Ungar, 1985.

Duffus, Robert. *Lillian Wald, Neighbor and Crusader.* New York: Macmillan, 1938.

Dye, Nancy Schrom. "Creating a Feminist Alliance: Sisterhood and Class Conflict in the New York Women's Trade Union League, 1902–1914." *FS* 2 (1975).

———. *As Equals and as Sisters: Feminism, the Labor Movement, and the Women's Trade Union League of New York.* Columbia and London: University of Missouri Press, 1980.

Eagle, Mary Kavanaugh Oldham, ed. *The Congress of Women.* 1894. Reprint ed. New York: Arno Press, 1974.

Elwell, Ellen Sue Levi. "The Founding and Early Programs of the National Council of Jewish Women: Study and Practice as Jewish Women's Religious Expression." Ph.D. diss., Indiana University, 1982. AJA.

Farrer, David. *The Warburgs: The Story of a Family.* New York: Stein & Day, 1975.

Feingold, Henry. "Introduction," *AJH* 71 (Dec. 1981).

Flexner, Eleanor. *Century of Struggle: The Woman's Rights Movement in the United States.* New York: Atheneum, 1974.

Foner, Philip S. *Women and the American Labor Movement: From Colonial Times to the Eve of World War I.* New York: The Free Press; London: Collier Macmillan, 1979.

Freedman, Estelle. "Separatism as Strategy: Female Institution Building and American Feminism, 1870–1930." *FS* 5 (Fall 1979).

Friedman, Murray, ed. *Jewish Life in Philadelphia: 1830–1940.* Philadelphia: ISHI Press, 1983.

Friess, Horace, and Vessey, Clifford, eds. *Memorial Service for Josephine Goldmark.* Dec. 18, 1950. Schlesinger Library, Radcliffe College.

Gifford, Carolyn de Swarte. "Women in Social Reform Movements." In *Women and Religion in America.* Vol. 1. Edited by Rosemary Radford Ruether and Rosemary Skinner Keller. San Francisco: Harper & Row, 1981.

Glanz, Rudolph. "The Rise of the Jewish Club in America." *Jewish Social Studies* 31 (Apr. 1969): 82–89.

———. *The Jewish Woman in America.* Vol. 2, *The German Jewish Woman.* New York: Ktav and National Council of Jewish Women, 1976.

Glazer, Nathan. *American Judaism.* Chicago and London: University of Chicago Press, 1972.

Goldman, Emma. *Living My Life.* 1931.

Golumb, Deborah Grand. "The 1893 Congress of Jewish Women: Evolution or Revolution in American Jewish Women's History?" *AJH* 70 (Sept. 1980): 52–67.

Gordon, Ann D., and Buhle, Mari Jo. "Sex and Class in Colonial and Nineteenth-Century America." In *Liberating Women's History.* Edited by Berenice Carroll. Urbana: University of Illinois Press, 1976.

Goren, Arthur A. *New York Jews and the Quest for Community.* New York: Columbia University Press, 1970.

———. "The Promises of *The Promised City*: Moses Rischin, American History, and the Jews." *AJH* 73 (Dec. 1983).

Grinstein, Hyman. *The Rise of the Jewish Community in New York.* Philadelphia: Jewish Publication Society, 1945.

Gurock, Jeffrey. "Jacob A. Riis: Christian Friend or Missionary Foe? Two Jewish Views." *AJH* 71 (Sept. 1981): 29–47.

———. *When Harlem Was Jewish, 1870–1930.* New York: Columbia University Press, 1979.

Halttunen, Karen. "The Domestic Drama of Louisa May Alcott." *FS* 10 (Summer 1984): 233–54.

Handlin, Oscar. *The Uprooted.* Boston: Little, Brown, 1951.

Hapgood, Hutchings. *The Spirit of the Ghetto: Studies of the Jewish Quarter of New York.* Rev. ed. New York: Schocken, 1976.

Harper, Ida Husted, ed. *History of Woman Suffrage.* Vols. 1–6. Indianapolis, 1902.

"Harry Redinger—A Jew of the Old West." In *To Make a Dream Come True: Stories of the Residents of the Hebrew Home of Greater Washington.* Edited by Linda Gordon Kuzmack and Shulamith Weisman. Rockville, Md.: Hebrew Home of Greater Washington, 1983.

Hartman, Mary, and Banner, Lois W., eds. *Clio's Consciousness Raised.* New York, Hagerstown, San Francisco, London: Harper Colophon Books, 1974.

Healey, Robert M. "Jefferson on Judaism and the Jews: 'Divided We Stand, United, We Fall!'" *AJH* 73 (June 1984).

Henry, Alice. *The Trade Union Woman.* New York: Burt Franklin, 1973.

———. *Women and the Labor Movement.* New York: Arno and New York Times, 1971.

Hill, Mary A. *Charlotte Perkins Gilman: The Making of a Radical Feminist, 1860–1896.* Philadelphia: Temple University Press, 1960.

Hirsch, Emil G. *My Religion.* New York, 1925.

———. "The Modern Jewess." *AJ* (July 1895): 10.

A History of B'nai B'rith Women. Washington: B'nai B'rith Women, n.d. Pamphlet.

Howe, Irving. *World of Our Fathers.* New York and London: Harcourt Brace Jovanovich, 1976.

Hyman, Paula. "Immigrant Women and Consumer Protest: The New York City Kosher Meat Boycott of 1902." *AJH* 70 (Sept. 1980): 91–105.

———. "The Volunteer Organizations: Vanguard or Rear Guard?" *Lilith* no. 5 (1978): 17–22.

Irwin, Inez Haynes. *Angels and Amazons: A Hundred Years of American Women*. Garden City, N.Y.: Doubleday, Doran & Co., 1933.

Jacoby, Robin Miller. "Feminism and Class Consciousness in the British and American Women's Trade Union Leagues, 1890–1925." In *Liberating Women's History*. Edited by Berenice Carroll. Urbana: University of Illinois Press, 1976.

———. "The Women's Trade Union League and American Feminism." In *Class, Sex and the Woman Worker*. Edited by Milton Cantor and Bruce Laurie. Westport, Conn., London: Greenwood Press, 1977.

Joselit, Jenna Weissman. *Our Gang: Jewish Crime and the New York Jewish Community, 1900–1940*. Bloomington: Indiana University Press, 1983.

Kaplan, Mordecai. *Judaism as a Civilization*. New York: Schocken, 1972.

Keller, Rosemary Skinner. "Women, Civil Religion, and the American Revolution." In *Women and Religion in America*. Edited by Rosemary Radford Ruether and Rosemary Skinner Keller. Vol. 2. San Francisco: Harper & Row, 1981.

———. "Lay Women in the Protestant Tradition." In *Women and Religion in America*. Edited by Rosemary Radford Ruether and Rosemary Skinner Keller. Vol. 1. San Francisco: Harper & Row, 1981.

Kenneally, James J. *Women and American Trade Unions*. Monographs in Women's Studies. St. Albans, Vt.: Eden Press, 1978.

Kennedy, Susan Estabrook. *If All We Did Was to Weep at Home: A History of White Working-Class Women in America*. Bloomington: Indiana University Press, 1979.

Kessler-Harris, Alice. *Women Have Always Worked*. Old Westbury, N.Y.: Feminist Press; New York, St. Louis, San Francisco: McGraw-Hill, 1981.

———. "Organizing the Unorganizable: Three Jewish Women and Their Unions." *Labor History* 17 (Winter 1976).

———. "Women, Work and the Social Order." In *Liberating Women's History*. Edited by Berenice Carroll. Urbana: University of Illinois Press, 1976.

Kessner, Thomas. *The Golden Door: Italian and Jewish Immigrant Mobility in New York City, 1880–1915*. New York: Oxford University Press, 1977.

———. "Jobs, Ghettos and the Urban Economy, 1880–1935." *AJH* 71 (Dec. 1881).

Kohler, Kaufman. "Origin and Function of Ceremonies in Judaism." Central Conference of American Rabbis *Yearbook* (1907): 205–230.

Kohut, Rebekah. "Jewish Women's Organizations." *American Jewish Yearbook* 33 (1932).

———. *My Portion*. New York: Boni & Liveright, 1925.

Kominsky, Neil. "Jennie Franklin Purvin: A Study in Womanpower." Cincinnati: HUC-JIR, 1968. Typescript. AJA.

Kraditor, Aileen. *Ideas of the Woman Suffrage Movement, 1890–1920.* New York and London: Columbia University Press, 1967.

———. *Up from the Pedestal: Selected Writings in the History of American Feminism.* Chicago: Quadrangle, 1968.

Kuhn, Anne L. *The Mother's Role in Childhood Education: New England Concepts, 1830–1860.* New Haven: Yale University Press, 1947.

Kuzmack, Linda Gordon, and Weisman, Shulamith, eds. *To Make a Dream Come True: Stories of the Residents of the Hebrew Home of Greater Washington.* Rockville, Md.: Hebrew Home of Greater Washington, 1983.

Lagemann, Ellen Condliffe. *A Generation of Women: Education in the Lives of Progressive Reformers.* Cambridge: Harvard University Press, 1979.

Lauterbach, Jacob Z. "Responsum on Question, 'Shall Women be ordained Rabbis?'" Central Conference of American Rabbis *Yearbook* 1922, pp. 156–62.

Learsi, Rufus. *The Jews in America.* New York, 1972.

Lebeson, Anita L. *Recall to Life—The Jewish Woman in America.* New York: Thomas Yoseloff, 1970.

Lemons, J. Stanley. *The Woman Citizen: Social Feminism in the 1920's.* Urbana, Chicago, London: University of Illinois Press, 1973.

Lerner, Elinor. "Jewish Involvement in the New York City Woman Suffrage Movement." *AJH* 70, no. 4 (June 1981).

Lerner, Gerda. *The Woman in American History.* Menlo Park, Calif.; Reading, Mass.; Don Mills, Ontario; London: Addison-Wesley, 1971.

Letters of the Franks Family, 1733–1748. The Lee Max Friedman Collection of American Jewish Colonial Correspondence. Studies in American History, no. 5. Waltham, Mass.: American Jewish Historical Society, 1968.

Liptzin, Sol. *The Jew in American Literature.* New York, Bloch, 1966.

Litman, Simon. *Ray Frank Litman: A Memoir.* New York: AJHS, 1957.

Loeb, Garry. "Jewish Women and the Reform Movement in America." M.H.L. thesis, Hebrew Union College-Jewish Institute of Religion, 1981.

Lorwin, Lewis L. *The American Federation of Labor.* Washington: Brookings Institution, 1933.

Louis, Minnie D. "Woman—The Inciter to Reform." In *The Congress of Women.* Edited by Mary Eagle. Reprint ed. New York: Arno Press, 1974.

Marcus, Jacob Rader. *The American Jewish Woman, 1654–1980.* New York: Ktav; Cincinnati: American Jewish Archives, 1981.

———. *The American Jewish Woman: A Documentary History.* New York: Ktav; Cincinnati: American Jewish Archives, 1981.

Martin, Bernard. "Yiddish Literature in the United States," *American Jewish Archives* 33 (Nov. 1981): 184–209.

Melder, Keith. *Beginnings of Sisterhood: The American Woman's Rights Movement 1800–1850.* New York: Schocken, 1977.

Meyer, Annie Nathan. *It's Been Fun.* 1951.

Meyer, Michael A. "German-Jewish Identity in Nineteenth Century America." In *The American Jewish Experience.* Edited by Jonathan Sarna. New York and London: Holmes & Meier, 1986.

Metzker, Isaac, ed. Harry Golden, foreword and notes. *A Bintel Brief: Sixty Years of Letters from the Lower East Side.* Garden City, N.Y.: Doubleday, 1971.

Miller, Sally M. "From Sweatshop Worker to Labor Leader: Theresa Malkiel, a Case Study." *AJH* 68 (Dec. 1978): 189–205.

Moore, Deborah Dash. *B'nai B'rith and the Challenge of Ethnic Leadership.* Albany: State University of New York Press, 1981.

Morton, Leah. *I am a Woman—and a Jew.* Rev. ed. Masterworks of Modern Jewish Writing series. Jonathan D. Sarna, ed. Ellen Umansky, intro. New York: Markus Wiener, 1986.

Nadell, Pamela S. "The Journey to America by Steam: The Jews of Eastern Europe in Transition." *AJH* 71 (Dec. 1981): 269–84.

Nathan, Maud. *Once upon a Time and Today.* New York: Arno, 1974.

———. *Story of an Epoch-Making Movement.*

National Council of Jewish Women. "A Brief Summary of Investigations and Inquiries Made between the Years of 1905 and 1915 by Government and Private Agencies into Typical Industries Prevalent in the State of New York and Affording Work to Large Numbers of Women." New York, 1916.

———. *The First Fifty Years.*

Newton, Judith L.; Ryan, Mary P.; and Walkowitz, Judith R. *Sex and Class in Women's History.* London, Boston, Melbourne, and Henley: Routledge & Kegan Paul, 1983.

Notable American Women, 1607–1950. S.v. "Einstein, Hannah"; "Loeb, Sophie Irene"; "Wise, Louise Waterman"; "Nathan, Maud."

O'Neill, William. *Everyone Was Brave: The Rise and Fall of Feminism in America.* New York: Quadrangle, 1969.

———. "Feminism as a Radical Ideology." In *Dissent: History of American Radicalism.* Edited by A. F. Young. De Kalb, Ill.: Northern Illinois University Press, 1968.

Papers of the Jewish Women's Congress. Philadelphia: Jewish Publication Society, 1894.

Perry, Elisabeth Israels. *Belle Moskowitz: Feminine Politics and the Exercise of Power in the Age of Alfred E. Smith.* New York: Oxford University Press, 1987.

———. " 'Doing Good': The German-Jewish Experience and the Career of Belle Moskowitz." Paper delivered at the Association for Jewish Studies Annual Conference, Boston, December 1980.

Philipson, David, ed. *Letters of Rebecca Gratz.* Philadelphia: Jewish Publication Society, 1929.

Porter, Jack Nusan. "Rosa Sonneschein and *The American Jewess*: The First Independent English Language Jewish Women's Journal in the United States." *AJH* 67 (Sept. 1978).

Pratt, Norma Fain. "Culture and Radical Politics: Yiddish Women Writers, 1890–1940." *AJH* 70 (Sept. 1980): 69–90.

Rabinowitz, Benjamin. *The Young Men's Hebrew Associations (1854–1913).* New York: National Jewish Welfare Board, 1948.

Razovsky, Cecelia. "Humanitarian Effects of the Immigration Law." New York: NCJW, 1927. AJHS.

———. "A Report on the Work of the Bureau of International Service of the National Council of Jewish Women." New York: NCJW, 1927. AJHS.

Reznick, Allan Edward. "Lillian D. Wald: The Years at Henry Street." Ph.D. diss., University of Wisconsin, 1973.

Ribuffo, Leo P. "Henry Ford and *The International Jew*," *AJH* 69 (June 1980).

Richman, Julia. "Women Wage-Workers: With Reference to Directing Immigrants." *Papers of the Jewish Women's Congress.* Philadelphia: Jewish Publication Society, 1894.

Riis, Jacob. *How the Other Half Lives: Studies among the Tenements of New York.* New York: Charles Scribner's Sons, 1890; reprint ed. New York: Dover, 1971.

Rischin, Moses. *The Jews of the West: The Metropolitan Years.* Waltham, Mass.: AJHS, 1979.

———. *The Promised City: New York's Jews, 1870–1914.* Cambridge, Mass., and London: Harvard University Press, 1977.

Roberts, Mary M. "Lavinia Lloyd Dock—Nurse, Feminist, Internationalist." *American Journal of Nursing* 56 (Jan.–June 1956): 176–79.

Rogow, Faith. " 'Gone to Another Meeting': A History of the National Council of Jewish Women." Ph.D. diss., State University of New York, Binghamton, 1988.

Rose, Ernestine. "On Legal Discrimination." Second Worcester Convention, 1851. In *History of Woman Suffrage.* Edited by Ida Husted Harper. Vol. 1. Indianapolis, 1902.

Rosen, Ruth. *The Lost Sisterhood: Prostitution in America, 1900–1918.* Baltimore and London: Johns Hopkins University Press, 1982.

Rosen, Ruth, and Davidson, Sue, eds. *The Mamie Papers.* Cambridge: The Feminist Press and Schlesinger Library of Radcliffe College, 1977.

Rosenberg, Rosalind. *Beyond Separate Spheres: Intellectual Roots of Modern Feminism.* New Haven and London: Yale University Press, 1982.

Rossi, Alice S., ed. *The Feminist Papers.* New York and London: Columbia University Press, 1973.

Ruether, Rosemary Radford. "Women in Utopian Movements." In *Women and Religion in America*, vol. 1. Edited by Rosemary Radford Ruether and Rosemary Skinner Keller. San Francisco: Harper & Row, 1981.

Ruether, Rosemary Radford, and Keller, Rosemary Skinner, eds. *Women and Religion in America*, 2 vols. San Francisco: Harper & Row, 1981, 1983.

Ryan, Mary P. "The Power of Women's Networks." In *Sex and Class in Women's History.* Edited by Judith L. Newton, Mary P. Ryan, and Judith R. Walkowitz. London, Boston, Melbourne, and Henley: Routledge & Kegan Paul, 1983.

"Sadie Hershey." In *To Make A Dream Come True.* Edited by Linda Gordon Kuzmack and Shulamith Weisman. Rockville, Md.: Hebrew Home of Greater Washington, 1983.

Sarna, Jonathan. *Jacksonian Jew: The Two Worlds of Mordecai Noah.* New York and London: Holmes & Meyer, 1981.

———. "The 'Mythical Jew' and the 'Jew Next Door' in Nineteenth Century America." Cincinnati: Hebrew Union College-Jewish Institute of Religion, 1983. Typescript.

Sarna, Jonathan, ed. *The American Jewish Experience.* New York and London: Holmes & Meier, 1986.

———, ed. *People Walk on Their Heads: Moses Weinberger's "Jews and Judaism in New York."* New York and London: Holmes & Meier, 1981.

Schechter, Mathilde. "A Task for Jewish Women." Address to United Synagogue women. Reprinted from the *American Jewish Chronicle.* Feb. 1, 1918, AJA.

Schneiderman, Rose. *All for One.* New York: Paul S. Eriksson, 1967.

Scott, Anne Firor. *Making the Invisible Woman Visible.* Urbana and Chicago: University of Illinois Press, 1984.

Scott, Anne Firor, and Scott, Andrew MacKay. *One Half the People: The Fight for Woman Suffrage.* Urbana, Chicago, London: University of Illinois Press, 1982.

Siegel, Beatrice. *Lillian Wald of Henry Street.* New York and London: Macmillan, 1983.

Simmons, Adele. "Education and Ideology in Nineteenth-Century America: The Response of Educational Institutions to the Changing Role of Women." In *Liberating Women's History.* Edited by Berenice Carroll. Urbana: University of Illinois Press, 1976.

Singerman, Robert. "The American Jewish Press, 1823–1983: A Bibliographic Survey of Research and Studies." *AJH* 73 (June 1984): 422–44.

Sklar, Kathryn Kish. *Catherine Beecher: A Study in American Domesticity.* New Haven: Yale University Press, 1973.

Sklare, Marshall. *America's Jews.* New York: Random House, 1971.

———. *The Jews: Social Patterns of an American Group.* New York: Free Press; London: Collier-Macmillan, 1958.

Smith-Rosenberg, Carroll. "The Female World of Love and Ritual: Relations between Women in Nineteenth-Century America." *Signs* 1 (Autumn 1975): 1–29.

Sochen, June. *Consecrate Every Day: The Public Lives of Jewish American Women, 1880–1980.* Albany: State University of New York Press, 1981.

———. "Jewish Volunteers." *AJH* 70 (Sept. 1980): 23.

———. *Herstory: A Woman's View of American History.* New York, 1967.

Solomon, Hannah Greenbaum. *A Sheaf of Leaves.* Privately printed, 1911.

———. *Fabric of My Life: The Story of a Social Pioneer.* 1946. Reprint ed. New York: Bloch & National Council of Jewish Women, 1974.

Sorin, Gerald. *The Prophetic Minority: American Jewish Immigrant Radicals 1880–1920.* Bloomington: Indiana University Press, 1985.

Stanton, Elizabeth Cady, et al. *The Woman's Bible.* Part 1, New York, 1895.

Strom, Sharon Hartman. "Leadership and Tactics in the American Woman

Suffrage Movement: A New Perspective from Massachusetts." *Journal of American History* 62, no. 2 (Sept. 1975).

Swerdlow, Amy, and Lessinger, Hanna. *Class, Race and Sex: The Dynamics of Control*. Boston: G. K. Hall, 1983.

Tax, Meredith. *The Rising of the Women*. New York: Monthly Review Press, 1980.

Tcherikower, Elias. *The Early Jewish Labor Movement in the United States*. New York: YIVO, 1961.

Temkin, Sefton. *The New World of Reform*. Bridgeport, 1974.

Toll, William. *The Making of an Ethnic Middle Class: Portland Jewry over Four Generations*. Modern Jewish History Series. Albany: State University of New York Press, 1982.

Trattner, Walter I. *From Poor Law to Welfare State: A History of Social Welfare in America*. New York: Free Press; London: Collier, 1974.

UAHC Committee on Legislation. *Report* (1923). Cited in *The American Jewish Woman: A Documentary History*. Edited by Jacob Marcus. New York: Ktav; Cincinnati: AJA, 1981.

Urofsky, Melvin I. *A Voice That Spoke for Justice: The Life and Times of Stephen S. Wise*. Albany: State University of New York Press, 1982.

Wald, Lillian. *The House on Henry Street*. New York: Henry Holt, 1915.

Waldron, Morris. *Nor by Power*. New York: International Universities Press, 1953.

Weinryb, Bernard D. "Jewish Immigration and Accommodation to America." In *The New Jews: Social Patterns of an American Group*. Edited by Marshall Sklare. New York: Free Press, 1958.

Weinberg, Sydney Stahl. *The World of Our Mothers*. Chapel Hill: University of North Carolina Press, 1988.

Welter, Barbara. "The Cult of True Womanhood." *American Quarterly* 18 (1966): 151–74.

———. "The Feminization of American Religion: 1800–1860." In *Clio's Consciousness Raised*. Edited by Mary Hartman and Lois W. Banner. New York, Hagerstown, San Francisco, London: Harper Colophon Books, 1974.

———. "Anti-Intellectualism and the American Woman, 1800–1860." In *Dimity Convictions: The American Woman in the Nineteenth Century*. Athens, Ohio: Ohio University Press, 1976.

Whitfield, Stephen J. "The Radical Persuasion in American Jewish History." *Judaism* 32 (Spring 1983).

Wiebe, Richard. *The Search for Order*. New York: Hill & Wang, 1967.

Wilson, Elizabeth. *Women and the Welfare State*. London: Tavistock, 1977.

Wilson, Margaret Gibbons. *The American Woman in Transition: The Urban Influence, 1879–1920*. New York: Greenwood Press, 1979.

Wise, Isaac M. "The Principles and Achievements of the Central Conference of American Rabbis, 1889–1913." In *Centenary Papers and Others*. Edited by David Philipson.

———. *Reminiscences*. New York: Ayer, 1945.

Woody, Thomas. *A History of Women's Education in the United States.* Vol. 1, 1929; New York: Octagon, 1966.

"Women in the Zionist World." Tel Aviv: WIZO, 1931.

Yellowitz, Irwin. "Jewish Immigrants and the American Labor Movement, 1900–1920." *AJH* 71 (Dec. 1981): 188–92.

Young, A. F., ed. *Dissent: History of American Radicalism.* De Kalb, Ill.: Northern Illinois University Press, 1968.

Zikmund, Barbara Brown. "The Struggle for the Right to Preach." In *Women and Religion in America.* Vol. 1. Edited by Rosemary Radford Ruether and Rosemary Skinner Keller. San Francisco: Harper & Row, 1981.

Index